CRISIS ON MULTIPLE EARTHS
THE TEAM-UPS

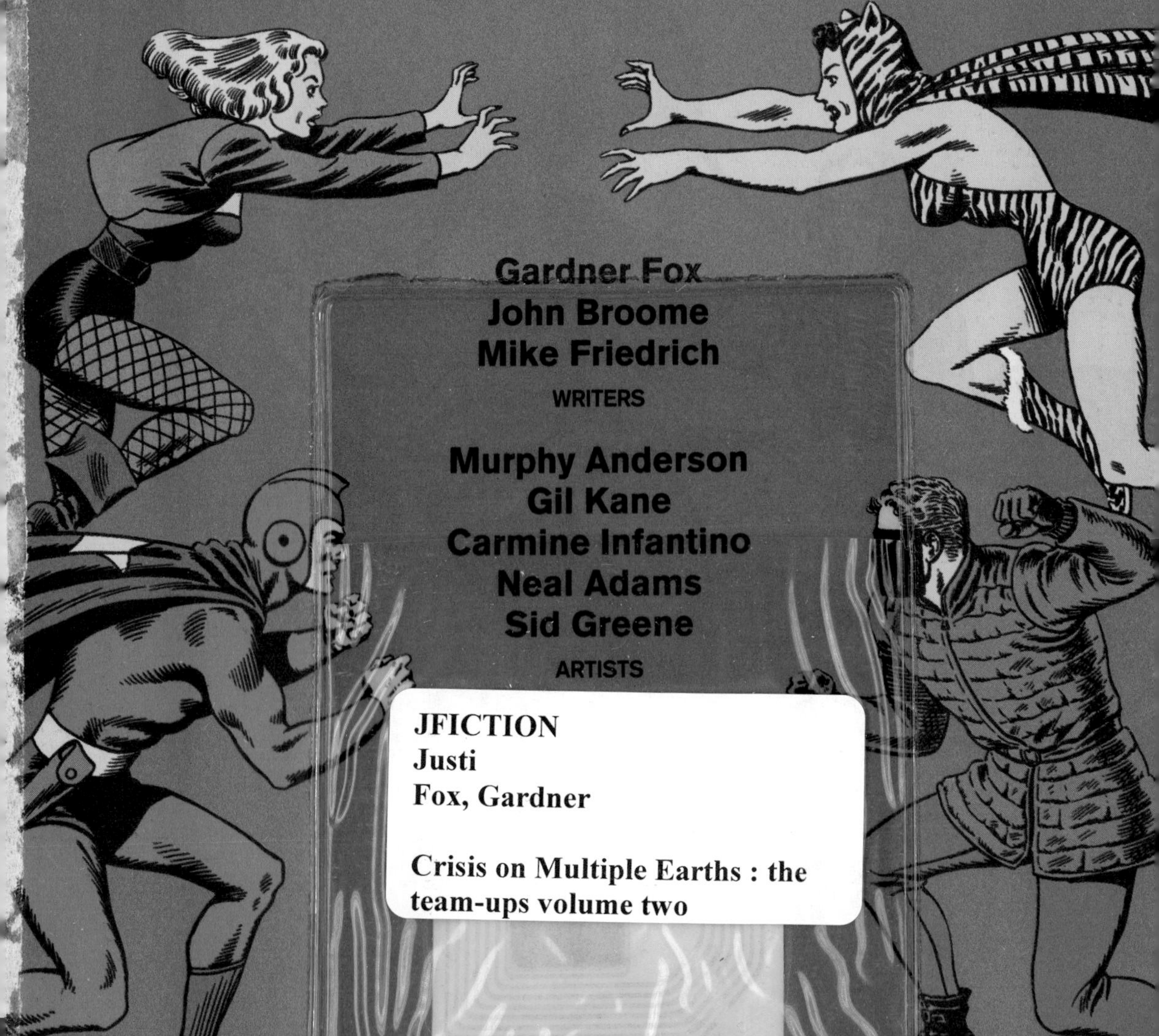

Gardner Fox
John Broome
Mike Friedrich
WRITERS

Murphy Anderson
Gil Kane
Carmine Infantino
Neal Adams
Sid Greene
ARTISTS

VOLUME TWO

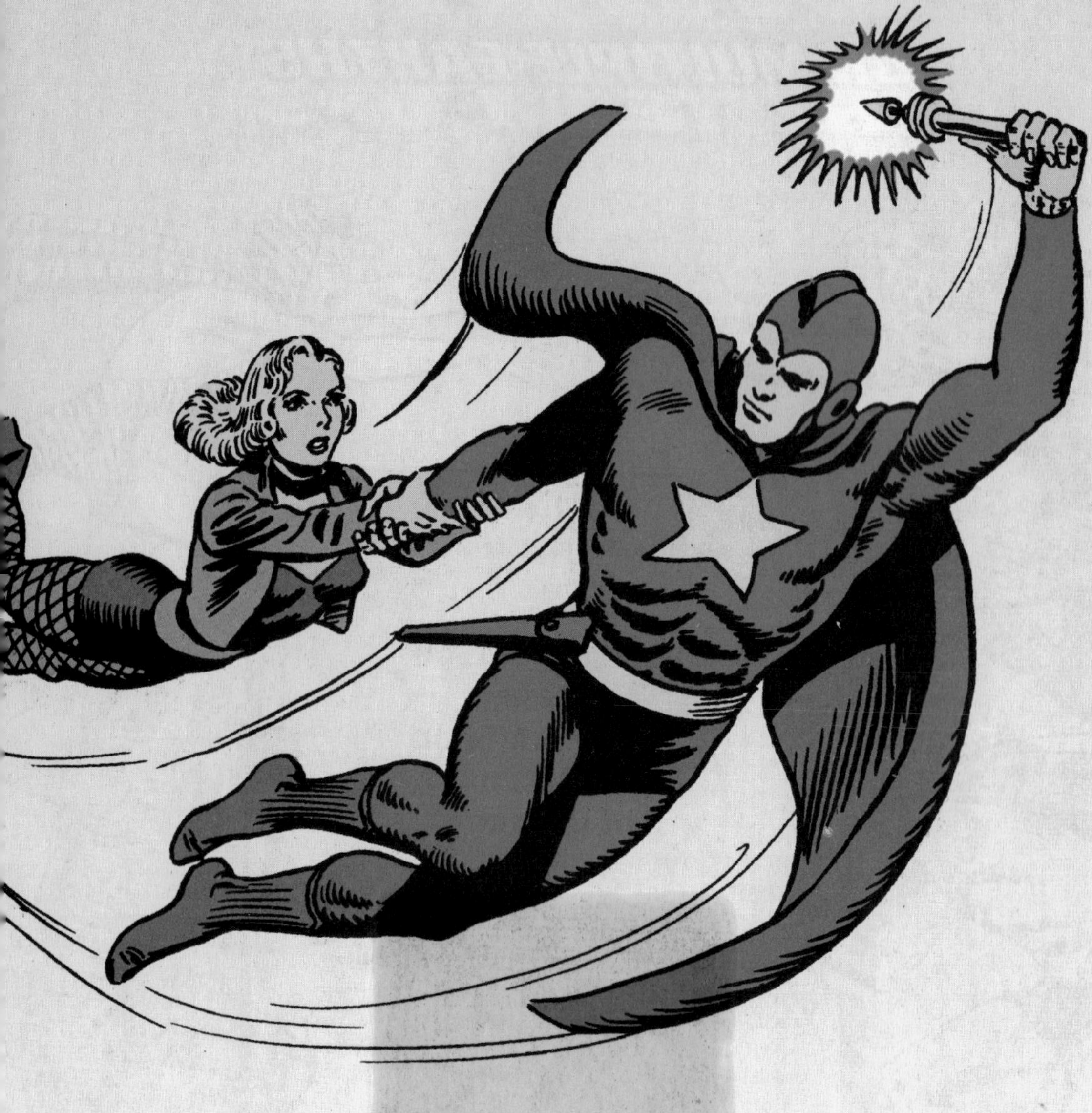

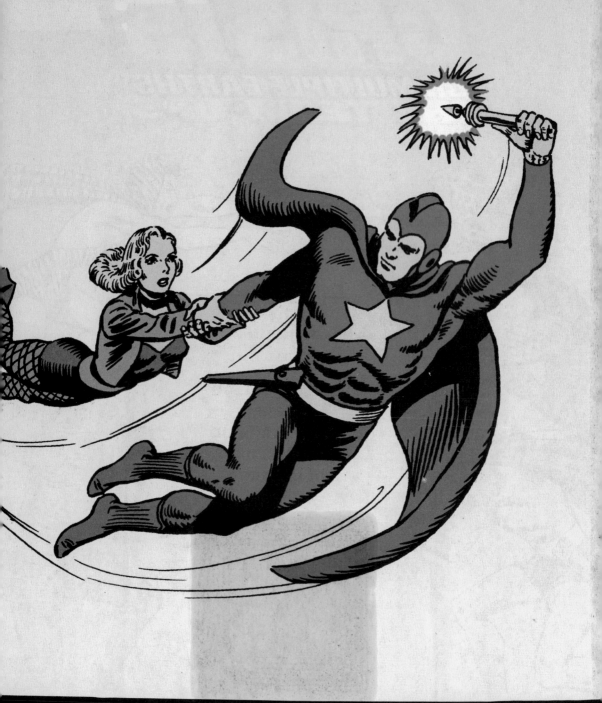

TABLE OF CONTENTS

CRISIS ON MULTIPLE EARTHS: TEAM-UPS VOLUME 2
Published by DC Comics. Cover and compilation copyright © 2007 DC Comics. All Rights Reserved.
Originally published in single magazine form in THE BRAVE AND THE BOLD 62; GREEN LANTERN 45, 52; ATOM 29, 36; FLASH 170, 173;
SPECTRE 3 Copyright © 1965-1968 DC Comics. All Rights Reserved. All characters, their distinctive likenesses and related elements featured in
this publication are trademarks of DC Comics. The stories, characters and incidents featured in this publication are entirely fictional.
DC Comics does not read or accept unsolicited submissions of ideas, stories or artwork.
DC Comics, 1700 Broadway, New York, NY 10019 • A Warner Bros. Entertainment Company • Printed in Canada. First Printing.
ISBN: 1-4012-1228-X ISBN 13: 978-1-4012-1228-5 • Cover illustration by Matt Wagner

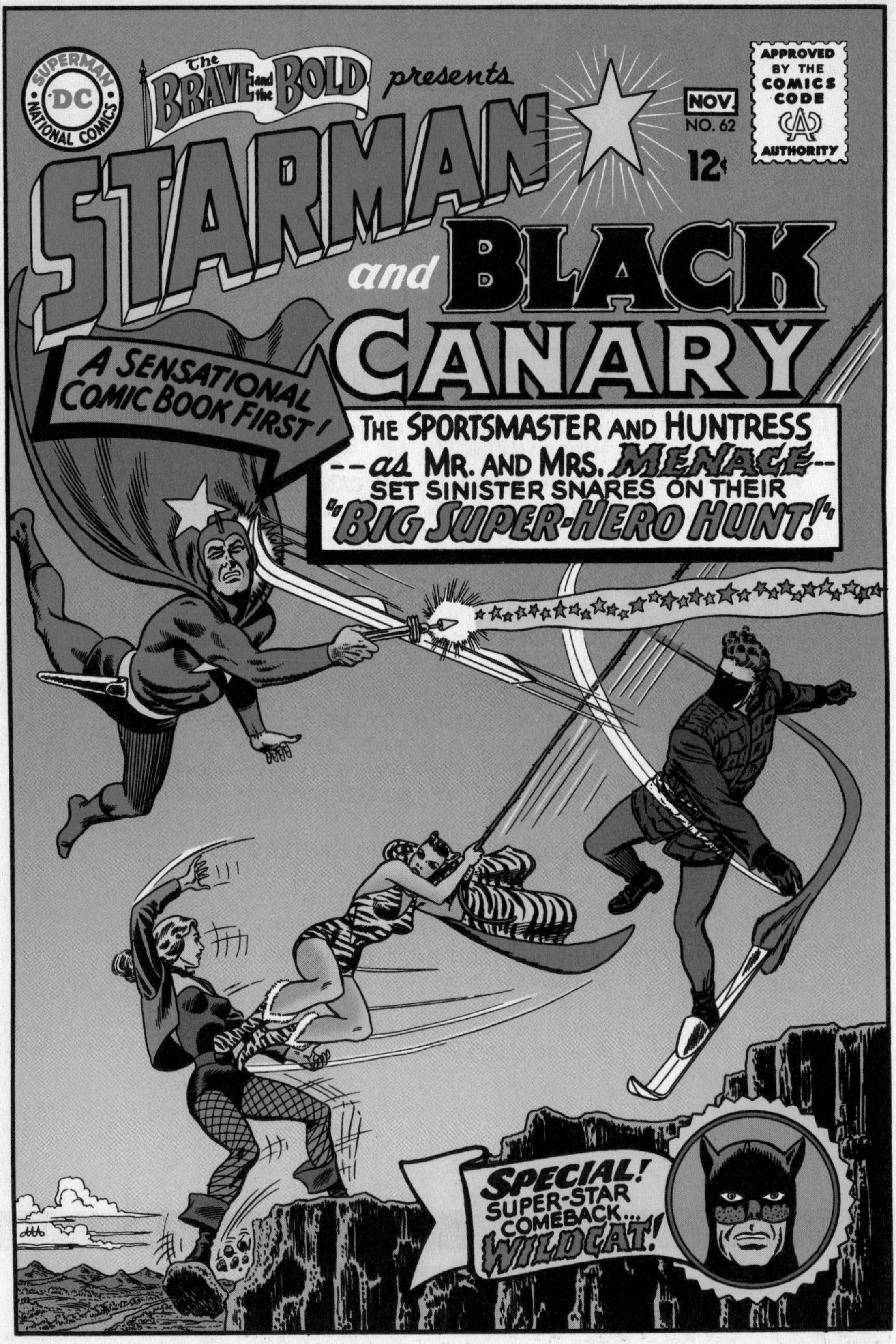
SUPERMAN DC NATIONAL COMICS
The BRAVE and the BOLD presents
STARMAN
NOV. NO. 62
12¢
APPROVED BY THE COMICS CODE AUTHORITY
and BLACK CANARY
A SENSATIONAL COMIC BOOK FIRST!
THE SPORTSMASTER AND HUNTRESS --as MR. AND MRS. MENACE-- SET SINISTER SNARES ON THEIR "BIG SUPER-HERO HUNT!"
SPECIAL! SUPER-STAR COMEBACK... WILDCAT!

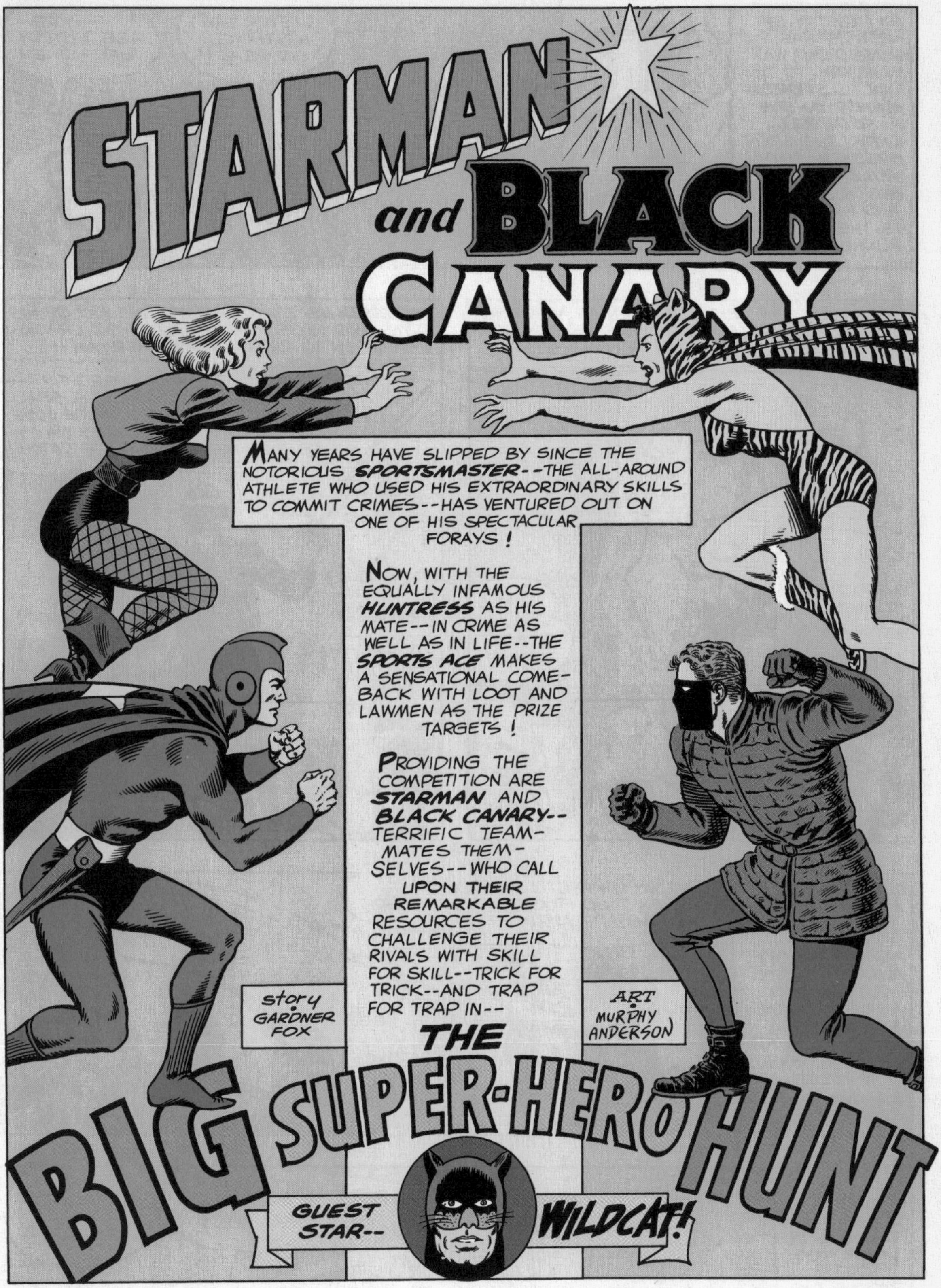
STARMAN and BLACK CANARY
MANY YEARS HAVE SLIPPED BY SINCE THE NOTORIOUS SPORTSMASTER--THE ALL-AROUND ATHLETE WHO USED HIS EXTRAORDINARY SKILLS TO COMMIT CRIMES--HAS VENTURED OUT ON ONE OF HIS SPECTACULAR FORAYS!
NOW, WITH THE EQUALLY INFAMOUS HUNTRESS AS HIS MATE--IN CRIME AS WELL AS IN LIFE--THE SPORTS ACE MAKES A SENSATIONAL COME-BACK WITH LOOT AND LAWMEN AS THE PRIZE TARGETS!
PROVIDING THE COMPETITION ARE STARMAN AND BLACK CANARY--TERRIFIC TEAM-MATES THEM-SELVES--WHO CALL UPON THEIR REMARKABLE RESOURCES TO CHALLENGE THEIR RIVALS WITH SKILL FOR SKILL--TRICK FOR TRICK--AND TRAP FOR TRAP IN--
story GARDNER FOX
ART MURPHY ANDERSON
THE BIG SUPER-HERO HUNT
GUEST STAR--WILDCAT!

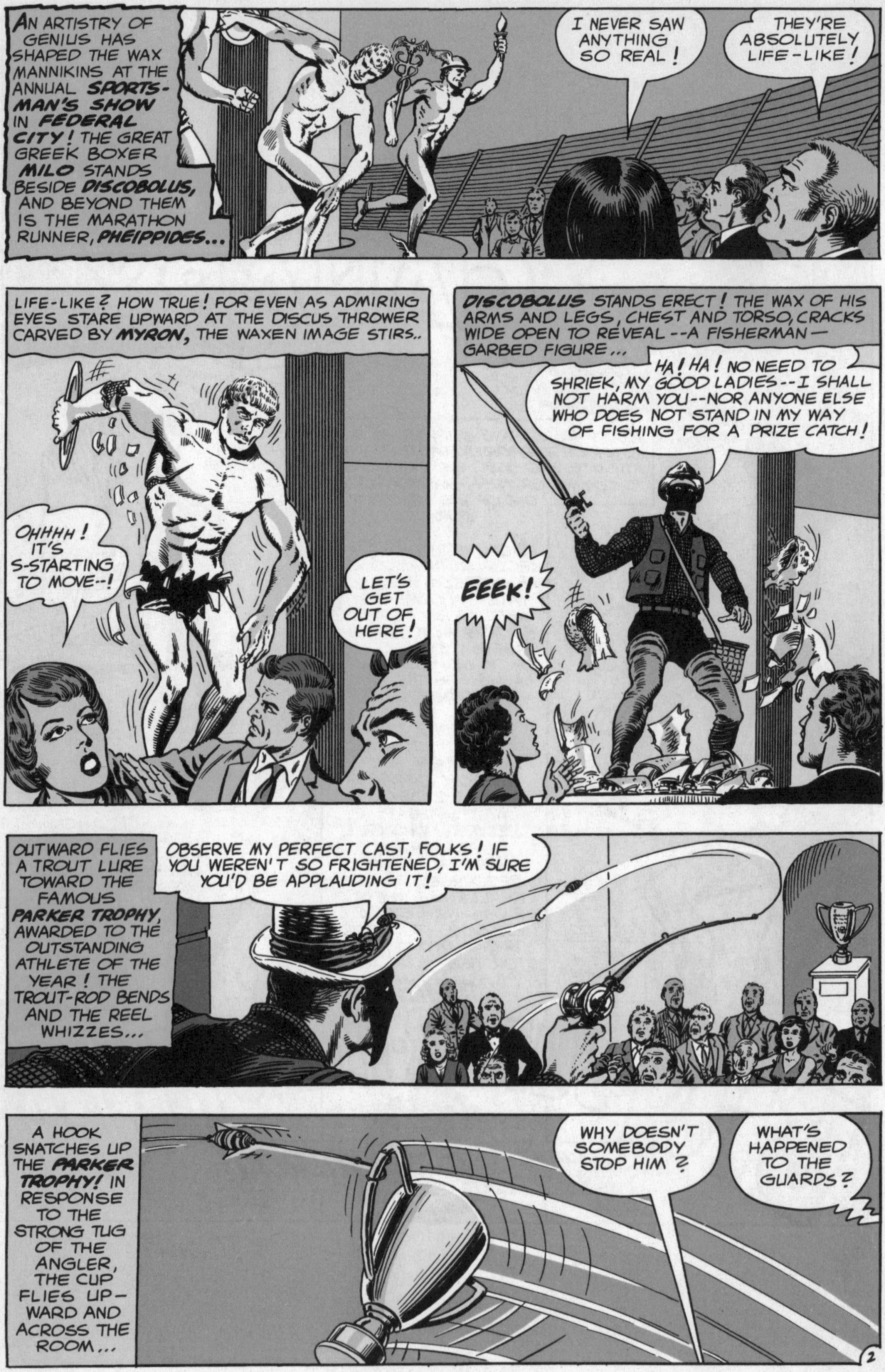
AN ARTISTRY OF GENIUS HAS SHAPED THE WAX MANNIKINS AT THE ANNUAL SPORTSMAN'S SHOW IN FEDERAL CITY! THE GREAT GREEK BOXER MILO STANDS BESIDE DISCOBOLUS, AND BEYOND THEM IS THE MARATHON RUNNER, PHEIPPIDES...
I NEVER SAW ANYTHING SO REAL!
THEY'RE ABSOLUTELY LIFE-LIKE!
LIFE-LIKE? HOW TRUE! FOR EVEN AS ADMIRING EYES STARE UPWARD AT THE DISCUS THROWER CARVED BY MYRON, THE WAXEN IMAGE STIRS..
OHHHH! IT'S S-STARTING TO MOVE--!
LET'S GET OUT OF HERE!
DISCOBOLUS STANDS ERECT! THE WAX OF HIS ARMS AND LEGS, CHEST AND TORSO, CRACKS WIDE OPEN TO REVEAL --A FISHERMAN-GARBED FIGURE...
HA! HA! NO NEED TO SHRIEK, MY GOOD LADIES--I SHALL NOT HARM YOU--NOR ANYONE ELSE WHO DOES NOT STAND IN MY WAY OF FISHING FOR A PRIZE CATCH!
EEEK!
OUTWARD FLIES A TROUT LURE TOWARD THE FAMOUS PARKER TROPHY, AWARDED TO THE OUTSTANDING ATHLETE OF THE YEAR! THE TROUT-ROD BENDS AND THE REEL WHIZZES...
OBSERVE MY PERFECT CAST, FOLKS! IF YOU WEREN'T SO FRIGHTENED, I'M SURE YOU'D BE APPLAUDING IT!
A HOOK SNATCHES UP THE PARKER TROPHY! IN RESPONSE TO THE STRONG TUG OF THE ANGLER, THE CUP FLIES UPWARD AND ACROSS THE ROOM...
WHY DOESN'T SOMEBODY STOP HIM?
WHAT'S HAPPENED TO THE GUARDS?
2

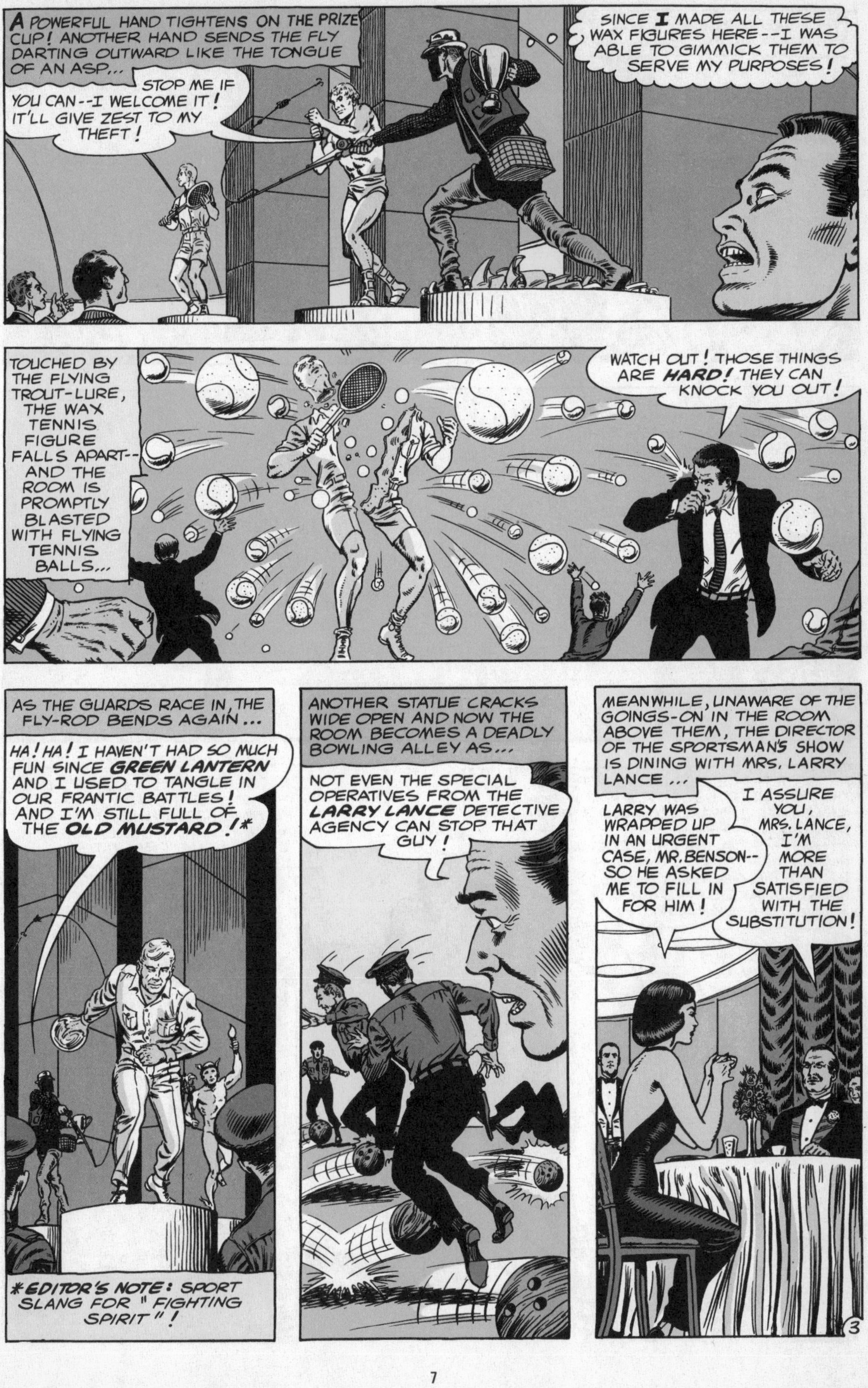
A POWERFUL HAND TIGHTENS ON THE PRIZE CUP! ANOTHER HAND SENDS THE FLY DARTING OUTWARD LIKE THE TONGUE OF AN ASP...
STOP ME IF YOU CAN--I WELCOME IT! IT'LL GIVE ZEST TO MY THEFT!
SINCE I MADE ALL THESE WAX FIGURES HERE--I WAS ABLE TO GIMMICK THEM TO SERVE MY PURPOSES!
TOUCHED BY THE FLYING TROUT-LURE, THE WAX TENNIS FIGURE FALLS APART--AND THE ROOM IS PROMPTLY BLASTED WITH FLYING TENNIS BALLS...
WATCH OUT! THOSE THINGS ARE HARD! THEY CAN KNOCK YOU OUT!
AS THE GUARDS RACE IN, THE FLY-ROD BENDS AGAIN...
HA! HA! I HAVEN'T HAD SO MUCH FUN SINCE GREEN LANTERN AND I USED TO TANGLE IN OUR FRANTIC BATTLES! AND I'M STILL FULL OF THE OLD MUSTARD!*
*EDITOR'S NOTE: SPORT SLANG FOR "FIGHTING SPIRIT"!
ANOTHER STATUE CRACKS WIDE OPEN AND NOW THE ROOM BECOMES A DEADLY BOWLING ALLEY AS...
NOT EVEN THE SPECIAL OPERATIVES FROM THE LARRY LANCE DETECTIVE AGENCY CAN STOP THAT GUY!
MEANWHILE, UNAWARE OF THE GOINGS-ON IN THE ROOM ABOVE THEM, THE DIRECTOR OF THE SPORTSMAN'S SHOW IS DINING WITH MRS. LARRY LANCE...
LARRY WAS WRAPPED UP IN AN URGENT CASE, MR. BENSON--SO HE ASKED ME TO FILL IN FOR HIM!
I ASSURE YOU, MRS. LANCE, I'M MORE THAN SATISFIED WITH THE SUBSTITUTION!
3

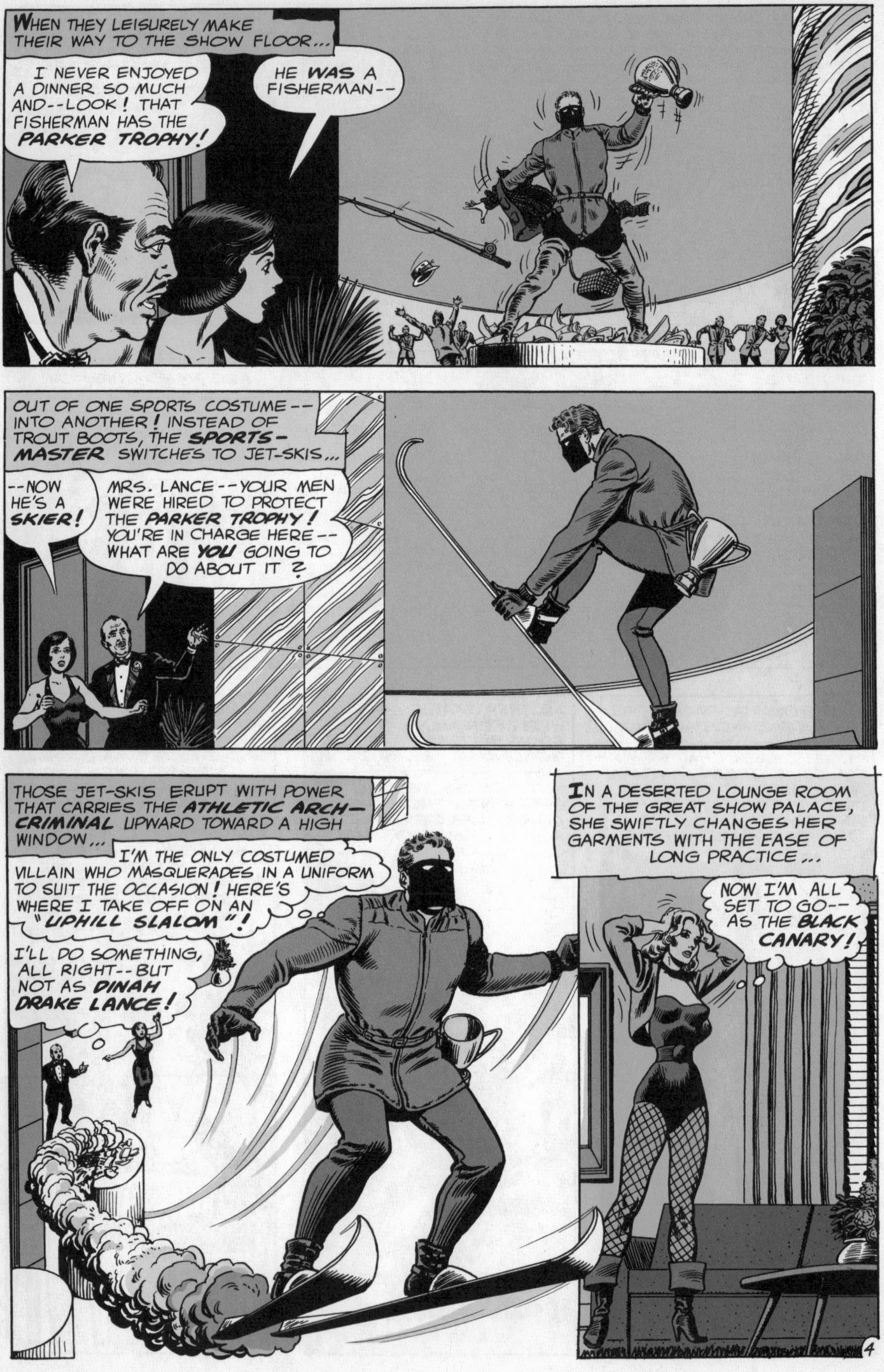
WHEN THEY LEISURELY MAKE THEIR WAY TO THE SHOW FLOOR...
I NEVER ENJOYED A DINNER SO MUCH AND--LOOK! THAT FISHERMAN HAS THE PARKER TROPHY!
HE WAS A FISHERMAN--
OUT OF ONE SPORTS COSTUME--INTO ANOTHER! INSTEAD OF TROUT BOOTS, THE SPORTS-MASTER SWITCHES TO JET-SKIS...
--NOW HE'S A SKIER!
MRS. LANCE--YOUR MEN WERE HIRED TO PROTECT THE PARKER TROPHY! YOU'RE IN CHARGE HERE--WHAT ARE YOU GOING TO DO ABOUT IT?
THOSE JET-SKIS ERUPT WITH POWER THAT CARRIES THE ATHLETIC ARCH-CRIMINAL UPWARD TOWARD A HIGH WINDOW...
I'M THE ONLY COSTUMED VILLAIN WHO MASQUERADES IN A UNIFORM TO SUIT THE OCCASION! HERE'S WHERE I TAKE OFF ON AN "UPHILL SLALOM"!
I'LL DO SOMETHING, ALL RIGHT--BUT NOT AS DINAH DRAKE LANCE!
IN A DESERTED LOUNGE ROOM OF THE GREAT SHOW PALACE, SHE SWIFTLY CHANGES HER GARMENTS WITH THE EASE OF LONG PRACTICE...
NOW I'M ALL SET TO GO--AS THE BLACK CANARY!
4

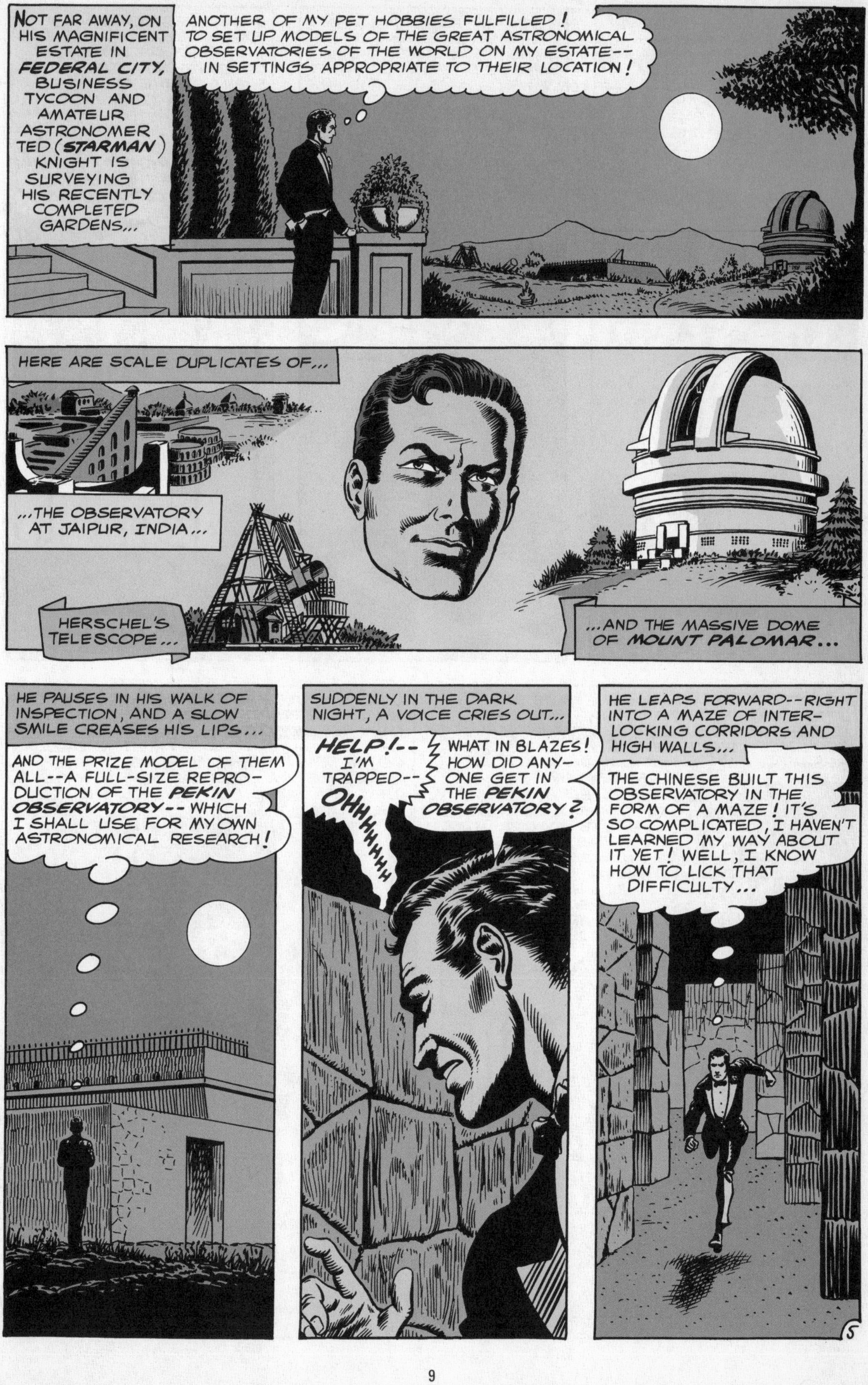
NOT FAR AWAY, ON HIS MAGNIFICENT ESTATE IN FEDERAL CITY, BUSINESS TYCOON AND AMATEUR ASTRONOMER TED (STARMAN) KNIGHT IS SURVEYING HIS RECENTLY COMPLETED GARDENS...
ANOTHER OF MY PET HOBBIES FULFILLED! TO SET UP MODELS OF THE GREAT ASTRONOMICAL OBSERVATORIES OF THE WORLD ON MY ESTATE-- IN SETTINGS APPROPRIATE TO THEIR LOCATION!
HERE ARE SCALE DUPLICATES OF...
...THE OBSERVATORY AT JAIPUR, INDIA...
HERSCHEL'S TELESCOPE...
...AND THE MASSIVE DOME OF MOUNT PALOMAR...
HE PAUSES IN HIS WALK OF INSPECTION, AND A SLOW SMILE CREASES HIS LIPS...
AND THE PRIZE MODEL OF THEM ALL--A FULL-SIZE REPRODUCTION OF THE PEKIN OBSERVATORY-- WHICH I SHALL USE FOR MY OWN ASTRONOMICAL RESEARCH!
SUDDENLY IN THE DARK NIGHT, A VOICE CRIES OUT...
HELP!-- I'M TRAPPED-- OHHHHHHH
WHAT IN BLAZES! HOW DID ANYONE GET IN THE PEKIN OBSERVATORY?
HE LEAPS FORWARD--RIGHT INTO A MAZE OF INTERLOCKING CORRIDORS AND HIGH WALLS...
THE CHINESE BUILT THIS OBSERVATORY IN THE FORM OF A MAZE! IT'S SO COMPLICATED, I HAVEN'T LEARNED MY WAY ABOUT IT YET! WELL, I KNOW HOW TO LICK THAT DIFFICULTY...
5

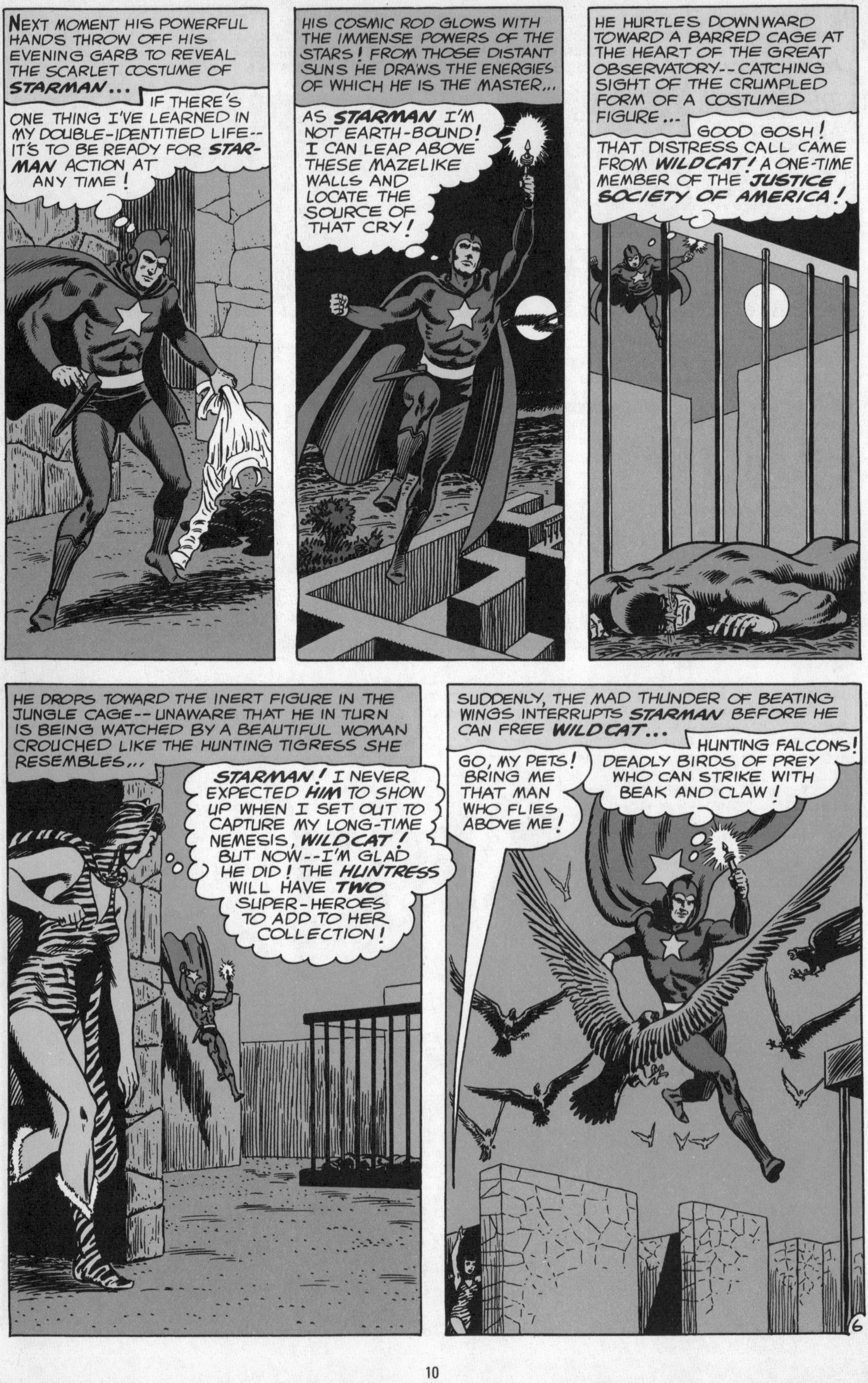
NEXT MOMENT HIS POWERFUL HANDS THROW OFF HIS EVENING GARB TO REVEAL THE SCARLET COSTUME OF STARMAN...
IF THERE'S ONE THING I'VE LEARNED IN MY DOUBLE-IDENTITIED LIFE-- IT'S TO BE READY FOR STAR-MAN ACTION AT ANY TIME!
HIS COSMIC ROD GLOWS WITH THE IMMENSE POWERS OF THE STARS! FROM THOSE DISTANT SUNS HE DRAWS THE ENERGIES OF WHICH HE IS THE MASTER...
AS STARMAN I'M NOT EARTH-BOUND! I CAN LEAP ABOVE THESE MAZELIKE WALLS AND LOCATE THE SOURCE OF THAT CRY!
HE HURTLES DOWNWARD TOWARD A BARRED CAGE AT THE HEART OF THE GREAT OBSERVATORY--CATCHING SIGHT OF THE CRUMPLED FORM OF A COSTUMED FIGURE...
GOOD GOSH! THAT DISTRESS CALL CAME FROM WILDCAT! A ONE-TIME MEMBER OF THE JUSTICE SOCIETY OF AMERICA!
HE DROPS TOWARD THE INERT FIGURE IN THE JUNGLE CAGE--UNAWARE THAT HE IN TURN IS BEING WATCHED BY A BEAUTIFUL WOMAN CROUCHED LIKE THE HUNTING TIGRESS SHE RESEMBLES...
STARMAN! I NEVER EXPECTED HIM TO SHOW UP WHEN I SET OUT TO CAPTURE MY LONG-TIME NEMESIS, WILDCAT! BUT NOW--I'M GLAD HE DID! THE HUNTRESS WILL HAVE TWO SUPER-HEROES TO ADD TO HER COLLECTION!
SUDDENLY, THE MAD THUNDER OF BEATING WINGS INTERRUPTS STARMAN BEFORE HE CAN FREE WILDCAT...
GO, MY PETS! BRING ME THAT MAN WHO FLIES ABOVE ME!
HUNTING FALCONS! DEADLY BIRDS OF PREY WHO CAN STRIKE WITH BEAK AND CLAW!
6

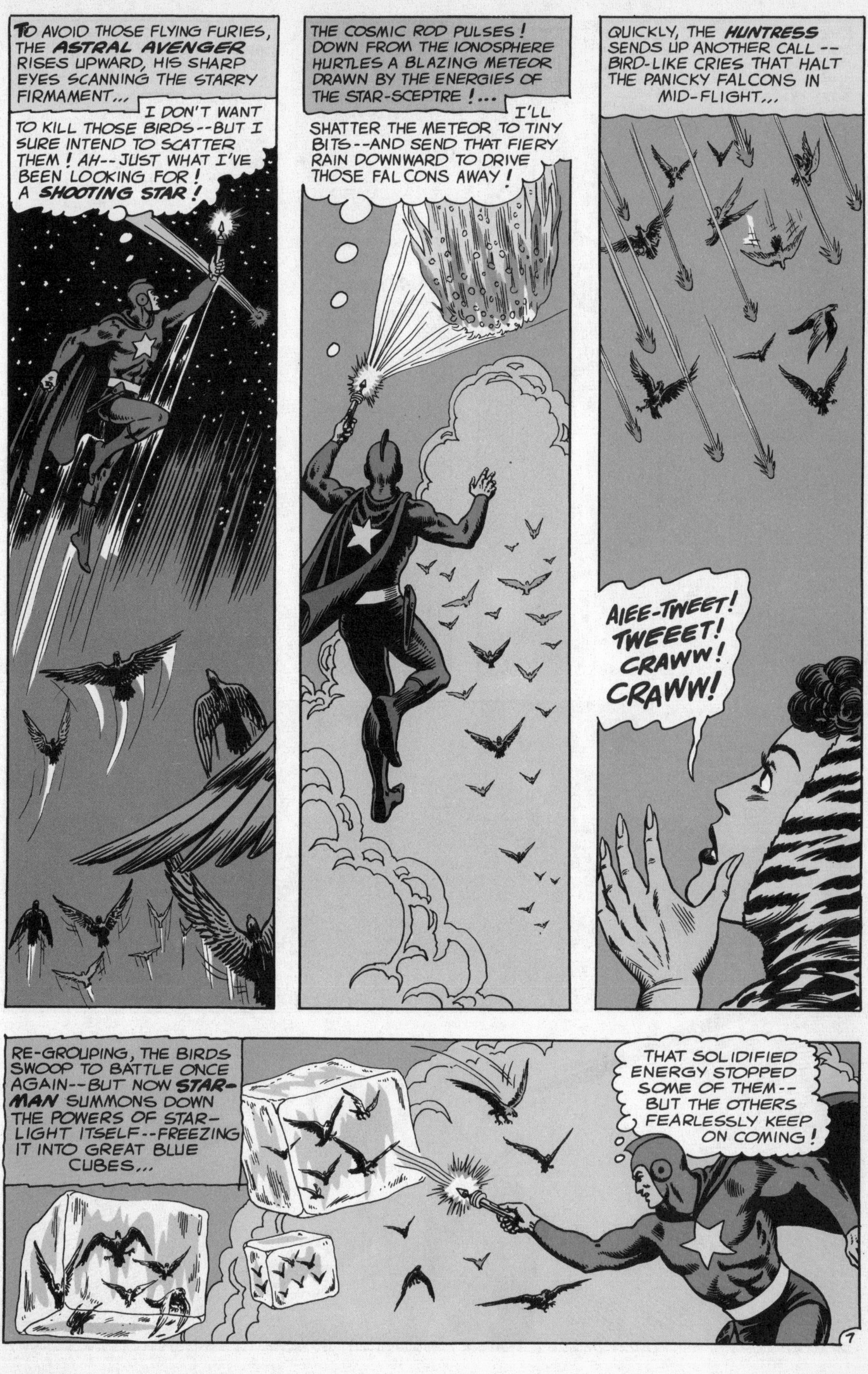

TO AVOID THOSE FLYING FURIES, THE ASTRAL AVENGER RISES UPWARD, HIS SHARP EYES SCANNING THE STARRY FIRMAMENT...
I DON'T WANT TO KILL THOSE BIRDS--BUT I SURE INTEND TO SCATTER THEM! AH--JUST WHAT I'VE BEEN LOOKING FOR! A SHOOTING STAR!
THE COSMIC ROD PULSES! DOWN FROM THE IONOSPHERE HURTLES A BLAZING METEOR DRAWN BY THE ENERGIES OF THE STAR-SCEPTRE!...
I'LL SHATTER THE METEOR TO TINY BITS--AND SEND THAT FIERY RAIN DOWNWARD TO DRIVE THOSE FALCONS AWAY!
QUICKLY, THE HUNTRESS SENDS UP ANOTHER CALL--BIRD-LIKE CRIES THAT HALT THE PANICKY FALCONS IN MID-FLIGHT...
AIEE-TWEET! TWEEET! CRAWW! CRAWW!
RE-GROUPING, THE BIRDS SWOOP TO BATTLE ONCE AGAIN--BUT NOW STAR-MAN SUMMONS DOWN THE POWERS OF STAR-LIGHT ITSELF--FREEZING IT INTO GREAT BLUE CUBES...
THAT SOLIDIFIED ENERGY STOPPED SOME OF THEM--BUT THE OTHERS FEARLESSLY KEEP ON COMING!
7

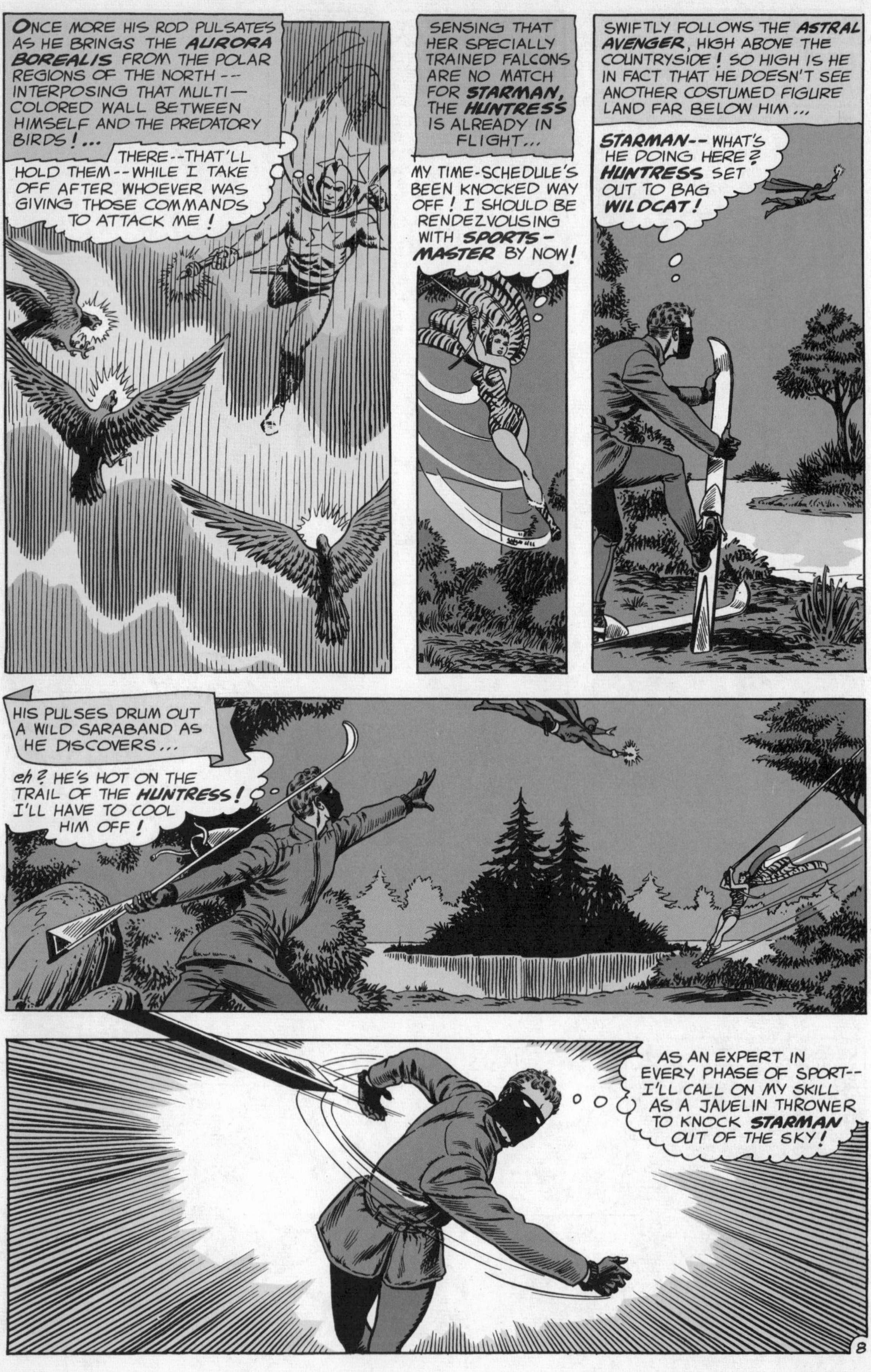
ONCE MORE HIS ROD PULSATES AS HE BRINGS THE AURORA BOREALIS FROM THE POLAR REGIONS OF THE NORTH -- INTERPOSING THAT MULTI-COLORED WALL BETWEEN HIMSELF AND THE PREDATORY BIRDS!...
THERE--THAT'LL HOLD THEM--WHILE I TAKE OFF AFTER WHOEVER WAS GIVING THOSE COMMANDS TO ATTACK ME!
SENSING THAT HER SPECIALLY TRAINED FALCONS ARE NO MATCH FOR STARMAN, THE HUNTRESS IS ALREADY IN FLIGHT...
MY TIME-SCHEDULE'S BEEN KNOCKED WAY OFF! I SHOULD BE RENDEZVOUSING WITH SPORTS-MASTER BY NOW!
SWIFTLY FOLLOWS THE ASTRAL AVENGER, HIGH ABOVE THE COUNTRYSIDE! SO HIGH IS HE IN FACT THAT HE DOESN'T SEE ANOTHER COSTUMED FIGURE LAND FAR BELOW HIM...
STARMAN-- WHAT'S HE DOING HERE? HUNTRESS SET OUT TO BAG WILDCAT!
HIS PULSES DRUM OUT A WILD SARABAND AS HE DISCOVERS...
eh? HE'S HOT ON THE TRAIL OF THE HUNTRESS! I'LL HAVE TO COOL HIM OFF!
AS AN EXPERT IN EVERY PHASE OF SPORT-- I'LL CALL ON MY SKILL AS A JAVELIN THROWER TO KNOCK STARMAN OUT OF THE SKY!
8

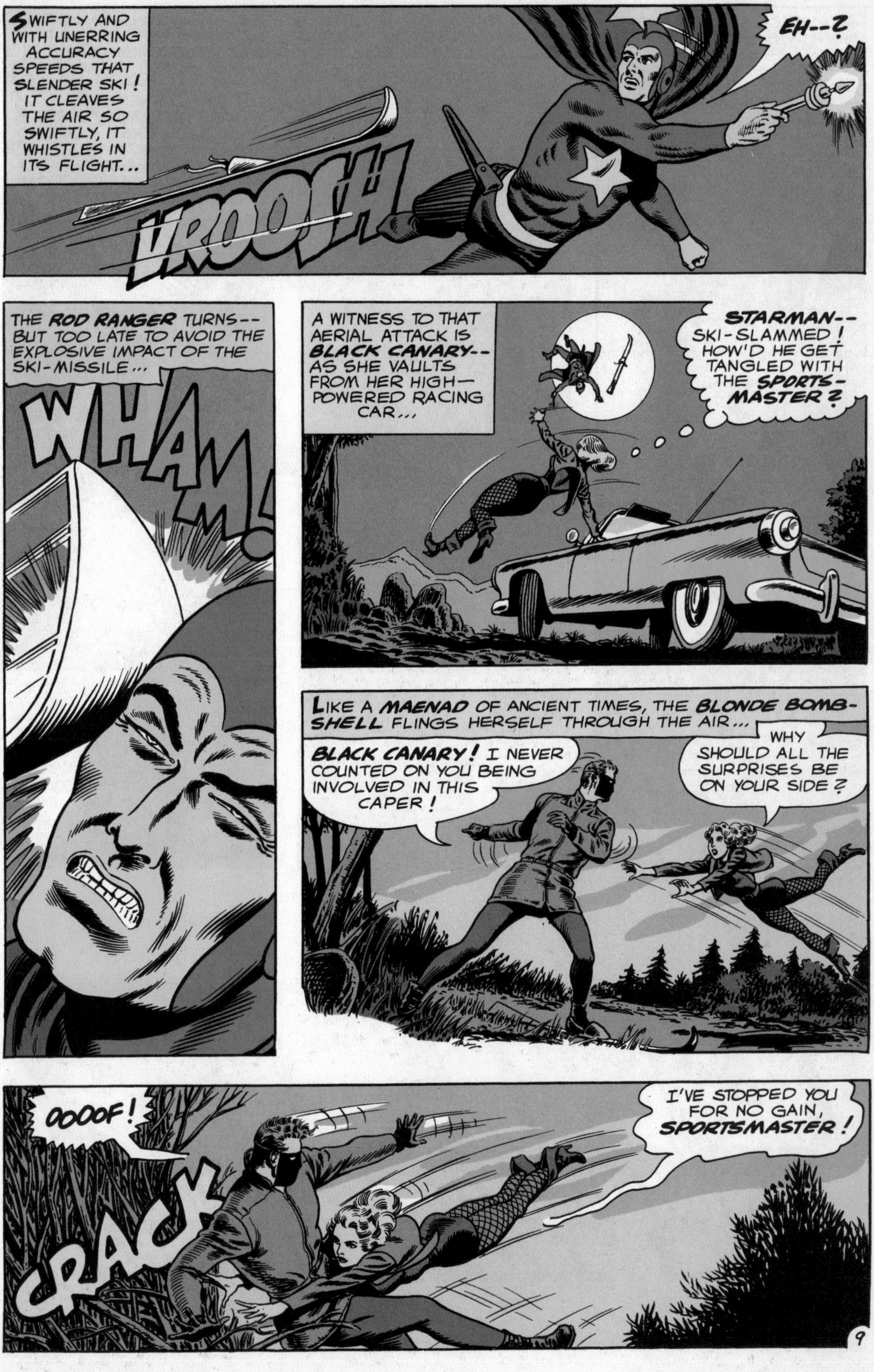
SWIFTLY AND WITH UNERRING ACCURACY SPEEDS THAT SLENDER SKI! IT CLEAVES THE AIR SO SWIFTLY, IT WHISTLES IN ITS FLIGHT...
EH--?
VROOSH
THE ROD RANGER TURNS-- BUT TOO LATE TO AVOID THE EXPLOSIVE IMPACT OF THE SKI-MISSILE...
WHAM!
A WITNESS TO THAT AERIAL ATTACK IS BLACK CANARY-- AS SHE VAULTS FROM HER HIGH-POWERED RACING CAR...
STARMAN-- SKI-SLAMMED! HOW'D HE GET TANGLED WITH THE SPORTS-MASTER?
LIKE A MAENAD OF ANCIENT TIMES, THE BLONDE BOMB-SHELL FLINGS HERSELF THROUGH THE AIR...
BLACK CANARY! I NEVER COUNTED ON YOU BEING INVOLVED IN THIS CAPER!
WHY SHOULD ALL THE SURPRISES BE ON YOUR SIDE?
OOOOF!
CRACK
I'VE STOPPED YOU FOR NO GAIN, SPORTSMASTER!
9

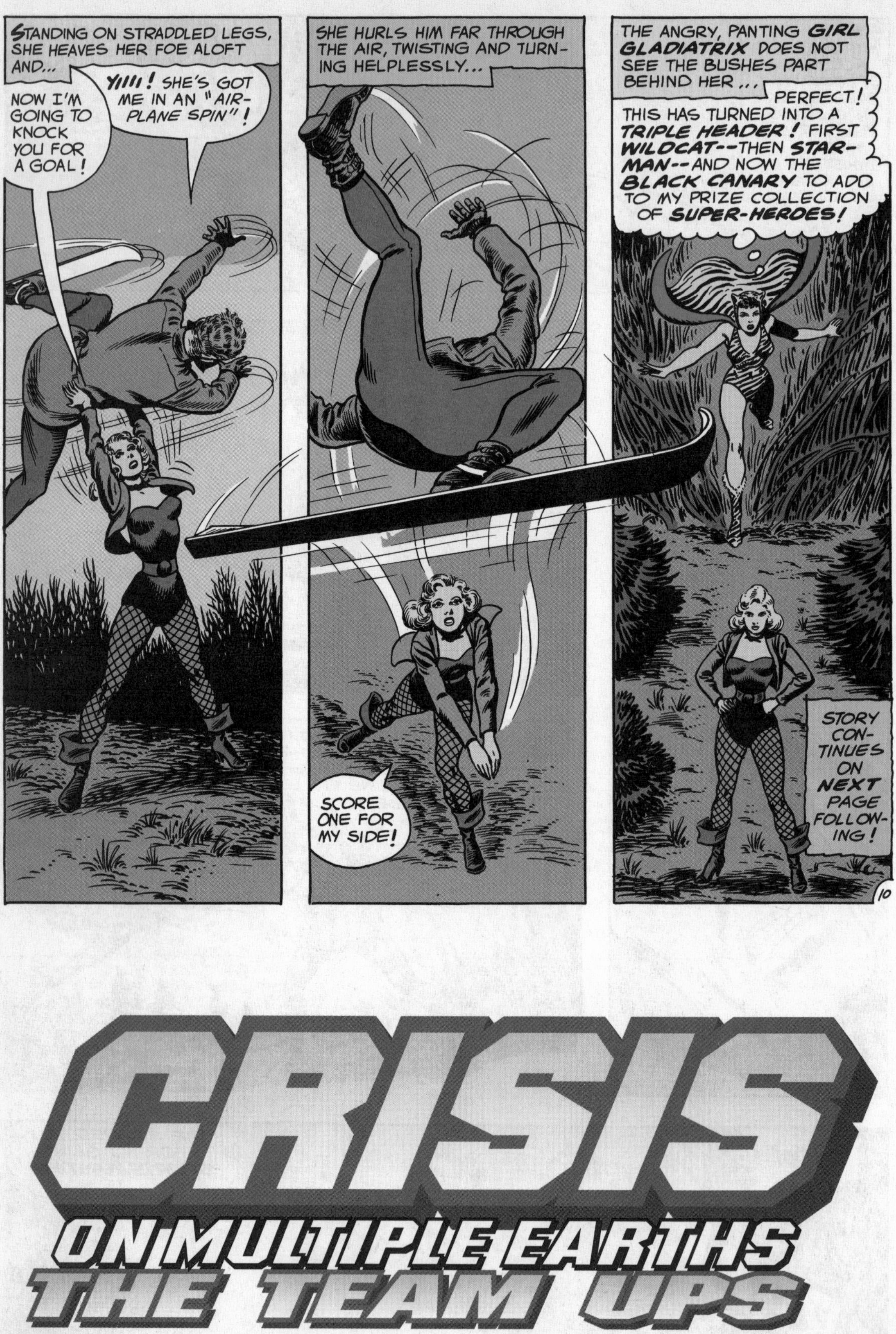
STANDING ON STRADDLED LEGS, SHE HEAVES HER FOE ALOFT AND...
NOW I'M GOING TO KNOCK YOU FOR A GOAL!
YIIII! SHE'S GOT ME IN AN "AIR-PLANE SPIN"!
SHE HURLS HIM FAR THROUGH THE AIR, TWISTING AND TURN-ING HELPLESSLY...
SCORE ONE FOR MY SIDE!
THE ANGRY, PANTING GIRL GLADIATRIX DOES NOT SEE THE BUSHES PART BEHIND HER...
PERFECT! THIS HAS TURNED INTO A TRIPLE HEADER! FIRST WILDCAT--THEN STAR-MAN--AND NOW THE BLACK CANARY TO ADD TO MY PRIZE COLLECTION OF SUPER-HEROES!
STORY CON-TINUES ON NEXT PAGE FOLLOW-ING!
10

CRISIS ON MULTIPLE EARTHS THE TEAM UPS

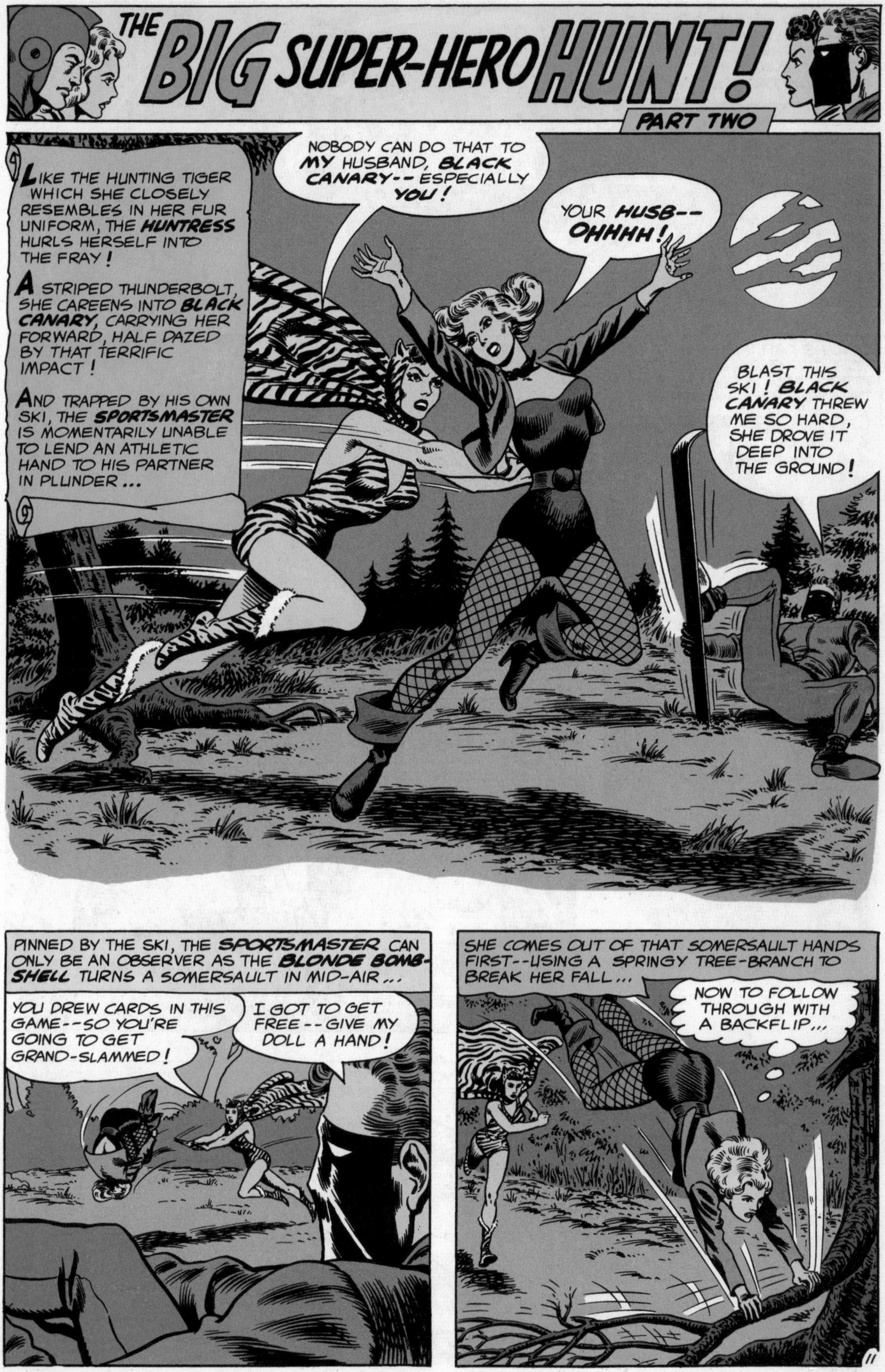
THE BIG SUPER-HERO HUNT!
PART TWO
LIKE THE HUNTING TIGER WHICH SHE CLOSELY RESEMBLES IN HER FUR UNIFORM, THE HUNTRESS HURLS HERSELF INTO THE FRAY!
A STRIPED THUNDERBOLT, SHE CAREENS INTO BLACK CANARY, CARRYING HER FORWARD, HALF DAZED BY THAT TERRIFIC IMPACT!
AND TRAPPED BY HIS OWN SKI, THE SPORTSMASTER IS MOMENTARILY UNABLE TO LEND AN ATHLETIC HAND TO HIS PARTNER IN PLUNDER...
NOBODY CAN DO THAT TO MY HUSBAND, BLACK CANARY-- ESPECIALLY YOU!
YOUR HUSB-- OHHHH!
BLAST THIS SKI! BLACK CANARY THREW ME SO HARD, SHE DROVE IT DEEP INTO THE GROUND!
PINNED BY THE SKI, THE SPORTSMASTER CAN ONLY BE AN OBSERVER AS THE BLONDE BOMB-SHELL TURNS A SOMERSAULT IN MID-AIR...
YOU DREW CARDS IN THIS GAME--SO YOU'RE GOING TO GET GRAND-SLAMMED!
I GOT TO GET FREE--GIVE MY DOLL A HAND!
SHE COMES OUT OF THAT SOMERSAULT HANDS FIRST--USING A SPRINGY TREE-BRANCH TO BREAK HER FALL...
NOW TO FOLLOW THROUGH WITH A BACKFLIP...
11

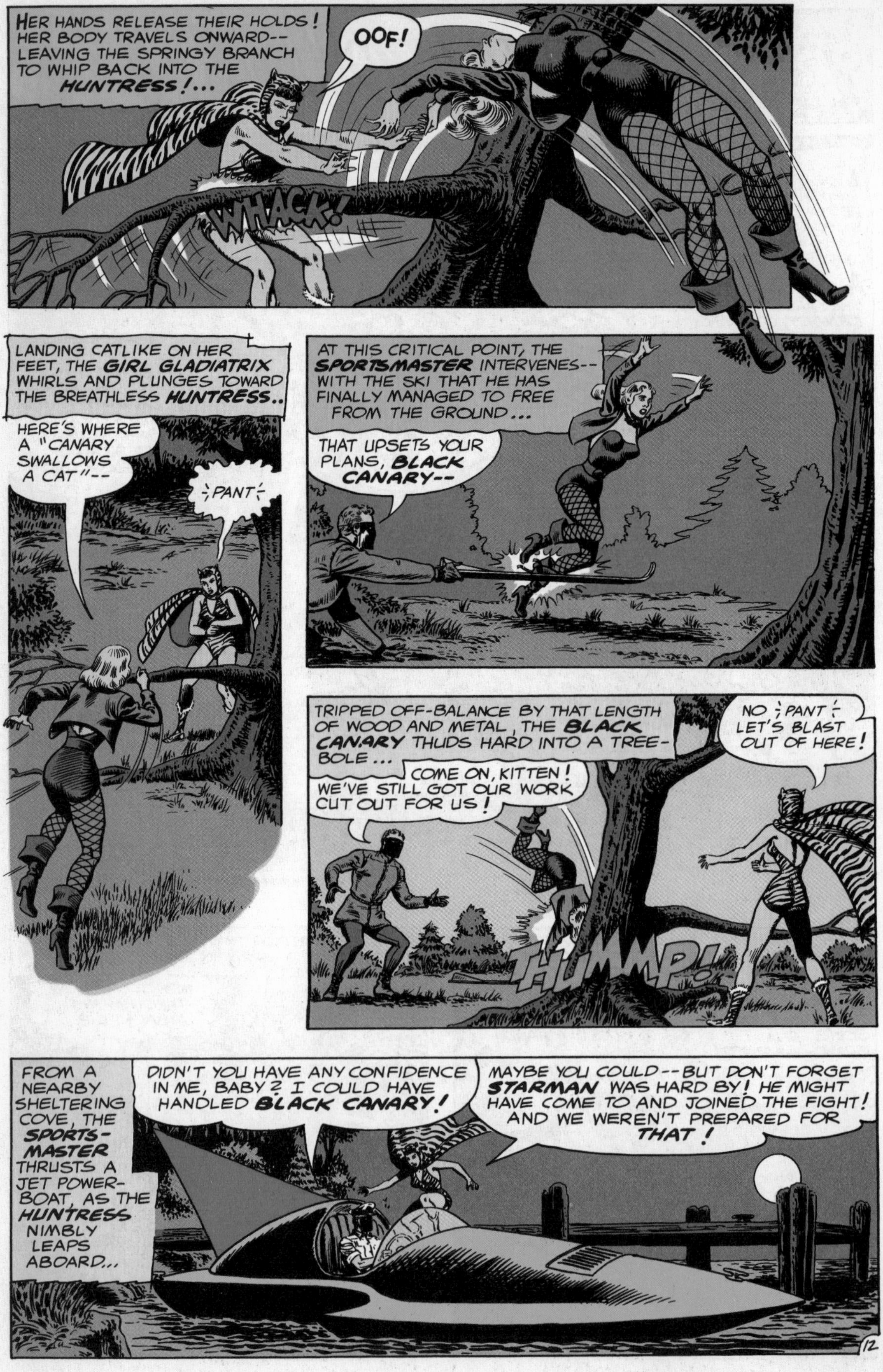

HER HANDS RELEASE THEIR HOLDS! HER BODY TRAVELS ONWARD-- LEAVING THE SPRINGY BRANCH TO WHIP BACK INTO THE HUNTRESS!...
OOF!
WHACK!
LANDING CATLIKE ON HER FEET, THE GIRL GLADIATRIX WHIRLS AND PLUNGES TOWARD THE BREATHLESS HUNTRESS..
HERE'S WHERE A "CANARY SWALLOWS A CAT"--
PANT
AT THIS CRITICAL POINT, THE SPORTSMASTER INTERVENES-- WITH THE SKI THAT HE HAS FINALLY MANAGED TO FREE FROM THE GROUND...
THAT UPSETS YOUR PLANS, BLACK CANARY--
TRIPPED OFF-BALANCE BY THAT LENGTH OF WOOD AND METAL, THE BLACK CANARY THUDS HARD INTO A TREE-BOLE...
COME ON, KITTEN! WE'VE STILL GOT OUR WORK CUT OUT FOR US!
NO PANT LET'S BLAST OUT OF HERE!
THUMMP!
FROM A NEARBY SHELTERING COVE, THE SPORTSMASTER THRUSTS A JET POWER-BOAT, AS THE HUNTRESS NIMBLY LEAPS ABOARD...
DIDN'T YOU HAVE ANY CONFIDENCE IN ME, BABY? I COULD HAVE HANDLED BLACK CANARY!
MAYBE YOU COULD--BUT DON'T FORGET STARMAN WAS HARD BY! HE MIGHT HAVE COME TO AND JOINED THE FIGHT! AND WE WEREN'T PREPARED FOR THAT!
12

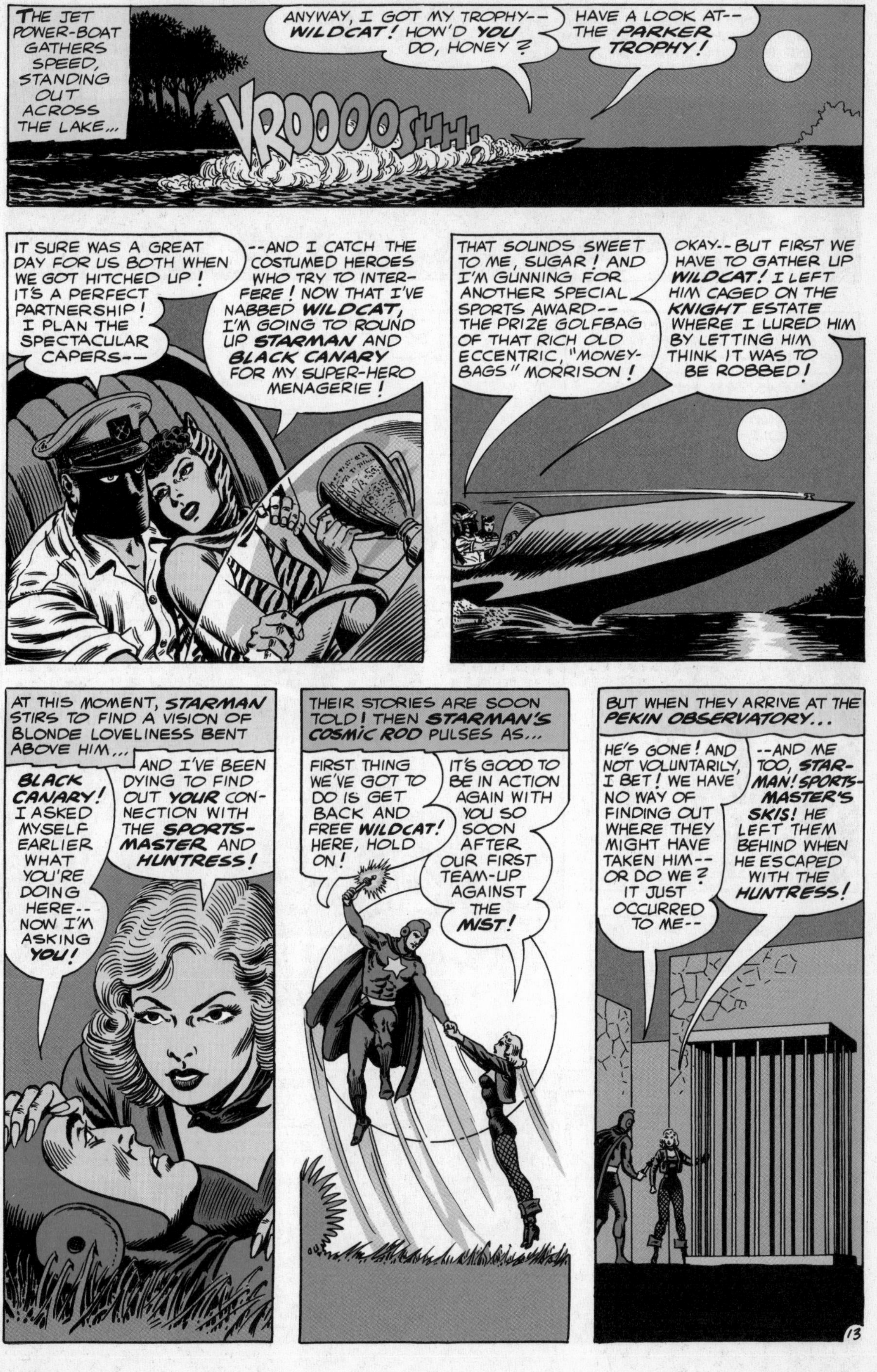
THE JET POWER-BOAT GATHERS SPEED, STANDING OUT ACROSS THE LAKE...
ANYWAY, I GOT MY TROPHY-- WILDCAT! HOW'D YOU DO, HONEY?
HAVE A LOOK AT-- THE PARKER TROPHY!
VROOOOOSHH!
IT SURE WAS A GREAT DAY FOR US BOTH WHEN WE GOT HITCHED UP! IT'S A PERFECT PARTNERSHIP! I PLAN THE SPECTACULAR CAPERS--
--AND I CATCH THE COSTUMED HEROES WHO TRY TO INTERFERE! NOW THAT I'VE NABBED WILDCAT, I'M GOING TO ROUND UP STARMAN AND BLACK CANARY FOR MY SUPER-HERO MENAGERIE!
THAT SOUNDS SWEET TO ME, SUGAR! AND I'M GUNNING FOR ANOTHER SPECIAL SPORTS AWARD-- THE PRIZE GOLFBAG OF THAT RICH OLD ECCENTRIC, "MONEY-BAGS" MORRISON!
OKAY-- BUT FIRST WE HAVE TO GATHER UP WILDCAT! I LEFT HIM CAGED ON THE KNIGHT ESTATE WHERE I LURED HIM BY LETTING HIM THINK IT WAS TO BE ROBBED!
AT THIS MOMENT, STARMAN STIRS TO FIND A VISION OF BLONDE LOVELINESS BENT ABOVE HIM...
BLACK CANARY! I ASKED MYSELF EARLIER WHAT YOU'RE DOING HERE-- NOW I'M ASKING YOU!
AND I'VE BEEN DYING TO FIND OUT YOUR CONNECTION WITH THE SPORTS-MASTER AND HUNTRESS!
THEIR STORIES ARE SOON TOLD! THEN STARMAN'S COSMIC ROD PULSES AS...
FIRST THING WE'VE GOT TO DO IS GET BACK AND FREE WILDCAT! HERE, HOLD ON!
IT'S GOOD TO BE IN ACTION AGAIN WITH YOU SO SOON AFTER OUR FIRST TEAM-UP AGAINST THE MIST!
BUT WHEN THEY ARRIVE AT THE PEKIN OBSERVATORY...
HE'S GONE! AND NOT VOLUNTARILY, I BET! WE HAVE NO WAY OF FINDING OUT WHERE THEY MIGHT HAVE TAKEN HIM-- OR DO WE? IT JUST OCCURRED TO ME--
--AND ME TOO, STARMAN! SPORTSMASTER'S SKIS! HE LEFT THEM BEHIND WHEN HE ESCAPED WITH THE HUNTRESS!
13

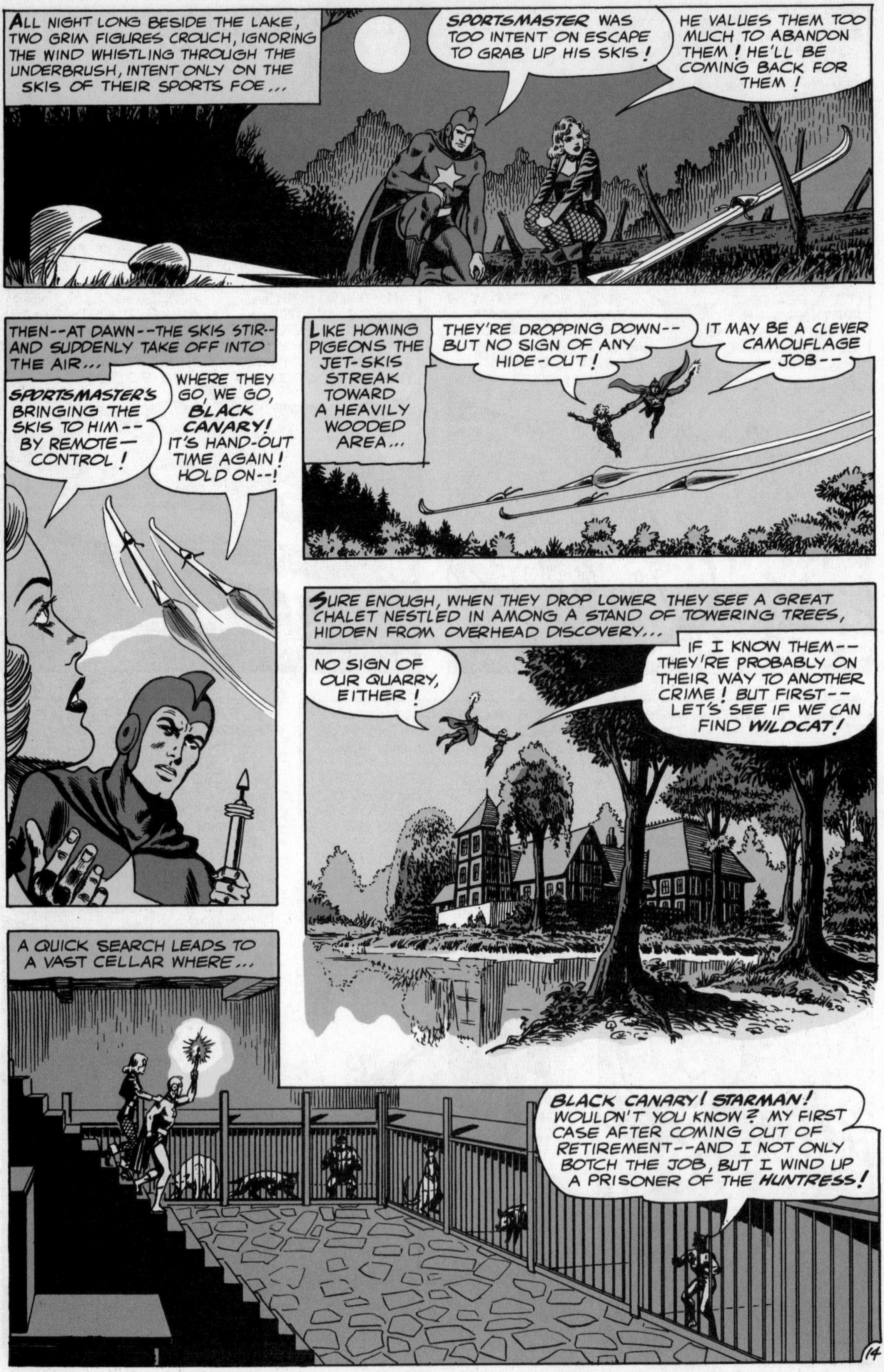
ALL NIGHT LONG BESIDE THE LAKE, TWO GRIM FIGURES CROUCH, IGNORING THE WIND WHISTLING THROUGH THE UNDERBRUSH, INTENT ONLY ON THE SKIS OF THEIR SPORTS FOE...
SPORTSMASTER WAS TOO INTENT ON ESCAPE TO GRAB UP HIS SKIS!
HE VALUES THEM TOO MUCH TO ABANDON THEM! HE'LL BE COMING BACK FOR THEM!
THEN--AT DAWN--THE SKIS STIR--AND SUDDENLY TAKE OFF INTO THE AIR...
SPORTSMASTER'S BRINGING THE SKIS TO HIM--BY REMOTE-CONTROL!
WHERE THEY GO, WE GO, BLACK CANARY! IT'S HAND-OUT TIME AGAIN! HOLD ON--!
LIKE HOMING PIGEONS THE JET-SKIS STREAK TOWARD A HEAVILY WOODED AREA...
THEY'RE DROPPING DOWN--BUT NO SIGN OF ANY HIDE-OUT!
IT MAY BE A CLEVER CAMOUFLAGE JOB--
SURE ENOUGH, WHEN THEY DROP LOWER THEY SEE A GREAT CHALET NESTLED IN AMONG A STAND OF TOWERING TREES, HIDDEN FROM OVERHEAD DISCOVERY...
NO SIGN OF OUR QUARRY, EITHER!
IF I KNOW THEM--THEY'RE PROBABLY ON THEIR WAY TO ANOTHER CRIME! BUT FIRST--LET'S SEE IF WE CAN FIND WILDCAT!
A QUICK SEARCH LEADS TO A VAST CELLAR WHERE...
BLACK CANARY! STARMAN! WOULDN'T YOU KNOW? MY FIRST CASE AFTER COMING OUT OF RETIREMENT--AND I NOT ONLY BOTCH THE JOB, BUT I WIND UP A PRISONER OF THE HUNTRESS!
14

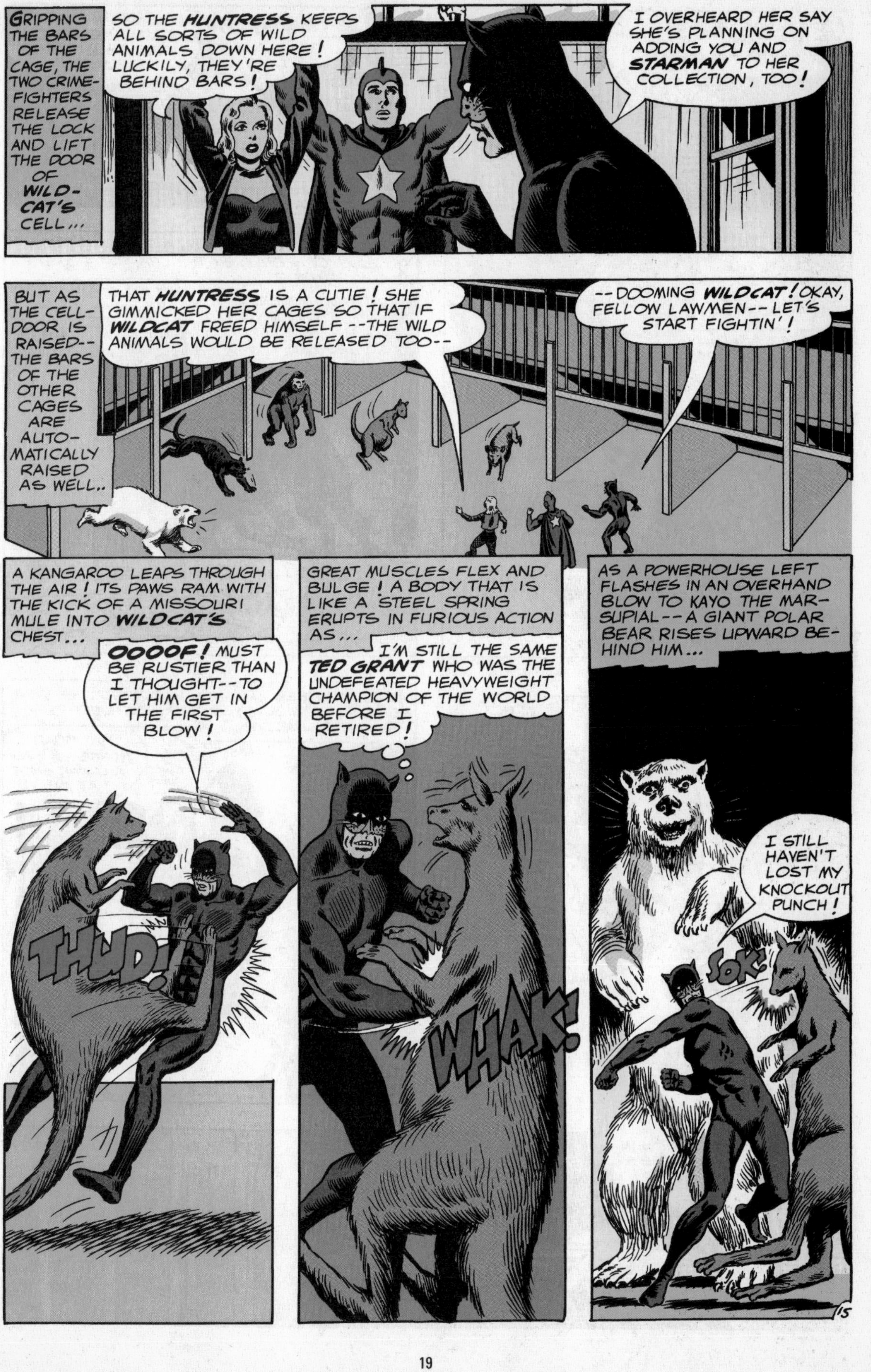
GRIPPING THE BARS OF THE CAGE, THE TWO CRIME-FIGHTERS RELEASE THE LOCK AND LIFT THE DOOR OF WILD-CAT'S CELL...
SO THE HUNTRESS KEEPS ALL SORTS OF WILD ANIMALS DOWN HERE! LUCKILY, THEY'RE BEHIND BARS!
I OVERHEARD HER SAY SHE'S PLANNING ON ADDING YOU AND STARMAN TO HER COLLECTION, TOO!
BUT AS THE CELL-DOOR IS RAISED-- THE BARS OF THE OTHER CAGES ARE AUTO-MATICALLY RAISED AS WELL..
THAT HUNTRESS IS A CUTIE! SHE GIMMICKED HER CAGES SO THAT IF WILDCAT FREED HIMSELF --THE WILD ANIMALS WOULD BE RELEASED TOO--
--DOOMING WILDCAT! OKAY, FELLOW LAWMEN--LET'S START FIGHTIN'!
A KANGAROO LEAPS THROUGH THE AIR! ITS PAWS RAM WITH THE KICK OF A MISSOURI MULE INTO WILDCAT'S CHEST...
OOOOF! MUST BE RUSTIER THAN I THOUGHT--TO LET HIM GET IN THE FIRST BLOW!
THUD!
GREAT MUSCLES FLEX AND BULGE! A BODY THAT IS LIKE A STEEL SPRING ERUPTS IN FURIOUS ACTION AS...
I'M STILL THE SAME TED GRANT WHO WAS THE UNDEFEATED HEAVYWEIGHT CHAMPION OF THE WORLD BEFORE I RETIRED!
WHAK!
AS A POWERHOUSE LEFT FLASHES IN AN OVERHAND BLOW TO KAYO THE MAR-SUPIAL--A GIANT POLAR BEAR RISES UPWARD BE-HIND HIM...
I STILL HAVEN'T LOST MY KNOCKOUT PUNCH!
SOK!
15

FROM BEHIND, A GREAT WHITE-FURRED PAW SLAMS INTO **WILDCAT**...

GRRRKRRROWW!

MMMOOPFFF!?

I'LL SHOW THAT ARCTIC BEAST I'M STILL ABLE TO "TAKE" A PUNCH!

WITHOUT TAKING A COUNT, THE EX-CHAMP ZOOMS BACK AT HIS OPPONENT...

BROTHER BEAR-- YOU'RE A SUCKER FOR A LEFT!

MEANWHILE, **STARMAN** HAS BEEN RAMMED INTO THE BARS OF A CELL BY THE LEAP OF A GREAT BLACK PANTHER...

GOT TO COSMIC-ROD HIM AWAY FROM ME!

FROM THE COSMIC RAYS THAT TRAVEL EVERYWHERE, HE SUMMONS ANTI-GRAVITIC POWER TO LIFT THE SCREECHING FELINE HIGH INTO THE AIR...

UP YOU GO, FELLA!

AS THE PANTHER CRASHES HARD INTO THE STONE CEILING--A WILD-EYED TUSKER THUNDERS FROM THE SHADOWS...

THAT BOAR THINKS HE HAS A CLEAR SHOT AT ME--!

THUMMP!

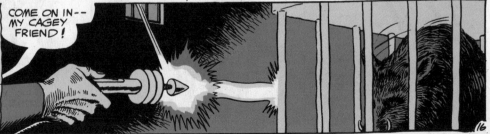

DRAWING AN ERRANT MOONBEAM THROUGH A BARRED WINDOW, THE **ROD RANGER** CONVERTS IT INTO A CAGE BEFORE THE ONRUSHING ANIMAL...

COME ON IN-- MY CAGEY FRIEND!

16

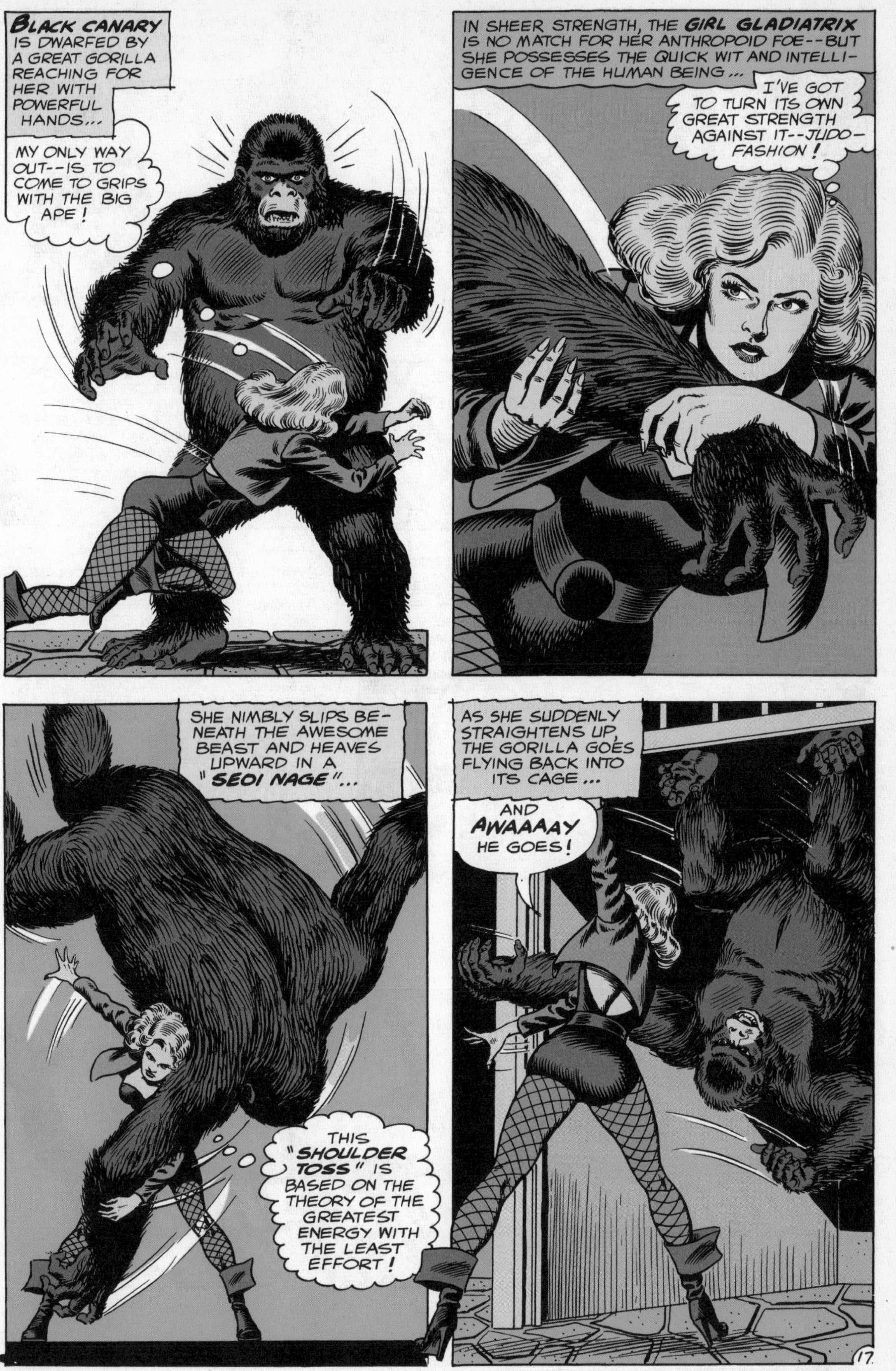
BLACK CANARY IS DWARFED BY A GREAT GORILLA REACHING FOR HER WITH POWERFUL HANDS...
MY ONLY WAY OUT--IS TO COME TO GRIPS WITH THE BIG APE!
IN SHEER STRENGTH, THE GIRL GLADIATRIX IS NO MATCH FOR HER ANTHROPOID FOE--BUT SHE POSSESSES THE QUICK WIT AND INTELLIGENCE OF THE HUMAN BEING...
I'VE GOT TO TURN ITS OWN GREAT STRENGTH AGAINST IT--JUDO-FASHION!
SHE NIMBLY SLIPS BENEATH THE AWESOME BEAST AND HEAVES UPWARD IN A "SEOI NAGE"...
THIS "SHOULDER TOSS" IS BASED ON THE THEORY OF THE GREATEST ENERGY WITH THE LEAST EFFORT!
AS SHE SUDDENLY STRAIGHTENS UP, THE GORILLA GOES FLYING BACK INTO ITS CAGE...
AND AWAAAAY HE GOES!
17

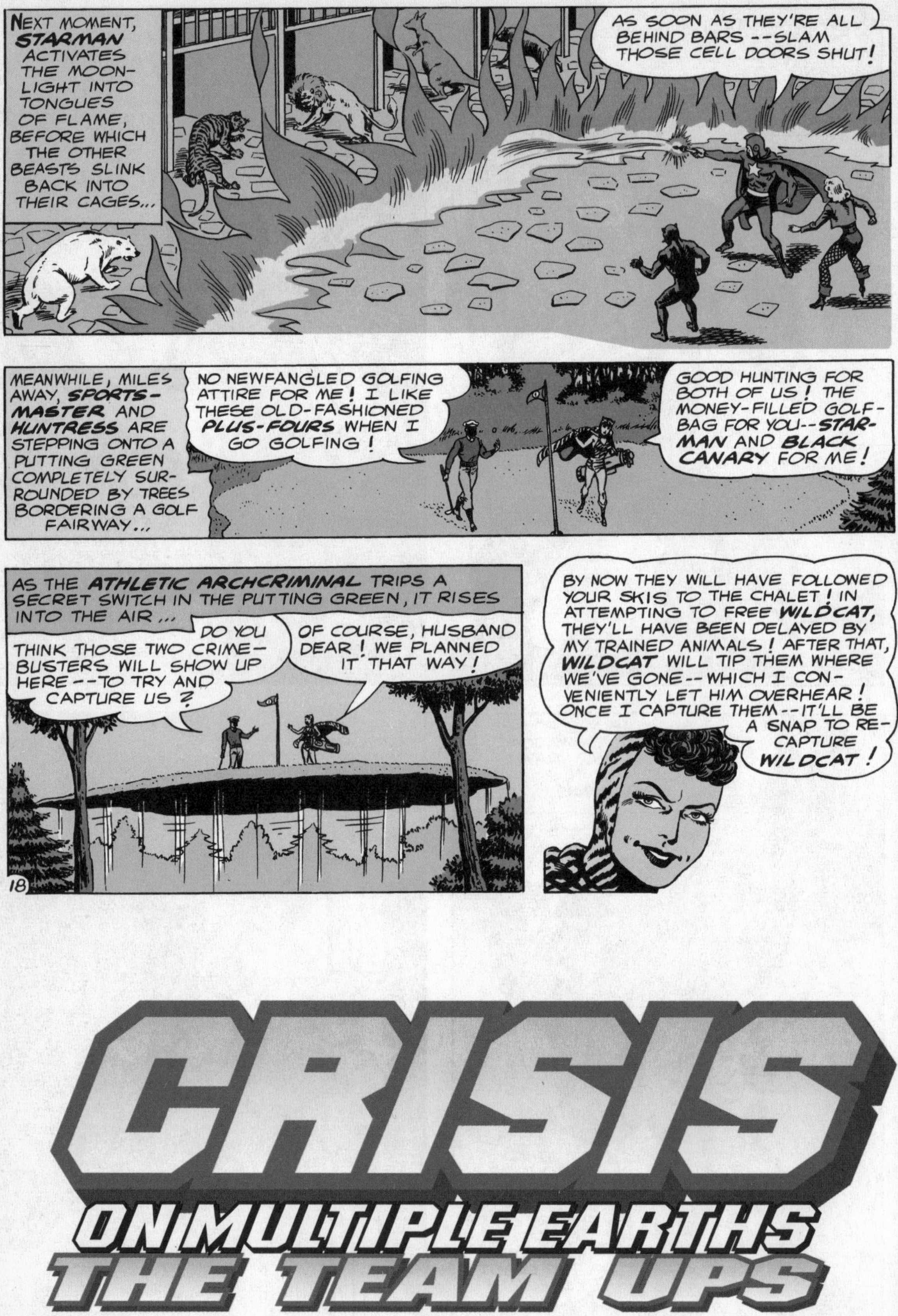
NEXT MOMENT, STARMAN ACTIVATES THE MOON-LIGHT INTO TONGUES OF FLAME, BEFORE WHICH THE OTHER BEASTS SLINK BACK INTO THEIR CAGES...
AS SOON AS THEY'RE ALL BEHIND BARS --SLAM THOSE CELL DOORS SHUT!
MEANWHILE, MILES AWAY, SPORTSMASTER AND HUNTRESS ARE STEPPING ONTO A PUTTING GREEN COMPLETELY SURROUNDED BY TREES BORDERING A GOLF FAIRWAY...
NO NEWFANGLED GOLFING ATTIRE FOR ME! I LIKE THESE OLD-FASHIONED PLUS-FOURS WHEN I GO GOLFING!
GOOD HUNTING FOR BOTH OF US! THE MONEY-FILLED GOLF-BAG FOR YOU--STARMAN AND BLACK CANARY FOR ME!
AS THE ATHLETIC ARCHCRIMINAL TRIPS A SECRET SWITCH IN THE PUTTING GREEN, IT RISES INTO THE AIR...
DO YOU THINK THOSE TWO CRIME-BUSTERS WILL SHOW UP HERE--TO TRY AND CAPTURE US?
OF COURSE, HUSBAND DEAR! WE PLANNED IT THAT WAY!
18
BY NOW THEY WILL HAVE FOLLOWED YOUR SKIS TO THE CHALET! IN ATTEMPTING TO FREE WILDCAT, THEY'LL HAVE BEEN DELAYED BY MY TRAINED ANIMALS! AFTER THAT, WILDCAT WILL TIP THEM WHERE WE'VE GONE--WHICH I CONVENIENTLY LET HIM OVERHEAR! ONCE I CAPTURE THEM--IT'LL BE A SNAP TO RECAPTURE WILDCAT!

CRISIS ON MULTIPLE EARTHS THE TEAM UPS

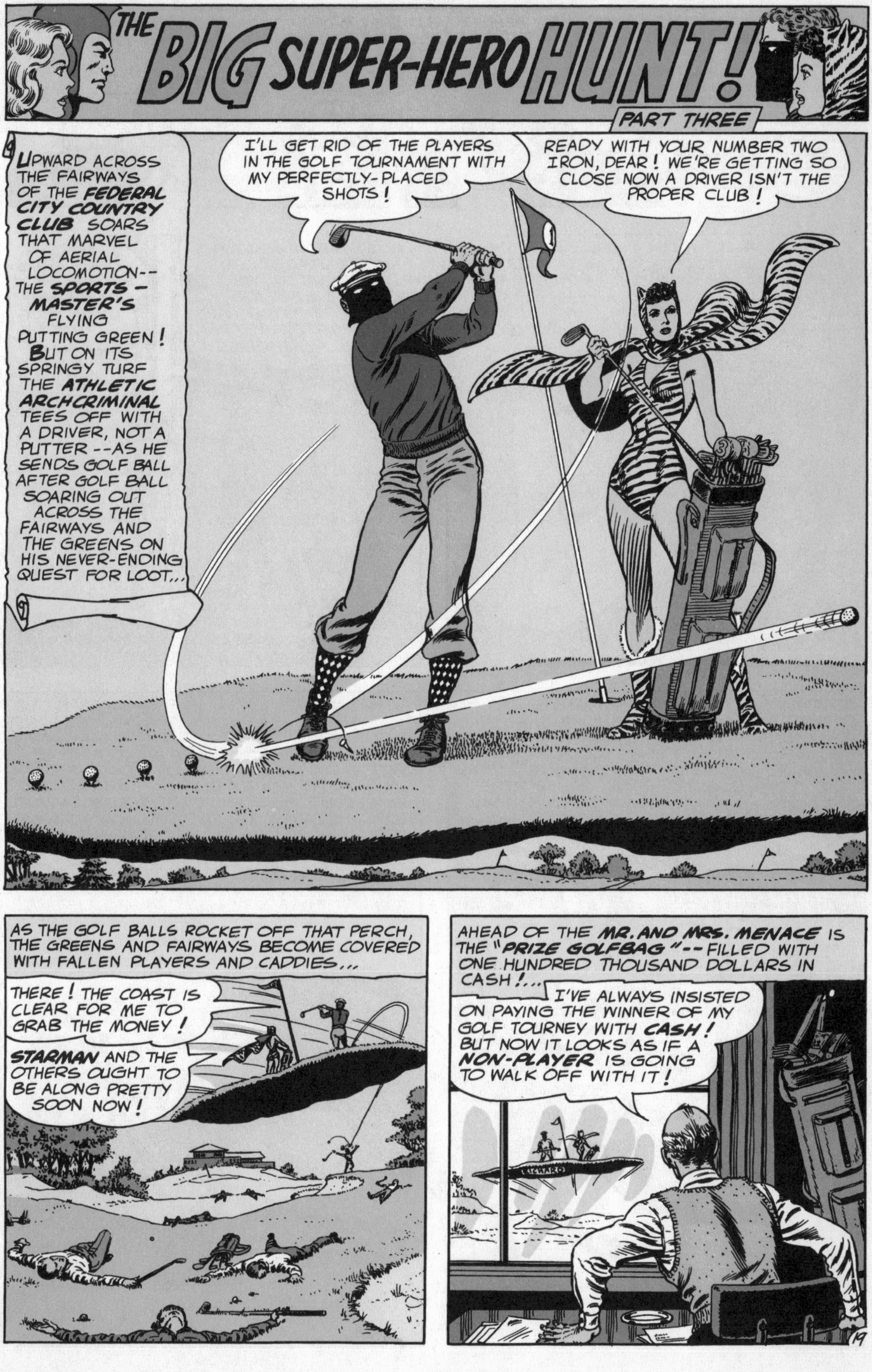
THE BIG SUPER-HERO HUNT!
PART THREE
UPWARD ACROSS THE FAIRWAYS OF THE FEDERAL CITY COUNTRY CLUB SOARS THAT MARVEL OF AERIAL LOCOMOTION-- THE SPORTS-MASTER'S FLYING PUTTING GREEN! BUT ON ITS SPRINGY TURF THE ATHLETIC ARCHCRIMINAL TEES OFF WITH A DRIVER, NOT A PUTTER --AS HE SENDS GOLF BALL AFTER GOLF BALL SOARING OUT ACROSS THE FAIRWAYS AND THE GREENS ON HIS NEVER-ENDING QUEST FOR LOOT...
I'LL GET RID OF THE PLAYERS IN THE GOLF TOURNAMENT WITH MY PERFECTLY-PLACED SHOTS!
READY WITH YOUR NUMBER TWO IRON, DEAR! WE'RE GETTING SO CLOSE NOW A DRIVER ISN'T THE PROPER CLUB!
AS THE GOLF BALLS ROCKET OFF THAT PERCH, THE GREENS AND FAIRWAYS BECOME COVERED WITH FALLEN PLAYERS AND CADDIES...
THERE! THE COAST IS CLEAR FOR ME TO GRAB THE MONEY!
STARMAN AND THE OTHERS OUGHT TO BE ALONG PRETTY SOON NOW!
AHEAD OF THE MR. AND MRS. MENACE IS THE "PRIZE GOLFBAG"-- FILLED WITH ONE HUNDRED THOUSAND DOLLARS IN CASH!...
I'VE ALWAYS INSISTED ON PAYING THE WINNER OF MY GOLF TOURNEY WITH CASH! BUT NOW IT LOOKS AS IF A NON-PLAYER IS GOING TO WALK OFF WITH IT!
19

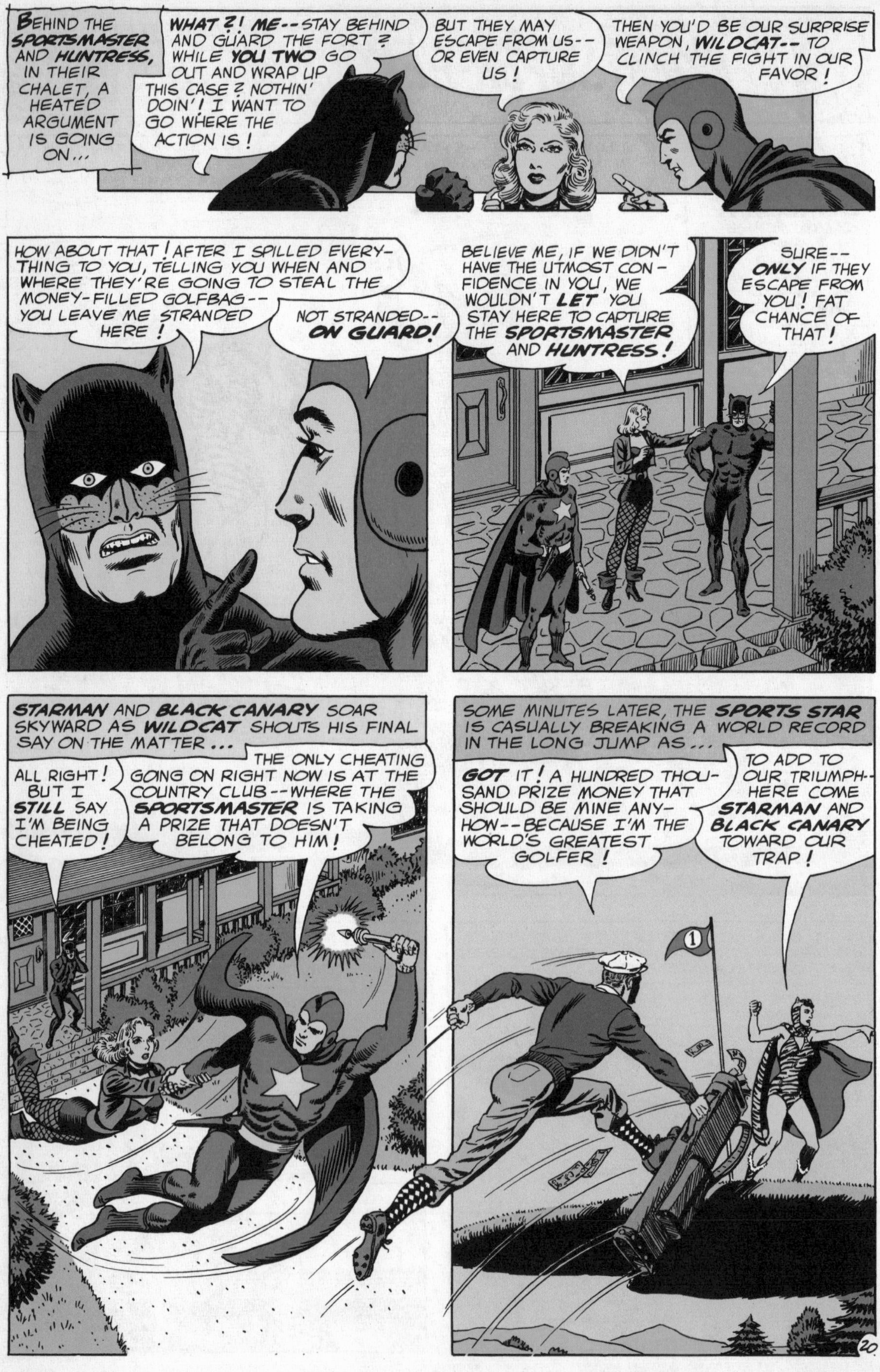
BEHIND THE SPORTSMASTER AND HUNTRESS, IN THEIR CHALET, A HEATED ARGUMENT IS GOING ON...
WHAT?! ME--STAY BEHIND AND GUARD THE FORT? WHILE YOU TWO GO OUT AND WRAP UP THIS CASE? NOTHIN' DOIN'! I WANT TO GO WHERE THE ACTION IS!
BUT THEY MAY ESCAPE FROM US--OR EVEN CAPTURE US!
THEN YOU'D BE OUR SURPRISE WEAPON, WILDCAT-- TO CLINCH THE FIGHT IN OUR FAVOR!
HOW ABOUT THAT! AFTER I SPILLED EVERYTHING TO YOU, TELLING YOU WHEN AND WHERE THEY'RE GOING TO STEAL THE MONEY-FILLED GOLFBAG--YOU LEAVE ME STRANDED HERE!
NOT STRANDED--ON GUARD!
BELIEVE ME, IF WE DIDN'T HAVE THE UTMOST CONFIDENCE IN YOU, WE WOULDN'T LET YOU STAY HERE TO CAPTURE THE SPORTSMASTER AND HUNTRESS!
SURE--ONLY IF THEY ESCAPE FROM YOU! FAT CHANCE OF THAT!
STARMAN AND BLACK CANARY SOAR SKYWARD AS WILDCAT SHOUTS HIS FINAL SAY ON THE MATTER...
ALL RIGHT! BUT I STILL SAY I'M BEING CHEATED!
THE ONLY CHEATING GOING ON RIGHT NOW IS AT THE COUNTRY CLUB--WHERE THE SPORTSMASTER IS TAKING A PRIZE THAT DOESN'T BELONG TO HIM!
SOME MINUTES LATER, THE SPORTS STAR IS CASUALLY BREAKING A WORLD RECORD IN THE LONG JUMP AS...
GOT IT! A HUNDRED THOUSAND PRIZE MONEY THAT SHOULD BE MINE ANYHOW--BECAUSE I'M THE WORLD'S GREATEST GOLFER!
TO ADD TO OUR TRIUMPH--HERE COME STARMAN AND BLACK CANARY TOWARD OUR TRAP!
1
20

THE FLYING PUTTING GREEN TAKES TO THE AIR AGAIN...

THEN WE ATTACK THEM AS PLANNED--STARTING WITH MY "BRASSIE BEANIE" AT *STARMAN*!

I'LL WRAP UP THE *BLACK CANARY*!

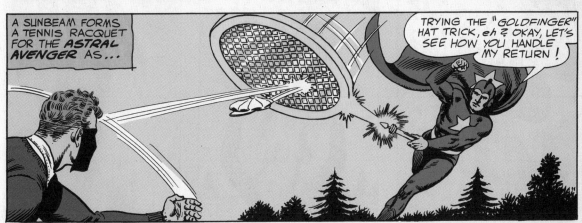

A SUNBEAM FORMS A TENNIS RACQUET FOR THE *ASTRAL AVENGER* AS...

TRYING THE "GOLDFINGER" HAT TRICK, *eh*? OKAY, LET'S SEE HOW YOU HANDLE MY *RETURN*!

THE *SPORTS ACE* DUCKS JUST IN TIME TO AVOID AN OVERHEAD EXPLOSION...

NICE PLAY, *STARMAN*! BUT I'M SWITCHING GAMES--WITH THIS CUP-POLE!

WHAM!

HERE'S WHERE THIS DISGUISED GUIDED MISSILE MAKES A FALL GUY OUT OF *STARMAN*!

THE WAY *SPORTSMASTER* KEEPS BOMBARDING ME WITH HIS WEAPONS-- AS IF TRYING TO MANEUVER ME TOWARD *BLACK CANARY*!

200 YDS.

21

JUST BELOW HIM, THE *HUNTRESS* HAS LURED THE *GIRL GLADIATOR* INTO A CUNNINGLY HIDDEN TRAP...

OHHHHH!

I CATCH WILD ANIMALS IN SUCH PITS, *BLACK CANARY*-- BUT I HAVE A BETTER PRISON PREPARED FOR YOU!

TURNING ABOUT, THE JUNGLE AMAZON LEAPS OVER THE *BLACK CANARY*, GRASPING HER WRISTS...

NOW TO COORDINATE MY MOVEMENTS WITH THOSE OF MY MATE-- AND TRAP THEM BOTH!

THE WEIGHT OF THE *HUNTRESS'* FLYING BODY AND HER SUPERB MUSCLES LIFTS HER VICTIM OUT OF THE PIT...

A WELL-TIMED FLIP AND *BLACK CANARY* WILL BE IN *TRAP-POSITION!*

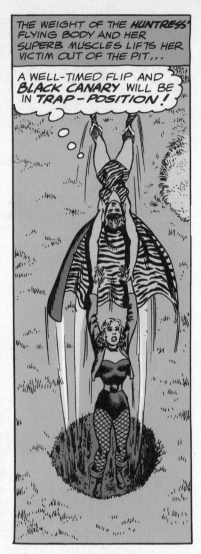

CHASED ALONG BY THE GUIDED MISSILE, *STARMAN* SIZES UP THE SITUATION...

THE TEAMWORK OF *SPORTSMASTER* AND *HUNTRESS* IS AIMED AT GETTING ME AND *BLACK CANARY* UNDER-NEATH THE GOLF GREEN! IT ALL ADDS UP TO AN UNSEEN TRAP...

SUDDENLY, THE *COSMIC ROD* PULSES...

I'LL HAVE TO DO SOME GOLFING OF MY OWN TO BLAST OUT OF THAT TRAP-- WHER-EVER AND WHATEVER IT MAY BE!

22

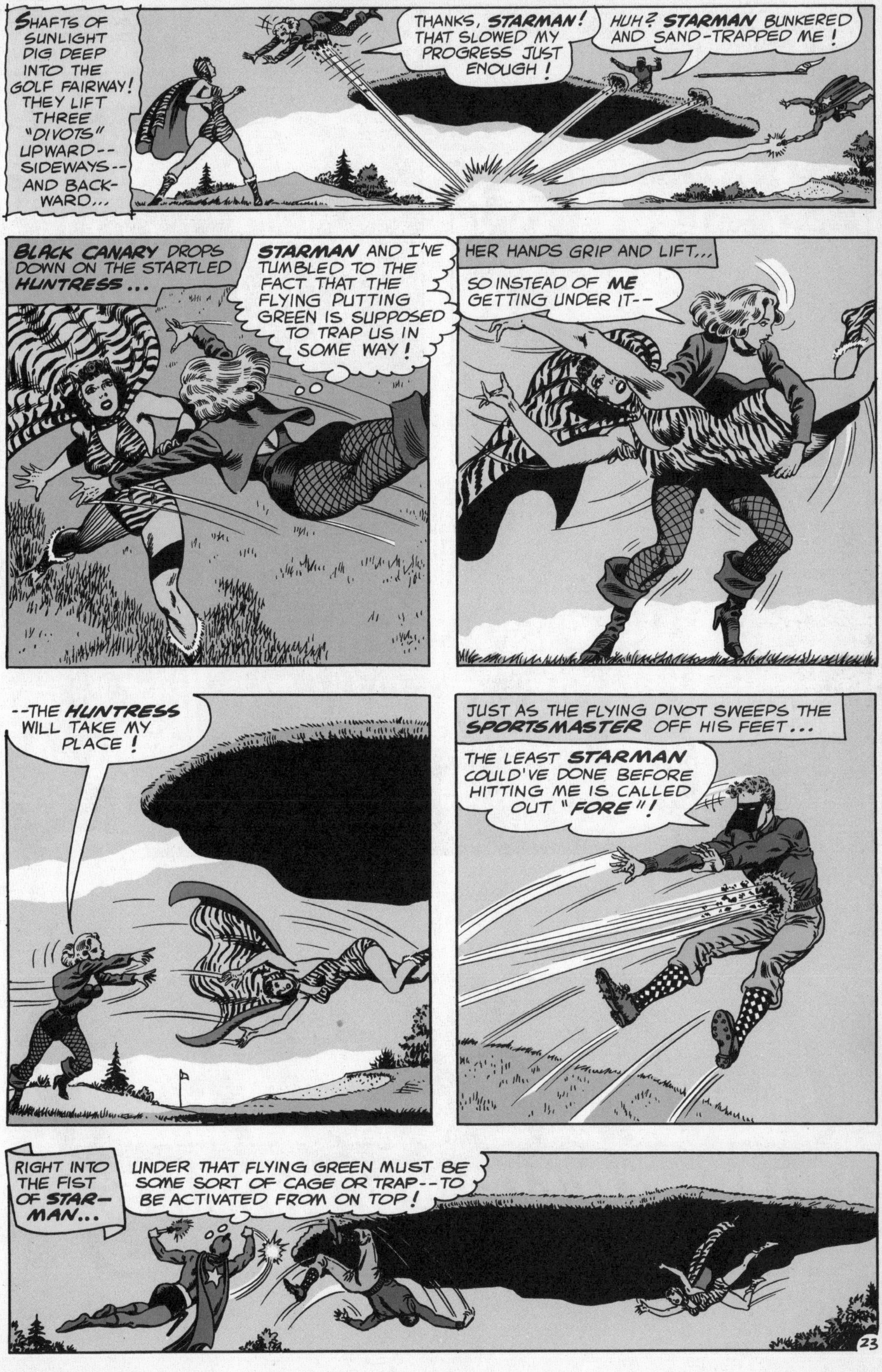
SHAFTS OF SUNLIGHT DIG DEEP INTO THE GOLF FAIRWAY! THEY LIFT THREE "DIVOTS" UPWARD--SIDEWAYS--AND BACKWARD...
THANKS, STARMAN! THAT SLOWED MY PROGRESS JUST ENOUGH!
HUH? STARMAN BUNKERED AND SAND-TRAPPED ME!
BLACK CANARY DROPS DOWN ON THE STARTLED HUNTRESS...
STARMAN AND I'VE TUMBLED TO THE FACT THAT THE FLYING PUTTING GREEN IS SUPPOSED TO TRAP US IN SOME WAY!
HER HANDS GRIP AND LIFT...
SO INSTEAD OF ME GETTING UNDER IT--
--THE HUNTRESS WILL TAKE MY PLACE!
JUST AS THE FLYING DIVOT SWEEPS THE SPORTSMASTER OFF HIS FEET...
THE LEAST STARMAN COULD'VE DONE BEFORE HITTING ME IS CALLED OUT "FORE"!
RIGHT INTO THE FIST OF STAR-MAN...
UNDER THAT FLYING GREEN MUST BE SOME SORT OF CAGE OR TRAP--TO BE ACTIVATED FROM ON TOP!
23

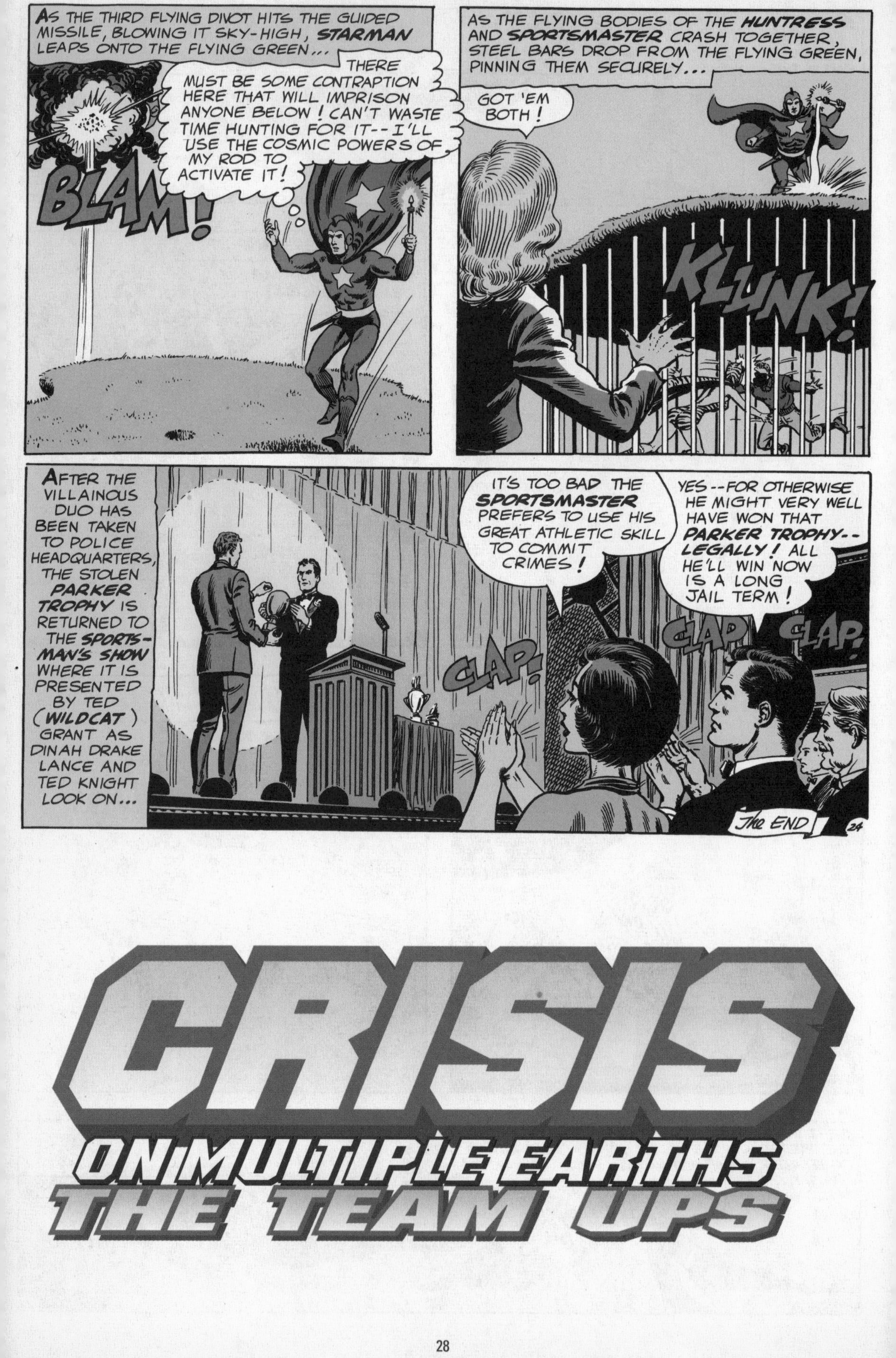
AS THE THIRD FLYING DIVOT HITS THE GUIDED MISSILE, BLOWING IT SKY-HIGH, STARMAN LEAPS ONTO THE FLYING GREEN...
THERE MUST BE SOME CONTRAPTION HERE THAT WILL IMPRISON ANYONE BELOW! CAN'T WASTE TIME HUNTING FOR IT-- I'LL USE THE COSMIC POWERS OF MY ROD TO ACTIVATE IT!
BLAM!
AS THE FLYING BODIES OF THE HUNTRESS AND SPORTSMASTER CRASH TOGETHER, STEEL BARS DROP FROM THE FLYING GREEN, PINNING THEM SECURELY...
GOT 'EM BOTH!
KLUNK!
AFTER THE VILLAINOUS DUO HAS BEEN TAKEN TO POLICE HEADQUARTERS, THE STOLEN PARKER TROPHY IS RETURNED TO THE SPORTSMAN'S SHOW WHERE IT IS PRESENTED BY TED (WILDCAT) GRANT AS DINAH DRAKE LANCE AND TED KNIGHT LOOK ON...
IT'S TOO BAD THE SPORTSMASTER PREFERS TO USE HIS GREAT ATHLETIC SKILL TO COMMIT CRIMES!
YES--FOR OTHERWISE HE MIGHT VERY WELL HAVE WON THAT PARKER TROPHY--LEGALLY! ALL HE'LL WIN NOW IS A LONG JAIL TERM!
CLAP!
CLAP
CLAP.
The END
24

CRISIS ON MULTIPLE EARTHS THE TEAM UPS

THE ORIGIN OF STARMAN

From his boyhood, Ted Knight had an absorbing interest in astronomy. Born to wealth, he was able to devote much time to this hobby, and eventually made a remarkable discovery. He found a way to utilize infra-rays from distant stars with his amazing *gravity rod*, which was first described as "an invention that overcomes the forces of gravity and launches bolts of energy" by radiating starlight.

Having perfected this instrument, Ted next created the red-and-green costume the world was soon to know as the uniform of *Starman*. He made his debut in ADVENTURE COMICS No. 61 (April, 1941) the cover of which is reproduced below.

The *Astral Avenger* battled many villains, but none more ingenious than *The Mist*. These arch-foes first met in "The Menace of the Invisible Raiders" (ADVENTURE No. 67, October, 1941.)

When *Hourman* was granted a leave of absence from the *Justice Society of America*, *Starman* was selected as his replacement. He and *Dr. Mid-Nite* both "won their spurs" in ALL-STAR COMICS No. 8 (December, 1941-January, 1942) by helping the *JSA* defeat the evil plots of *Professor Elba*.

Soon after the Japanese attack on Pearl Harbor brought the United States into World War II, the *Justice Society* became the *Justice Battalion*, under orders from the War Department. *Starman* joined his fellow *JSA-ers* in fighting spies and saboteurs on the home front, as well as performing missions behind enemy lines. During one such expedition, in occupied Poland, he kept Nazi officials busy trying to decode a "secret message" consisting of the lifetime batting averages of big league baseball stars Ty Cobb, Tris Speaker and "Rabbit" Maranville!

On another occasion, a German rocket scientist tried to get rid of eight *JSA* members by trapping them and shooting them into space. *Starman* wound up on the planet *Jupiter*, where he overcame a threat to the native *Jovians* by building a huge replica of his *gravity rod* and using it to hurl the menace off that world. The towering instrument also provided the power which returned the *Astral Avenger* to Earth.

Of course, there were domestic villains to deal with, too, and *Starman* was in the thick of the battles with such foes as *The Brain Wave, The King Bee,* and the original *Psycho-Pirate*.

Starman's last appearance with the *Justice Society* was in "The Plunder of the Psycho-Pirate" (ALL-STAR No. 23, Winter, 1944-5.) He and *The Spectre*, who dropped out at the same time, were replaced by *Green Lantern* and *The Flash*. A year later, he last saw action in the pages of ADVENTURE (No. 102, February-March, 1946.)

During his years of retirement, Ted Knight continued to improve his *gravity rod* until he developed the highly superior *cosmic rod*, which draws its incredible power from the cosmic forces of the universe. He first put this new instrument to use against the *Crime Syndicate of America* of *Earth-Three*, when he returned to action with his fellow *JSA-ers*, *Hawkman*, *Doctor Fate*, *Dr. Mid-Nite*, and *Black Canary*.

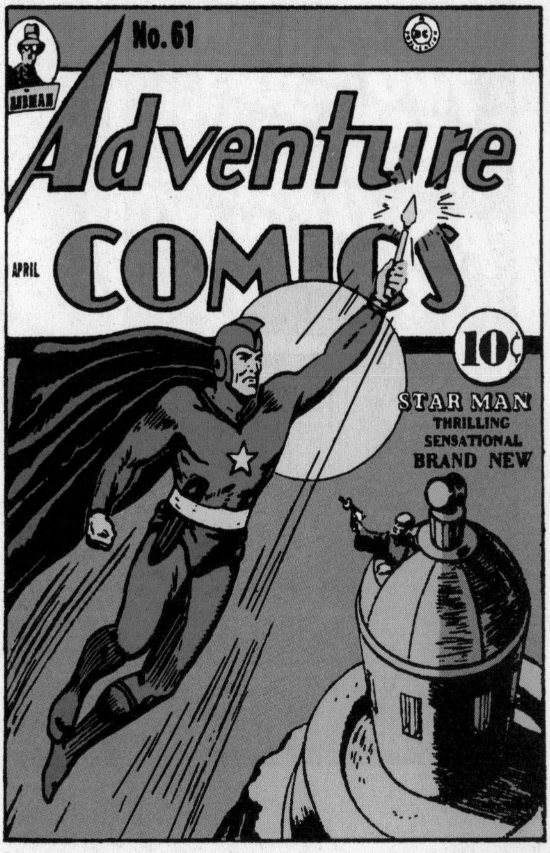
No. 61
Adventure
COMICS
APRIL
10¢
STAR MAN
THRILLING
SENSATIONAL
BRAND NEW

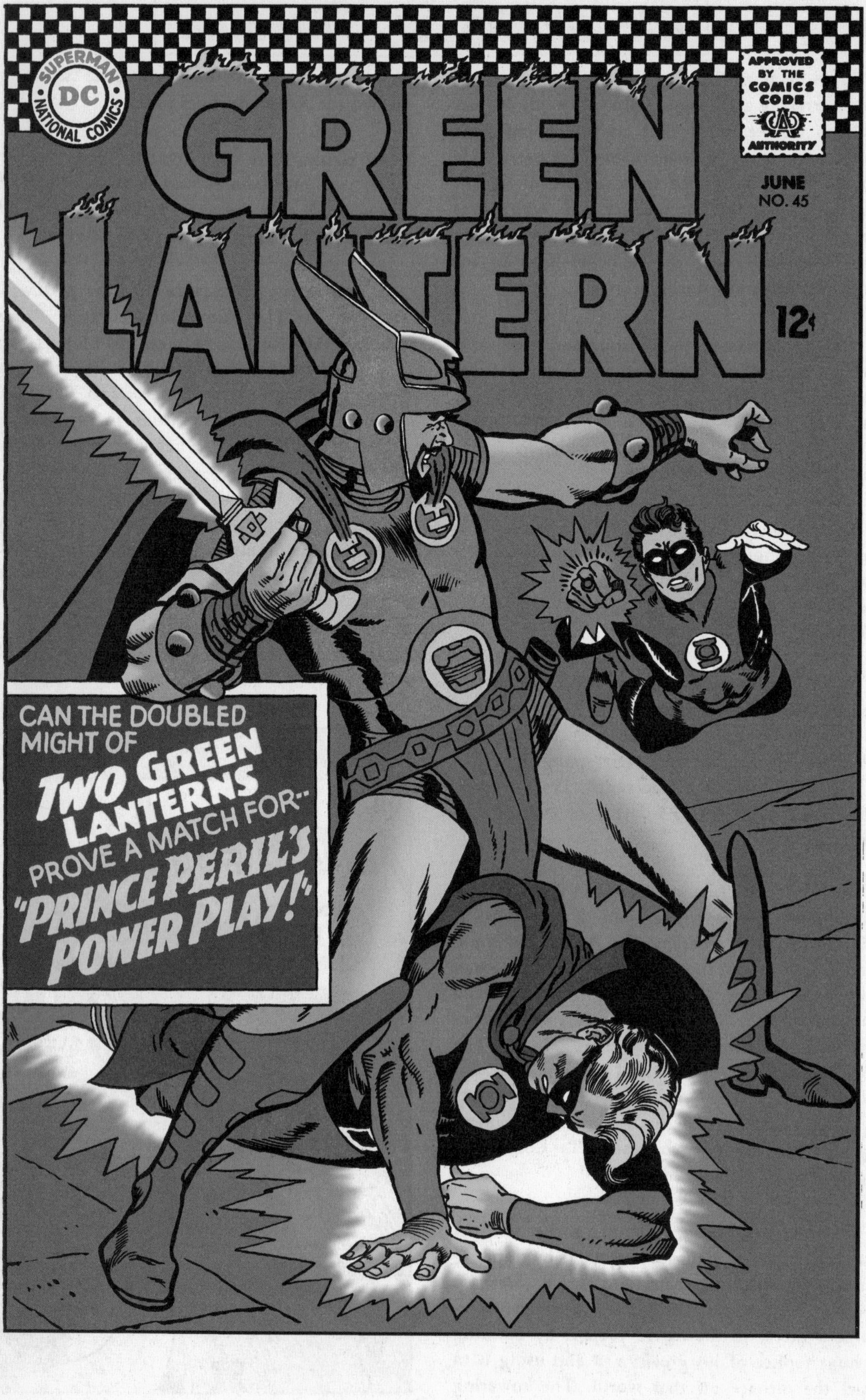
SUPERMAN DC NATIONAL COMICS
GREEN LANTERN
APPROVED BY THE COMICS CODE AUTHORITY
JUNE
NO. 45
12¢
CAN THE DOUBLED MIGHT OF
TWO GREEN LANTERNS
PROVE A MATCH FOR--
"PRINCE PERIL'S POWER PLAY!"

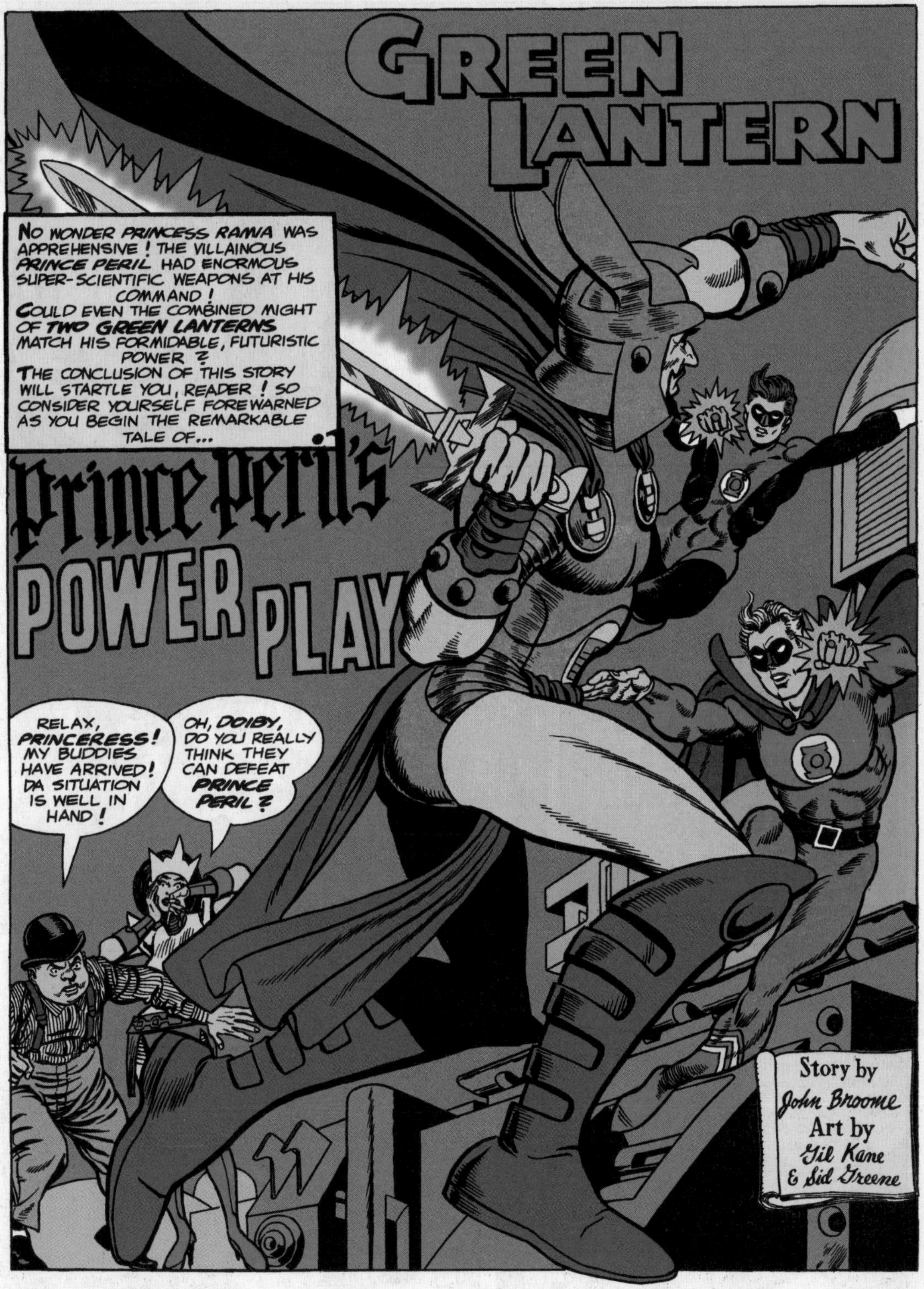
GREEN LANTERN
NO WONDER PRINCESS RAMA WAS APPREHENSIVE! THE VILLAINOUS PRINCE PERIL HAD ENORMOUS SUPER-SCIENTIFIC WEAPONS AT HIS COMMAND! COULD EVEN THE COMBINED MIGHT OF TWO GREEN LANTERNS MATCH HIS FORMIDABLE, FUTURISTIC POWER? THE CONCLUSION OF THIS STORY WILL STARTLE YOU, READER! SO CONSIDER YOURSELF FOREWARNED AS YOU BEGIN THE REMARKABLE TALE OF...
Prince Peril's POWER PLAY
RELAX, PRINCERESS! MY BUDDIES HAVE ARRIVED! DA SITUATION IS WELL IN HAND!
OH, DOIBY, DO YOU REALLY THINK THEY CAN DEFEAT PRINCE PERIL?
Story by John Broome Art by Gil Kane & Sid Greene

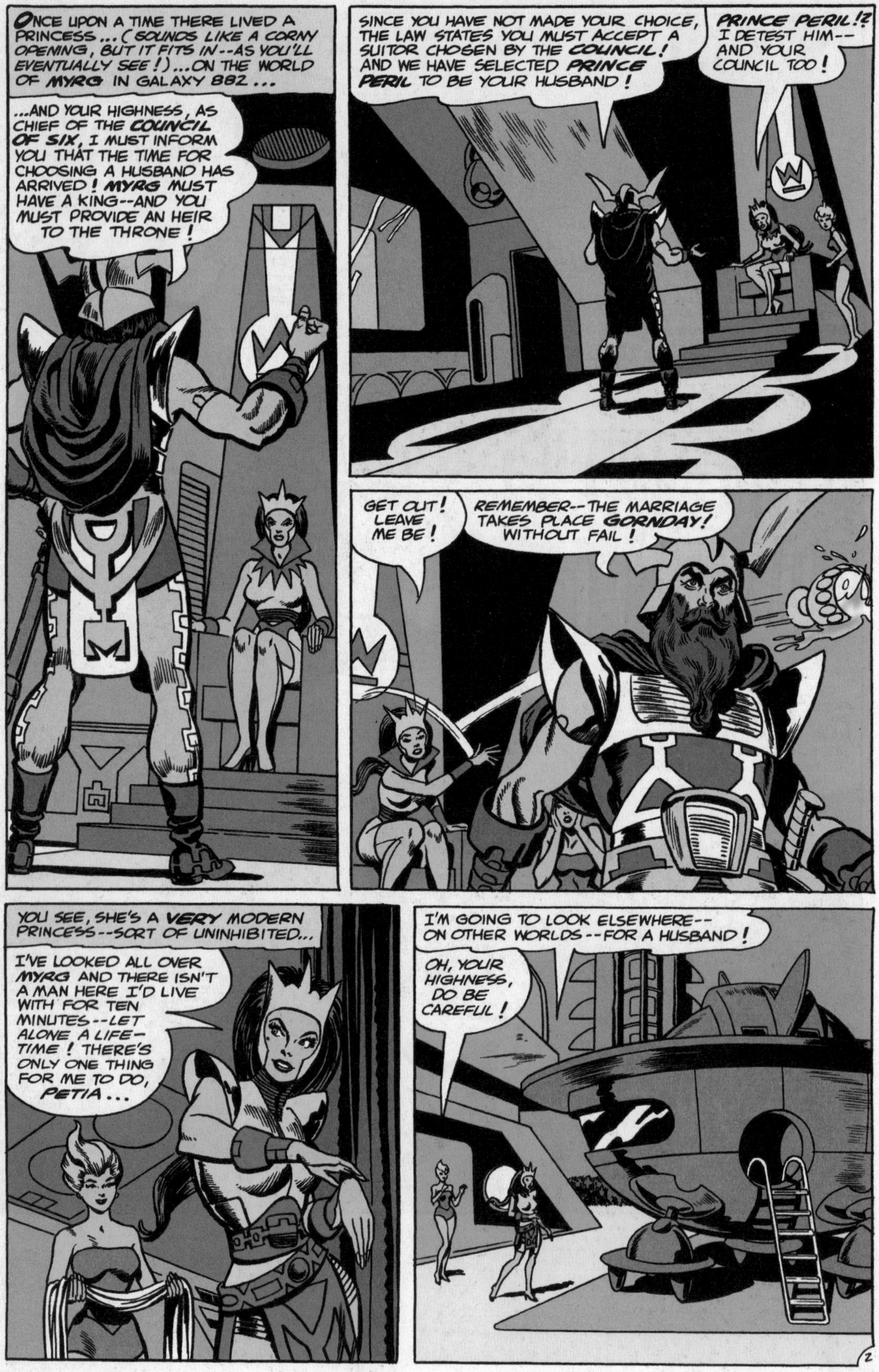
ONCE UPON A TIME THERE LIVED A PRINCESS... (SOUNDS LIKE A CORNY OPENING, BUT IT FITS IN--AS YOU'LL EVENTUALLY SEE!)...ON THE WORLD OF MYRG IN GALAXY 882...
...AND YOUR HIGHNESS, AS CHIEF OF THE COUNCIL OF SIX, I MUST INFORM YOU THAT THE TIME FOR CHOOSING A HUSBAND HAS ARRIVED! MYRG MUST HAVE A KING--AND YOU MUST PROVIDE AN HEIR TO THE THRONE!
SINCE YOU HAVE NOT MADE YOUR CHOICE, THE LAW STATES YOU MUST ACCEPT A SUITOR CHOSEN BY THE COUNCIL! AND WE HAVE SELECTED PRINCE PERIL TO BE YOUR HUSBAND!
PRINCE PERIL!? I DETEST HIM--AND YOUR COUNCIL TOO!
GET OUT! LEAVE ME BE!
REMEMBER--THE MARRIAGE TAKES PLACE GORNDAY! WITHOUT FAIL!
YOU SEE, SHE'S A VERY MODERN PRINCESS--SORT OF UNINHIBITED...
I'VE LOOKED ALL OVER MYRG AND THERE ISN'T A MAN HERE I'D LIVE WITH FOR TEN MINUTES--LET ALONE A LIFE-TIME! THERE'S ONLY ONE THING FOR ME TO DO, PETIA...
I'M GOING TO LOOK ELSEWHERE--ON OTHER WORLDS--FOR A HUSBAND!
OH, YOUR HIGHNESS, DO BE CAREFUL!
2

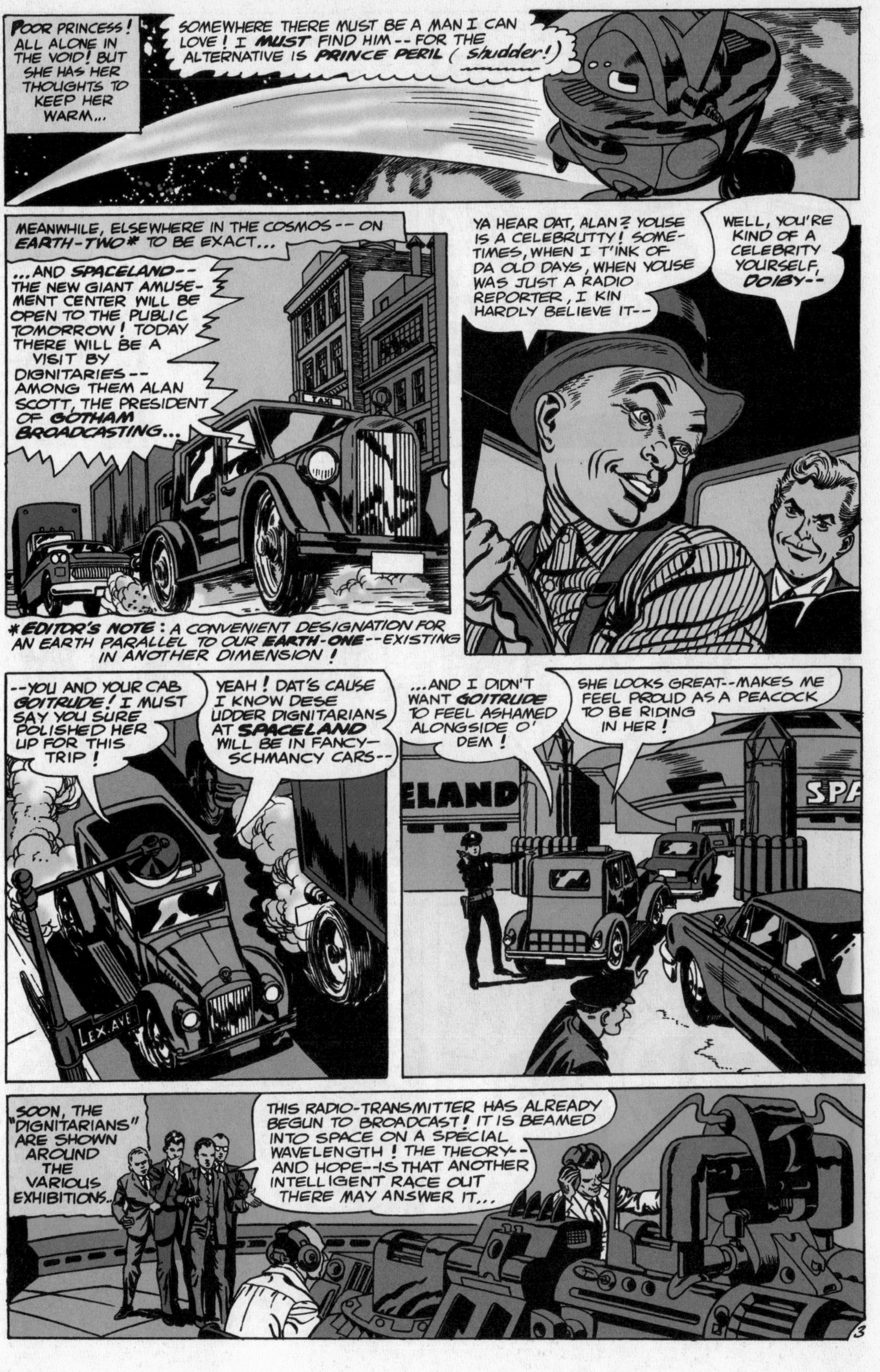
POOR PRINCESS! ALL ALONE IN THE VOID! BUT SHE HAS HER THOUGHTS TO KEEP HER WARM...
SOMEWHERE THERE MUST BE A MAN I CAN LOVE! I MUST FIND HIM--FOR THE ALTERNATIVE IS PRINCE PERIL (shudder!)
MEANWHILE, ELSEWHERE IN THE COSMOS--ON EARTH-TWO* TO BE EXACT...
...AND SPACELAND--THE NEW GIANT AMUSEMENT CENTER WILL BE OPEN TO THE PUBLIC TOMORROW! TODAY THERE WILL BE A VISIT BY DIGNITARIES--AMONG THEM ALAN SCOTT, THE PRESIDENT OF GOTHAM BROADCASTING...
TAXI
*EDITOR'S NOTE: A CONVENIENT DESIGNATION FOR AN EARTH PARALLEL TO OUR EARTH-ONE--EXISTING IN ANOTHER DIMENSION!
YA HEAR DAT, ALAN? YOUSE IS A CELEBRUTTY! SOMETIMES, WHEN I T'INK OF DA OLD DAYS, WHEN YOUSE WAS JUST A RADIO REPORTER, I KIN HARDLY BELIEVE IT--
WELL, YOU'RE KIND OF A CELEBRITY YOURSELF, DOIBY--
--YOU AND YOUR CAB GOITRUDE! I MUST SAY YOU SURE POLISHED HER UP FOR THIS TRIP!
YEAH! DAT'S CAUSE I KNOW DESE UDDER DIGNITARIANS AT SPACELAND WILL BE IN FANCY-SCHMANCY CARS--
LEX. AVE
...AND I DIDN'T WANT GOITRUDE TO FEEL ASHAMED ALONGSIDE O' DEM!
SHE LOOKS GREAT--MAKES ME FEEL PROUD AS A PEACOCK TO BE RIDING IN HER!
ELAND
SPA
SOON, THE "DIGNITARIANS" ARE SHOWN AROUND THE VARIOUS EXHIBITIONS...
THIS RADIO-TRANSMITTER HAS ALREADY BEGUN TO BROADCAST! IT IS BEAMED INTO SPACE ON A SPECIAL WAVELENGTH! THE THEORY--AND HOPE--IS THAT ANOTHER INTELLIGENT RACE OUT THERE MAY ANSWER IT...
3

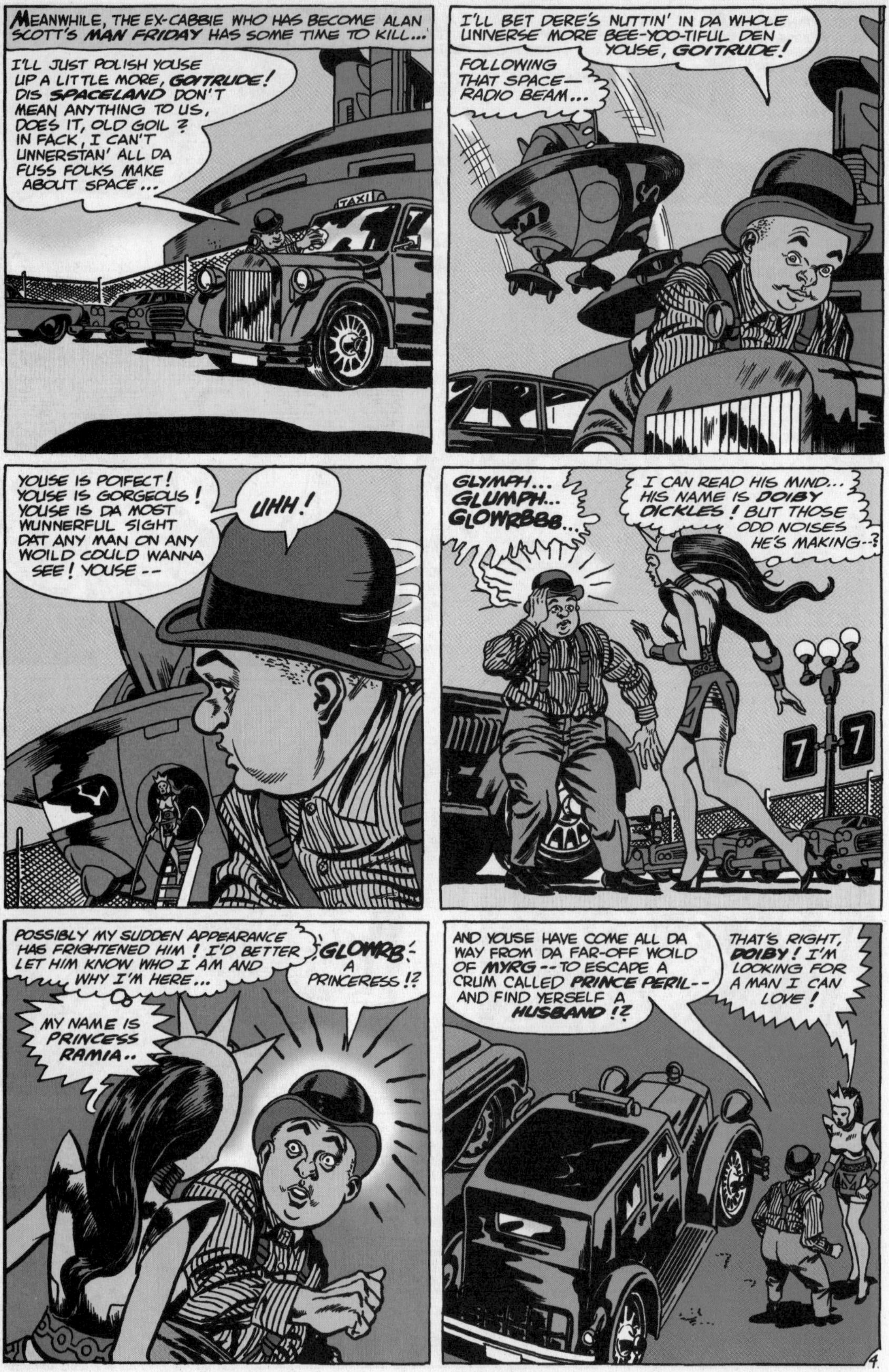

MEANWHILE, THE EX-CABBIE WHO HAS BECOME ALAN SCOTT'S MAN FRIDAY HAS SOME TIME TO KILL...
I'LL JUST POLISH YOUSE UP A LITTLE MORE, GOITRUDE! DIS SPACELAND DON'T MEAN ANYTHING TO US, DOES IT, OLD GOIL? IN FACK, I CAN'T UNNERSTAN' ALL DA FUSS FOLKS MAKE ABOUT SPACE...
TAXI
I'LL BET DERE'S NUTTIN' IN DA WHOLE UNIVERSE MORE BEE-YOO-TIFUL DEN YOUSE, GOITRUDE!
FOLLOWING THAT SPACE-RADIO BEAM...
YOUSE IS POIFECT! YOUSE IS GORGEOUS! YOUSE IS DA MOST WUNNERFUL SIGHT DAT ANY MAN ON ANY WOILD COULD WANNA SEE! YOUSE --
UHH!
GLYMPH... GLUMPH... GLOWRBBB...
I CAN READ HIS MIND... HIS NAME IS DOIBY DICKLES! BUT THOSE ODD NOISES HE'S MAKING--?
7
7
POSSIBLY MY SUDDEN APPEARANCE HAS FRIGHTENED HIM! I'D BETTER LET HIM KNOW WHO I AM AND WHY I'M HERE...
MY NAME IS PRINCESS RAMIA..
GLOWRB- A PRINCERESS!?
AND YOUSE HAVE COME ALL DA WAY FROM DA FAR-OFF WOILD OF MYRG -- TO ESCAPE A CRUM CALLED PRINCE PERIL-- AND FIND YERSELF A HUSBAND!?
THAT'S RIGHT, DOIBY! I'M LOOKING FOR A MAN I CAN LOVE!
4.

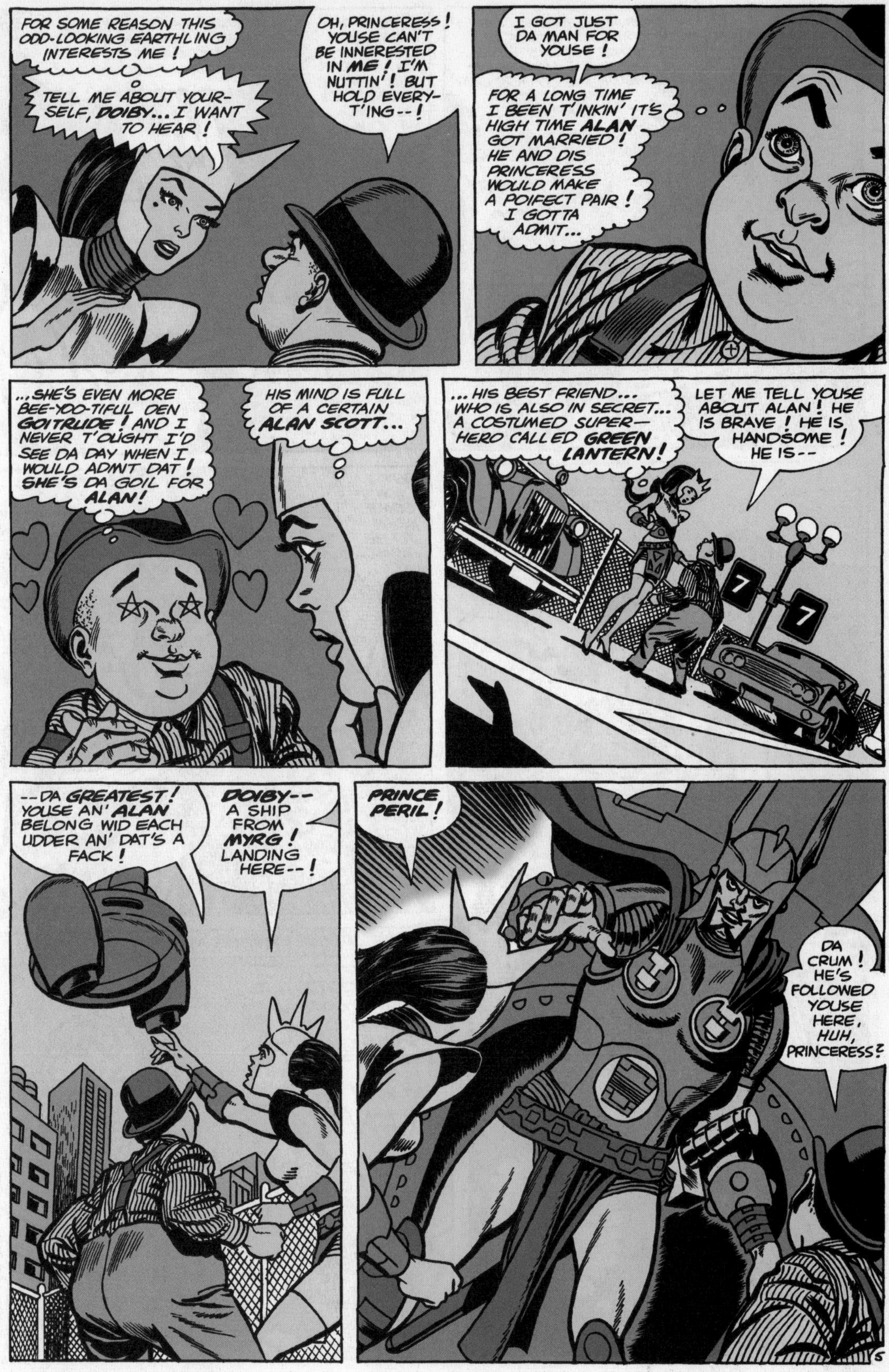
FOR SOME REASON THIS ODD-LOOKING EARTHLING INTERESTS ME!
TELL ME ABOUT YOURSELF, DOIBY... I WANT TO HEAR!
OH, PRINCERESS! YOUSE CAN'T BE INNERESTED IN ME! I'M NUTTIN'! BUT HOLD EVERYT'ING--!
I GOT JUST DA MAN FOR YOUSE!
FOR A LONG TIME I BEEN T'INKIN' IT'S HIGH TIME ALAN GOT MARRIED! HE AND DIS PRINCERESS WOULD MAKE A POIFECT PAIR! I GOTTA ADMIT...
...SHE'S EVEN MORE BEE-YOO-TIFUL DEN GOITRUDE! AND I NEVER T'OUGHT I'D SEE DA DAY WHEN I WOULD ADMIT DAT! SHE'S DA GOIL FOR ALAN!
HIS MIND IS FULL OF A CERTAIN ALAN SCOTT...
...HIS BEST FRIEND... WHO IS ALSO IN SECRET... A COSTUMED SUPER-HERO CALLED GREEN LANTERN!
LET ME TELL YOUSE ABOUT ALAN! HE IS BRAVE! HE IS HANDSOME! HE IS--
7
7
--DA GREATEST! YOUSE AN' ALAN BELONG WID EACH UDDER AN' DAT'S A FACK!
DOIBY-- A SHIP FROM MYRG! LANDING HERE--!
PRINCE PERIL!
DA CRUM! HE'S FOLLOWED YOUSE HERE, HUH, PRINCERESS?
5

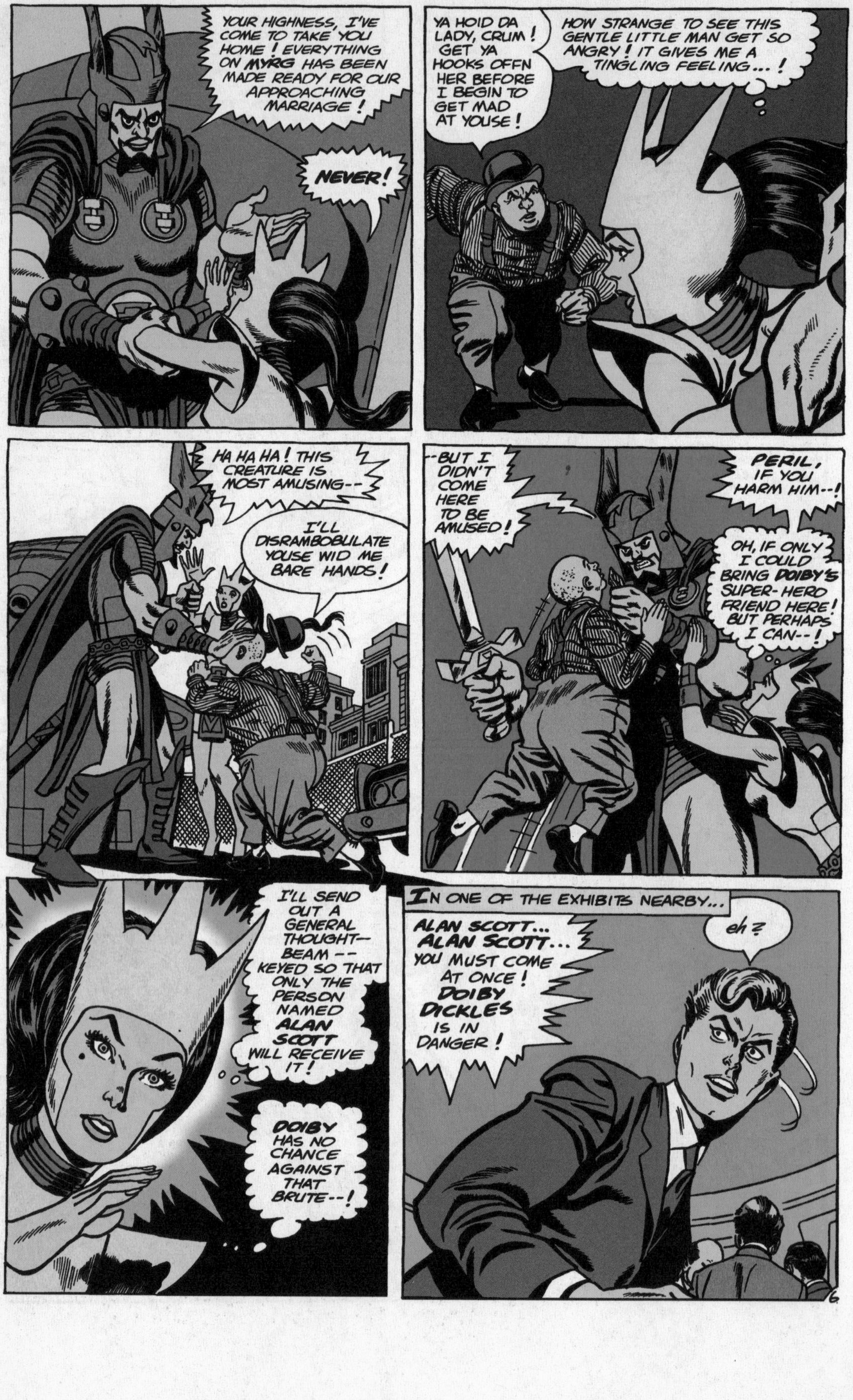
YOUR HIGHNESS, I'VE COME TO TAKE YOU HOME! EVERYTHING ON MYRG HAS BEEN MADE READY FOR OUR APPROACHING MARRIAGE!
NEVER!
YA HOID DA LADY, CRUM! GET YA HOOKS OFFN HER BEFORE I BEGIN TO GET MAD AT YOUSE!
HOW STRANGE TO SEE THIS GENTLE LITTLE MAN GET SO ANGRY! IT GIVES ME A TINGLING FEELING...!
HA HA HA! THIS CREATURE IS MOST AMUSING--
I'LL DISRAMBOBULATE YOUSE WID ME BARE HANDS!
--BUT I DIDN'T COME HERE TO BE AMUSED!
PERIL, IF YOU HARM HIM--!
OH, IF ONLY I COULD BRING DOIBY'S SUPER-HERO FRIEND HERE! BUT PERHAPS I CAN--!
I'LL SEND OUT A GENERAL THOUGHT-BEAM -- KEYED SO THAT ONLY THE PERSON NAMED ALAN SCOTT WILL RECEIVE IT!
DOIBY HAS NO CHANCE AGAINST THAT BRUTE--!
IN ONE OF THE EXHIBITS NEARBY...
ALAN SCOTT... ALAN SCOTT... YOU MUST COME AT ONCE! DOIBY DICKLES IS IN DANGER!
eh?
6

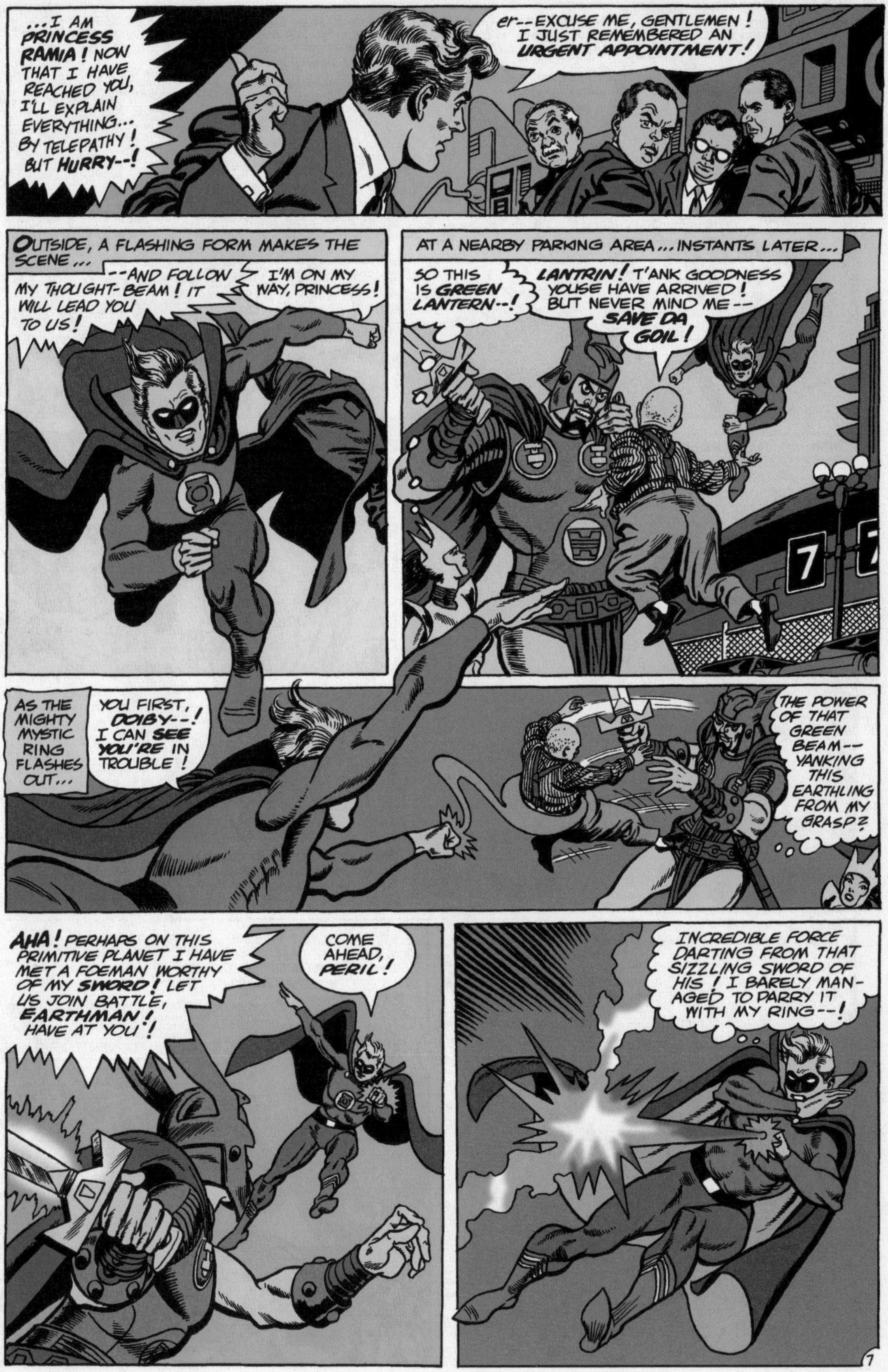
...I AM PRINCESS RAMIA! NOW THAT I HAVE REACHED YOU, I'LL EXPLAIN EVERYTHING... BY TELEPATHY! BUT HURRY--!
er--EXCUSE ME, GENTLEMEN! I JUST REMEMBERED AN URGENT APPOINTMENT!
OUTSIDE, A FLASHING FORM MAKES THE SCENE...
--AND FOLLOW MY THOUGHT-BEAM! IT WILL LEAD YOU TO US!
I'M ON MY WAY, PRINCESS!
AT A NEARBY PARKING AREA... INSTANTS LATER...
SO THIS IS GREEN LANTERN--!
LANTRIN! T'ANK GOODNESS YOUSE HAVE ARRIVED! BUT NEVER MIND ME -- SAVE DA GOIL!
AS THE MIGHTY MYSTIC RING FLASHES OUT...
YOU FIRST, DOIBY--! I CAN SEE YOU'RE IN TROUBLE!
THE POWER OF THAT GREEN BEAM-- YANKING THIS EARTHLING FROM MY GRASP?
AHA! PERHAPS ON THIS PRIMITIVE PLANET I HAVE MET A FOEMAN WORTHY OF MY SWORD! LET US JOIN BATTLE, EARTHMAN! HAVE AT YOU!
COME AHEAD, PERIL!
INCREDIBLE FORCE DARTING FROM THAT SIZZLING SWORD OF HIS! I BARELY MANAGED TO PARRY IT WITH MY RING--!
7

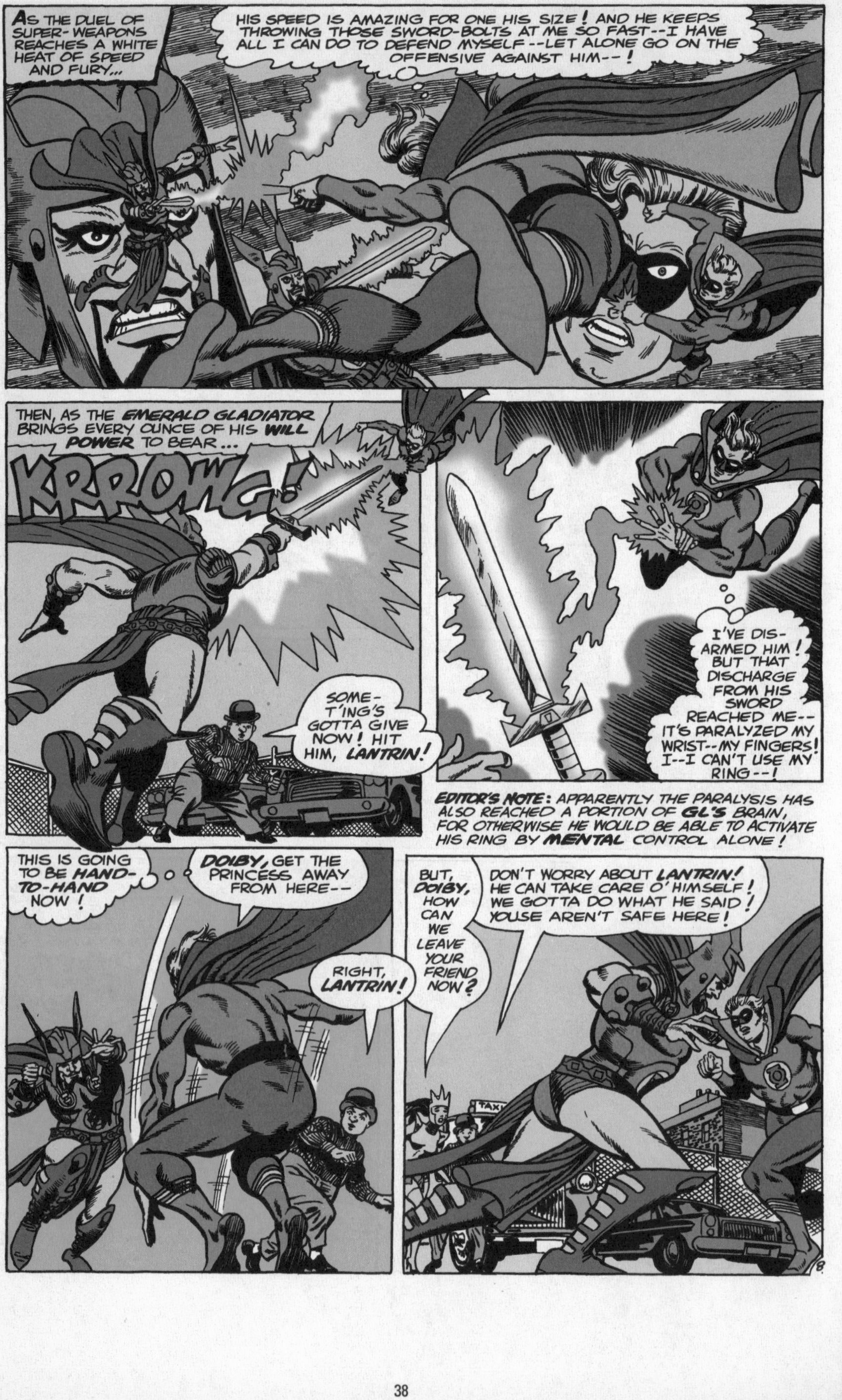
AS THE DUEL OF SUPER-WEAPONS REACHES A WHITE HEAT OF SPEED AND FURY...
HIS SPEED IS AMAZING FOR ONE HIS SIZE! AND HE KEEPS THROWING THOSE SWORD-BOLTS AT ME SO FAST--I HAVE ALL I CAN DO TO DEFEND MYSELF--LET ALONE GO ON THE OFFENSIVE AGAINST HIM--!
THEN, AS THE EMERALD GLADIATOR BRINGS EVERY OUNCE OF HIS WILL POWER TO BEAR...
KRROWG!
SOME-T'ING'S GOTTA GIVE NOW! HIT HIM, LANTRIN!
I'VE DIS-ARMED HIM! BUT DISCHARGE FROM HIS SWORD REACHED ME--IT'S PARALYZED MY WRIST--MY FINGERS! I--I CAN'T USE MY RING--!
EDITOR'S NOTE: APPARENTLY THE PARALYSIS HAS ALSO REACHED A PORTION OF GL'S BRAIN, FOR OTHERWISE HE WOULD BE ABLE TO ACTIVATE HIS RING BY MENTAL CONTROL ALONE!
THIS IS GOING TO BE HAND-TO-HAND NOW!
DOIBY, GET THE PRINCESS AWAY FROM HERE--
RIGHT, LANTRIN!
BUT, DOIBY, HOW CAN WE LEAVE YOUR FRIEND NOW?
DON'T WORRY ABOUT LANTRIN! HE CAN TAKE CARE O' HIMSELF! WE GOTTA DO WHAT HE SAID! YOUSE AREN'T SAFE HERE!
TAXI
8

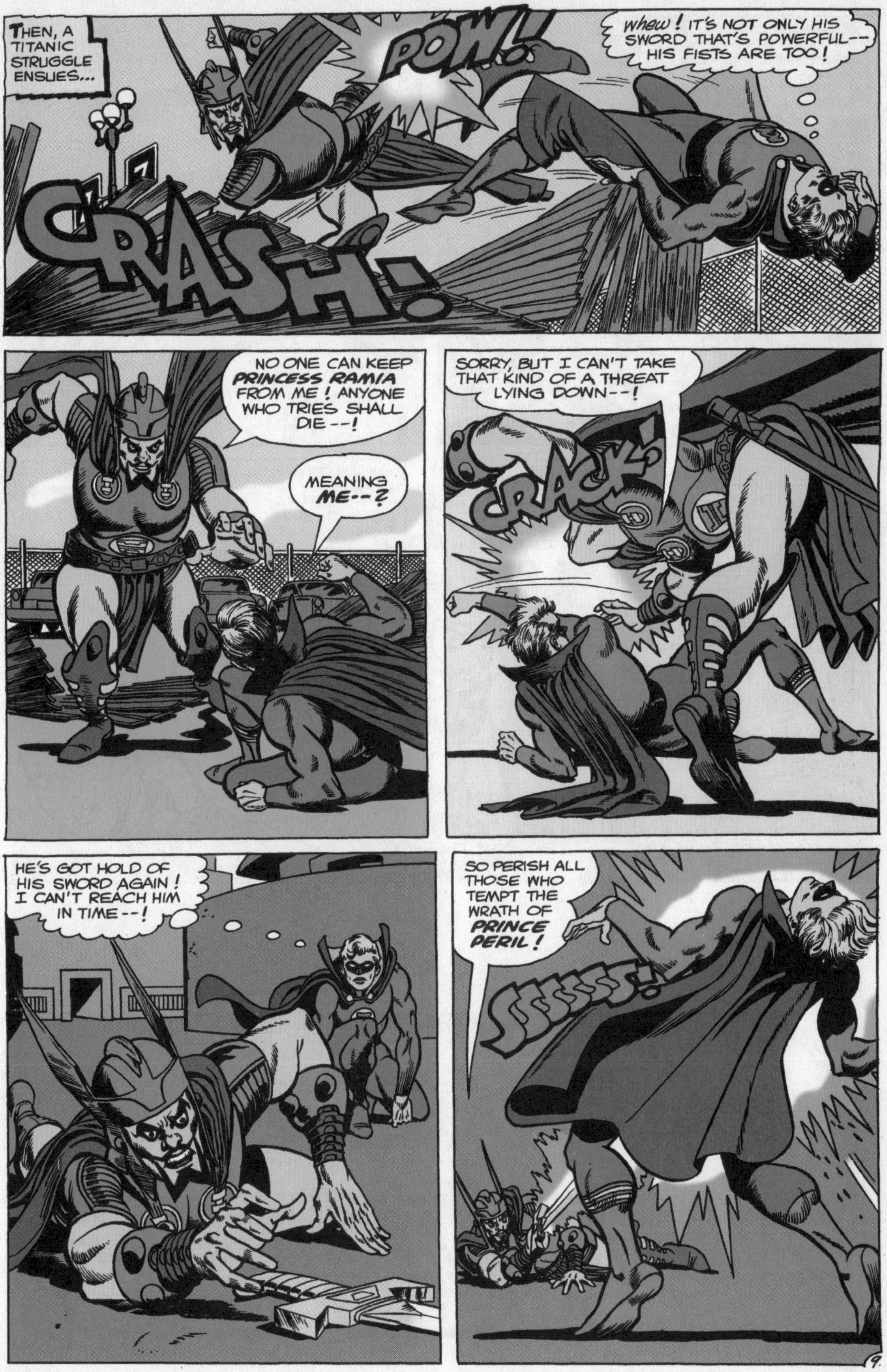
THEN, A TITANIC STRUGGLE ENSUES...
POW!
WHEW! IT'S NOT ONLY HIS SWORD THAT'S POWERFUL-- HIS FISTS ARE TOO!
CRASH!
NO ONE CAN KEEP PRINCESS RAMIA FROM ME! ANYONE WHO TRIES SHALL DIE--!
MEANING ME--?
SORRY, BUT I CAN'T TAKE THAT KIND OF A THREAT LYING DOWN--!
CRACK!
HE'S GOT HOLD OF HIS SWORD AGAIN! I CAN'T REACH HIM IN TIME--!
SO PERISH ALL THOSE WHO TEMPT THE WRATH OF PRINCE PERIL!
SSSSSS!
9.

MOMENTS LATER...
DOIBY! IT'S PRINCE PERIL--COMING AFTER US! HE MUST HAVE DEFEATED GREEN LANTERN--!
DAT AIN'T HUMANLY POSSIBLE!
BUT DON'T YOUSE WORRY, PRINCERESS! I WILL PROTECT YOUSE WID ME LIFE!
ONLY ONE WAY TO ESCAPE NOW--MY DIMENSION-CHANGER--!
YER WOT--?!
THIS SPECIAL DEVICE! IT WILL SWITCH US FROM THIS DIMENSION TO THE NEXT ONE--ALONG WITH YOUR VEHICLE! WE DON'T KNOW WHERE WE MAY LAND--BUT WE MUST TAKE THE CHANCE! HERE GOES--
AS AN EXTRAORDINARY CHANGE TAKES PLACE...
HOLY MACREE! DIS IS DA MOST AMAZING T'ING I EVER HOID OF!
IT WORKED!
STORY CONTINUES ON THE FOLLOWING PAGE!
10

CRISIS ON MULTIPLE EARTHS THE TEAM UPS

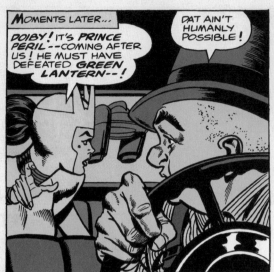

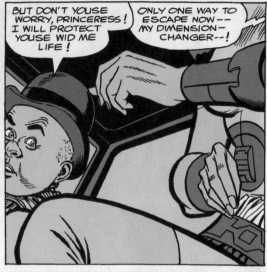

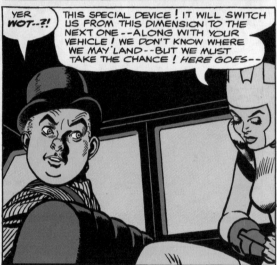

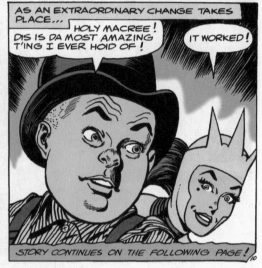

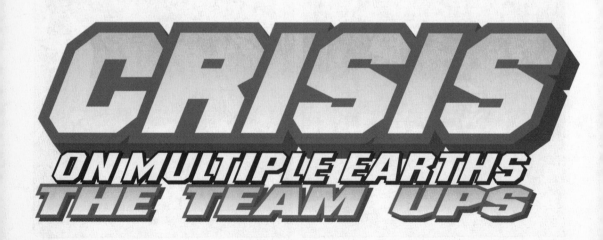

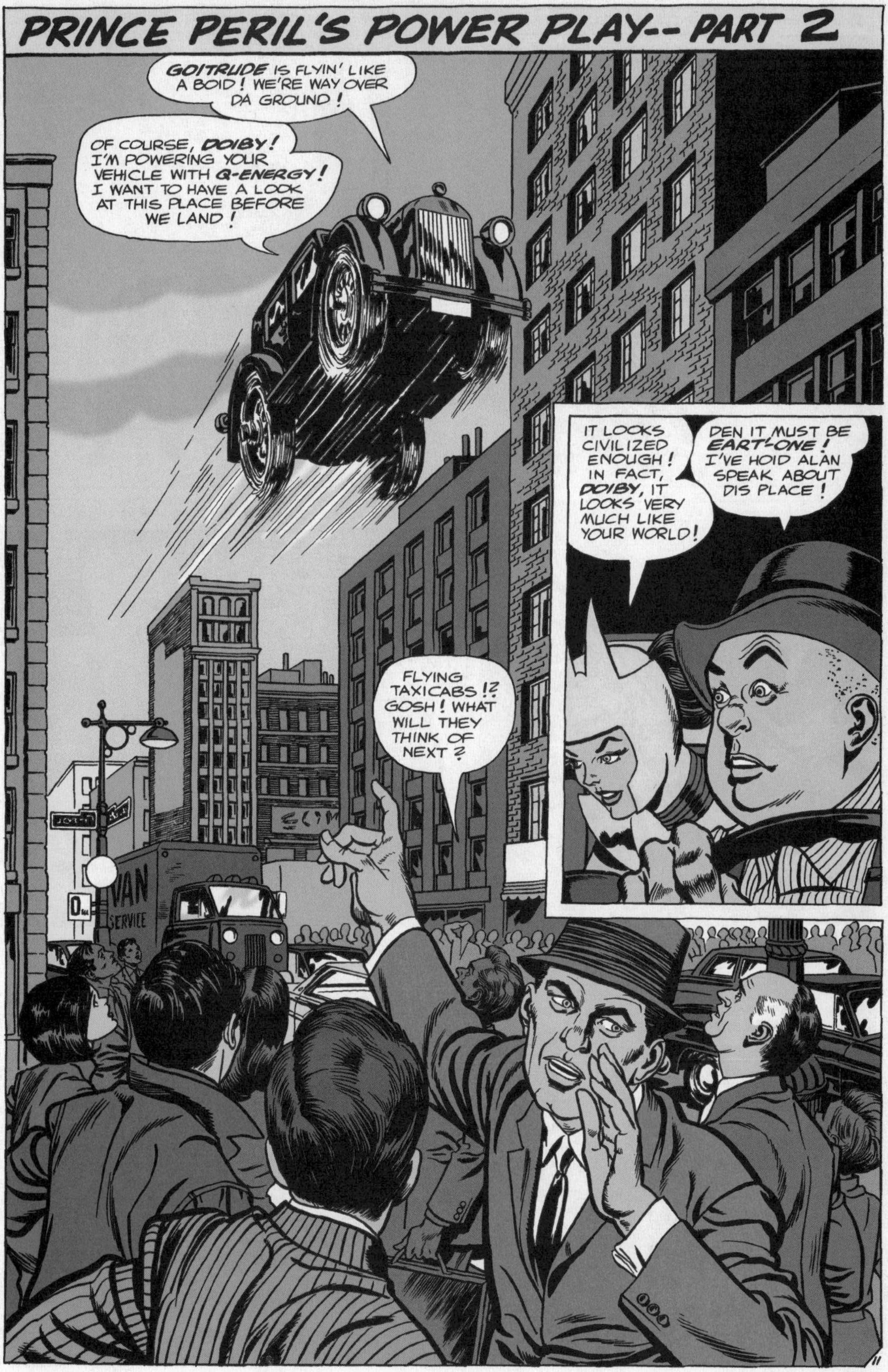
PRINCE PERIL'S POWER PLAY-- PART 2
GOITRUDE IS FLYIN' LIKE A BOID! WE'RE WAY OVER DA GROUND!
OF COURSE, DOIBY! I'M POWERING YOUR VEHICLE WITH Q-ENERGY! I WANT TO HAVE A LOOK AT THIS PLACE BEFORE WE LAND!
IT LOOKS CIVILIZED ENOUGH! IN FACT, DOIBY, IT LOOKS VERY MUCH LIKE YOUR WORLD!
DEN IT MUST BE EART'-ONE! I'VE HOID ALAN SPEAK ABOUT DIS PLACE!
FLYING TAXICABS!? GOSH! WHAT WILL THEY THINK OF NEXT?
VAN SERVICE
11

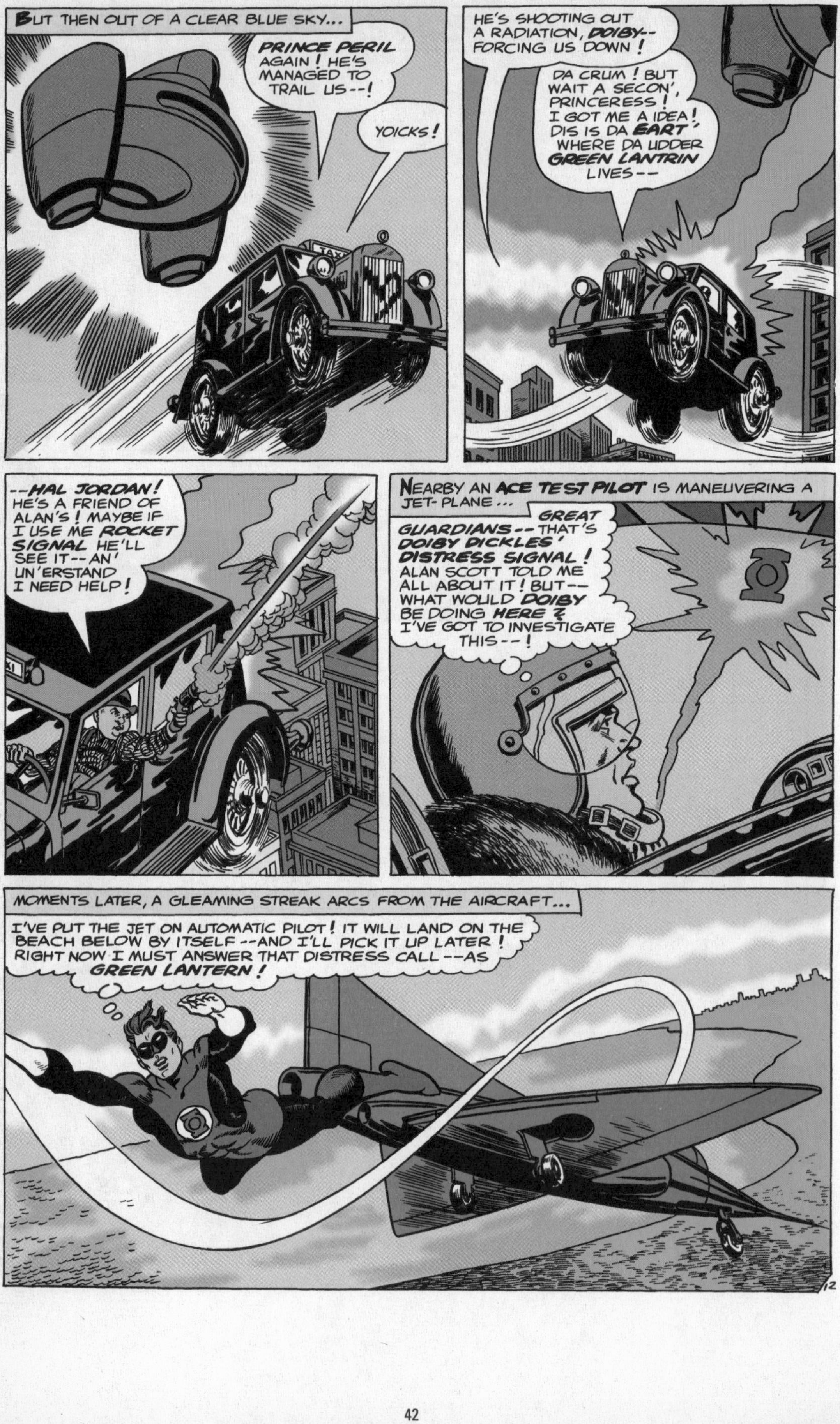
BUT THEN OUT OF A CLEAR BLUE SKY...
PRINCE PERIL AGAIN! HE'S MANAGED TO TRAIL US--!
YOICKS!
HE'S SHOOTING OUT A RADIATION, DOIBY-- FORCING US DOWN!
DA CRUM! BUT WAIT A SECON', PRINCERESS! I GOT ME A IDEA! DIS IS DA EART' WHERE DA UDDER GREEN LANTRIN LIVES--
--HAL JORDAN! HE'S A FRIEND OF ALAN'S! MAYBE IF I USE ME ROCKET SIGNAL HE'LL SEE IT--AN' UN'ERSTAND I NEED HELP!
NEARBY AN ACE TEST PILOT IS MANEUVERING A JET-PLANE...
GREAT GUARDIANS--THAT'S DOIBY DICKLES' DISTRESS SIGNAL! ALAN SCOTT TOLD ME ALL ABOUT IT! BUT--WHAT WOULD DOIBY BE DOING HERE? I'VE GOT TO INVESTIGATE THIS--!
MOMENTS LATER, A GLEAMING STREAK ARCS FROM THE AIRCRAFT...
I'VE PUT THE JET ON AUTOMATIC PILOT! IT WILL LAND ON THE BEACH BELOW BY ITSELF--AND I'LL PICK IT UP LATER! RIGHT NOW I MUST ANSWER THAT DISTRESS CALL--AS GREEN LANTERN!
12

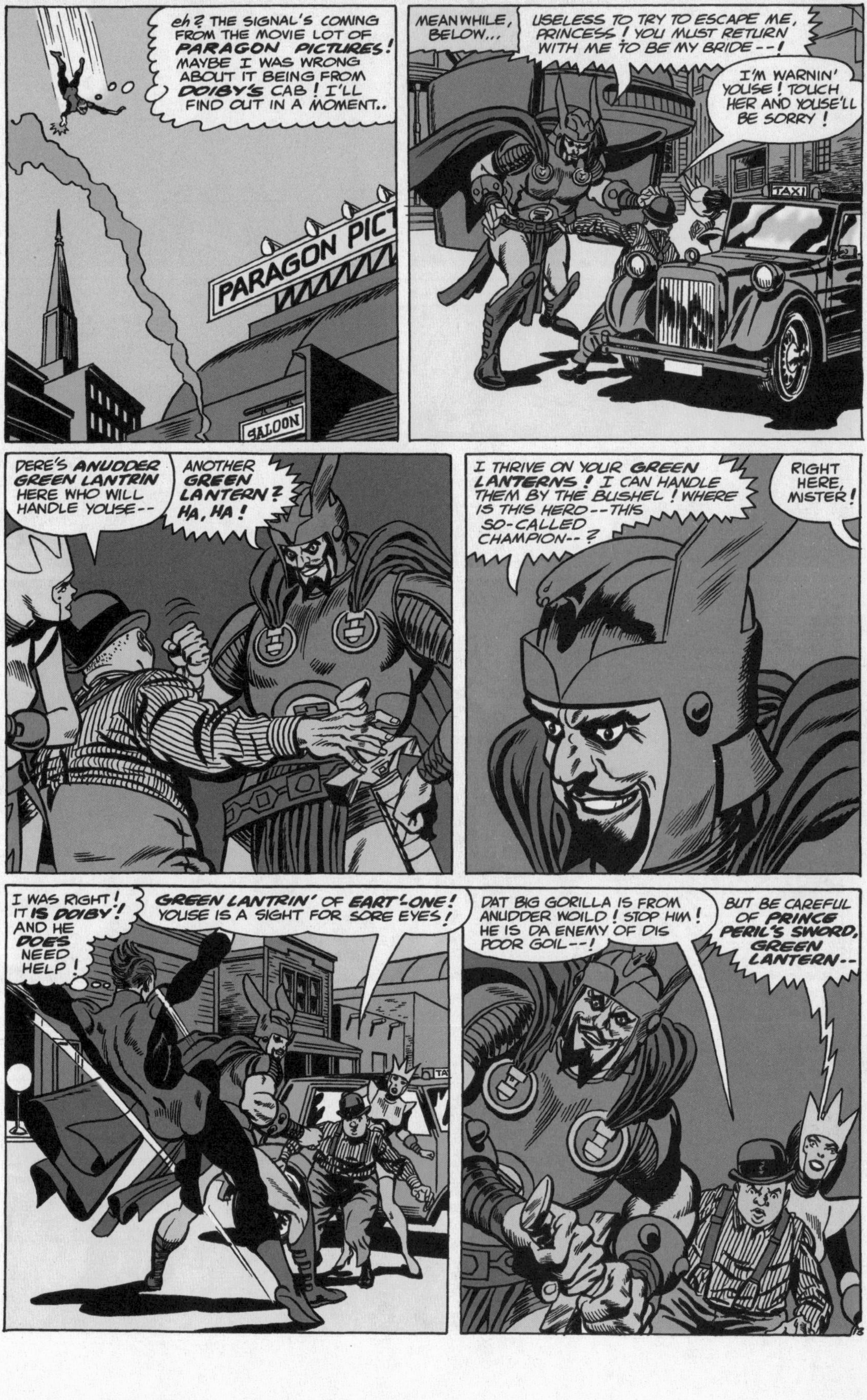
eh? THE SIGNAL'S COMING FROM THE MOVIE LOT OF PARAGON PICTURES! MAYBE I WAS WRONG ABOUT IT BEING FROM DOIBY'S CAB! I'LL FIND OUT IN A MOMENT..
PARAGON PICT
SALOON
MEANWHILE, BELOW...
USELESS TO TRY TO ESCAPE ME, PRINCESS! YOU MUST RETURN WITH ME TO BE MY BRIDE--!
I'M WARNIN' YOUSE! TOUCH HER AND YOUSE'LL BE SORRY!
TAXI
DERE'S ANUDDER GREEN LANTRIN HERE WHO WILL HANDLE YOUSE--
ANOTHER GREEN LANTERN? HA, HA!
I THRIVE ON YOUR GREEN LANTERNS! I CAN HANDLE THEM BY THE BUSHEL! WHERE IS THIS HERO--THIS SO-CALLED CHAMPION--?
RIGHT HERE, MISTER!
I WAS RIGHT! IT IS DOIBY! AND HE DOES NEED HELP!
GREEN LANTRIN' OF EART'-ONE! YOUSE IS A SIGHT FOR SORE EYES!
DAT BIG GORILLA IS FROM ANUDDER WOILD! STOP HIM! HE IS DA ENEMY OF DIS POOR GOIL--!
BUT BE CAREFUL OF PRINCE PERIL'S SWORD, GREEN LANTERN--
13

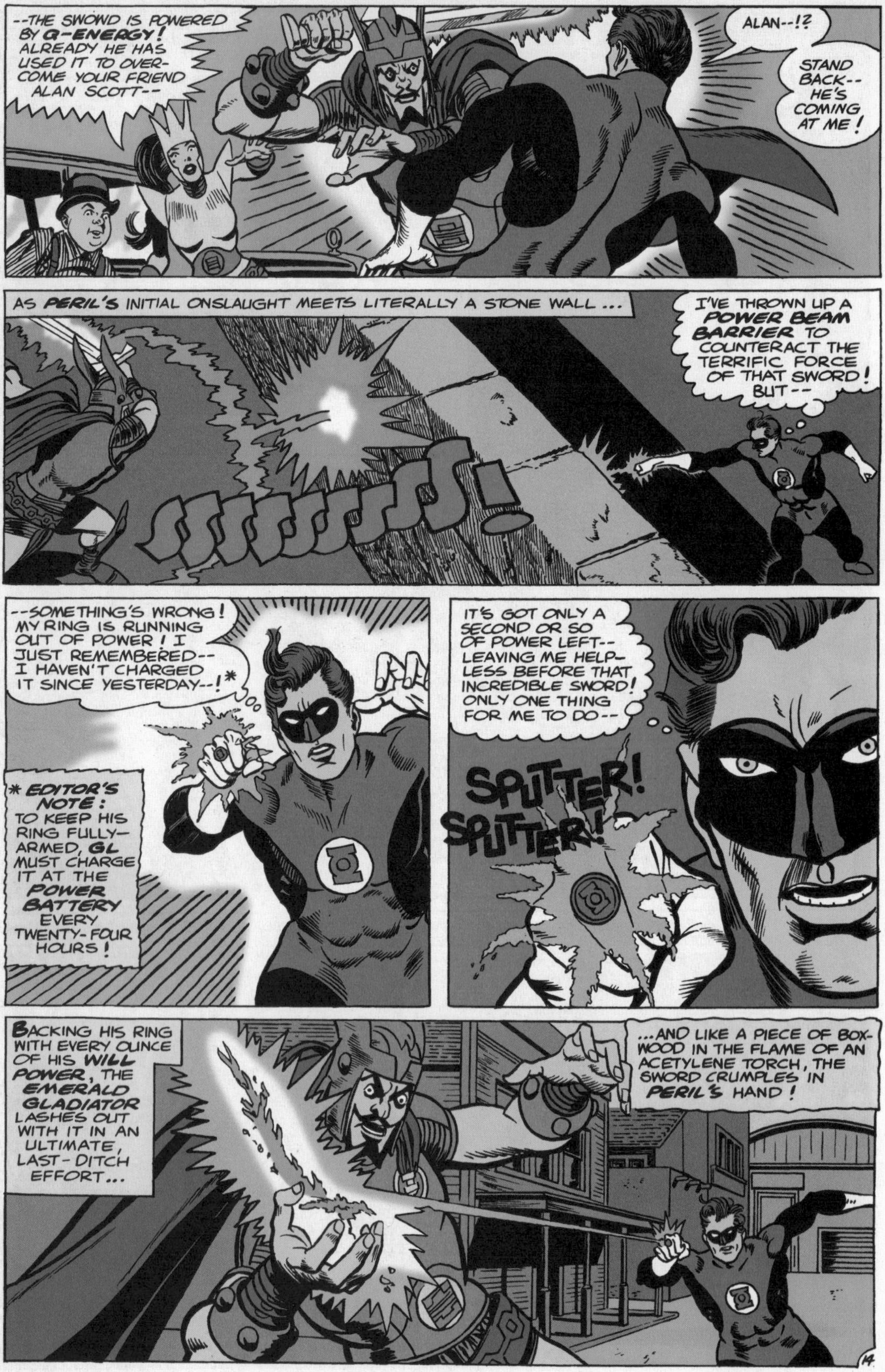
--THE SWORD IS POWERED BY Q-ENERGY! ALREADY HE HAS USED IT TO OVER-COME YOUR FRIEND ALAN SCOTT--
ALAN--!?
STAND BACK--HE'S COMING AT ME!
AS PERIL'S INITIAL ONSLAUGHT MEETS LITERALLY A STONE WALL ...
I'VE THROWN UP A POWER BEAM BARRIER TO COUNTERACT THE TERRIFIC FORCE OF THAT SWORD! BUT--
SSSSSSSSSS!
--SOMETHING'S WRONG! MY RING IS RUNNING OUT OF POWER! I JUST REMEMBERED--I HAVEN'T CHARGED IT SINCE YESTERDAY--!*
* EDITOR'S NOTE: TO KEEP HIS RING FULLY-ARMED, GL MUST CHARGE IT AT THE POWER BATTERY EVERY TWENTY-FOUR HOURS!
IT'S GOT ONLY A SECOND OR SO OF POWER LEFT--LEAVING ME HELP-LESS BEFORE THAT INCREDIBLE SWORD! ONLY ONE THING FOR ME TO DO--
SPUTTER! SPUTTER!
BACKING HIS RING WITH EVERY OUNCE OF HIS WILL POWER, THE EMERALD GLADIATOR LASHES OUT WITH IT IN AN ULTIMATE, LAST-DITCH EFFORT...
...AND LIKE A PIECE OF BOX-WOOD IN THE FLAME OF AN ACETYLENE TORCH, THE SWORD CRUMPLES IN PERIL'S HAND!
14

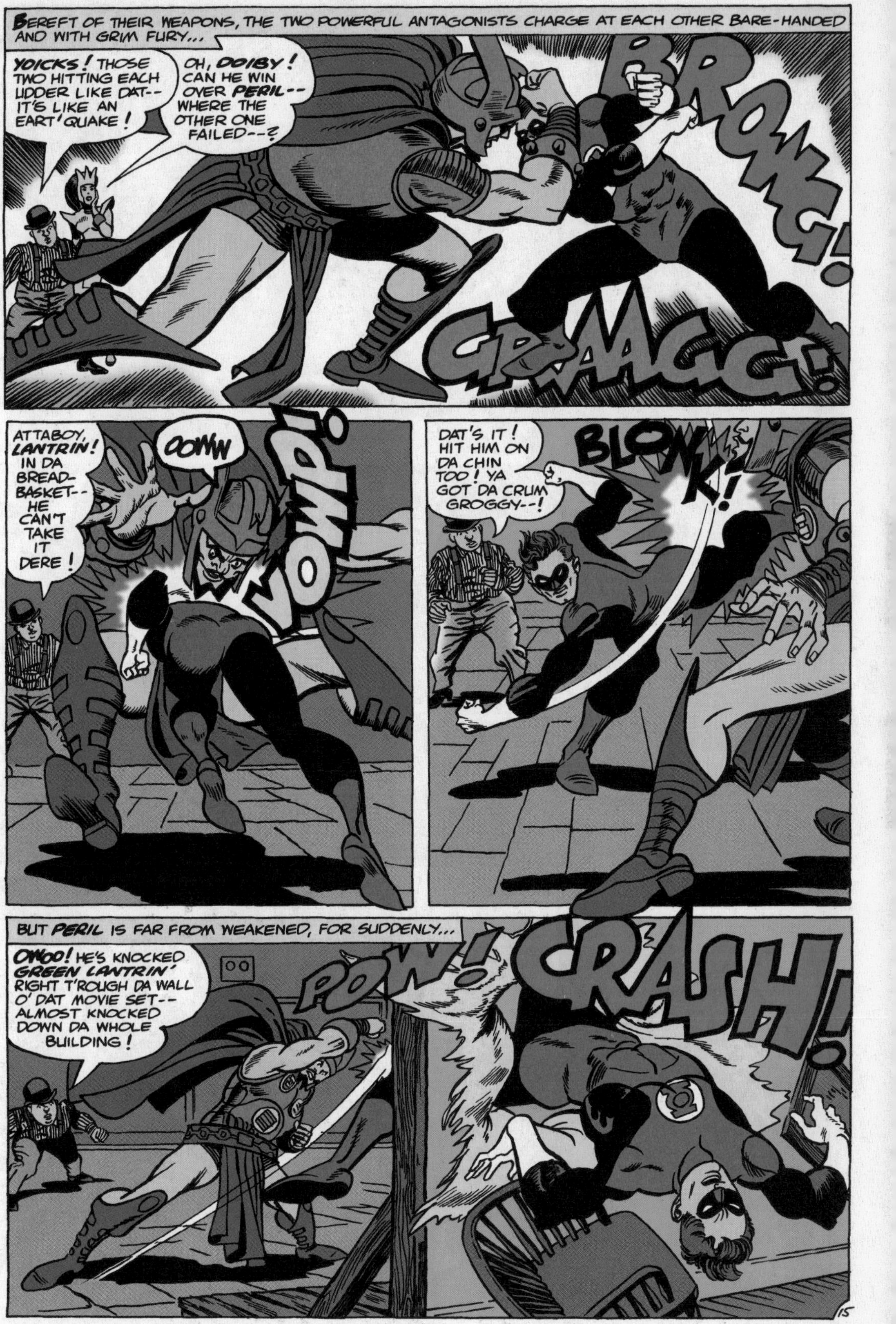

BEREFT OF THEIR WEAPONS, THE TWO POWERFUL ANTAGONISTS CHARGE AT EACH OTHER BARE-HANDED AND WITH GRIM FURY...
YOICKS! THOSE TWO HITTING EACH UDDER LIKE DAT-- IT'S LIKE AN EART'QUAKE!
OH, DOIBY! CAN HE WIN OVER PERIL-- WHERE THE OTHER ONE FAILED--?
BRONG!
GRAAGG!
ATTABOY, LANTRIN! IN DA BREAD-BASKET-- HE CAN'T TAKE IT DERE!
OOMW
WOMP!
DAT'S IT! HIT HIM ON DA CHIN TOO! YA GOT DA CRUM GROGGY--!
BLONK!
BUT PERIL IS FAR FROM WEAKENED, FOR SUDDENLY...
OWOO! HE'S KNOCKED GREEN LANTRIN' RIGHT T'ROUGH DA WALL O' DAT MOVIE SET-- ALMOST KNOCKED DOWN DA WHOLE BUILDING!
POW!
CRASH!
15

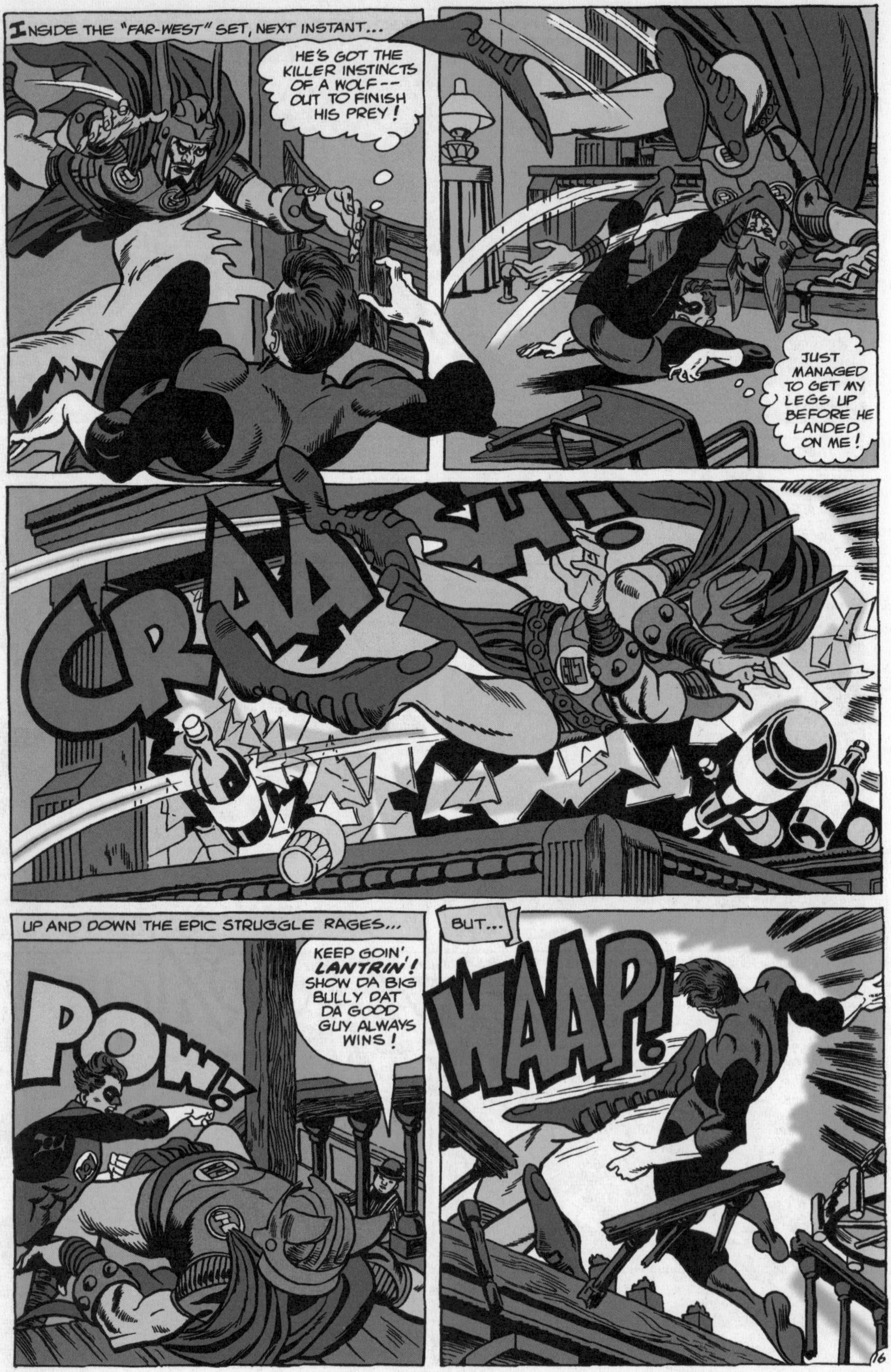
INSIDE THE "FAR-WEST" SET, NEXT INSTANT...
HE'S GOT THE KILLER INSTINCTS OF A WOLF-- OUT TO FINISH HIS PREY!
JUST MANAGED TO GET MY LEGS UP BEFORE HE LANDED ON ME!
CRAASH!
UP AND DOWN THE EPIC STRUGGLE RAGES...
POW!
KEEP GOIN', LANTRIN! SHOW DA BIG BULLY DAT DA GOOD GUY ALWAYS WINS!
BUT...
WAAP!
16

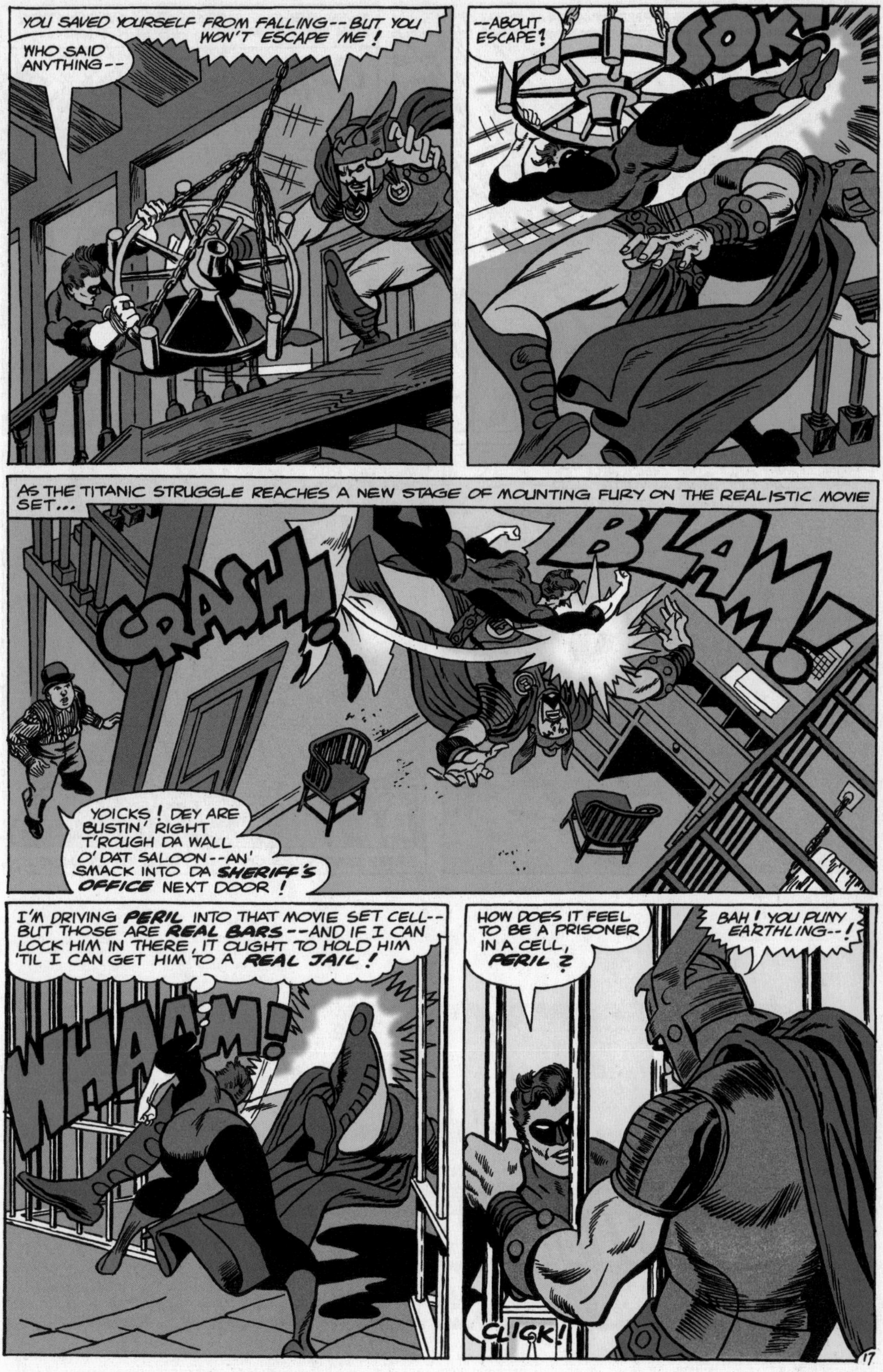
YOU SAVED YOURSELF FROM FALLING--BUT YOU WON'T ESCAPE ME!
WHO SAID ANYTHING--
--ABOUT ESCAPE?
SOK!
AS THE TITANIC STRUGGLE REACHES A NEW STAGE OF MOUNTING FURY ON THE REALISTIC MOVIE SET...
CRASH!
BLAM!
YOICKS! DEY ARE BUSTIN' RIGHT T'ROUGH DA WALL O' DAT SALOON--AN' SMACK INTO DA SHERIFF'S OFFICE NEXT DOOR!
I'M DRIVING PERIL INTO THAT MOVIE SET CELL--BUT THOSE ARE REAL BARS--AND IF I CAN LOCK HIM IN THERE, IT OUGHT TO HOLD HIM 'TIL I CAN GET HIM TO A REAL JAIL!
WHAAM!
HOW DOES IT FEEL TO BE A PRISONER IN A CELL, PERIL?
BAH! YOU PUNY EARTHLING--!
CLICK!
17

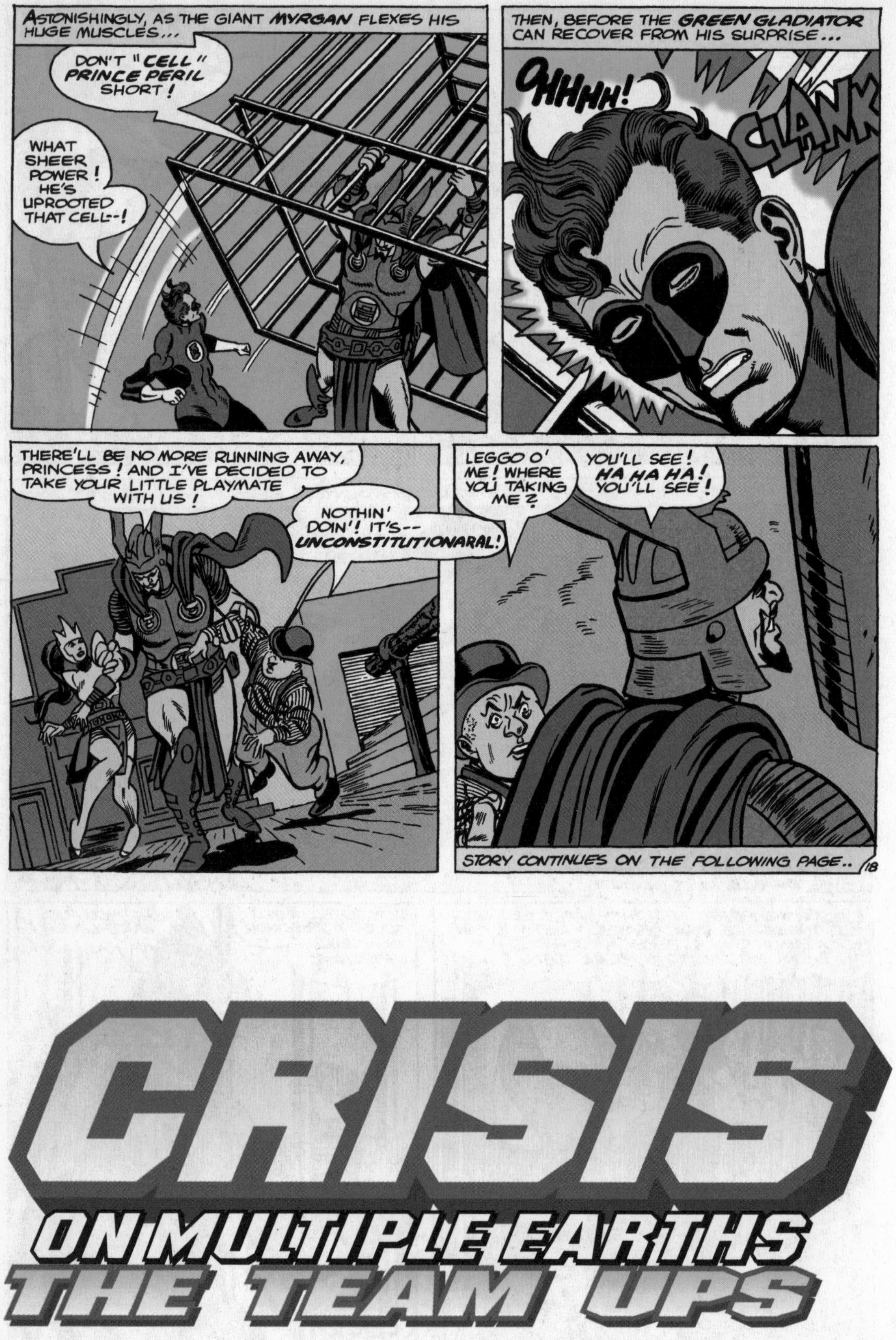
ASTONISHINGLY, AS THE GIANT MYRGAN FLEXES HIS HUGE MUSCLES...
DON'T "CELL" PRINCE PERIL SHORT!
WHAT SHEER POWER! HE'S UPROOTED THAT CELL--!
THEN, BEFORE THE GREEN GLADIATOR CAN RECOVER FROM HIS SURPRISE...
OHHHH!
CLANK
THERE'LL BE NO MORE RUNNING AWAY, PRINCESS! AND I'VE DECIDED TO TAKE YOUR LITTLE PLAYMATE WITH US!
NOTHIN' DOIN'! IT'S-- UNCONSTITUTIONARAL!
LEGGO O' ME! WHERE YOU TAKING ME?
YOU'LL SEE! HA HA HA! YOU'LL SEE!
STORY CONTINUES ON THE FOLLOWING PAGE..
18

CRISIS ON MULTIPLE EARTHS THE TEAM UPS

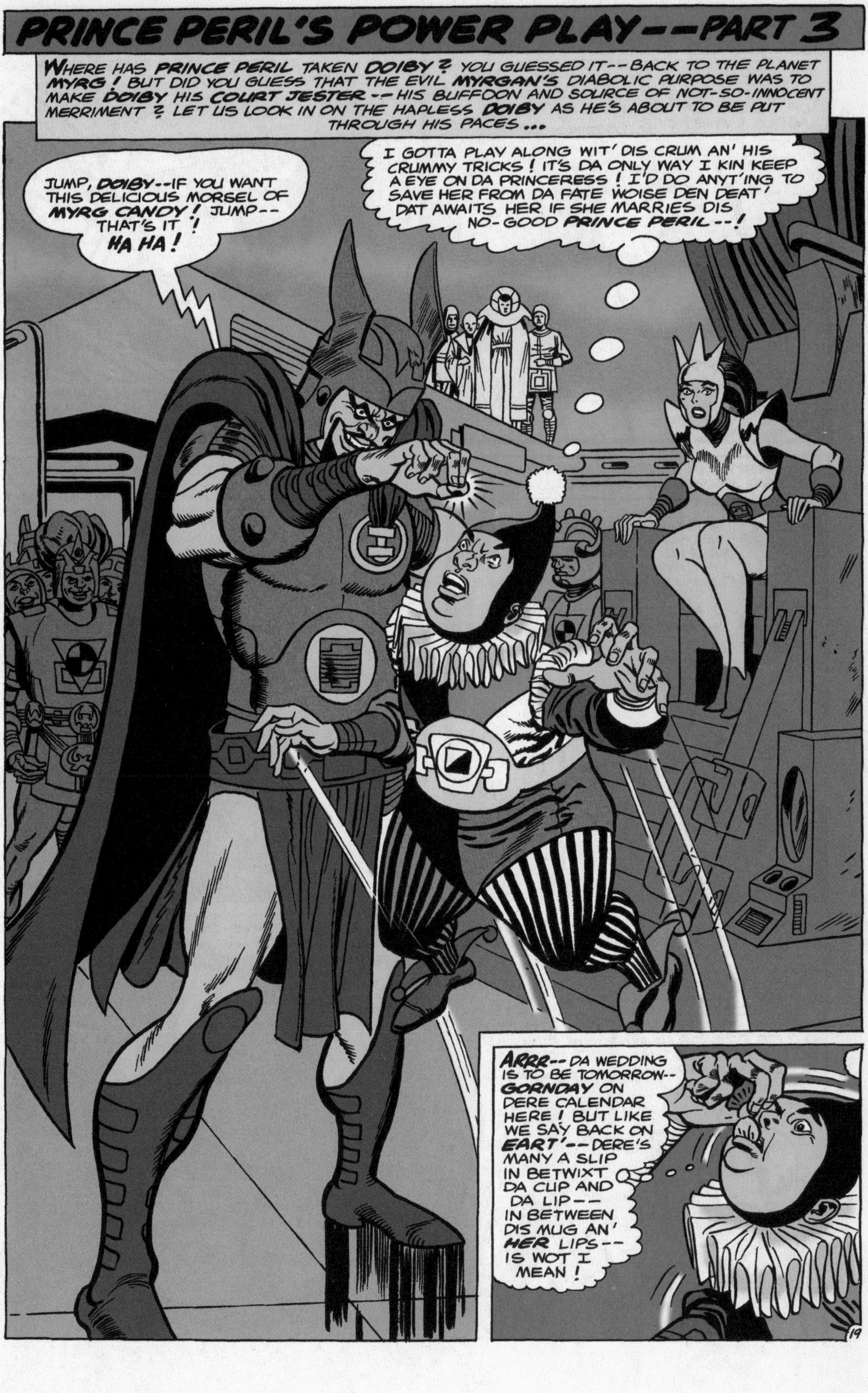
PRINCE PERIL'S POWER PLAY--PART 3
WHERE HAS PRINCE PERIL TAKEN DOIBY? YOU GUESSED IT--BACK TO THE PLANET MYRG! BUT DID YOU GUESS THAT THE EVIL MYRGAN'S DIABOLIC PURPOSE WAS TO MAKE DOIBY HIS COURT JESTER--HIS BUFFOON AND SOURCE OF NOT-SO-INNOCENT MERRIMENT? LET US LOOK IN ON THE HAPLESS DOIBY AS HE'S ABOUT TO BE PUT THROUGH HIS PACES...
JUMP, DOIBY--IF YOU WANT THIS DELICIOUS MORSEL OF MYRG CANDY! JUMP--THAT'S IT! HA HA!
I GOTTA PLAY ALONG WIT' DIS CRUM AN' HIS CRUMMY TRICKS! IT'S DA ONLY WAY I KIN KEEP A EYE ON DA PRINCERESS! I'D DO ANYT'ING TO SAVE HER FROM DA FATE WOISE DEN DEAT' DAT AWAITS HER IF SHE MARRIES DIS NO-GOOD PRINCE PERIL--!
ARRR--DA WEDDING IS TO BE TOMORROW--GORNDAY ON DERE CALENDAR HERE! BUT LIKE WE SAY BACK ON EART'--DERE'S MANY A SLIP IN BETWIXT DA CUP AND DA LIP--IN BETWEEN DIS MUG AN' HER LIPS--IS WOT I MEAN!
19

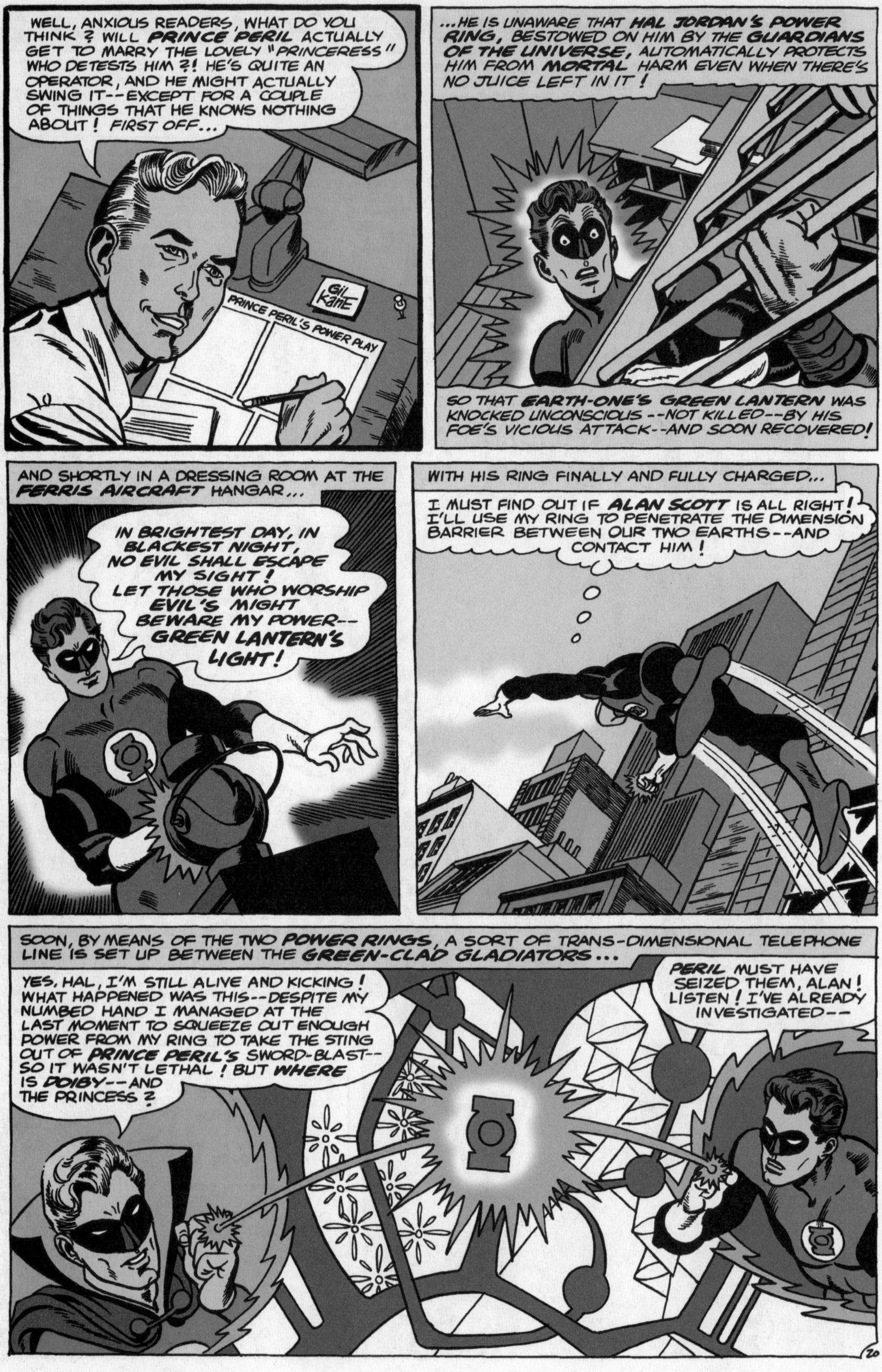
WELL, ANXIOUS READERS, WHAT DO YOU THINK ? WILL PRINCE PERIL ACTUALLY GET TO MARRY THE LOVELY "PRINCERESS" WHO DETESTS HIM ?! HE'S QUITE AN OPERATOR, AND HE MIGHT ACTUALLY SWING IT--EXCEPT FOR A COUPLE OF THINGS THAT HE KNOWS NOTHING ABOUT ! FIRST OFF...
GIL KANE
PRINCE PERIL'S POWER PLAY
...HE IS UNAWARE THAT HAL JORDAN'S POWER RING, BESTOWED ON HIM BY THE GUARDIANS OF THE UNIVERSE, AUTOMATICALLY PROTECTS HIM FROM MORTAL HARM EVEN WHEN THERE'S NO JUICE LEFT IN IT !
SO THAT EARTH-ONE'S GREEN LANTERN WAS KNOCKED UNCONSCIOUS--NOT KILLED--BY HIS FOE'S VICIOUS ATTACK--AND SOON RECOVERED!
AND SHORTLY IN A DRESSING ROOM AT THE FERRIS AIRCRAFT HANGAR...
IN BRIGHTEST DAY, IN BLACKEST NIGHT, NO EVIL SHALL ESCAPE MY SIGHT ! LET THOSE WHO WORSHIP EVIL'S MIGHT BEWARE MY POWER-- GREEN LANTERN'S LIGHT!
WITH HIS RING FINALLY AND FULLY CHARGED...
I MUST FIND OUT IF ALAN SCOTT IS ALL RIGHT! I'LL USE MY RING TO PENETRATE THE DIMENSION BARRIER BETWEEN OUR TWO EARTHS--AND CONTACT HIM !
SOON, BY MEANS OF THE TWO POWER RINGS, A SORT OF TRANS-DIMENSIONAL TELEPHONE LINE IS SET UP BETWEEN THE GREEN-CLAD GLADIATORS...
YES, HAL, I'M STILL ALIVE AND KICKING ! WHAT HAPPENED WAS THIS--DESPITE MY NUMBED HAND I MANAGED AT THE LAST MOMENT TO SQUEEZE OUT ENOUGH POWER FROM MY RING TO TAKE THE STING OUT OF PRINCE PERIL'S SWORD-BLAST--SO IT WASN'T LETHAL ! BUT WHERE IS DOIBY--AND THE PRINCESS ?
PERIL MUST HAVE SEIZED THEM, ALAN ! LISTEN ! I'VE ALREADY INVESTIGATED--
20

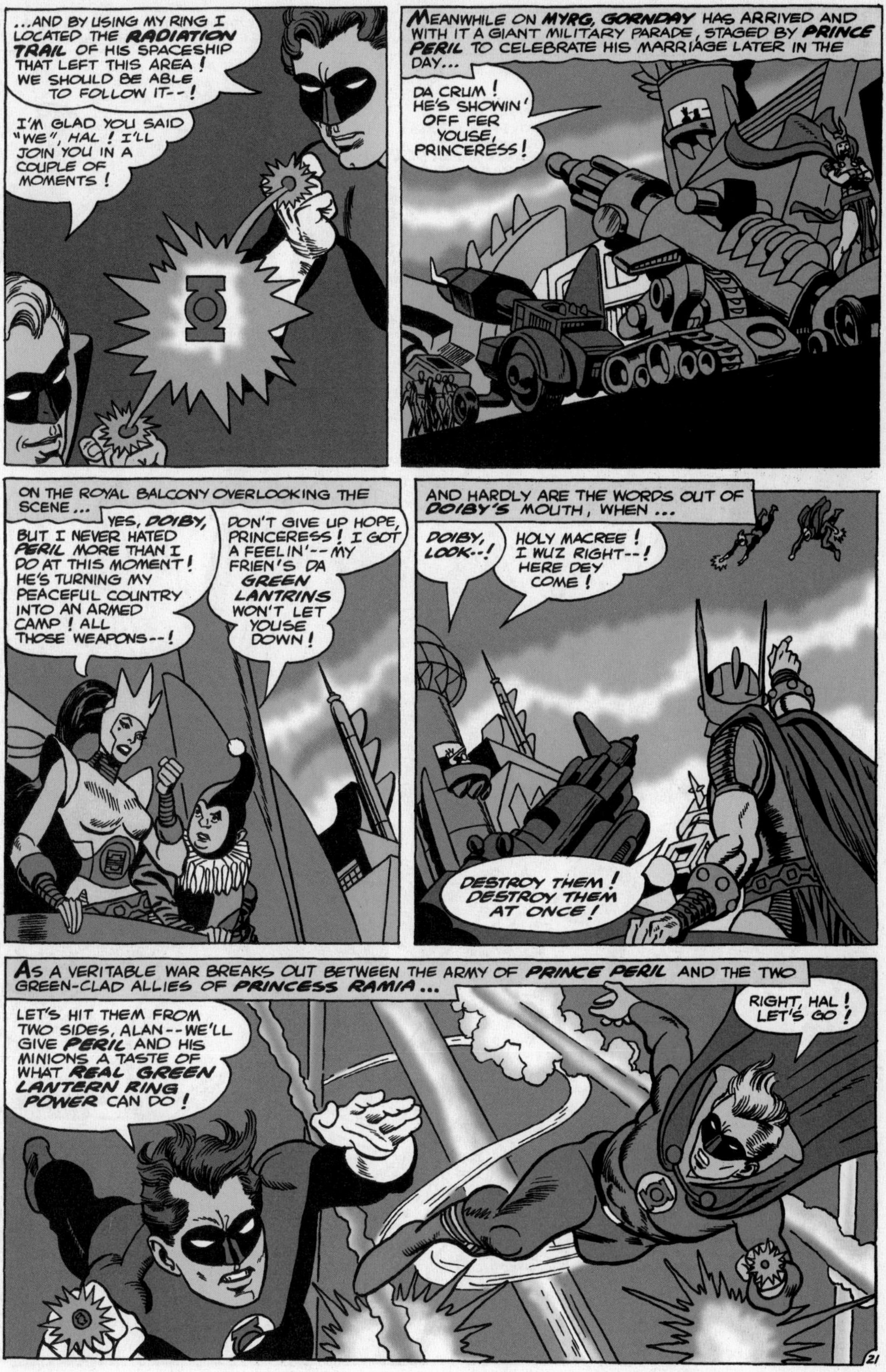
...AND BY USING MY RING I LOCATED THE RADIATION TRAIL OF HIS SPACESHIP THAT LEFT THIS AREA! WE SHOULD BE ABLE TO FOLLOW IT--!
I'M GLAD YOU SAID "WE", HAL! I'LL JOIN YOU IN A COUPLE OF MOMENTS!
MEANWHILE ON MYRG, GORNDAY HAS ARRIVED AND WITH IT A GIANT MILITARY PARADE, STAGED BY PRINCE PERIL TO CELEBRATE HIS MARRIAGE LATER IN THE DAY...
DA CRUM! HE'S SHOWIN' OFF FER YOUSE, PRINCERESS!
ON THE ROYAL BALCONY OVERLOOKING THE SCENE...
YES, DOIBY, BUT I NEVER HATED PERIL MORE THAN I DO AT THIS MOMENT! HE'S TURNING MY PEACEFUL COUNTRY INTO AN ARMED CAMP! ALL THOSE WEAPONS--!
DON'T GIVE UP HOPE, PRINCERESS! I GOT A FEELIN'--MY FRIEN'S DA GREEN LANTRINS WON'T LET YOUSE DOWN!
AND HARDLY ARE THE WORDS OUT OF DOIBY'S MOUTH, WHEN...
DOIBY, LOOK--!
HOLY MACREE! I WUZ RIGHT--! HERE DEY COME!
DESTROY THEM! DESTROY THEM AT ONCE!
AS A VERITABLE WAR BREAKS OUT BETWEEN THE ARMY OF PRINCE PERIL AND THE TWO GREEN-CLAD ALLIES OF PRINCESS RAMIA...
LET'S HIT THEM FROM TWO SIDES, ALAN--WE'LL GIVE PERIL AND HIS MINIONS A TASTE OF WHAT REAL GREEN LANTERN RING POWER CAN DO!
RIGHT, HAL! LET'S GO!
21

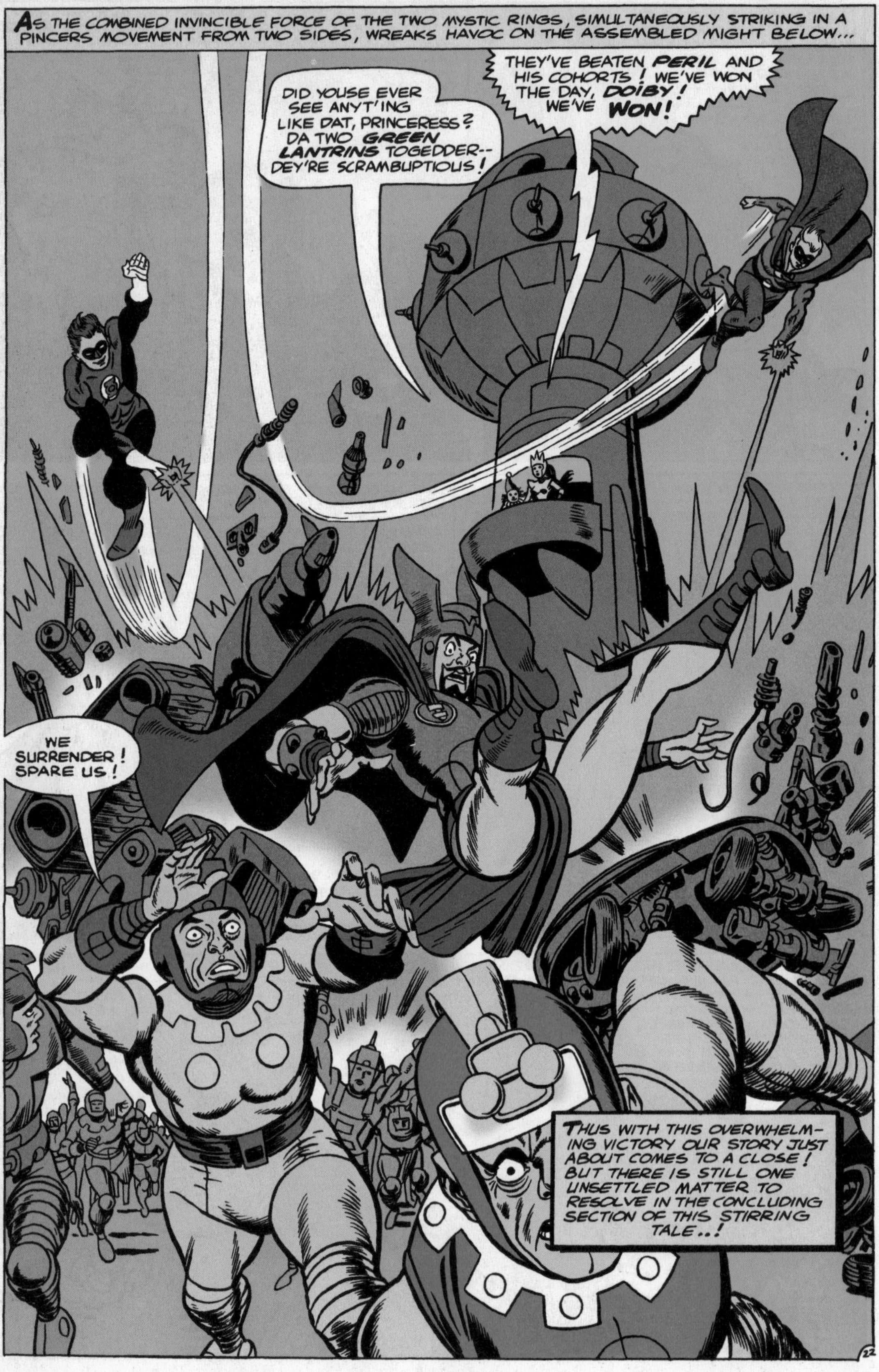
AS THE COMBINED INVINCIBLE FORCE OF THE TWO MYSTIC RINGS, SIMULTANEOUSLY STRIKING IN A PINCERS MOVEMENT FROM TWO SIDES, WREAKS HAVOC ON THE ASSEMBLED MIGHT BELOW...
DID YOUSE EVER SEE ANYT'ING LIKE DAT, PRINCERESS? DA TWO GREEN LANTRINS TOGEDDER-- DEY'RE SCRAMBUPTIOUS!
THEY'VE BEATEN PERIL AND HIS COHORTS! WE'VE WON THE DAY, DOIBY! WE'VE WON!
WE SURRENDER! SPARE US!
THUS WITH THIS OVERWHELMING VICTORY OUR STORY JUST ABOUT COMES TO A CLOSE! BUT THERE IS STILL ONE UNSETTLED MATTER TO RESOLVE IN THE CONCLUDING SECTION OF THIS STIRRING TALE..!
22

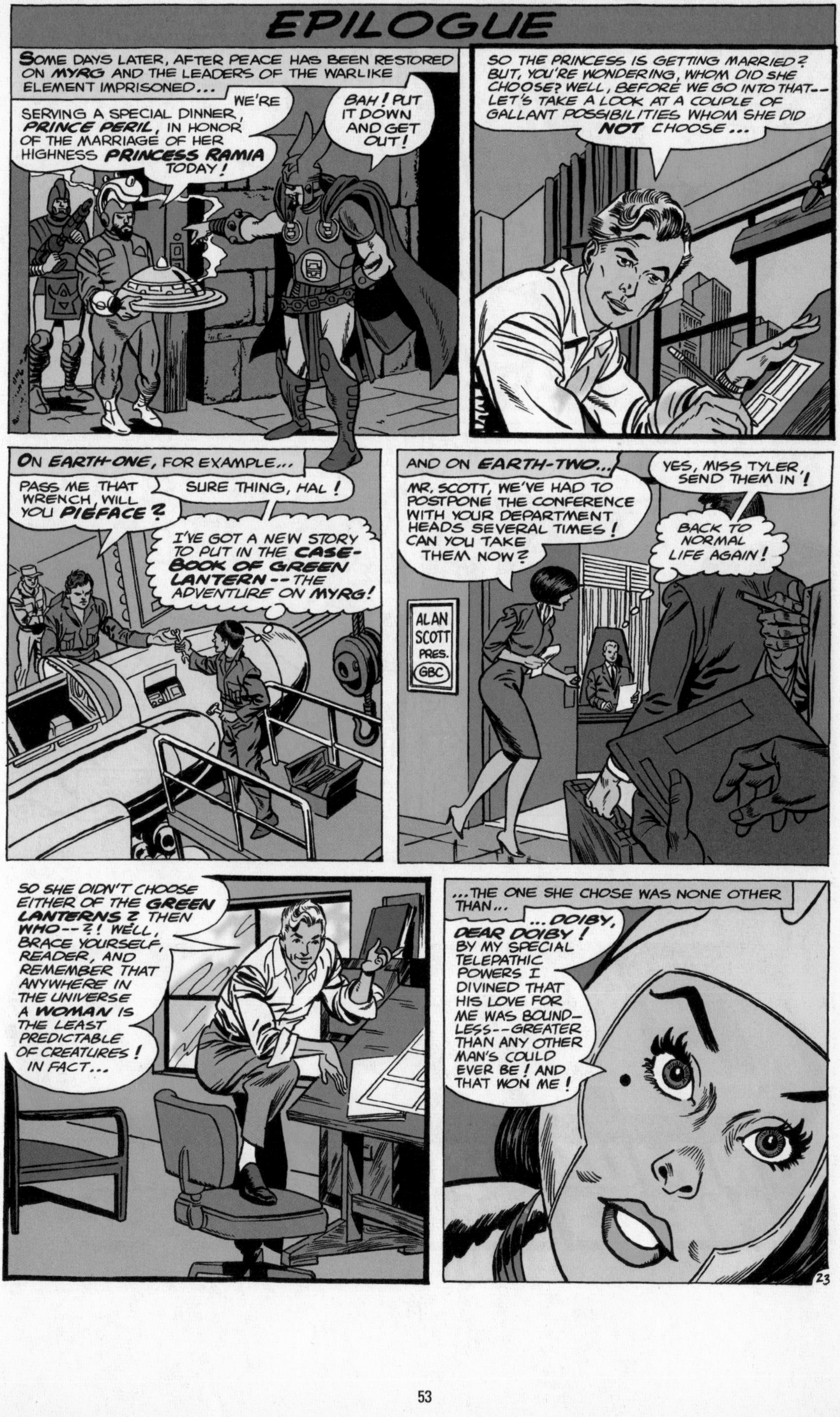
EPILOGUE
SOME DAYS LATER, AFTER PEACE HAS BEEN RESTORED ON MYRG AND THE LEADERS OF THE WARLIKE ELEMENT IMPRISONED...
WE'RE SERVING A SPECIAL DINNER, PRINCE PERIL, IN HONOR OF THE MARRIAGE OF HER HIGHNESS PRINCESS RAMIA TODAY!
BAH! PUT IT DOWN AND GET OUT!
SO THE PRINCESS IS GETTING MARRIED? BUT, YOU'RE WONDERING, WHOM DID SHE CHOOSE? WELL, BEFORE WE GO INTO THAT--LET'S TAKE A LOOK AT A COUPLE OF GALLANT POSSIBILITIES WHOM SHE DID NOT CHOOSE...
ON EARTH-ONE, FOR EXAMPLE...
PASS ME THAT WRENCH, WILL YOU PIEFACE?
SURE THING, HAL!
I'VE GOT A NEW STORY TO PUT IN THE CASE-BOOK OF GREEN LANTERN--THE ADVENTURE ON MYRG!
AND ON EARTH-TWO...
MR. SCOTT, WE'VE HAD TO POSTPONE THE CONFERENCE WITH YOUR DEPARTMENT HEADS SEVERAL TIMES! CAN YOU TAKE THEM NOW?
YES, MISS TYLER, SEND THEM IN!
BACK TO NORMAL LIFE AGAIN!
ALAN SCOTT PRES. GBC
SO SHE DIDN'T CHOOSE EITHER OF THE GREEN LANTERNS? THEN WHO--?! WELL, BRACE YOURSELF, READER, AND REMEMBER THAT ANYWHERE IN THE UNIVERSE A WOMAN IS THE LEAST PREDICTABLE OF CREATURES! IN FACT...
...THE ONE SHE CHOSE WAS NONE OTHER THAN...
...DOIBY, DEAR DOIBY! BY MY SPECIAL TELEPATHIC POWERS I DIVINED THAT HIS LOVE FOR ME WAS BOUNDLESS--GREATER THAN ANY OTHER MAN'S COULD EVER BE! AND THAT WON ME!
23

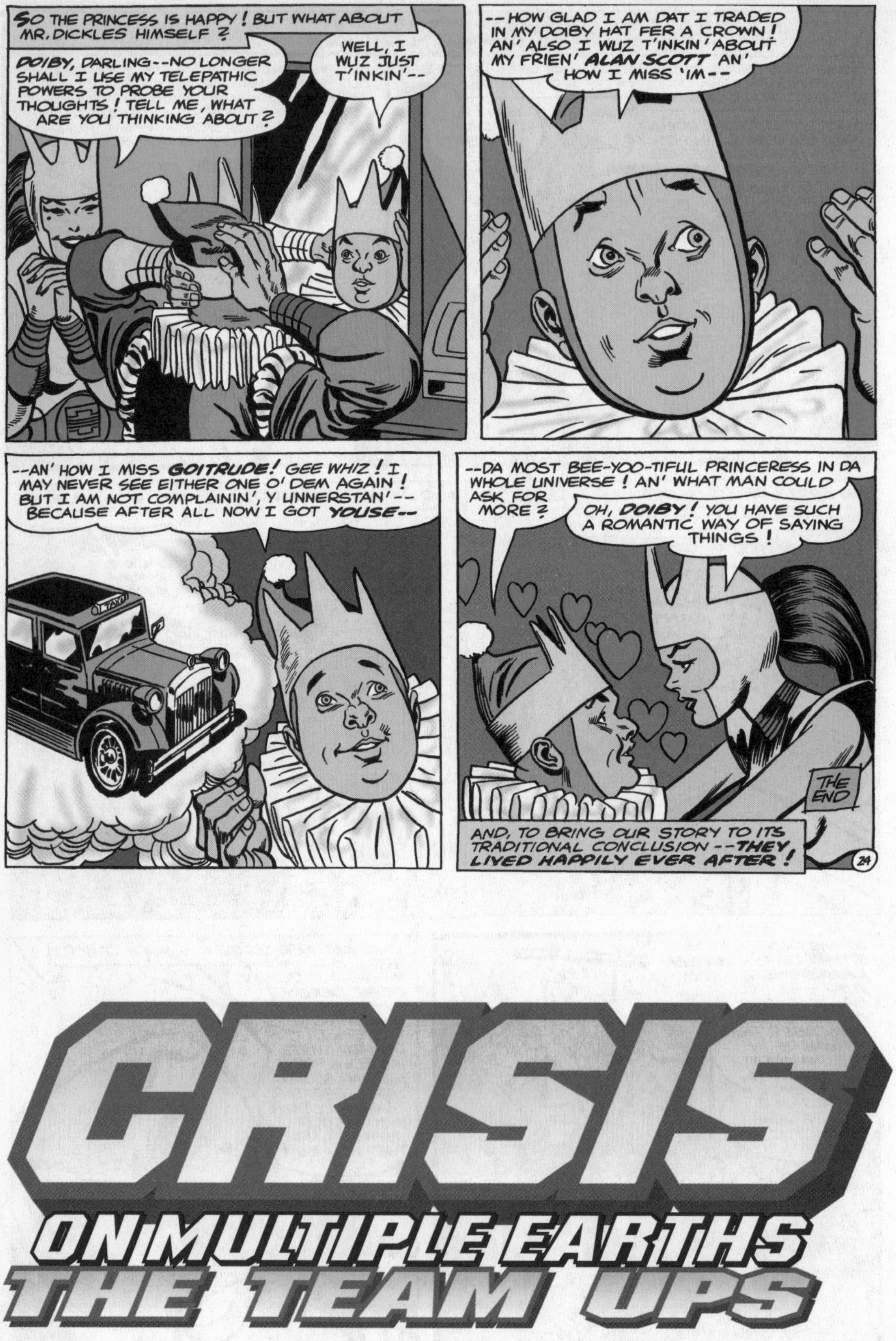
SO THE PRINCESS IS HAPPY! BUT WHAT ABOUT MR. DICKLES HIMSELF?
DOIBY, DARLING--NO LONGER SHALL I USE MY TELEPATHIC POWERS TO PROBE YOUR THOUGHTS! TELL ME, WHAT ARE YOU THINKING ABOUT?
WELL, I WUZ JUST T'INKIN'--
--HOW GLAD I AM DAT I TRADED IN MY DOIBY HAT FER A CROWN! AN' ALSO I WUZ T'INKIN' ABOUT MY FRIEN' ALAN SCOTT AN' HOW I MISS 'IM--
--AN' HOW I MISS GOITRUDE! GEE WHIZ! I MAY NEVER SEE EITHER ONE O' DEM AGAIN! BUT I AM NOT COMPLAININ', Y UNNERSTAN'--BECAUSE AFTER ALL NOW I GOT YOUSE--
TAXI
--DA MOST BEE-YOO-TIFUL PRINCESS IN DA WHOLE UNIVERSE! AN' WHAT MAN COULD ASK FOR MORE?
OH, DOIBY! YOU HAVE SUCH A ROMANTIC WAY OF SAYING THINGS!
THE END
AND, TO BRING OUR STORY TO ITS TRADITIONAL CONCLUSION--THEY LIVED HAPPILY EVER AFTER!
24

CRISIS ON MULTIPLE EARTHS
THE TEAM UPS

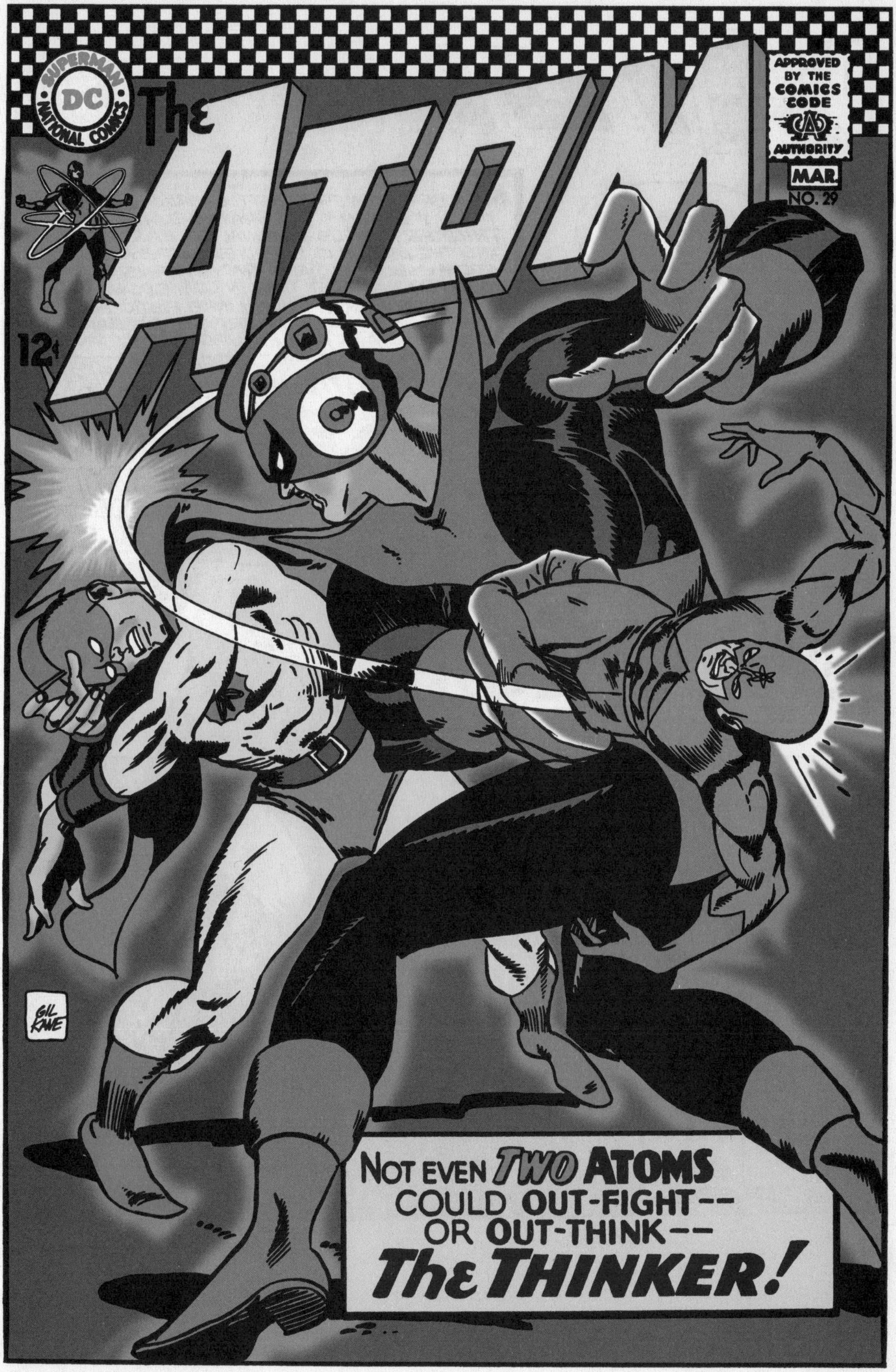

SUPERMAN DC NATIONAL COMICS
The ATOM
APPROVED BY THE COMICS CODE AUTHORITY
MAR. NO. 29
12¢
GIL KANE
NOT EVEN TWO ATOMS COULD OUT-FIGHT-- OR OUT-THINK-- The THINKER!

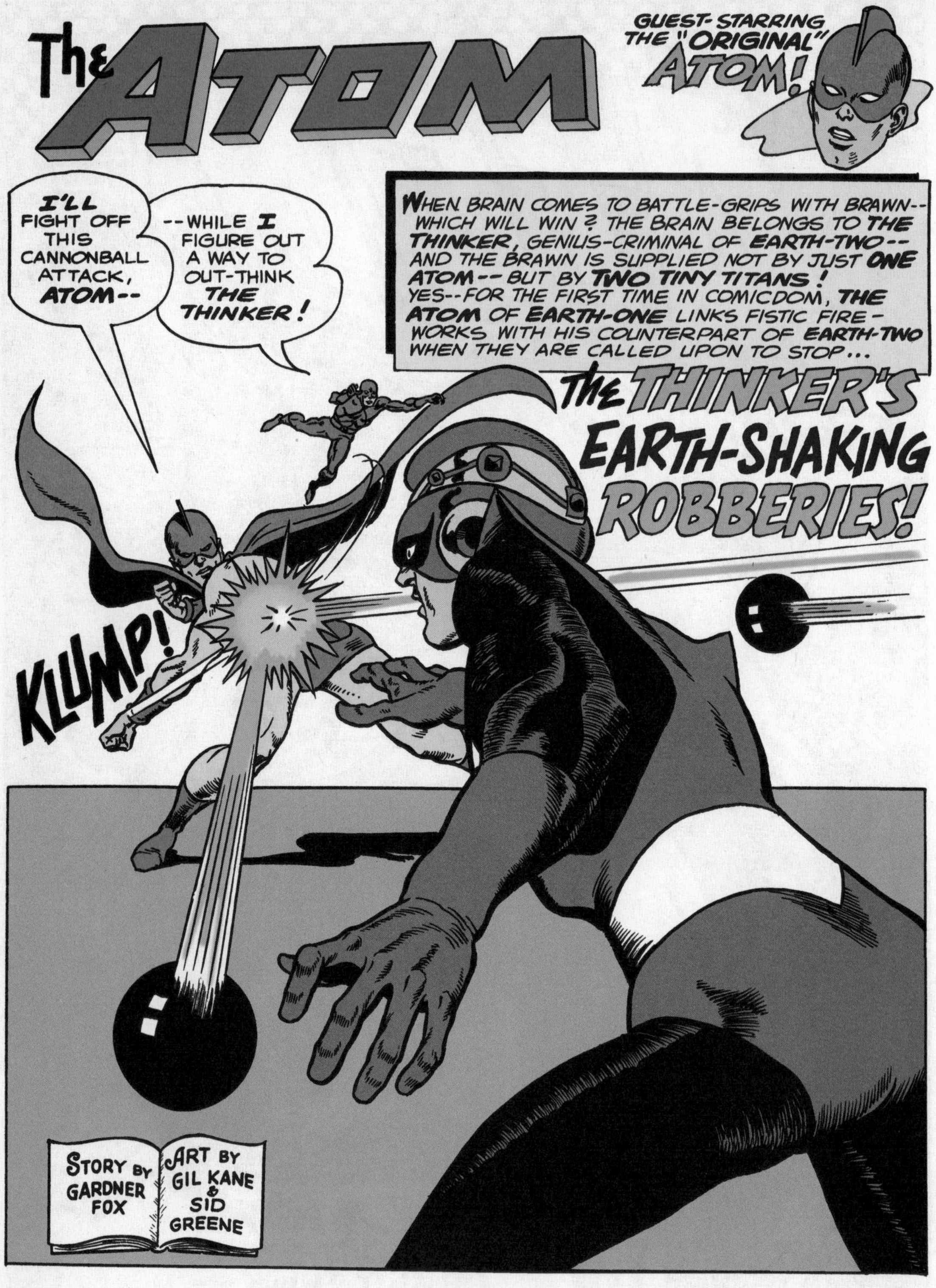

The ATOM
GUEST-STARRING THE "ORIGINAL" ATOM!
I'LL FIGHT OFF THIS CANNONBALL ATTACK, ATOM--
--WHILE I FIGURE OUT A WAY TO OUT-THINK THE THINKER!
WHEN BRAIN COMES TO BATTLE-GRIPS WITH BRAWN--WHICH WILL WIN? THE BRAIN BELONGS TO THE THINKER, GENIUS-CRIMINAL OF EARTH-TWO--AND THE BRAWN IS SUPPLIED NOT BY JUST ONE ATOM--BUT BY TWO TINY TITANS! YES--FOR THE FIRST TIME IN COMICDOM, THE ATOM OF EARTH-ONE LINKS FISTIC FIRE-WORKS WITH HIS COUNTERPART OF EARTH-TWO WHEN THEY ARE CALLED UPON TO STOP...
The THINKER'S EARTH-SHAKING ROBBERIES!
KLUMP!
STORY BY GARDNER FOX
ART BY GIL KANE & SID GREENE

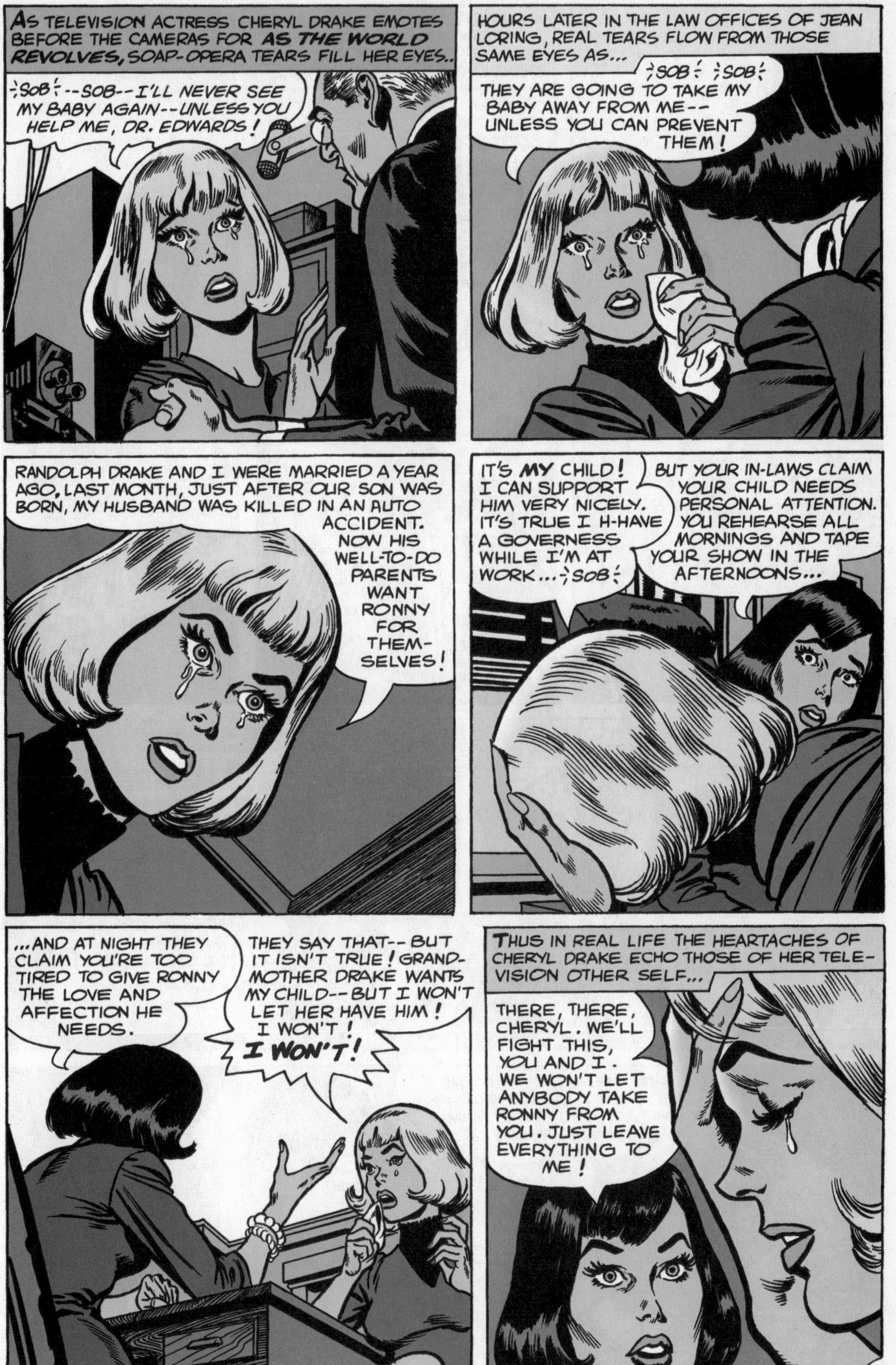

AS TELEVISION ACTRESS CHERYL DRAKE EMOTES BEFORE THE CAMERAS FOR AS THE WORLD REVOLVES, SOAP-OPERA TEARS FILL HER EYES...
SOB --SOB-- I'LL NEVER SEE MY BABY AGAIN--UNLESS YOU HELP ME, DR. EDWARDS!
HOURS LATER IN THE LAW OFFICES OF JEAN LORING, REAL TEARS FLOW FROM THOSE SAME EYES AS...
SOB SOB
THEY ARE GOING TO TAKE MY BABY AWAY FROM ME-- UNLESS YOU CAN PREVENT THEM!
RANDOLPH DRAKE AND I WERE MARRIED A YEAR AGO. LAST MONTH, JUST AFTER OUR SON WAS BORN, MY HUSBAND WAS KILLED IN AN AUTO ACCIDENT. NOW HIS WELL-TO-DO PARENTS WANT RONNY FOR THEMSELVES!
IT'S MY CHILD! I CAN SUPPORT HIM VERY NICELY. IT'S TRUE I H-HAVE A GOVERNESS WHILE I'M AT WORK... SOB
BUT YOUR IN-LAWS CLAIM YOUR CHILD NEEDS PERSONAL ATTENTION. YOU REHEARSE ALL MORNINGS AND TAPE YOUR SHOW IN THE AFTERNOONS...
...AND AT NIGHT THEY CLAIM YOU'RE TOO TIRED TO GIVE RONNY THE LOVE AND AFFECTION HE NEEDS.
THEY SAY THAT-- BUT IT ISN'T TRUE! GRANDMOTHER DRAKE WANTS MY CHILD--BUT I WON'T LET HER HAVE HIM! I WON'T! I WON'T!
THUS IN REAL LIFE THE HEARTACHES OF CHERYL DRAKE ECHO THOSE OF HER TELEVISION OTHER SELF...
THERE, THERE, CHERYL. WE'LL FIGHT THIS, YOU AND I. WE WON'T LET ANYBODY TAKE RONNY FROM YOU. JUST LEAVE EVERYTHING TO ME!
2.

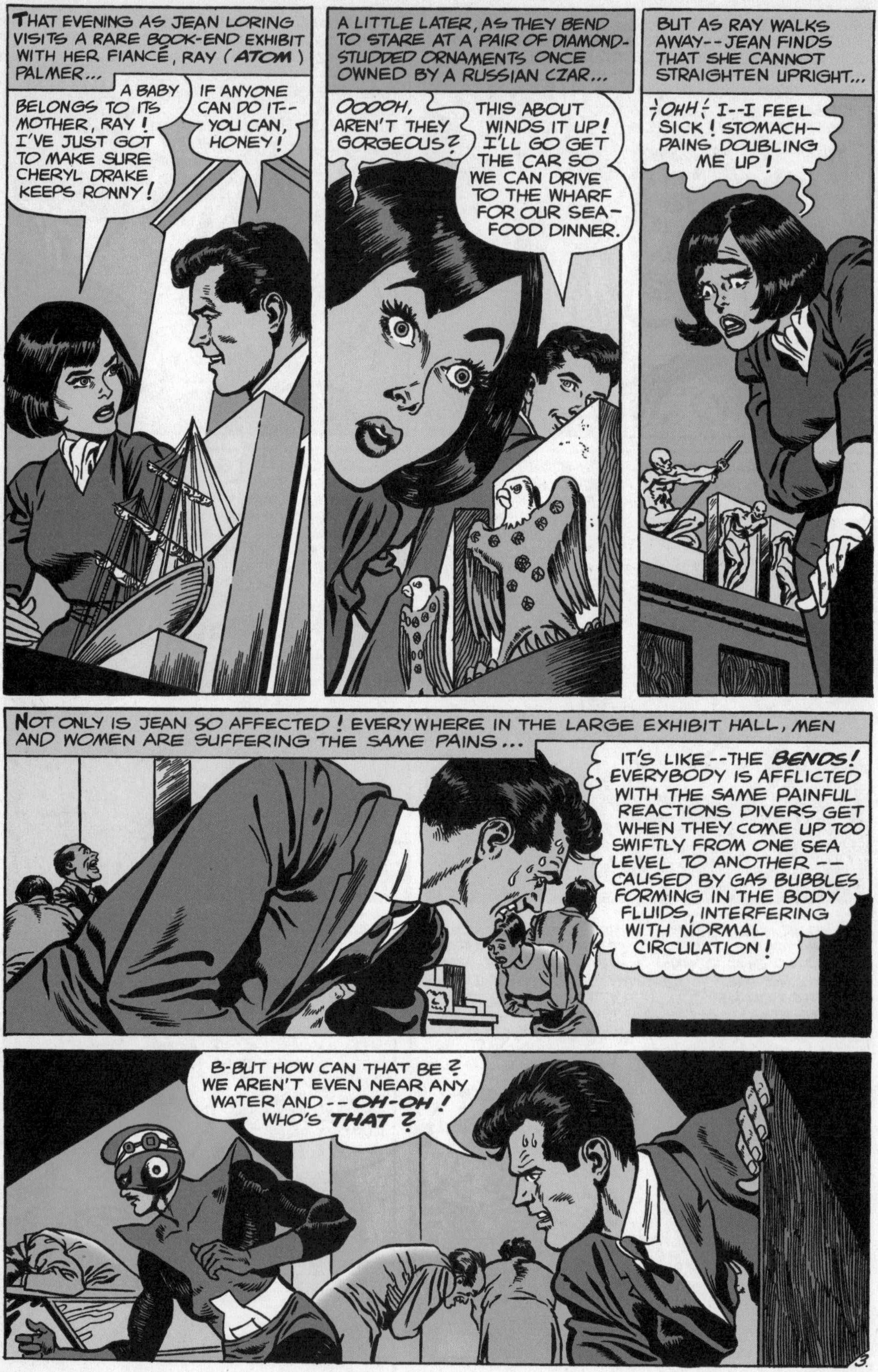
THAT EVENING AS JEAN LORING VISITS A RARE BOOK-END EXHIBIT WITH HER FIANCÉ, RAY (ATOM) PALMER...
A BABY BELONGS TO ITS MOTHER, RAY! I'VE JUST GOT TO MAKE SURE CHERYL DRAKE KEEPS RONNY!
IF ANYONE CAN DO IT--YOU CAN, HONEY!
A LITTLE LATER, AS THEY BEND TO STARE AT A PAIR OF DIAMOND-STUDDED ORNAMENTS ONCE OWNED BY A RUSSIAN CZAR...
OOOOH, AREN'T THEY GORGEOUS?
THIS ABOUT WINDS IT UP! I'LL GO GET THE CAR SO WE CAN DRIVE TO THE WHARF FOR OUR SEA-FOOD DINNER.
BUT AS RAY WALKS AWAY--JEAN FINDS THAT SHE CANNOT STRAIGHTEN UPRIGHT...
OHH! I--I FEEL SICK! STOMACH-PAINS DOUBLING ME UP!
NOT ONLY IS JEAN SO AFFECTED! EVERYWHERE IN THE LARGE EXHIBIT HALL, MEN AND WOMEN ARE SUFFERING THE SAME PAINS...
IT'S LIKE--THE BENDS! EVERYBODY IS AFFLICTED WITH THE SAME PAINFUL REACTIONS DIVERS GET WHEN THEY COME UP TOO SWIFTLY FROM ONE SEA LEVEL TO ANOTHER--CAUSED BY GAS BUBBLES FORMING IN THE BODY FLUIDS, INTERFERING WITH NORMAL CIRCULATION!
B-BUT HOW CAN THAT BE? WE AREN'T EVEN NEAR ANY WATER AND--OH-OH! WHO'S THAT?
3.

BATTLING THE AGONIES OF THE DIVER'S NIGHTMARE, RAY'S POWERFUL FINGERS FUMBLE AT THE SIZE-AND-WEIGHT CONTROLS HIDDEN IN THE PALMS OF HIS INVISIBLE-WHEN-EXPANDED UNIFORM...

NO ONE'S LOOKING AT ME... IT'S SAFE TO SWITCH... AND FIGHT...

NEXT INSTANT THE *TINY TITAN* IS HITTING THE TAUT WIRE THAT FORMS PART OF AN UNUSUAL BOOK-END...

HUH?! WHO'S THAT?!

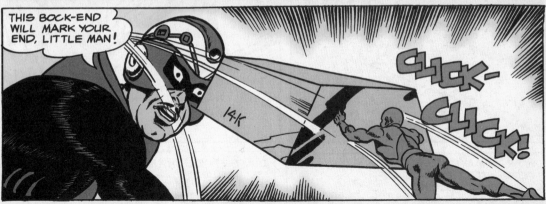

THIS BOOK-END WILL MARK YOUR END, LITTLE MAN!

CLICK-CLICK!

14K

MADE MYSELF SO SMALL, I SLIPPED BETWEEN THE ATOMS OF THE BOOK-END -- SO I WOULDN'T GET HURT!

CRASH!

IT IS THE WORK OF AN INSTANT FOR THE *WORLD'S SMALLEST SUPER-HERO* TO RESUME HIS SIX-INCH SIZE -- THROW OFF THE SHARDS OF BROKEN GLASS AND...

FIRST SCORE TO YOU, WHOEVER YOU ARE! NOW IT'S MY TURN TO RACK UP THE POINTS!

YOU LITTLE FOOL! I HAVE MEN TO BACK ME UP! YOU DON'T THINK I CAME HERE ALONE, DO YOU? TAKE A LOOK!

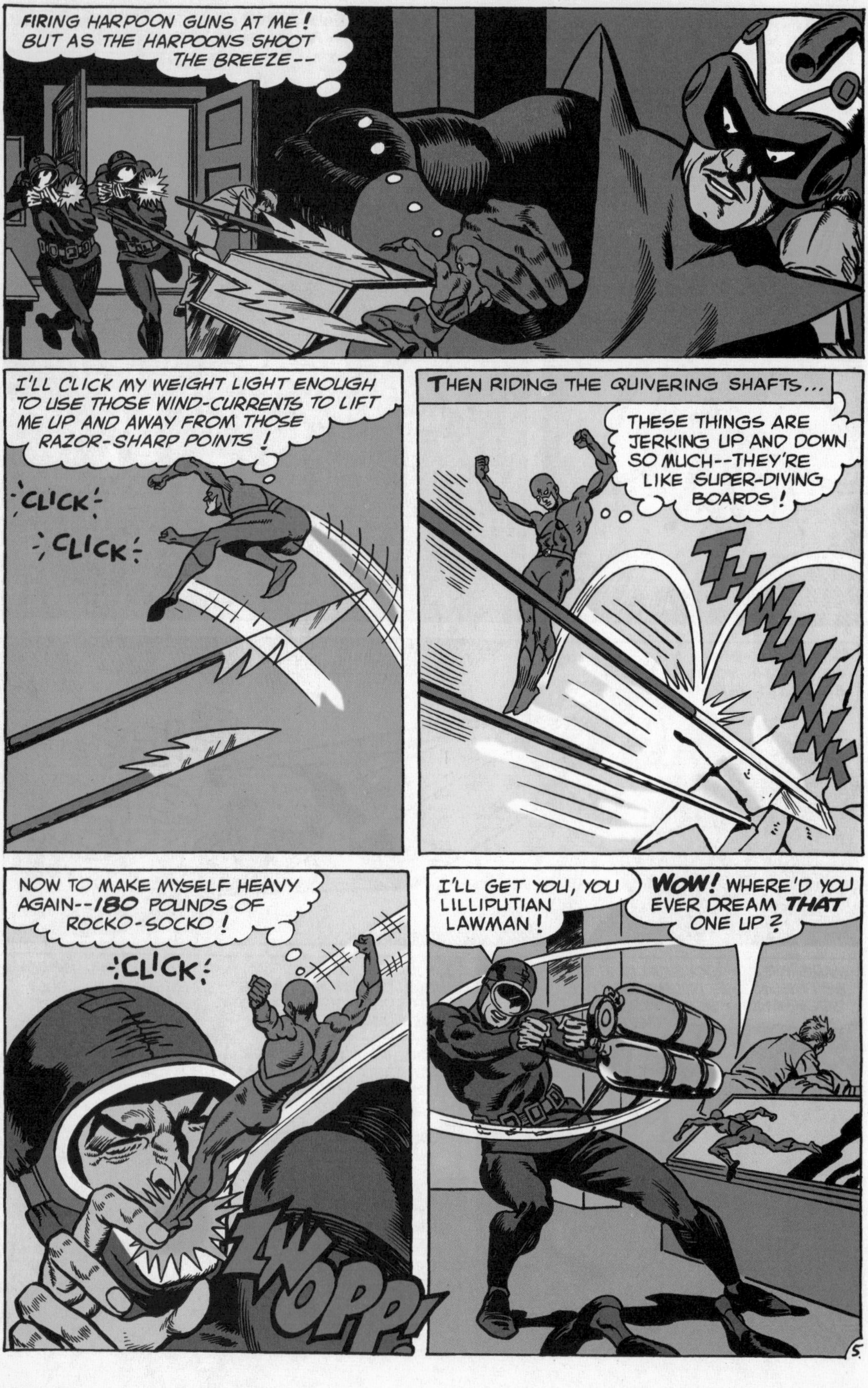
FIRING HARPOON GUNS AT ME! BUT AS THE HARPOONS SHOOT THE BREEZE--
I'LL CLICK MY WEIGHT LIGHT ENOUGH TO USE THOSE WIND-CURRENTS TO LIFT ME UP AND AWAY FROM THOSE RAZOR-SHARP POINTS!
CLICK
CLICK
THEN RIDING THE QUIVERING SHAFTS...
THESE THINGS ARE JERKING UP AND DOWN SO MUCH--THEY'RE LIKE SUPER-DIVING BOARDS!
THWUNNNK
NOW TO MAKE MYSELF HEAVY AGAIN--180 POUNDS OF ROCKO-SOCKO!
CLICK
ZWOPP!
I'LL GET YOU, YOU LILLIPUTIAN LAWMAN!
WOW! WHERE'D YOU EVER DREAM THAT ONE UP?
5.

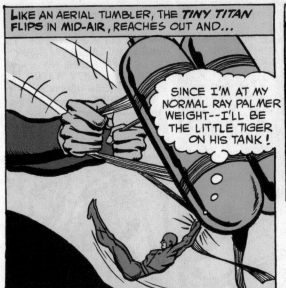

LIKE AN AERIAL TUMBLER, THE *TINY TITAN* FLIPS IN MID-AIR, REACHES OUT AND...

SINCE I'M AT MY NORMAL RAY PALMER WEIGHT--I'LL BE THE LITTLE TIGER ON HIS TANK!

KLONK!

UHH! I FEEL ODD VIBRATIONS OF SOME SORT! WHAT'S THAT GUY WITH THE STRANGE HEAD-GEAR UP TO NOW?

HUH? HE'S LEAPING OUT OF HERE-- THROUGH THAT OVAL NIMBUS OF LIGHT--!

BEYOND IT--A WORLD JUST LIKE *EARTH!* IT CAN'T BE THIS *EARTH*-- IT'S RAINING HERE! IN THAT OTHER WORLD--IT'S A CLEAR MOONLIT NIGHT! UNLESS IT'S A DIFFERENT PART OF *EARTH*-- BUT THAT CAN'T BE BECAUSE OF THE POSITION OF THE STARS! THEN THAT MUST MEAN --

--IT'S *EARTH-TWO!*

THAT WORLD IS ALMOST A PARALLEL OF OUR OWN--GEO-GRAPHICALLY AND HISTORICALLY! IT EVEN HAS ITS OWN SUPER-HEROES --THE MEMBERS OF THE *JUSTICE SOCIETY OF AMERICA!*

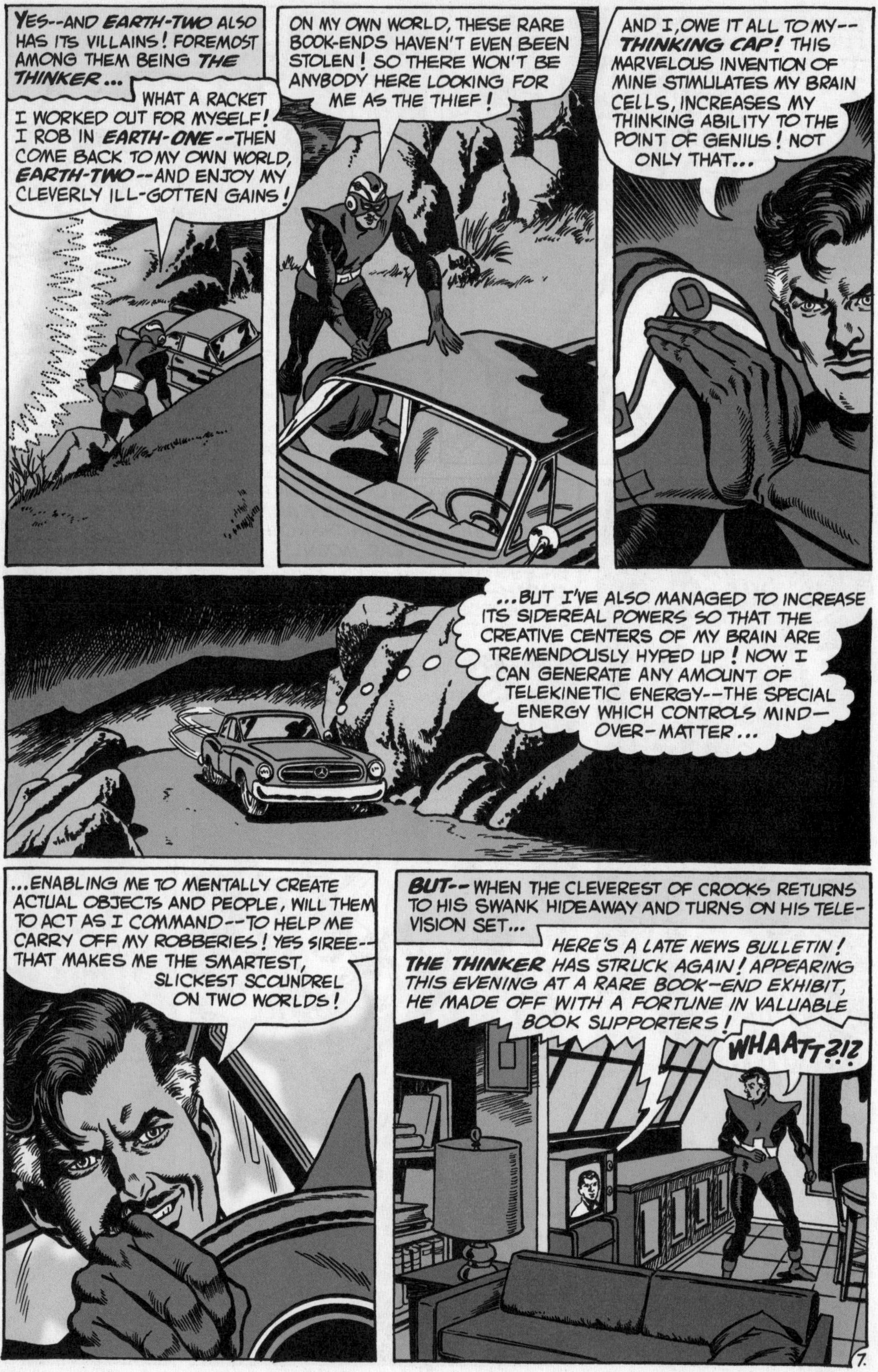

YES--AND EARTH-TWO ALSO HAS ITS VILLAINS! FOREMOST AMONG THEM BEING THE THINKER...
WHAT A RACKET I WORKED OUT FOR MYSELF! I ROB IN EARTH-ONE--THEN COME BACK TO MY OWN WORLD, EARTH-TWO--AND ENJOY MY CLEVERLY ILL-GOTTEN GAINS!
ON MY OWN WORLD, THESE RARE BOOK-ENDS HAVEN'T EVEN BEEN STOLEN! SO THERE WON'T BE ANYBODY HERE LOOKING FOR ME AS THE THIEF!
AND I, OWE IT ALL TO MY--THINKING CAP! THIS MARVELOUS INVENTION OF MINE STIMULATES MY BRAIN CELLS, INCREASES MY THINKING ABILITY TO THE POINT OF GENIUS! NOT ONLY THAT...
...BUT I'VE ALSO MANAGED TO INCREASE ITS SIDEREAL POWERS SO THAT THE CREATIVE CENTERS OF MY BRAIN ARE TREMENDOUSLY HYPED UP! NOW I CAN GENERATE ANY AMOUNT OF TELEKINETIC ENERGY--THE SPECIAL ENERGY WHICH CONTROLS MIND-OVER-MATTER...
...ENABLING ME TO MENTALLY CREATE ACTUAL OBJECTS AND PEOPLE, WILL THEM TO ACT AS I COMMAND--TO HELP ME CARRY OFF MY ROBBERIES! YES SIREE--THAT MAKES ME THE SMARTEST, SLICKEST SCOUNDREL ON TWO WORLDS!
BUT--WHEN THE CLEVEREST OF CROOKS RETURNS TO HIS SWANK HIDEAWAY AND TURNS ON HIS TELEVISION SET...
HERE'S A LATE NEWS BULLETIN! THE THINKER HAS STRUCK AGAIN! APPEARING THIS EVENING AT A RARE BOOK-END EXHIBIT, HE MADE OFF WITH A FORTUNE IN VALUABLE BOOK SUPPORTERS!
WHAATT?!?
7.

B-BUT IT CA-CAN'T BE--UNLESS BY SOME INCREDIBLE COINCIDENCE A CROOK ON THIS WORLD DREAMED UP THE SAME IDEA I DID! AFTER ALL, WHAT HAPPENS ON ONE EARTH SOMETIMES HAPPENS ON THE OTHER--

OF ALL THE BLASTED LUCK! JUST WHEN I HAD THINGS FIGURED OUT TO PERFECTION! NOW THE LAW WILL BE OUT HUNTING FOR ME! AND THERE ISN'T ANYTHING I CAN DO ABOUT IT!

CRASH

OR--IS THERE? WITH MY THINKING CAP I SHOULD BE ABLE TO FIGURE A WAY OUT OF MY DIFFICULTY!

WHAT ODD FATE HAS STRUCK *THE THINKER* RIGHT IN THE MIDDLE OF HIS CLEVEREST SCHEME? FOR THE AMAZING ANSWER-- READ ON! STORY CONTINUES ON NEXT PAGE FOLLOWING! 8.

CRISIS
ON MULTIPLE EARTHS
THE TEAM UPS

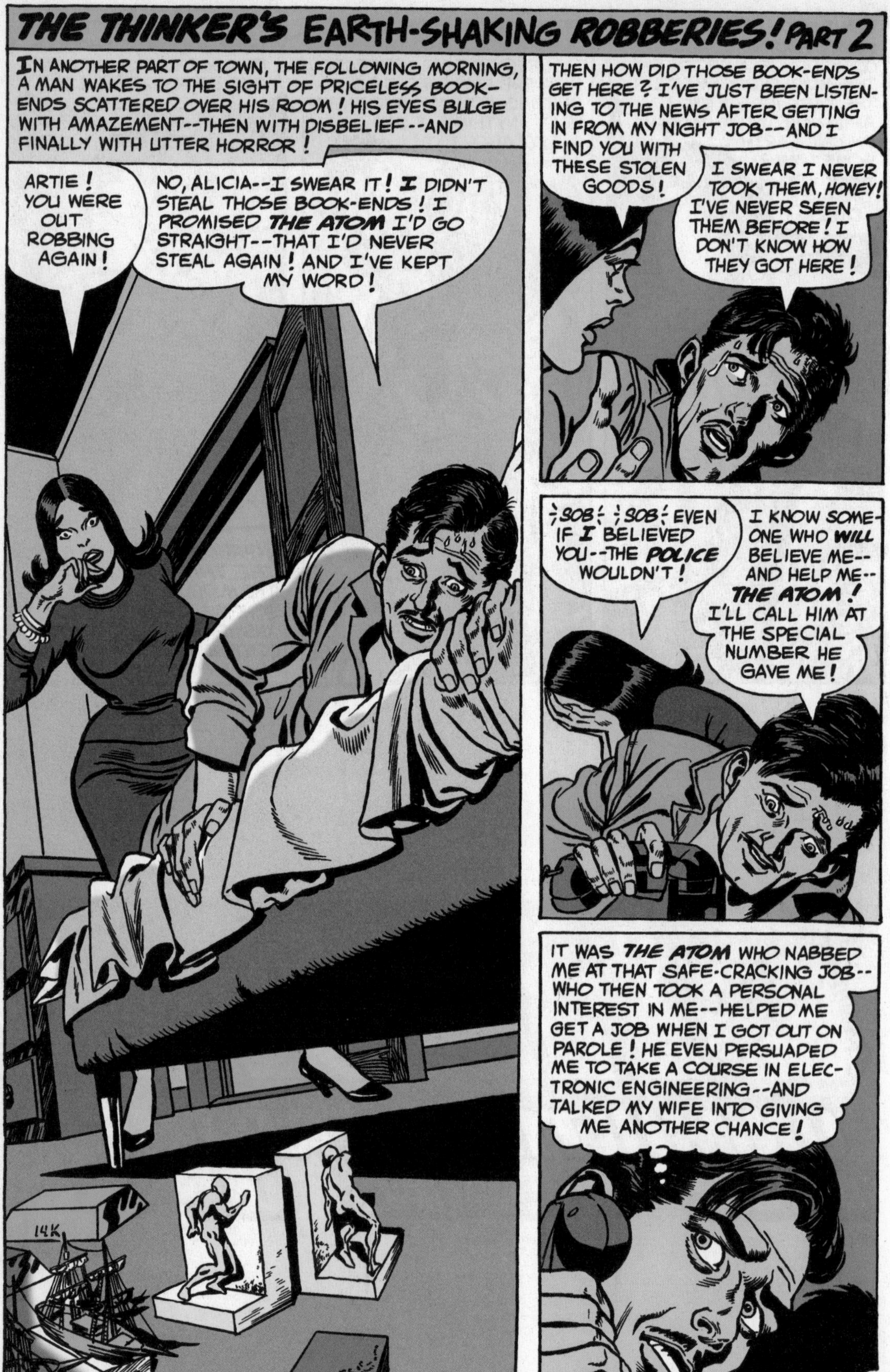
THE THINKER'S EARTH-SHAKING ROBBERIES! PART 2
IN ANOTHER PART OF TOWN, THE FOLLOWING MORNING, A MAN WAKES TO THE SIGHT OF PRICELESS BOOK-ENDS SCATTERED OVER HIS ROOM! HIS EYES BULGE WITH AMAZEMENT--THEN WITH DISBELIEF--AND FINALLY WITH UTTER HORROR!
ARTIE! YOU WERE OUT ROBBING AGAIN!
NO, ALICIA--I SWEAR IT! I DIDN'T STEAL THOSE BOOK-ENDS! I PROMISED THE ATOM I'D GO STRAIGHT--THAT I'D NEVER STEAL AGAIN! AND I'VE KEPT MY WORD!
14K
THEN HOW DID THOSE BOOK-ENDS GET HERE? I'VE JUST BEEN LISTENING TO THE NEWS AFTER GETTING IN FROM MY NIGHT JOB--AND I FIND YOU WITH THESE STOLEN GOODS!
I SWEAR I NEVER TOOK THEM, HONEY! I'VE NEVER SEEN THEM BEFORE! I DON'T KNOW HOW THEY GOT HERE!
-SOB- -SOB- EVEN IF I BELIEVED YOU--THE POLICE WOULDN'T!
I KNOW SOMEONE WHO WILL BELIEVE ME--AND HELP ME--THE ATOM! I'LL CALL HIM AT THE SPECIAL NUMBER HE GAVE ME!
IT WAS THE ATOM WHO NABBED ME AT THAT SAFE-CRACKING JOB--WHO THEN TOOK A PERSONAL INTEREST IN ME--HELPED ME GET A JOB WHEN I GOT OUT ON PAROLE! HE EVEN PERSUADED ME TO TAKE A COURSE IN ELECTRONIC ENGINEERING--AND TALKED MY WIFE INTO GIVING ME ANOTHER CHANCE!
9

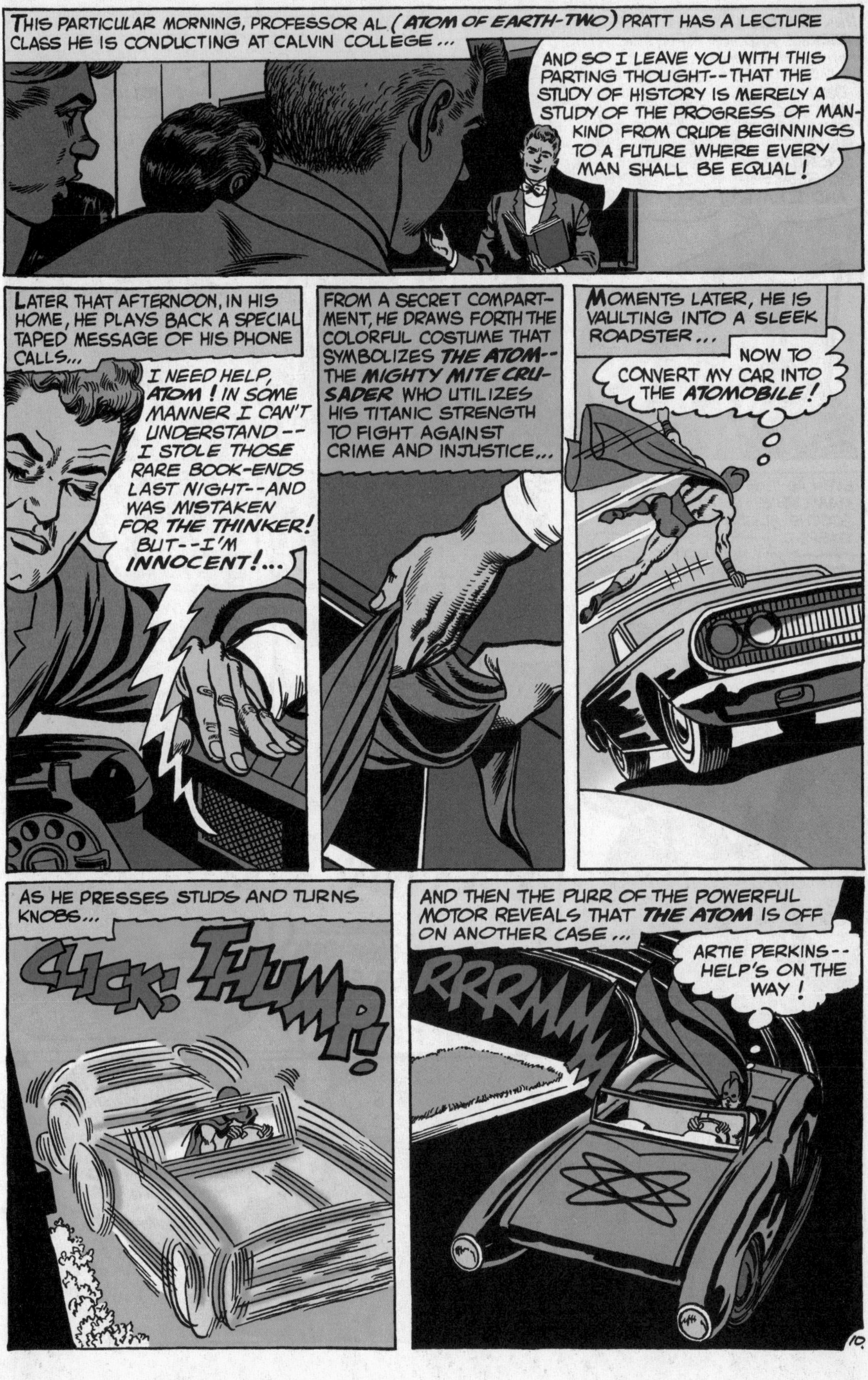
THIS PARTICULAR MORNING, PROFESSOR AL (ATOM OF EARTH-TWO) PRATT HAS A LECTURE CLASS HE IS CONDUCTING AT CALVIN COLLEGE...
AND SO I LEAVE YOU WITH THIS PARTING THOUGHT--THAT THE STUDY OF HISTORY IS MERELY A STUDY OF THE PROGRESS OF MAN-KIND FROM CRUDE BEGINNINGS TO A FUTURE WHERE EVERY MAN SHALL BE EQUAL!
LATER THAT AFTERNOON, IN HIS HOME, HE PLAYS BACK A SPECIAL TAPED MESSAGE OF HIS PHONE CALLS...
I NEED HELP, ATOM! IN SOME MANNER I CAN'T UNDERSTAND-- I STOLE THOSE RARE BOOK-ENDS LAST NIGHT--AND WAS MISTAKEN FOR THE THINKER! BUT--I'M INNOCENT!...
FROM A SECRET COMPART-MENT, HE DRAWS FORTH THE COLORFUL COSTUME THAT SYMBOLIZES THE ATOM-- THE MIGHTY MITE CRU-SADER WHO UTILIZES HIS TITANIC STRENGTH TO FIGHT AGAINST CRIME AND INJUSTICE...
MOMENTS LATER, HE IS VAULTING INTO A SLEEK ROADSTER...
NOW TO CONVERT MY CAR INTO THE ATOMOBILE!
AS HE PRESSES STUDS AND TURNS KNOBS...
CLICK! THUMP!
AND THEN THE PURR OF THE POWERFUL MOTOR REVEALS THAT THE ATOM IS OFF ON ANOTHER CASE...
RRRMMM
ARTIE PERKINS-- HELP'S ON THE WAY!
10.

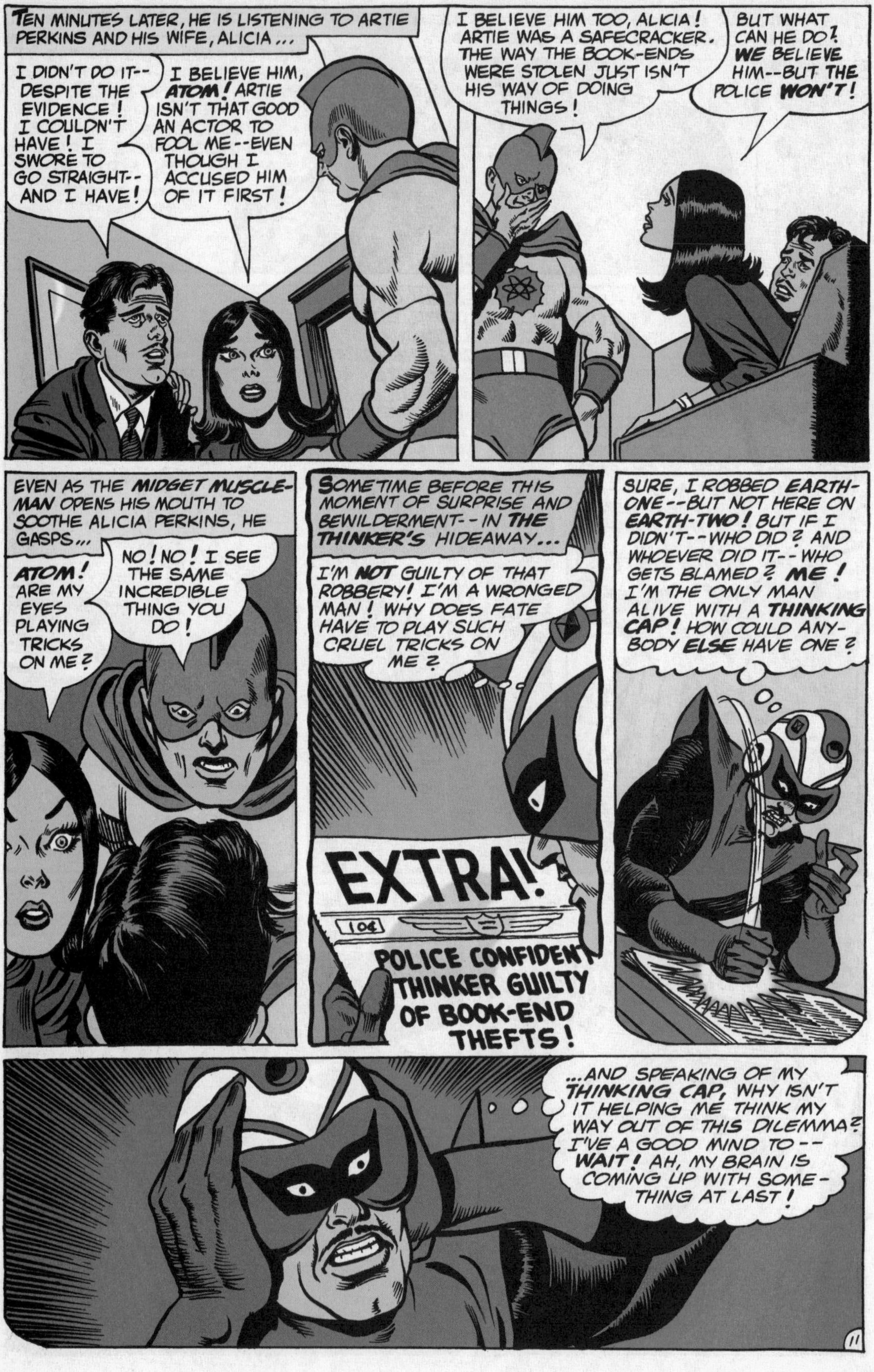
TEN MINUTES LATER, HE IS LISTENING TO ARTIE PERKINS AND HIS WIFE, ALICIA...
I DIDN'T DO IT-- DESPITE THE EVIDENCE! I COULDN'T HAVE! I SWORE TO GO STRAIGHT-- AND I HAVE!
I BELIEVE HIM, ATOM! ARTIE ISN'T THAT GOOD AN ACTOR TO FOOL ME--EVEN THOUGH I ACCUSED HIM OF IT FIRST!
I BELIEVE HIM TOO, ALICIA! ARTIE WAS A SAFECRACKER. THE WAY THE BOOK-ENDS WERE STOLEN JUST ISN'T HIS WAY OF DOING THINGS!
BUT WHAT CAN HE DO? WE BELIEVE HIM--BUT THE POLICE WON'T!
EVEN AS THE MIDGET MUSCLE-MAN OPENS HIS MOUTH TO SOOTHE ALICIA PERKINS, HE GASPS...
ATOM! ARE MY EYES PLAYING TRICKS ON ME?
NO! NO! I SEE THE SAME INCREDIBLE THING YOU DO!
SOMETIME BEFORE THIS MOMENT OF SURPRISE AND BEWILDERMENT-- IN THE THINKER'S HIDEAWAY...
I'M NOT GUILTY OF THAT ROBBERY! I'M A WRONGED MAN! WHY DOES FATE HAVE TO PLAY SUCH CRUEL TRICKS ON ME?
EXTRA!
10¢
POLICE CONFIDENT THINKER GUILTY OF BOOK-END THEFTS!
SURE, I ROBBED EARTH-ONE--BUT NOT HERE ON EARTH-TWO! BUT IF I DIDN'T--WHO DID? AND WHOEVER DID IT--WHO GETS BLAMED? ME! I'M THE ONLY MAN ALIVE WITH A THINKING CAP! HOW COULD ANY-BODY ELSE HAVE ONE?
...AND SPEAKING OF MY THINKING CAP, WHY ISN'T IT HELPING ME THINK MY WAY OUT OF THIS DILEMMA? I'VE A GOOD MIND TO-- WAIT! AH, MY BRAIN IS COMING UP WITH SOME-THING AT LAST!
11

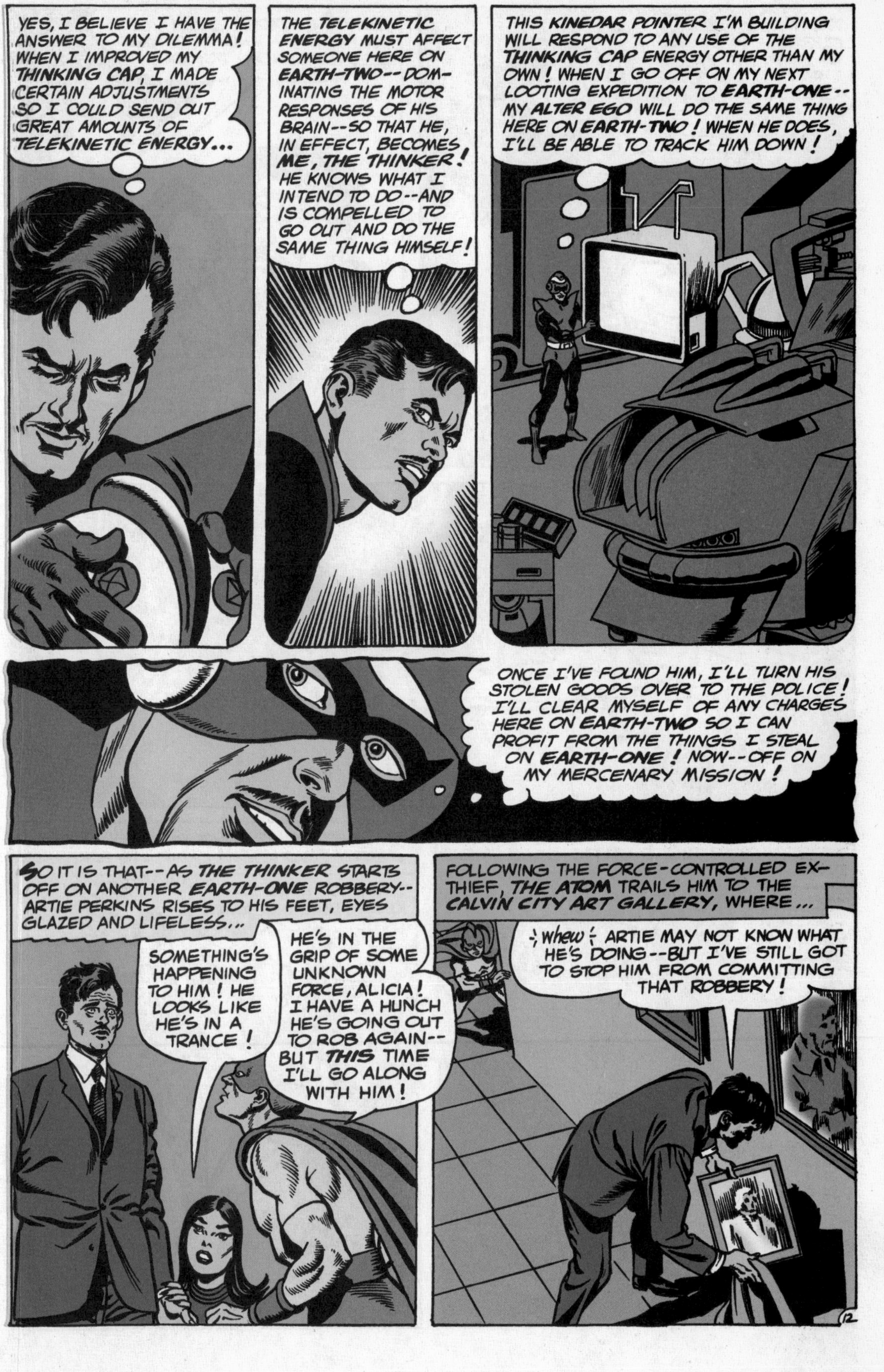
YES, I BELIEVE I HAVE THE ANSWER TO MY DILEMMA! WHEN I IMPROVED MY THINKING CAP, I MADE CERTAIN ADJUSTMENTS SO I COULD SEND OUT GREAT AMOUNTS OF TELEKINETIC ENERGY...
THE TELEKINETIC ENERGY MUST AFFECT SOMEONE HERE ON EARTH-TWO--DOMINATING THE MOTOR RESPONSES OF HIS BRAIN--SO THAT HE, IN EFFECT, BECOMES ME, THE THINKER! HE KNOWS WHAT I INTEND TO DO--AND IS COMPELLED TO GO OUT AND DO THE SAME THING HIMSELF!
THIS KINEDAR POINTER I'M BUILDING WILL RESPOND TO ANY USE OF THE THINKING CAP ENERGY OTHER THAN MY OWN! WHEN I GO OFF ON MY NEXT LOOTING EXPEDITION TO EARTH-ONE--MY ALTER EGO WILL DO THE SAME THING HERE ON EARTH-TWO! WHEN HE DOES, I'LL BE ABLE TO TRACK HIM DOWN!
ONCE I'VE FOUND HIM, I'LL TURN HIS STOLEN GOODS OVER TO THE POLICE! I'LL CLEAR MYSELF OF ANY CHARGES HERE ON EARTH-TWO SO I CAN PROFIT FROM THE THINGS I STEAL ON EARTH-ONE! NOW--OFF ON MY MERCENARY MISSION!
SO IT IS THAT--AS THE THINKER STARTS OFF ON ANOTHER EARTH-ONE ROBBERY--ARTIE PERKINS RISES TO HIS FEET, EYES GLAZED AND LIFELESS...
SOMETHING'S HAPPENING TO HIM! HE LOOKS LIKE HE'S IN A TRANCE!
HE'S IN THE GRIP OF SOME UNKNOWN FORCE, ALICIA! I HAVE A HUNCH HE'S GOING OUT TO ROB AGAIN--BUT THIS TIME I'LL GO ALONG WITH HIM!
FOLLOWING THE FORCE-CONTROLLED EX-THIEF, THE ATOM TRAILS HIM TO THE CALVIN CITY ART GALLERY, WHERE...
-; whew ;- ARTIE MAY NOT KNOW WHAT HE'S DOING--BUT I'VE STILL GOT TO STOP HIM FROM COMMITTING THAT ROBBERY!
12

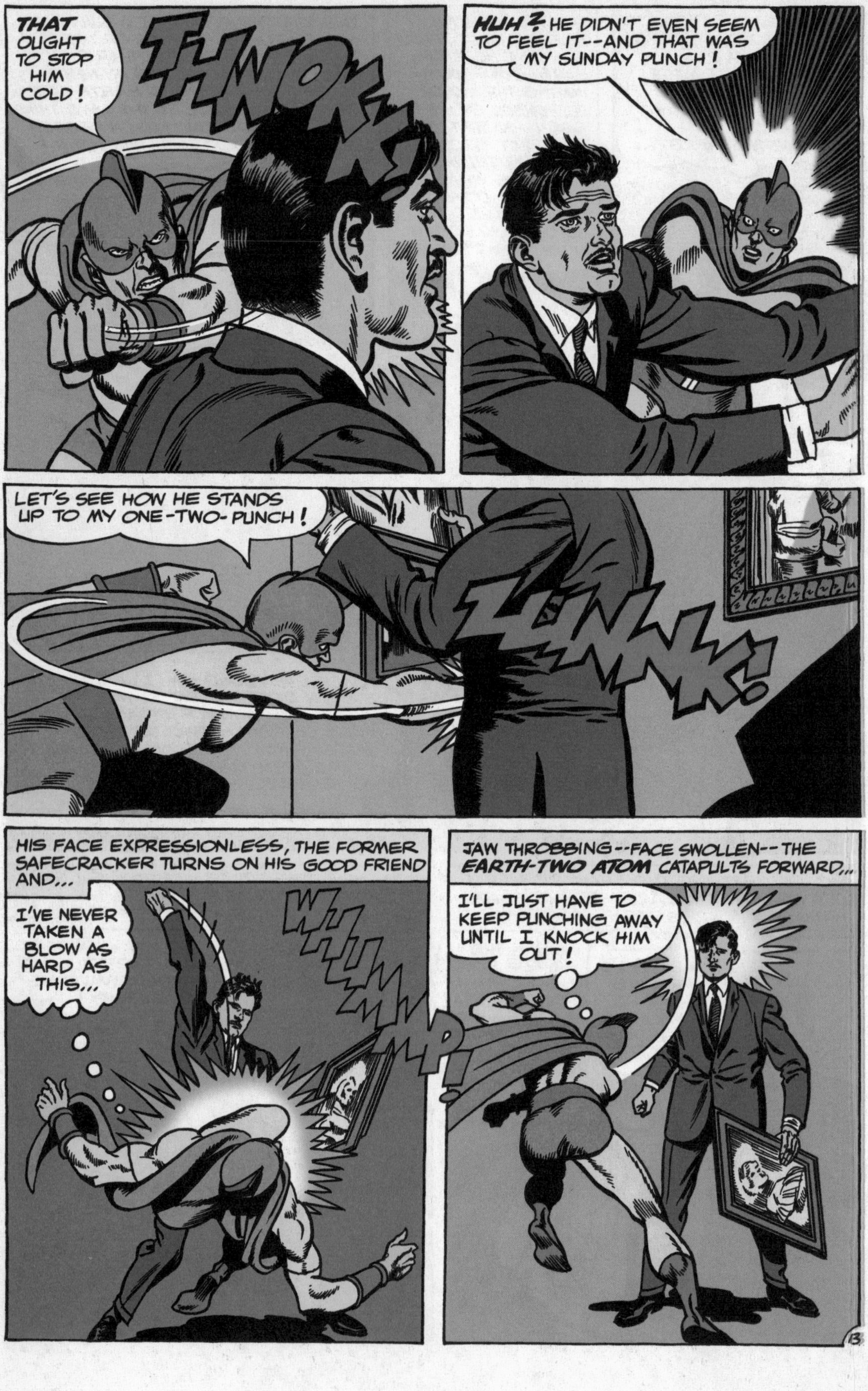
THAT OUGHT TO STOP HIM COLD!
THWOK!
HUH? HE DIDN'T EVEN SEEM TO FEEL IT--AND THAT WAS MY SUNDAY PUNCH!
LET'S SEE HOW HE STANDS UP TO MY ONE-TWO-PUNCH!
ZUNNK!
HIS FACE EXPRESSIONLESS, THE FORMER SAFECRACKER TURNS ON HIS GOOD FRIEND AND...
I'VE NEVER TAKEN A BLOW AS HARD AS THIS...
WHUMP!
JAW THROBBING--FACE SWOLLEN--THE EARTH-TWO ATOM CATAPULTS FORWARD...
I'LL JUST HAVE TO KEEP PUNCHING AWAY UNTIL I KNOCK HIM OUT!
13

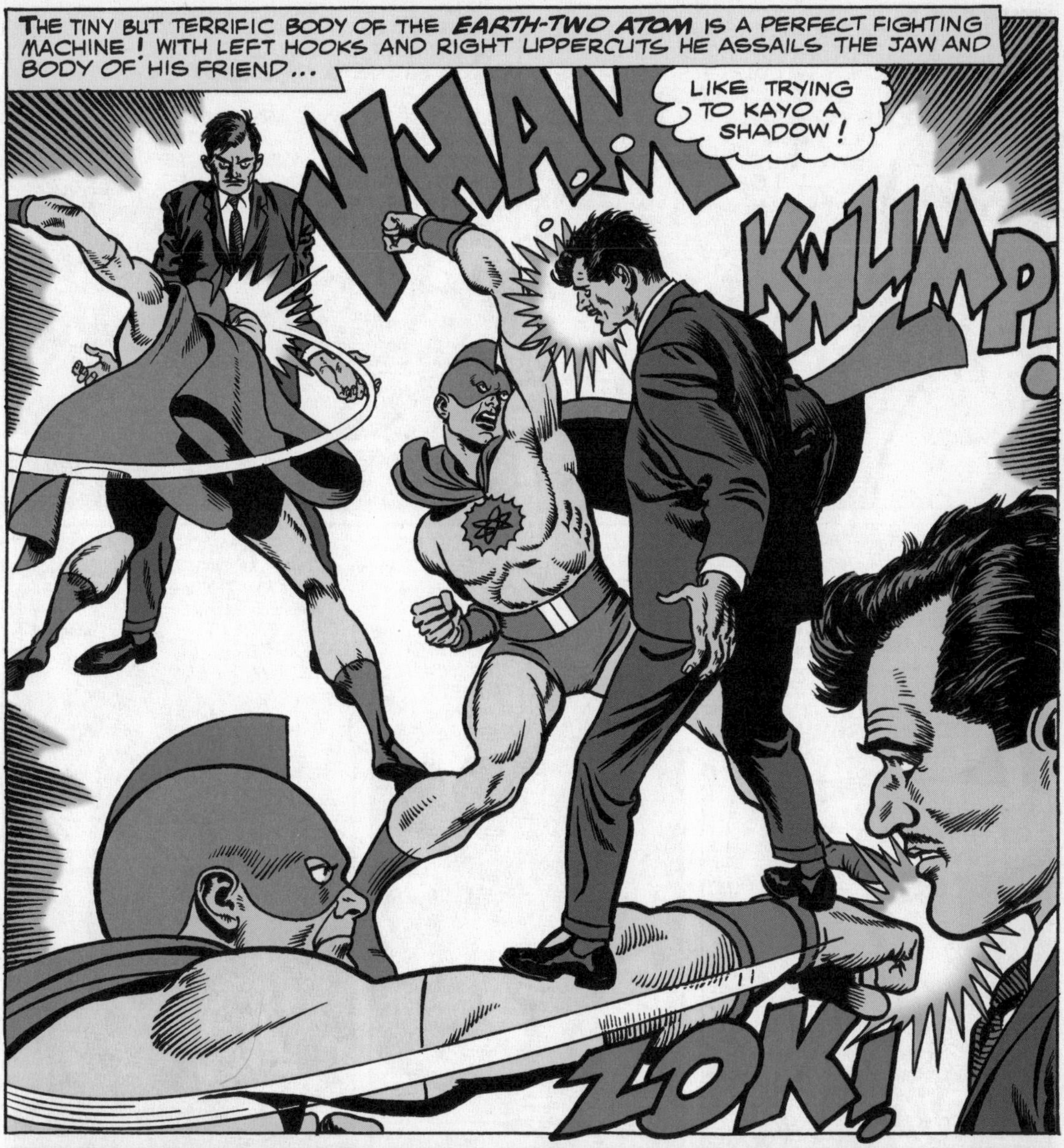

THE TINY BUT TERRIFIC BODY OF THE EARTH-TWO ATOM IS A PERFECT FIGHTING MACHINE! WITH LEFT HOOKS AND RIGHT UPPERCUTS HE ASSAILS THE JAW AND BODY OF HIS FRIEND...
WHAM!
LIKE TRYING TO KAYO A SHADOW!
KLUMP!
ZOK!

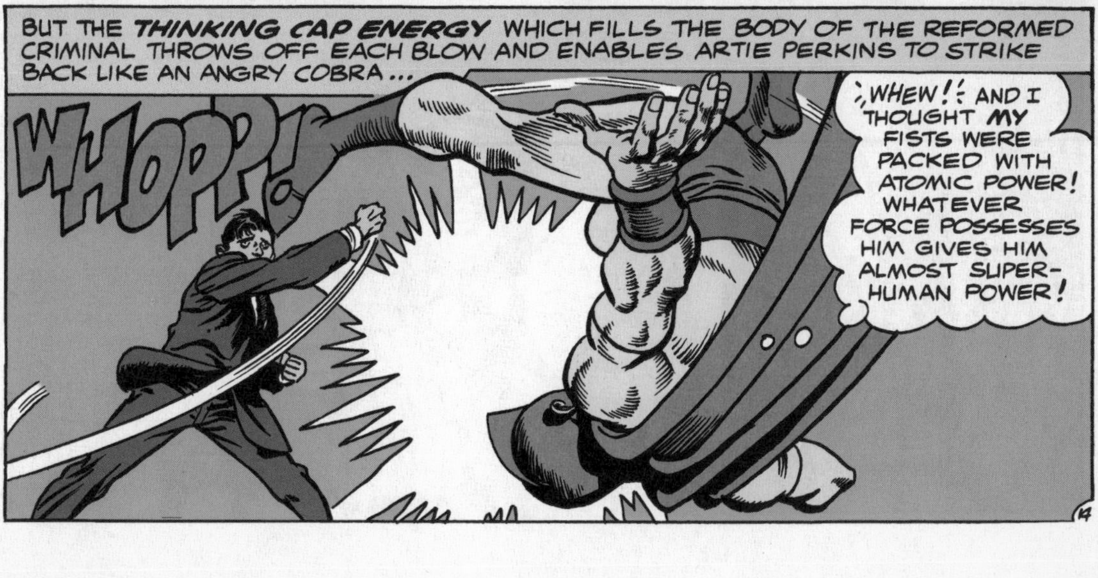

BUT THE THINKING CAP ENERGY WHICH FILLS THE BODY OF THE REFORMED CRIMINAL THROWS OFF EACH BLOW AND ENABLES ARTIE PERKINS TO STRIKE BACK LIKE AN ANGRY COBRA...
WHOPP!
WHEW! AND I THOUGHT MY FISTS WERE PACKED WITH ATOMIC POWER! WHATEVER FORCE POSSESSES HIM GIVES HIM ALMOST SUPER-HUMAN POWER!
14

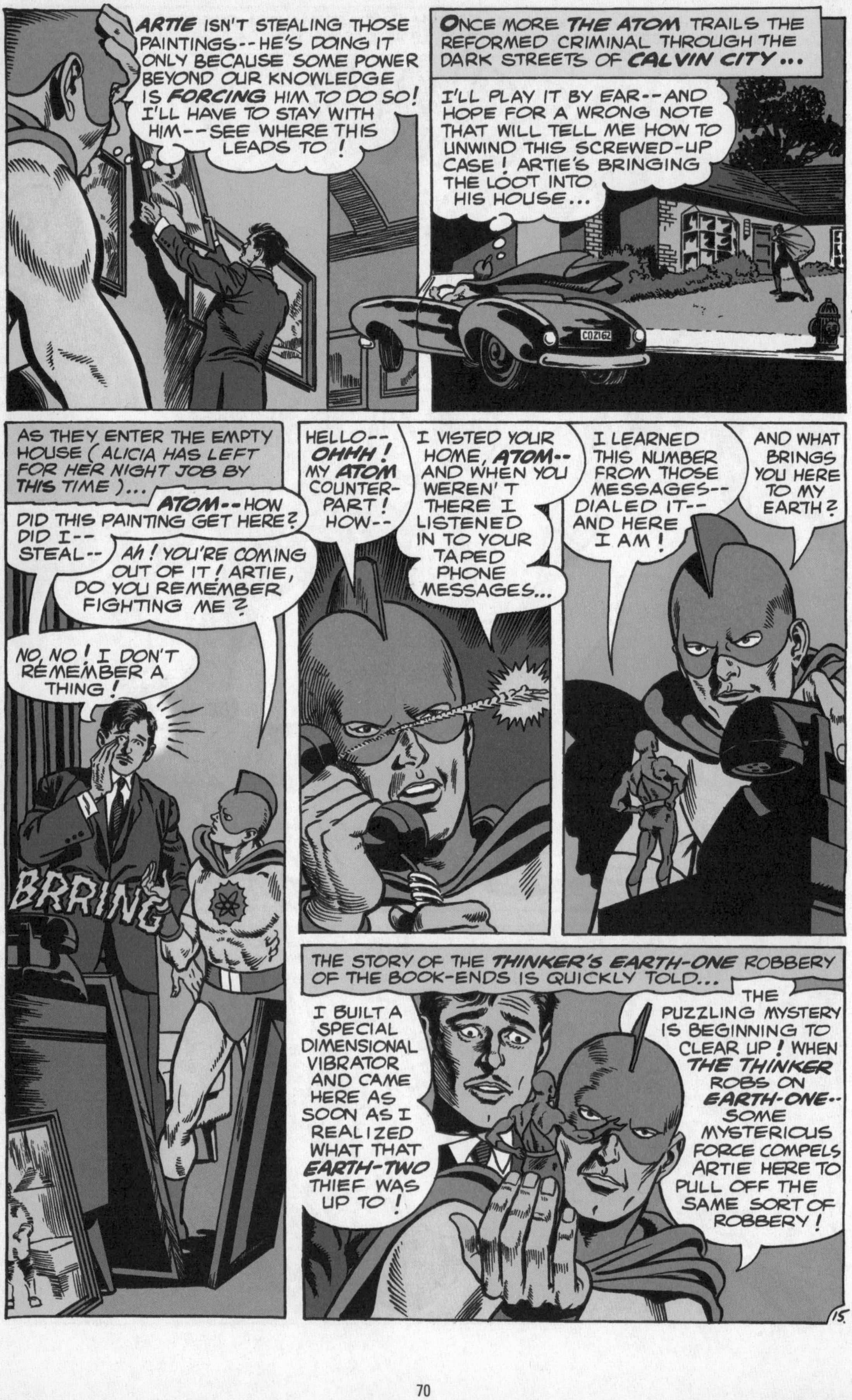
ARTIE ISN'T STEALING THOSE PAINTINGS--HE'S DOING IT ONLY BECAUSE SOME POWER BEYOND OUR KNOWLEDGE IS FORCING HIM TO DO SO! I'LL HAVE TO STAY WITH HIM--SEE WHERE THIS LEADS TO!
ONCE MORE THE ATOM TRAILS THE REFORMED CRIMINAL THROUGH THE DARK STREETS OF CALVIN CITY...
I'LL PLAY IT BY EAR--AND HOPE FOR A WRONG NOTE THAT WILL TELL ME HOW TO UNWIND THIS SCREWED-UP CASE! ARTIE'S BRINGING THE LOOT INTO HIS HOUSE...
CO2162
AS THEY ENTER THE EMPTY HOUSE (ALICIA HAS LEFT FOR HER NIGHT JOB BY THIS TIME)...
ATOM--HOW DID THIS PAINTING GET HERE? DID I--STEAL--
Ah! YOU'RE COMING OUT OF IT! ARTIE, DO YOU REMEMBER FIGHTING ME?
NO, NO! I DON'T REMEMBER A THING!
BRRING
HELLO--OHHH! MY ATOM COUNTER-PART! HOW--
I VISTED YOUR HOME, ATOM--AND WHEN YOU WEREN'T THERE I LISTENED IN TO YOUR TAPED PHONE MESSAGES...
I LEARNED THIS NUMBER FROM THOSE MESSAGES--DIALED IT--AND HERE I AM!
AND WHAT BRINGS YOU HERE TO MY EARTH?
THE STORY OF THE THINKER'S EARTH-ONE ROBBERY OF THE BOOK-ENDS IS QUICKLY TOLD...
I BUILT A SPECIAL DIMENSIONAL VIBRATOR AND CAME HERE AS SOON AS I REALIZED WHAT THAT EARTH-TWO THIEF WAS UP TO!
THE PUZZLING MYSTERY IS BEGINNING TO CLEAR UP! WHEN THE THINKER ROBS ON EARTH-ONE--SOME MYSTERIOUS FORCE COMPELS ARTIE HERE TO PULL OFF THE SAME SORT OF ROBBERY!
15.

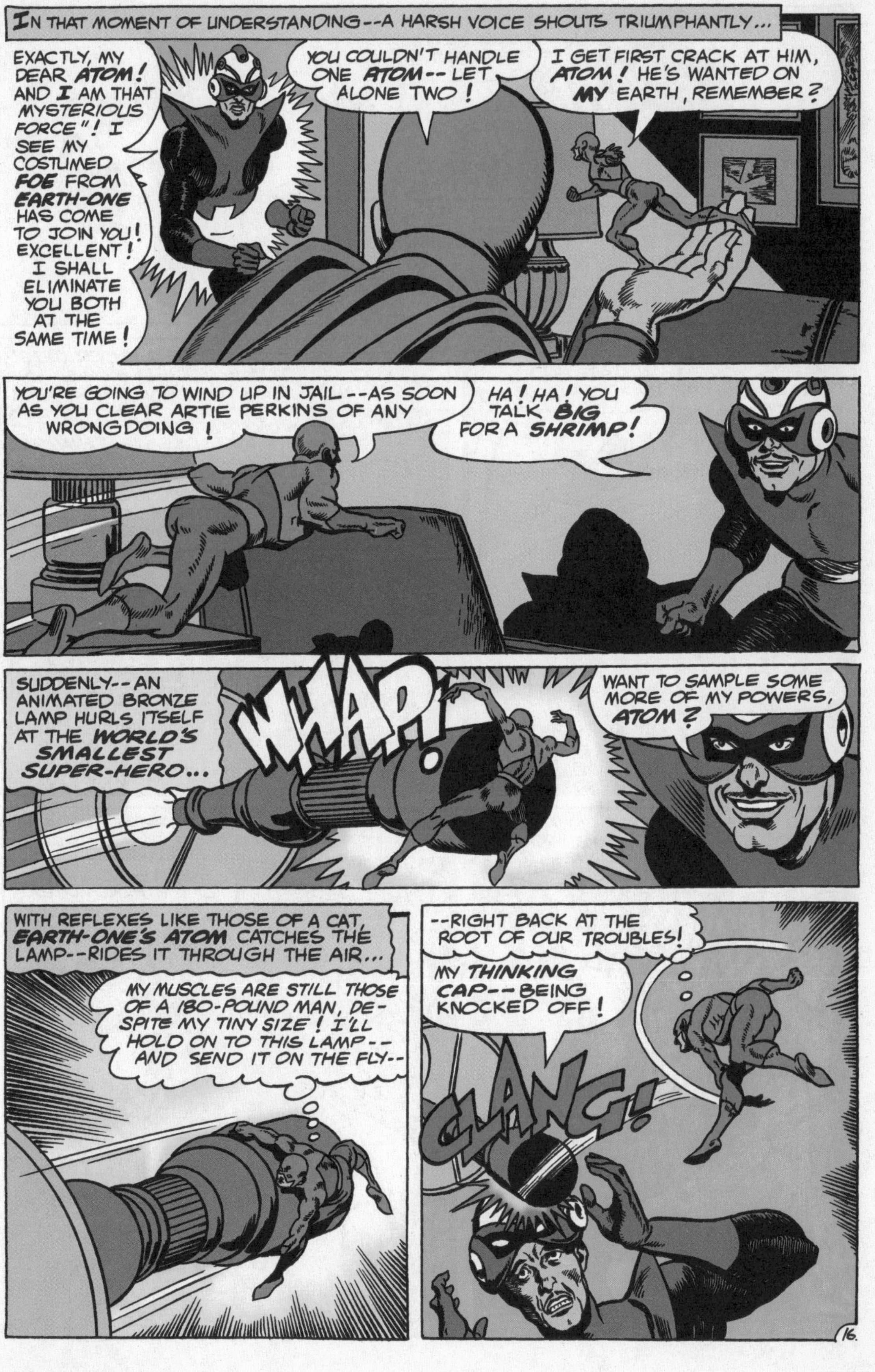
IN THAT MOMENT OF UNDERSTANDING--A HARSH VOICE SHOUTS TRIUMPHANTLY...
EXACTLY, MY DEAR ATOM! AND I AM THAT MYSTERIOUS FORCE"! I SEE MY COSTUMED FOE FROM EARTH-ONE HAS COME TO JOIN YOU! EXCELLENT! I SHALL ELIMINATE YOU BOTH AT THE SAME TIME!
YOU COULDN'T HANDLE ONE ATOM--LET ALONE TWO!
I GET FIRST CRACK AT HIM, ATOM! HE'S WANTED ON MY EARTH, REMEMBER?
YOU'RE GOING TO WIND UP IN JAIL--AS SOON AS YOU CLEAR ARTIE PERKINS OF ANY WRONGDOING!
HA! HA! YOU TALK BIG FOR A SHRIMP!
SUDDENLY--AN ANIMATED BRONZE LAMP HURLS ITSELF AT THE WORLD'S SMALLEST SUPER-HERO...
WHAP!
WANT TO SAMPLE SOME MORE OF MY POWERS, ATOM?
WITH REFLEXES LIKE THOSE OF A CAT, EARTH-ONE'S ATOM CATCHES THE LAMP--RIDES IT THROUGH THE AIR...
MY MUSCLES ARE STILL THOSE OF A 180-POUND MAN, DESPITE MY TINY SIZE! I'LL HOLD ON TO THIS LAMP--AND SEND IT ON THE FLY--
--RIGHT BACK AT THE ROOT OF OUR TROUBLES!
MY THINKING CAP--BEING KNOCKED OFF!
CLANG!
16.

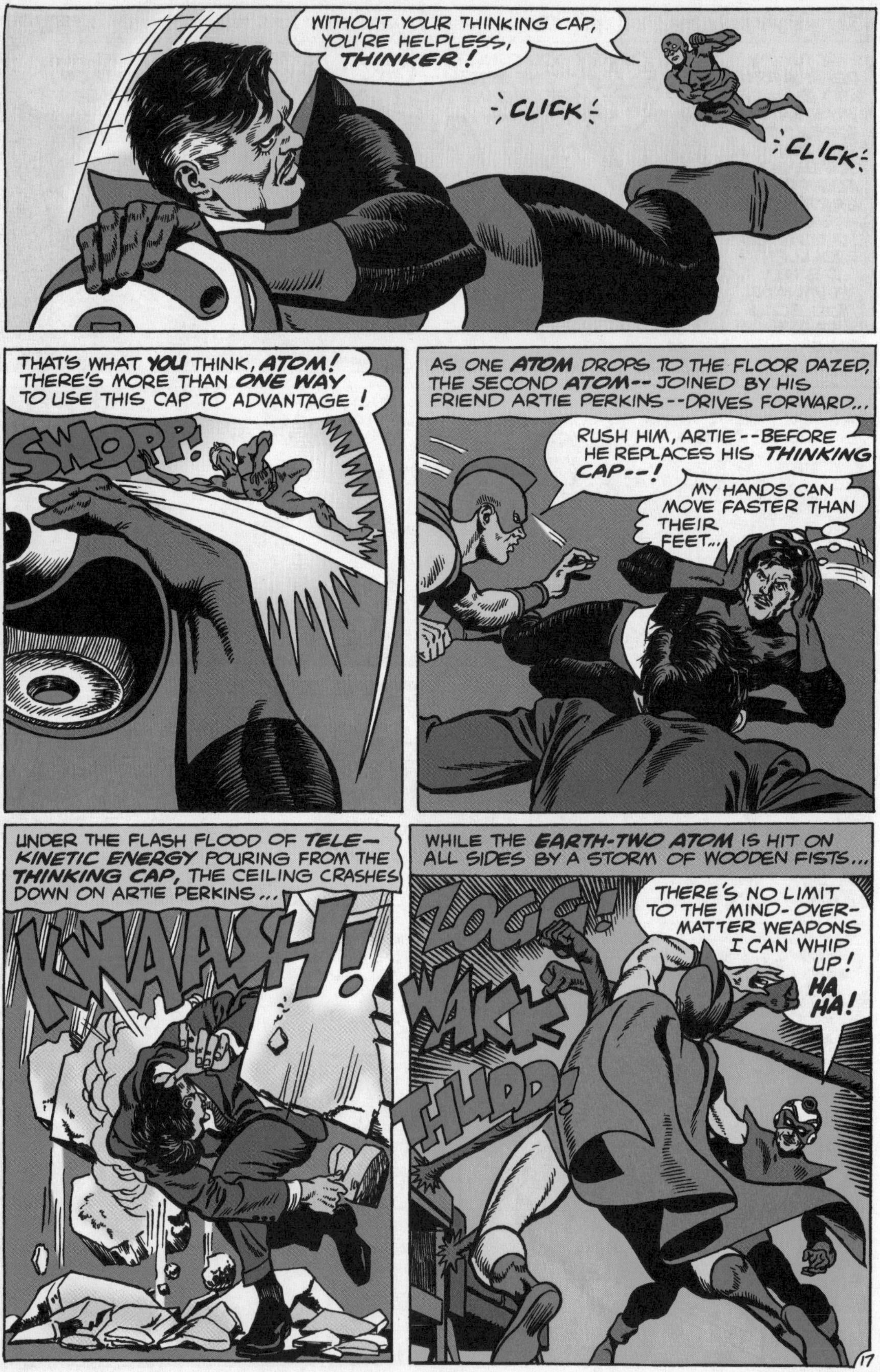
WITHOUT YOUR THINKING CAP, YOU'RE HELPLESS, THINKER!
CLICK
CLICK
THAT'S WHAT YOU THINK, ATOM! THERE'S MORE THAN ONE WAY TO USE THIS CAP TO ADVANTAGE!
SWOPP!
AS ONE ATOM DROPS TO THE FLOOR DAZED, THE SECOND ATOM-- JOINED BY HIS FRIEND ARTIE PERKINS--DRIVES FORWARD...
RUSH HIM, ARTIE--BEFORE HE REPLACES HIS THINKING CAP--!
MY HANDS CAN MOVE FASTER THAN THEIR FEET...
UNDER THE FLASH FLOOD OF TELE-KINETIC ENERGY POURING FROM THE THINKING CAP, THE CEILING CRASHES DOWN ON ARTIE PERKINS...
KWAASH!
WHILE THE EARTH-TWO ATOM IS HIT ON ALL SIDES BY A STORM OF WOODEN FISTS...
ZOGG!
WAKK
THUDD!
THERE'S NO LIMIT TO THE MIND-OVER-MATTER WEAPONS I CAN WHIP UP! HA HA!
17

AS BOTH *ATOMS* AND ARTIE PERKINS LIE UNCONSCIOUS, *THE THINKER* CONJURES UP A METALLIC CAGE ABOUT THEIR BODIES...

THERE! THAT CAGE OUGHT TO HOLD THEM UNTIL I CAN SEND BACK THE RARE BOOK-ENDS AND PAINTINGS ARTIE PERKINS STOLE HERE ON *EARTH-TWO* -- LEAVING ME INNOCENT AS A NEWBORN BABE!

AS AN ESCAPE-PROOF TOUCH--I'LL CHARGE THE CAGE WITH ENOUGH ELECTRICITY TO KILL THEM SHOULD THEY FOOLISHLY TRY TO GET OUT OF IT!

SAY, HEY! IT SURE LOOKS LIKE *THE THINKER* HAS PULLED HIS GREATEST THINK-TRICK! WITH BOTH *ATOMS* IMPRISONED BY HIS DIABOLICAL CAGE-- HE IS FREE TO ROAM BETWEEN WORLDS WITH-OUT PUNISHMENT! STORY CONTINUES ON THE NEXT PAGE FOLLOWING!

1B

CRISIS
ON MULTIPLE EARTHS
THE TEAM UPS

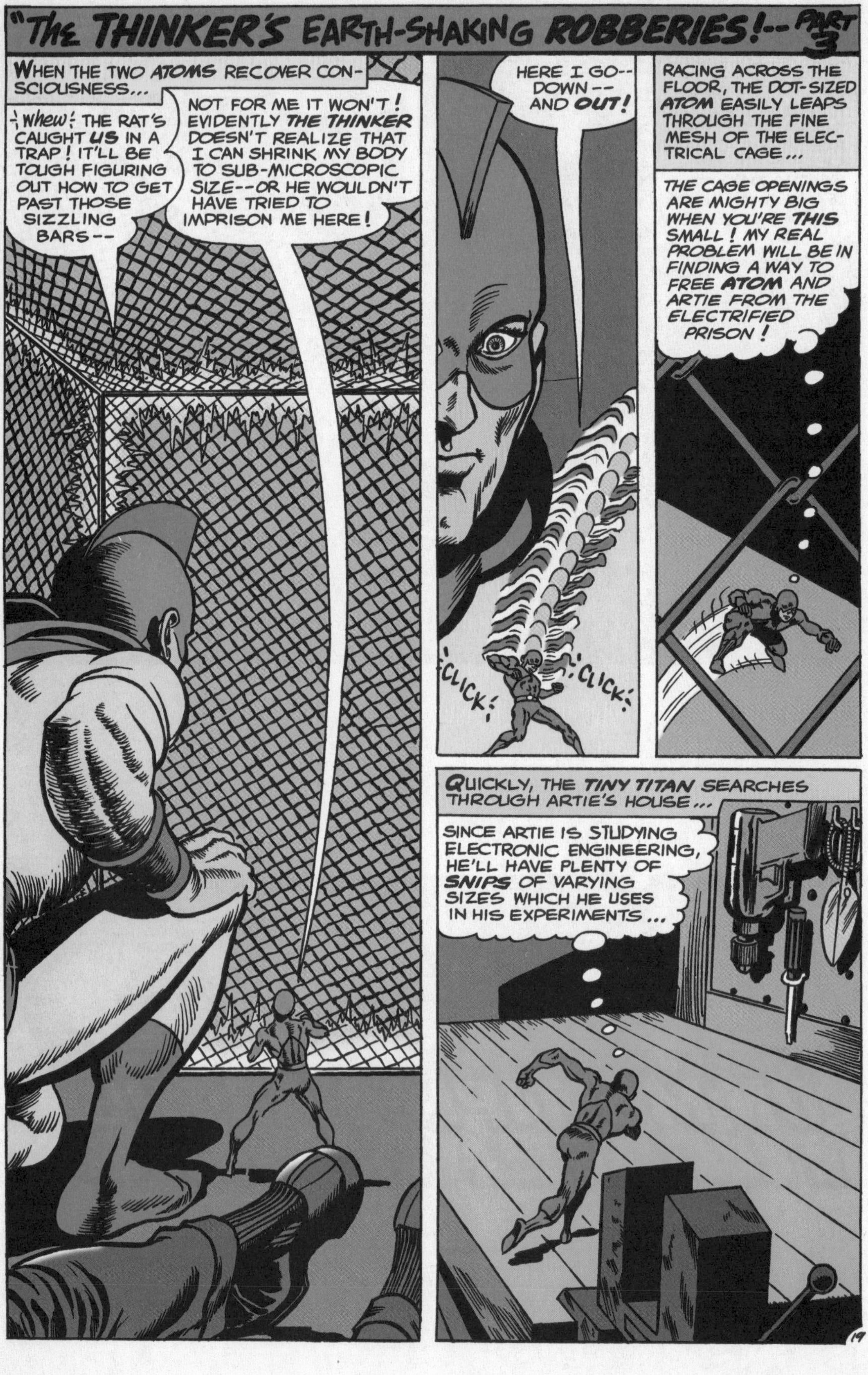
"THE THINKER'S EARTH-SHAKING ROBBERIES!-- PART 3
WHEN THE TWO ATOMS RECOVER CONSCIOUSNESS...
-WHEW- THE RAT'S CAUGHT US IN A TRAP! IT'LL BE TOUGH FIGURING OUT HOW TO GET PAST THOSE SIZZLING BARS--
NOT FOR ME IT WON'T! EVIDENTLY THE THINKER DOESN'T REALIZE THAT I CAN SHRINK MY BODY TO SUB-MICROSCOPIC SIZE--OR HE WOULDN'T HAVE TRIED TO IMPRISON ME HERE!
HERE I GO-- DOWN -- AND OUT!
CLICK!
CLICK!
RACING ACROSS THE FLOOR, THE DOT-SIZED ATOM EASILY LEAPS THROUGH THE FINE MESH OF THE ELECTRICAL CAGE...
THE CAGE OPENINGS ARE MIGHTY BIG WHEN YOU'RE THIS SMALL! MY REAL PROBLEM WILL BE IN FINDING A WAY TO FREE ATOM AND ARTIE FROM THE ELECTRIFIED PRISON!
QUICKLY, THE TINY TITAN SEARCHES THROUGH ARTIE'S HOUSE...
SINCE ARTIE IS STUDYING ELECTRONIC ENGINEERING, HE'LL HAVE PLENTY OF SNIPS OF VARYING SIZES WHICH HE USES IN HIS EXPERIMENTS...
19

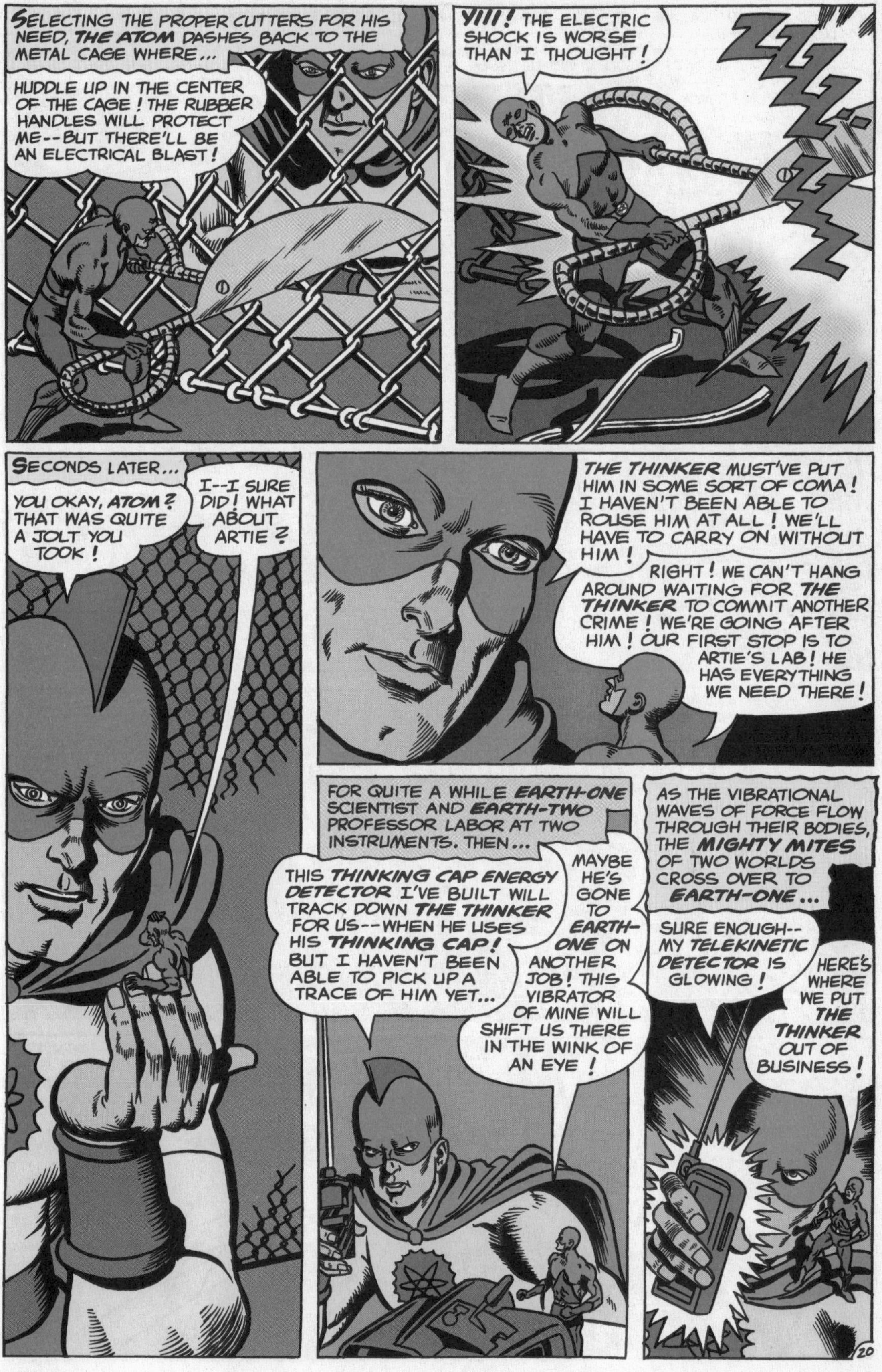
SELECTING THE PROPER CUTTERS FOR HIS NEED, THE ATOM DASHES BACK TO THE METAL CAGE WHERE...
HUDDLE UP IN THE CENTER OF THE CAGE! THE RUBBER HANDLES WILL PROTECT ME--BUT THERE'LL BE AN ELECTRICAL BLAST!
YIII! THE ELECTRIC SHOCK IS WORSE THAN I THOUGHT!
ZZZZ-ZZZZ
SECONDS LATER...
YOU OKAY, ATOM? THAT WAS QUITE A JOLT YOU TOOK!
I--I SURE DID! WHAT ABOUT ARTIE?
THE THINKER MUST'VE PUT HIM IN SOME SORT OF COMA! I HAVEN'T BEEN ABLE TO ROUSE HIM AT ALL! WE'LL HAVE TO CARRY ON WITHOUT HIM!
RIGHT! WE CAN'T HANG AROUND WAITING FOR THE THINKER TO COMMIT ANOTHER CRIME! WE'RE GOING AFTER HIM! OUR FIRST STOP IS TO ARTIE'S LAB! HE HAS EVERYTHING WE NEED THERE!
FOR QUITE A WHILE EARTH-ONE SCIENTIST AND EARTH-TWO PROFESSOR LABOR AT TWO INSTRUMENTS. THEN...
THIS THINKING CAP ENERGY DETECTOR I'VE BUILT WILL TRACK DOWN THE THINKER FOR US--WHEN HE USES HIS THINKING CAP! BUT I HAVEN'T BEEN ABLE TO PICK UP A TRACE OF HIM YET...
MAYBE HE'S GONE TO EARTH-ONE ON ANOTHER JOB! THIS VIBRATOR OF MINE WILL SHIFT US THERE IN THE WINK OF AN EYE!
AS THE VIBRATIONAL WAVES OF FORCE FLOW THROUGH THEIR BODIES, THE MIGHTY MITES OF TWO WORLDS CROSS OVER TO EARTH-ONE...
SURE ENOUGH--MY TELEKINETIC DETECTOR IS GLOWING!
HERE'S WHERE WE PUT THE THINKER OUT OF BUSINESS!
20

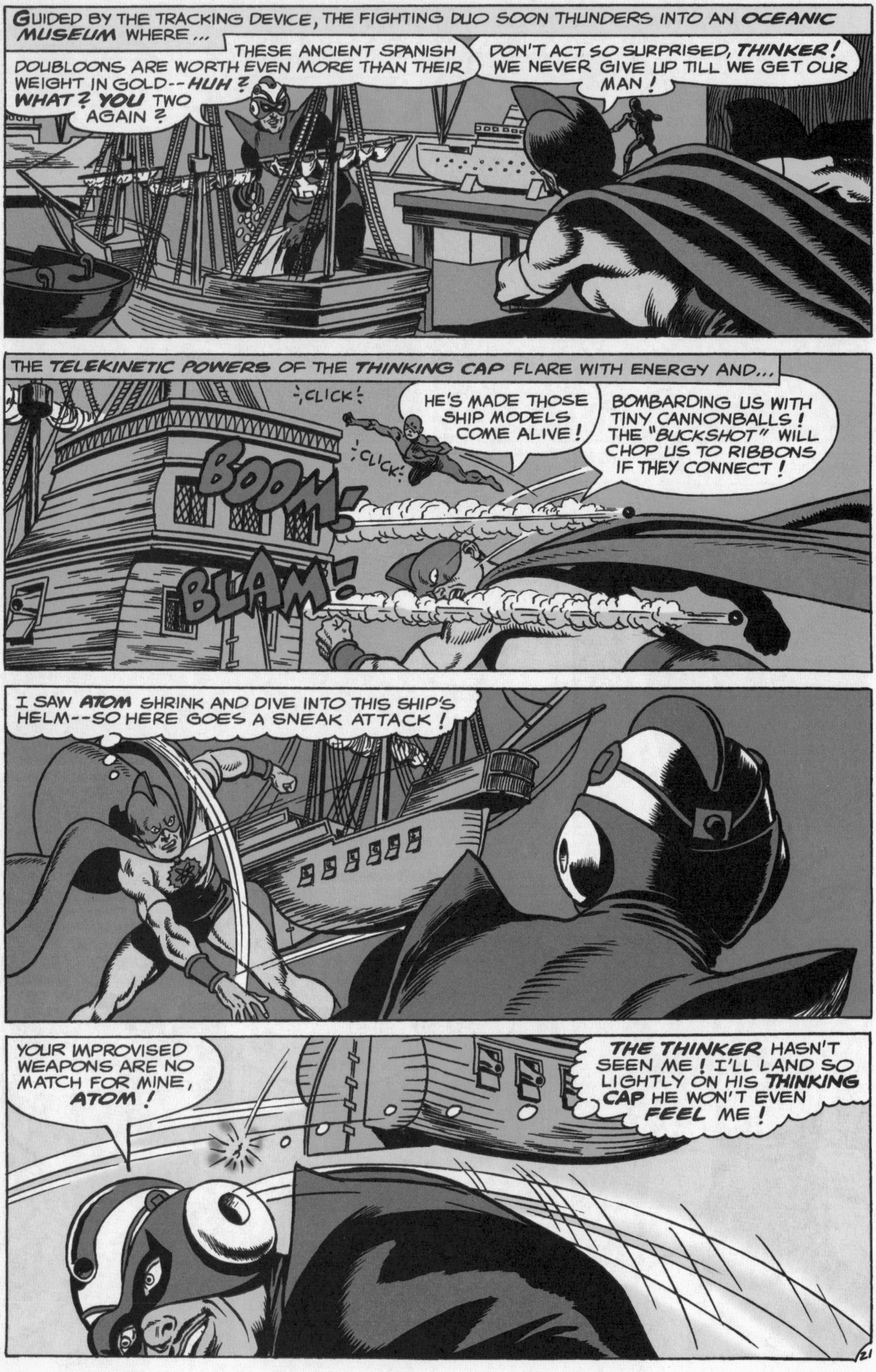
GUIDED BY THE TRACKING DEVICE, THE FIGHTING DUO SOON THUNDERS INTO AN OCEANIC MUSEUM WHERE...
THESE ANCIENT SPANISH DOUBLOONS ARE WORTH EVEN MORE THAN THEIR WEIGHT IN GOLD--HUH? WHAT? YOU TWO AGAIN?
DON'T ACT SO SURPRISED, THINKER! WE NEVER GIVE UP TILL WE GET OUR MAN!
THE TELEKINETIC POWERS OF THE THINKING CAP FLARE WITH ENERGY AND...
CLICK
CLICK
HE'S MADE THOSE SHIP MODELS COME ALIVE!
BOMBARDING US WITH TINY CANNONBALLS! THE "BUCKSHOT" WILL CHOP US TO RIBBONS IF THEY CONNECT!
BOOM!
BLAM!
I SAW ATOM SHRINK AND DIVE INTO THIS SHIP'S HELM--SO HERE GOES A SNEAK ATTACK!
YOUR IMPROVISED WEAPONS ARE NO MATCH FOR MINE, ATOM!
THE THINKER HASN'T SEEN ME! I'LL LAND SO LIGHTLY ON HIS THINKING CAP HE WON'T EVEN FEEL ME!
21

AS THE *TINY TITAN* NIMBLY STARTS PULLING AT CIRCUIT WIRES AND FILAMENTS ON THE *THINKING CAP*...

I'M DIRECTING THOSE IRON CANNONBALLS-- RELICS FROM THE CIVIL WAR-- TO POUND YOU TO A PULP BEFORE YOU CAN REACH ME!

BOOM!

BOOM!

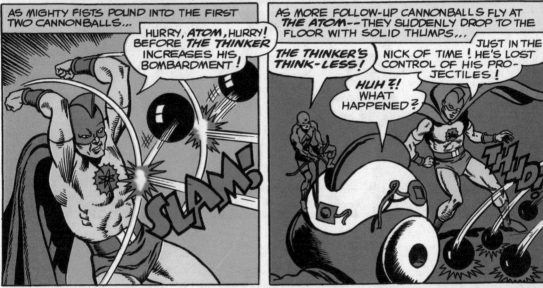

AS MIGHTY FISTS POUND INTO THE FIRST TWO CANNONBALLS...

HURRY, *ATOM*, HURRY! BEFORE *THE THINKER* INCREASES HIS BOMBARDMENT!

SLAM!

AS MORE FOLLOW-UP CANNONBALLS FLY AT *THE ATOM*--THEY SUDDENLY DROP TO THE FLOOR WITH SOLID THUMPS...

THE THINKER'S THINK-LESS!

JUST IN THE NICK OF TIME! HE'S LOST CONTROL OF HIS PRO- JECTILES!

HUH?! WHAT HAPPENED?

TH-UD!

WE HAPPENED TO YOU, *THINKER*!

ZWOK!

POW!

WE'LL LEAVE IT TO THE TWO *EARTHS* TO DEAL WITH *THE THINKER* AND HIS STOLEN LOOT!

I HAVE A FEELING THAT WHEN I DISCONNECTED THE *THINKING CAP* WIRES--ARTIE PERKINS RE- COVERED FROM HIS COMA! HIS NAME WILL BE CLEARED NOW--AND HE CAN CARRY ON HIS LAW-ABIDING LIFE!

22

LATER, WHEN RAY PALMER IS ALONE WITH HIS FIANCÉE...

AND HOW DID YOUR CASE OF THE TELEVISION-ACTRESS-MOTHER TURN OUT, JEAN?

THE JUDGE RULED THAT THE BABY BELONGED WITH HIS MOTHER! I MUST SAY, RAY, I NEVER PLEADED A CASE SO ELOQUENTLY! YOU SEE ...

WHEN WE ARE MARRIED AND I SHOULD DECIDE TO KEEP UP MY LAW PRACTICE, I'LL NEED A GOVERNESS TO CARE FOR OUR BABIES! IN PLEADING FOR CHERYL DRAKE-- I WAS ACTUALLY PLEADING FOR MYSELF!

AND WHO COULD RESIST SUCH AN APPEAL?

THE END

23

CRISIS ON MULTIPLE EARTHS THE TEAM UPS

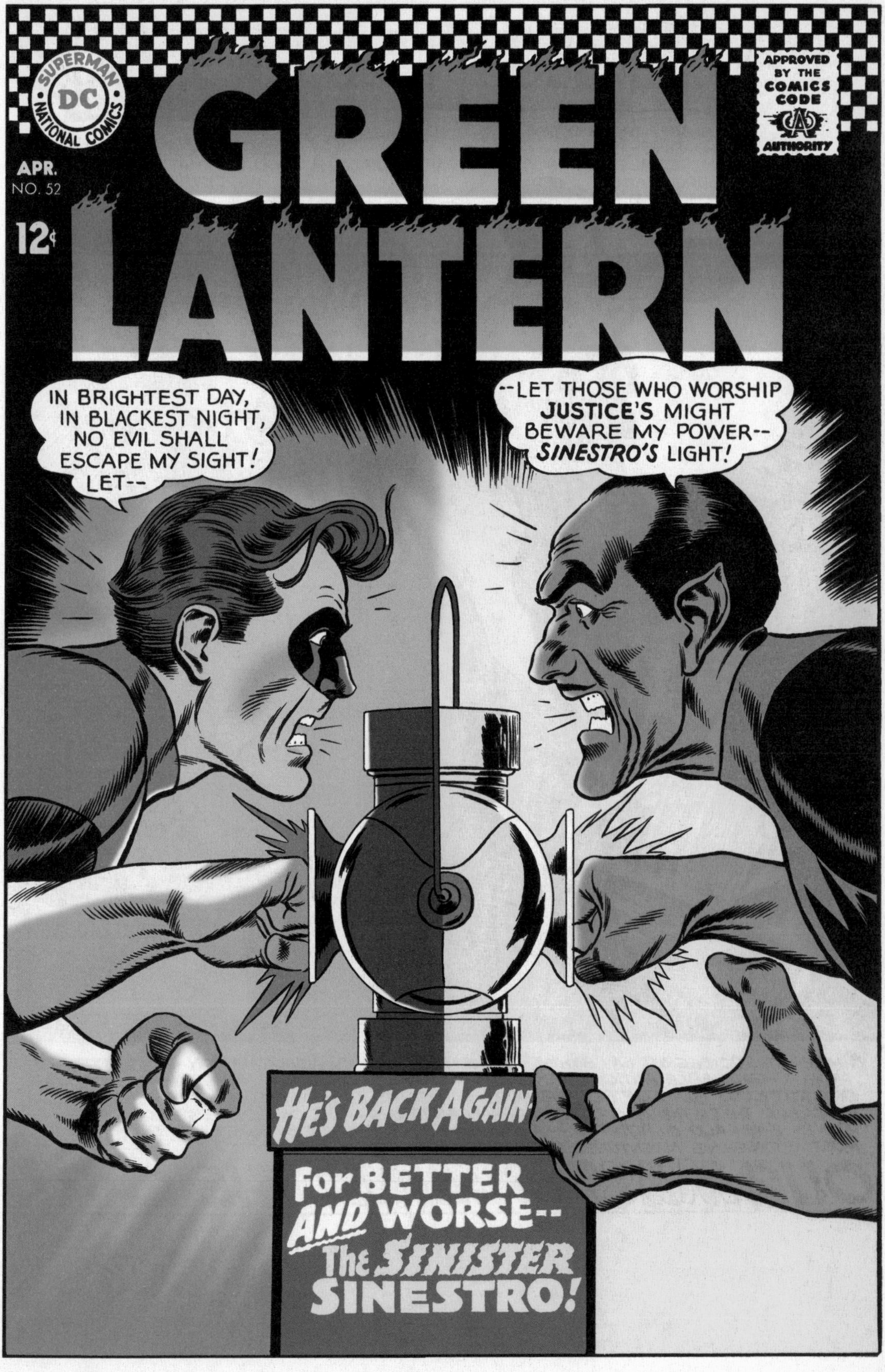
SUPERMAN DC NATIONAL COMICS
APPROVED BY THE COMICS CODE AUTHORITY
APR.
NO. 52
12¢
GREEN LANTERN
IN BRIGHTEST DAY, IN BLACKEST NIGHT, NO EVIL SHALL ESCAPE MY SIGHT! LET--
--LET THOSE WHO WORSHIP JUSTICE'S MIGHT BEWARE MY POWER-- SINESTRO'S LIGHT!
HE'S BACK AGAIN--
For BETTER AND WORSE-- The SINISTER SINESTRO!

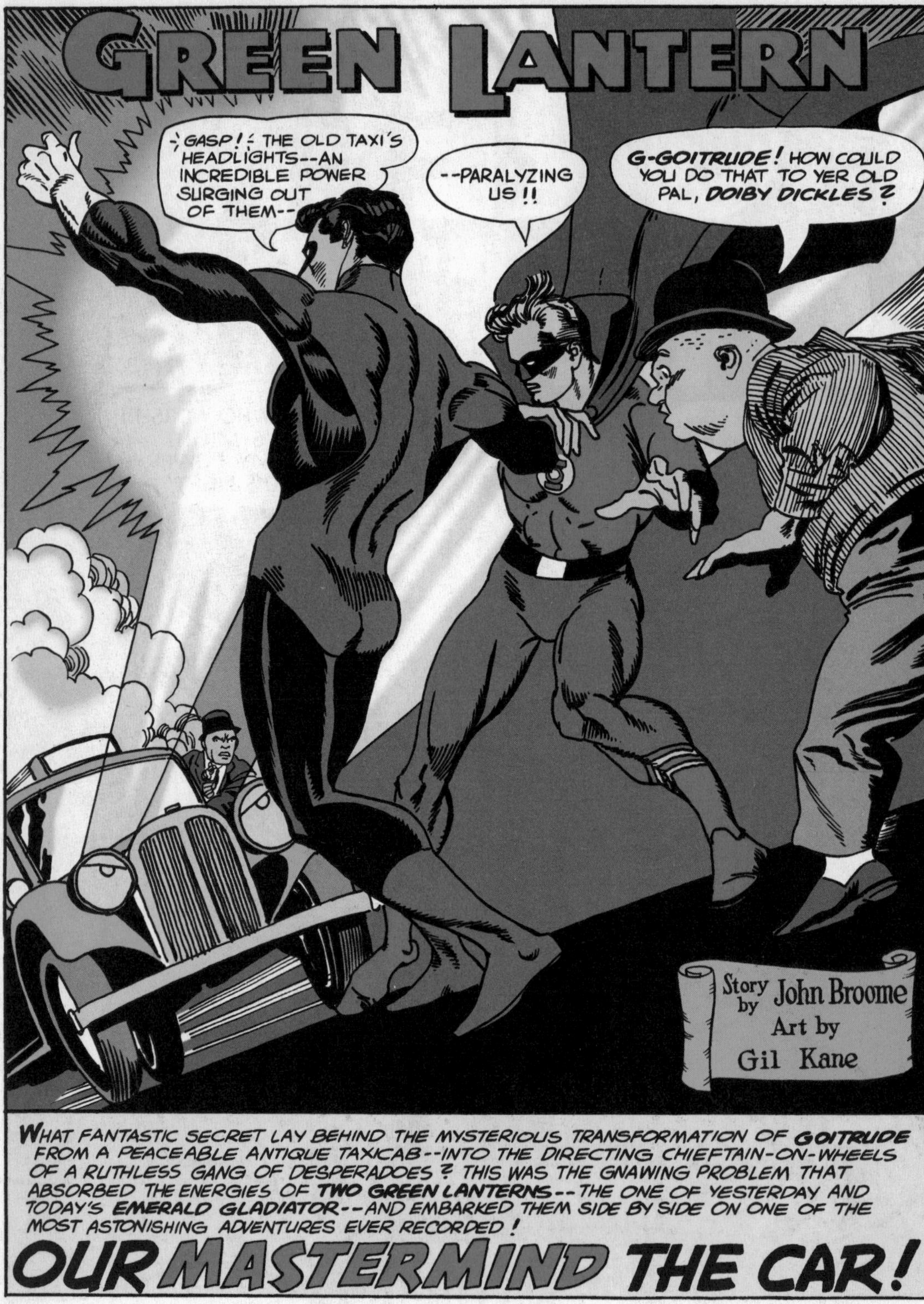

GREEN LANTERN
-GASP!- THE OLD TAXI'S HEADLIGHTS--AN INCREDIBLE POWER SURGING OUT OF THEM--
--PARALYZING US!!
G-GOITRUDE! HOW COULD YOU DO THAT TO YER OLD PAL, DOIBY DICKLES?
Story by John Broome
Art by Gil Kane
WHAT FANTASTIC SECRET LAY BEHIND THE MYSTERIOUS TRANSFORMATION OF GOITRUDE FROM A PEACEABLE ANTIQUE TAXICAB--INTO THE DIRECTING CHIEFTAIN-ON-WHEELS OF A RUTHLESS GANG OF DESPERADOES? THIS WAS THE GNAWING PROBLEM THAT ABSORBED THE ENERGIES OF TWO GREEN LANTERNS--THE ONE OF YESTERDAY AND TODAY'S EMERALD GLADIATOR--AND EMBARKED THEM SIDE BY SIDE ON ONE OF THE MOST ASTONISHING ADVENTURES EVER RECORDED!
OUR MASTERMIND THE CAR!

As airplane mechanic Thomas (Pieface) Kalmakli relays warm regards to his wife from a letter he has just received...

"...AND TELL *TERGA* I SURE MISS HER HOME-COOKED MEALS!"

THAT'S SWEET OF HAL JORDAN TO PRAISE MY COOKING, THOMAS! BUT TELL ME--

--HOW *IS* HE? WHAT HAS HE BEEN DOING SINCE HE LEFT *COAST CITY*?

er--NOTHING VERY MUCH, *TERGA*! HE'S STILL GOT THE WANDERLUST... GOING FROM PLACE TO PLACE--

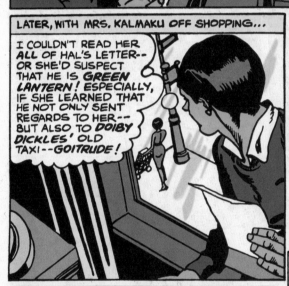

LATER, WITH MRS. KALMAKU OFF SHOPPING...

I COULDN'T READ HER ALL OF HAL'S LETTER-- OR SHE'D SUSPECT THAT HE IS *GREEN LANTERN*! ESPECIALLY, IF SHE LEARNED THAT HE NOT ONLY SENT REGARDS TO HER-- BUT ALSO TO *DOIBY DICKLES'* OLD TAXI--*GOITRUDE*!

OF COURSE *TERGA* DOESN'T KNOW ANY-THING ABOUT *GOITRUDE*--JUST AS SHE IS COMPLETELY UNAWARE THAT HERE IN MY DESK I KEEP A CERTAIN PRECIOUS NOTEBOOK UNDER LOCK AND KEY--MY PRECIOUS *CASEBOOK OF GREEN LANTERN!* *

* EDITOR'S NOTE: PIEFACE IS NOT ONLY GREEN LANTERN'S CONFIDANT BUT ALSO HIS FOREMOST FAN AND UNOFFICIAL BIOGRAPHER!

IT OCCURS TO ME, READER, THAT *YOU* STILL KNOW NOTHING ABOUT ONE OF MY IDOL'S MOST EXCITING ADVENTURES--INVOLVING *GOITRUDE*--WHICH TOOK PLACE AT A TIME WHEN HAL WAS STILL LIVING IN *COAST CITY* AND WORKING AS A TEST PILOT FOR THE *FERRIS AIRCRAFT COMPANY*...

IN MANY WAYS THIS IS THE *EMERALD GLADIATOR'S* MOST EXTRAORDINARY CASE! SETTLE BACK NOW AS I READ TO YOU THE ADVENTURE I'VE ENTITLED, *"OUR MASTERMIND THE CAR!"*

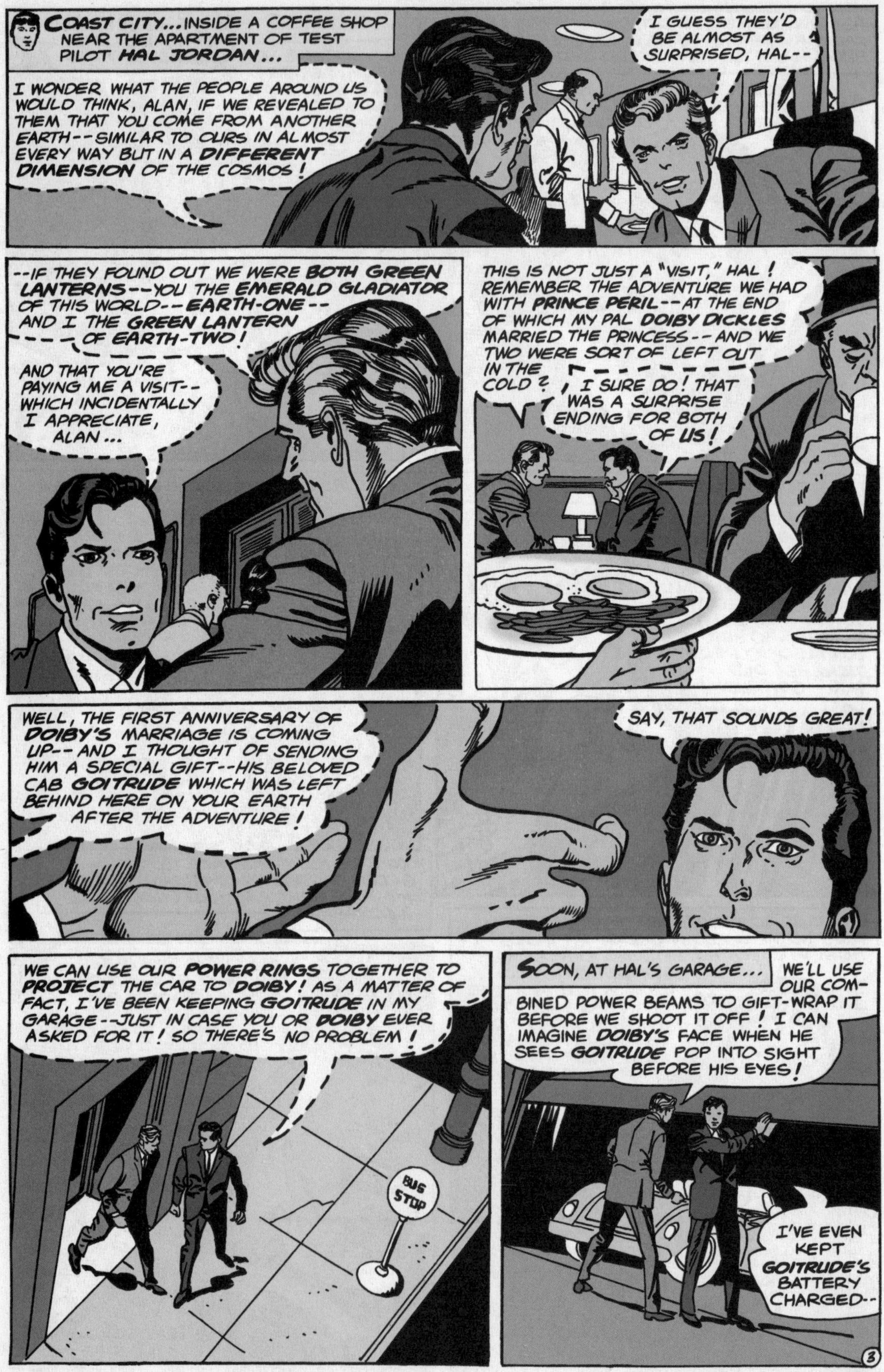
COAST CITY... INSIDE A COFFEE SHOP NEAR THE APARTMENT OF TEST PILOT HAL JORDAN...
I WONDER WHAT THE PEOPLE AROUND US WOULD THINK, ALAN, IF WE REVEALED TO THEM THAT YOU COME FROM ANOTHER EARTH--SIMILAR TO OURS IN ALMOST EVERY WAY BUT IN A DIFFERENT DIMENSION OF THE COSMOS!
I GUESS THEY'D BE ALMOST AS SURPRISED, HAL--
--IF THEY FOUND OUT WE WERE BOTH GREEN LANTERNS--YOU THE EMERALD GLADIATOR OF THIS WORLD--EARTH-ONE--AND I THE GREEN LANTERN OF EARTH-TWO!
AND THAT YOU'RE PAYING ME A VISIT--WHICH INCIDENTALLY I APPRECIATE, ALAN...
THIS IS NOT JUST A "VISIT," HAL! REMEMBER THE ADVENTURE WE HAD WITH PRINCE PERIL--AT THE END OF WHICH MY PAL DOIBY DICKLES MARRIED THE PRINCESS--AND WE TWO WERE SORT OF LEFT OUT IN THE COLD?
I SURE DO! THAT WAS A SURPRISE ENDING FOR BOTH OF US!
WELL, THE FIRST ANNIVERSARY OF DOIBY'S MARRIAGE IS COMING UP--AND I THOUGHT OF SENDING HIM A SPECIAL GIFT--HIS BELOVED CAB GOITRUDE WHICH WAS LEFT BEHIND HERE ON YOUR EARTH AFTER THE ADVENTURE!
SAY, THAT SOUNDS GREAT!
WE CAN USE OUR POWER RINGS TOGETHER TO PROJECT THE CAR TO DOIBY! AS A MATTER OF FACT, I'VE BEEN KEEPING GOITRUDE IN MY GARAGE--JUST IN CASE YOU OR DOIBY EVER ASKED FOR IT! SO THERE'S NO PROBLEM!
BUS STOP
SOON, AT HAL'S GARAGE...
WE'LL USE OUR COMBINED POWER BEAMS TO GIFT-WRAP IT BEFORE WE SHOOT IT OFF! I CAN IMAGINE DOIBY'S FACE WHEN HE SEES GOITRUDE POP INTO SIGHT BEFORE HIS EYES!
I'VE EVEN KEPT GOITRUDE'S BATTERY CHARGED--
3

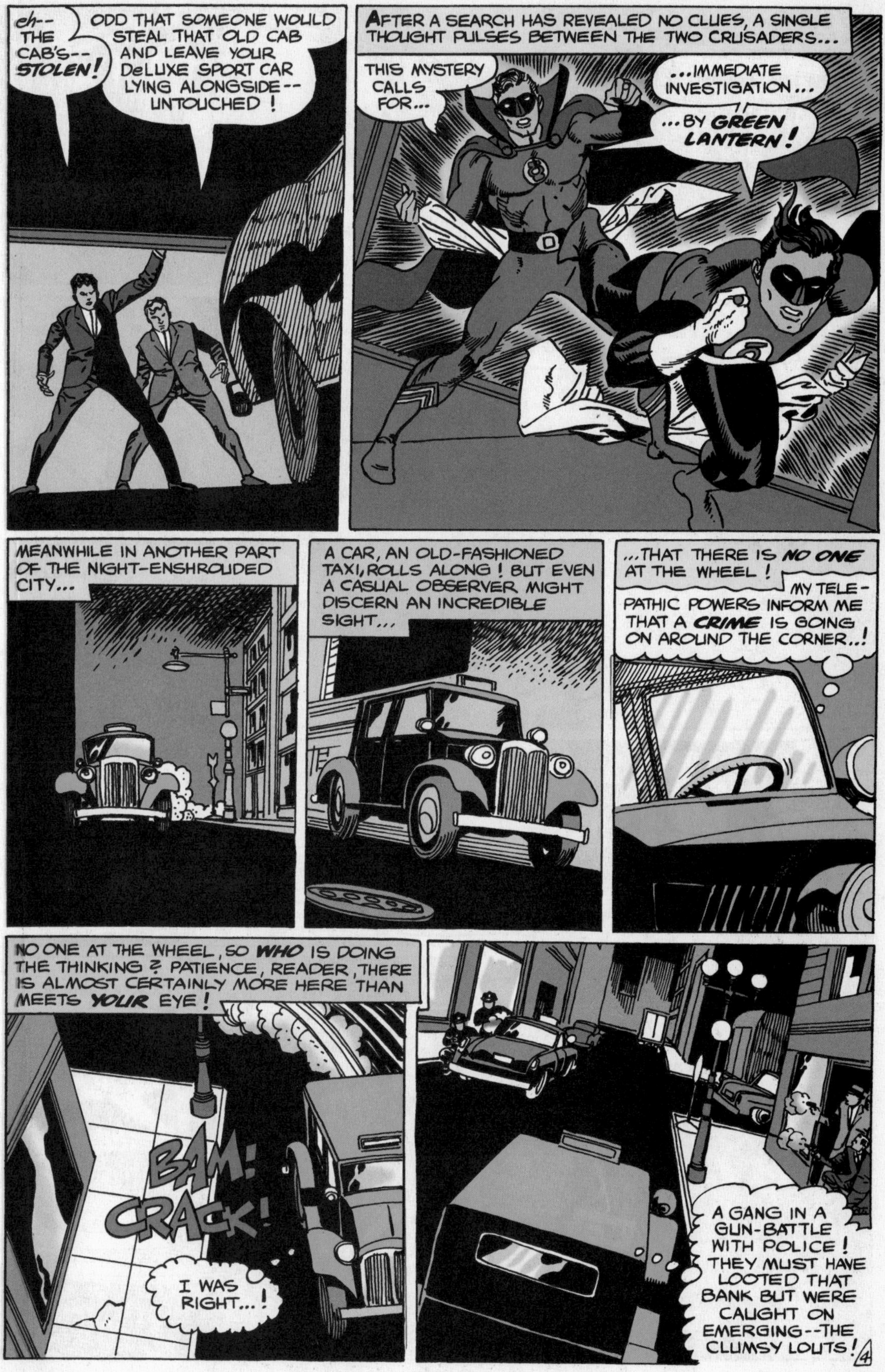
eh-- THE CAB'S-- STOLEN!
ODD THAT SOMEONE WOULD STEAL THAT OLD CAB AND LEAVE YOUR DeLUXE SPORT CAR LYING ALONGSIDE-- UNTOUCHED !
AFTER A SEARCH HAS REVEALED NO CLUES, A SINGLE THOUGHT PULSES BETWEEN THE TWO CRUSADERS...
THIS MYSTERY CALLS FOR...
...IMMEDIATE INVESTIGATION...
...BY GREEN LANTERN!
MEANWHILE IN ANOTHER PART OF THE NIGHT-ENSHROUDED CITY...
A CAR, AN OLD-FASHIONED TAXI, ROLLS ALONG ! BUT EVEN A CASUAL OBSERVER MIGHT DISCERN AN INCREDIBLE SIGHT...
...THAT THERE IS NO ONE AT THE WHEEL !
MY TELE-PATHIC POWERS INFORM ME THAT A CRIME IS GOING ON AROUND THE CORNER..!
NO ONE AT THE WHEEL, SO WHO IS DOING THE THINKING ? PATIENCE, READER, THERE IS ALMOST CERTAINLY MORE HERE THAN MEETS YOUR EYE !
BAM! CRACK!
I WAS RIGHT...!
A GANG IN A GUN-BATTLE WITH POLICE ! THEY MUST HAVE LOOTED THAT BANK BUT WERE CAUGHT ON EMERGING--THE CLUMSY LOUTS!
4

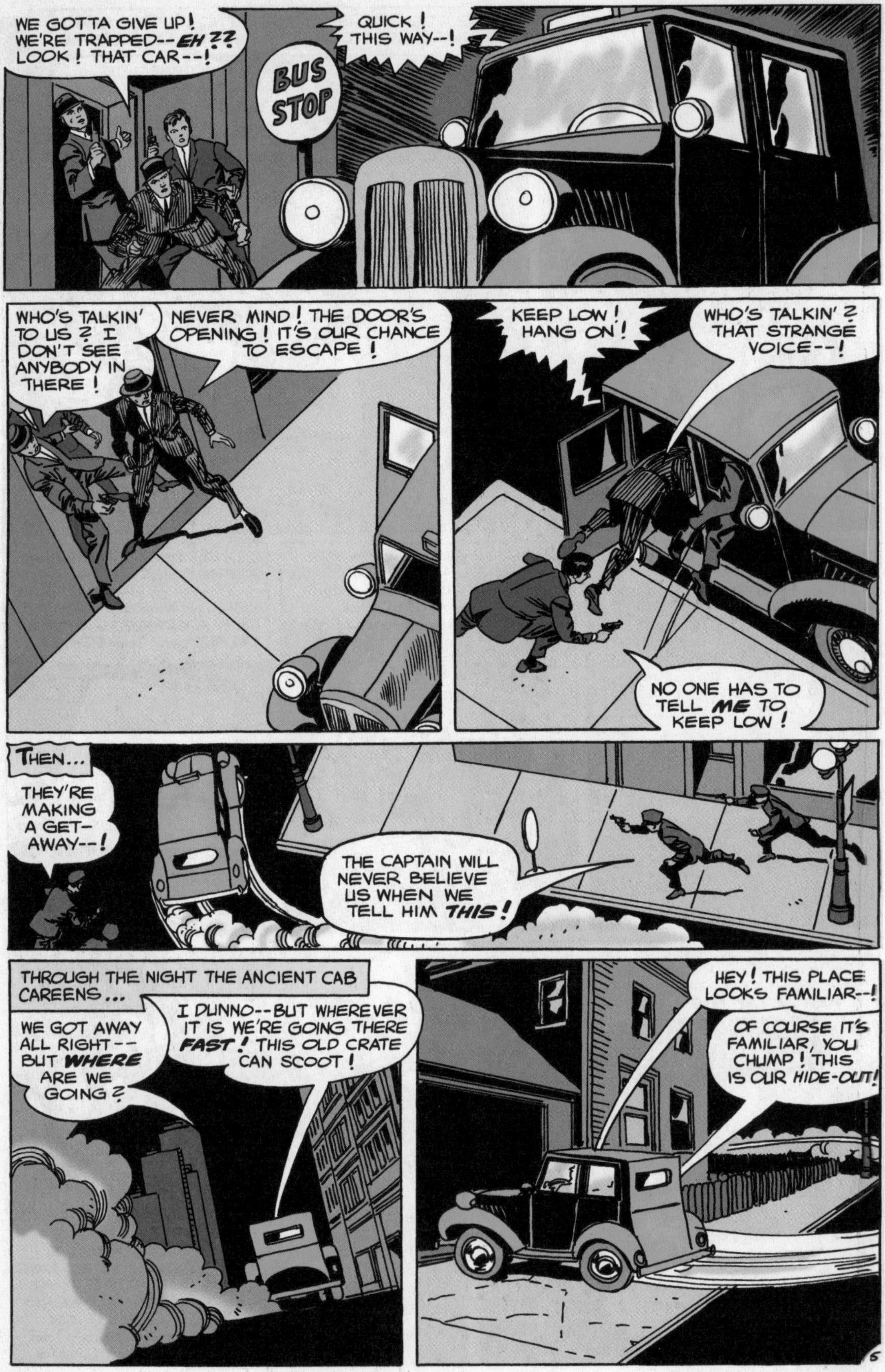

WE GOTTA GIVE UP! WE'RE TRAPPED--EH?? LOOK! THAT CAR--!
QUICK! THIS WAY--!
BUS STOP
WHO'S TALKIN' TO US? I DON'T SEE ANYBODY IN THERE!
NEVER MIND! THE DOOR'S OPENING! IT'S OUR CHANCE TO ESCAPE!
KEEP LOW! HANG ON!
WHO'S TALKIN'? THAT STRANGE VOICE--!
NO ONE HAS TO TELL ME TO KEEP LOW!
THEN...
THEY'RE MAKING A GET-AWAY--!
THE CAPTAIN WILL NEVER BELIEVE US WHEN WE TELL HIM THIS!
THROUGH THE NIGHT THE ANCIENT CAB CAREENS...
WE GOT AWAY ALL RIGHT--BUT WHERE ARE WE GOING?
I DUNNO--BUT WHEREVER IT IS WE'RE GOING THERE FAST! THIS OLD CRATE CAN SCOOT!
HEY! THIS PLACE LOOKS FAMILIAR--!
OF COURSE IT'S FAMILIAR, YOU CHUMP! THIS IS OUR HIDE-OUT!
6

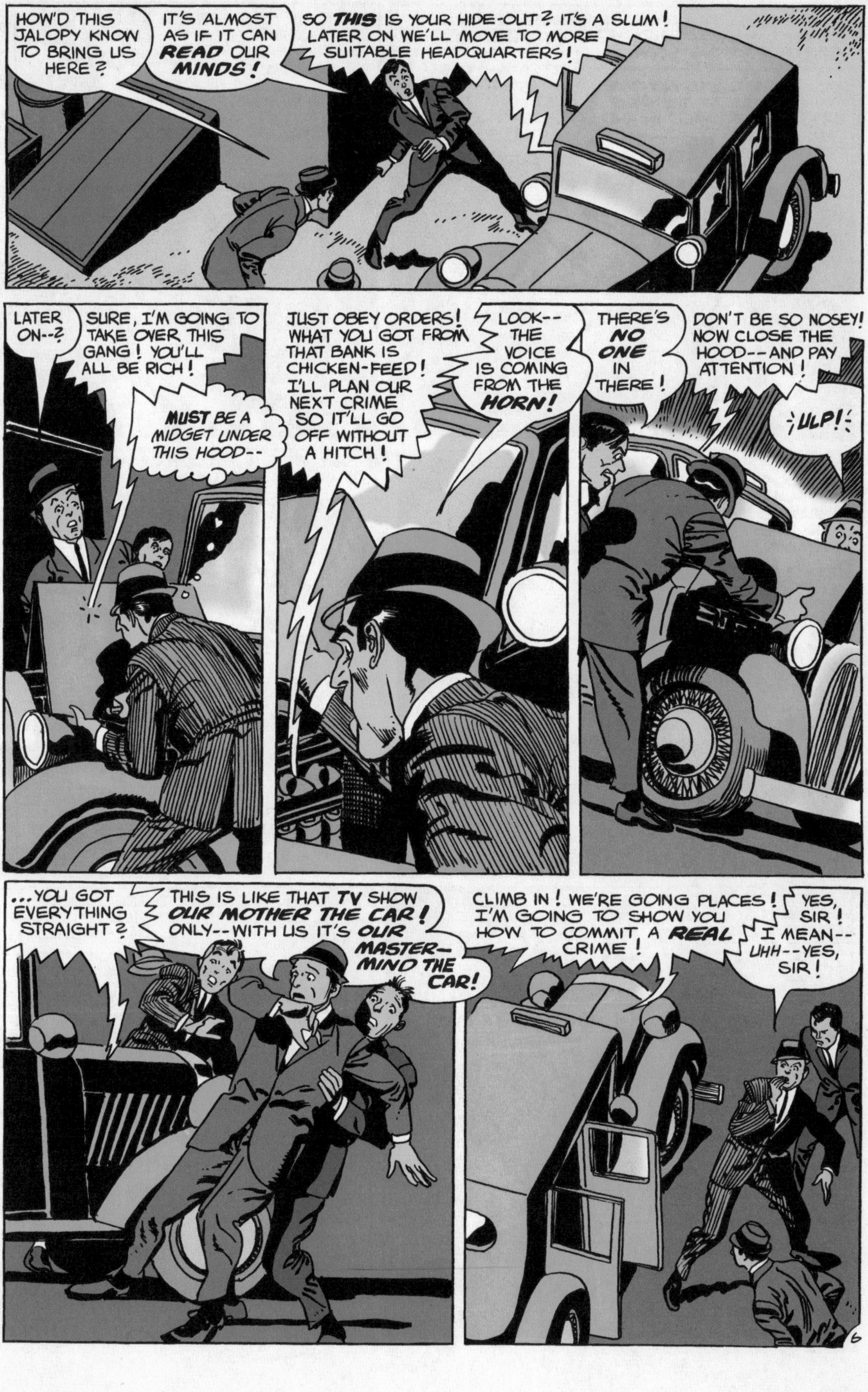
HOW'D THIS JALOPY KNOW TO BRING US HERE?
IT'S ALMOST AS IF IT CAN READ OUR MINDS!
SO THIS IS YOUR HIDE-OUT? IT'S A SLUM! LATER ON WE'LL MOVE TO MORE SUITABLE HEADQUARTERS!
LATER ON--?
SURE, I'M GOING TO TAKE OVER THIS GANG! YOU'LL ALL BE RICH!
MUST BE A MIDGET UNDER THIS HOOD--
JUST OBEY ORDERS! WHAT YOU GOT FROM THAT BANK IS CHICKEN-FEED! I'LL PLAN OUR NEXT CRIME SO IT'LL GO OFF WITHOUT A HITCH!
LOOK-- THE VOICE IS COMING FROM THE HORN!
THERE'S NO ONE IN THERE!
DON'T BE SO NOSEY! NOW CLOSE THE HOOD--AND PAY ATTENTION!
ULP!
...YOU GOT EVERYTHING STRAIGHT?
THIS IS LIKE THAT TV SHOW OUR MOTHER THE CAR! ONLY--WITH US IT'S OUR MASTER-MIND THE CAR!
CLIMB IN! WE'RE GOING PLACES! I'M GOING TO SHOW YOU HOW TO COMMIT A REAL CRIME!
YES, SIR! I MEAN-- UHH--YES, SIR!
6

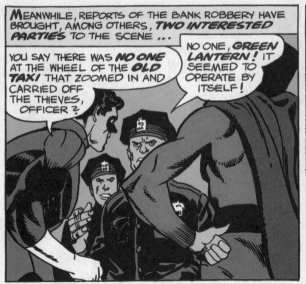

MEANWHILE, REPORTS OF THE BANK ROBBERY HAVE BROUGHT, AMONG OTHERS, *TWO INTERESTED PARTIES* TO THE SCENE ...

YOU SAY THERE WAS *NO ONE* AT THE WHEEL OF THE *OLD TAXI* THAT ZOOMED IN AND CARRIED OFF THE THIEVES, OFFICER?

NO ONE, *GREEN LANTERN!* IT SEEMED TO OPERATE BY ITSELF!

FROM THE DESCRIPTION, THAT GETAWAY CAR *COULD* HAVE BEEN *GOITRUDE!*

INCREDIBLE! IT'S AS IF THE OLD CAB HAS SOMEHOW *COME ALIVE* AND TAKEN UP *CRIME!*

IF THAT'S TRUE AND *DOIBY* EVER HEARS ABOUT IT, HE'LL ABSOLUTELY DIE OF SHAME! HIS *GOITRUDE* HELPING CRIMINALS--!

WE'VE GOT TO LOCATE IT! WE CAN'T REST UNTIL WE DO!

ELSEWHERE IN THE CITY...

FELLOW CRIMINALS, MY TELEPATHIC POWERS INFORM ME THAT AN ARMORED CAR CARRYING THE *CENTRAL INSURANCE COMPANY PAYROLL* WILL BE HERE *ANY MOMENT...*

WE'LL BE READY, CHIEF...

ATTENTION! HERE IT COMES! CARRY OUT THE ORDERS I'VE GIVEN YOU!

THEN...

THAT OLD JALOPY WON'T MOVE!

THERE'S NOBODY INSIDE IT! LOOKS ABANDONED--!

HONK!

HONK!

HONK!

7.

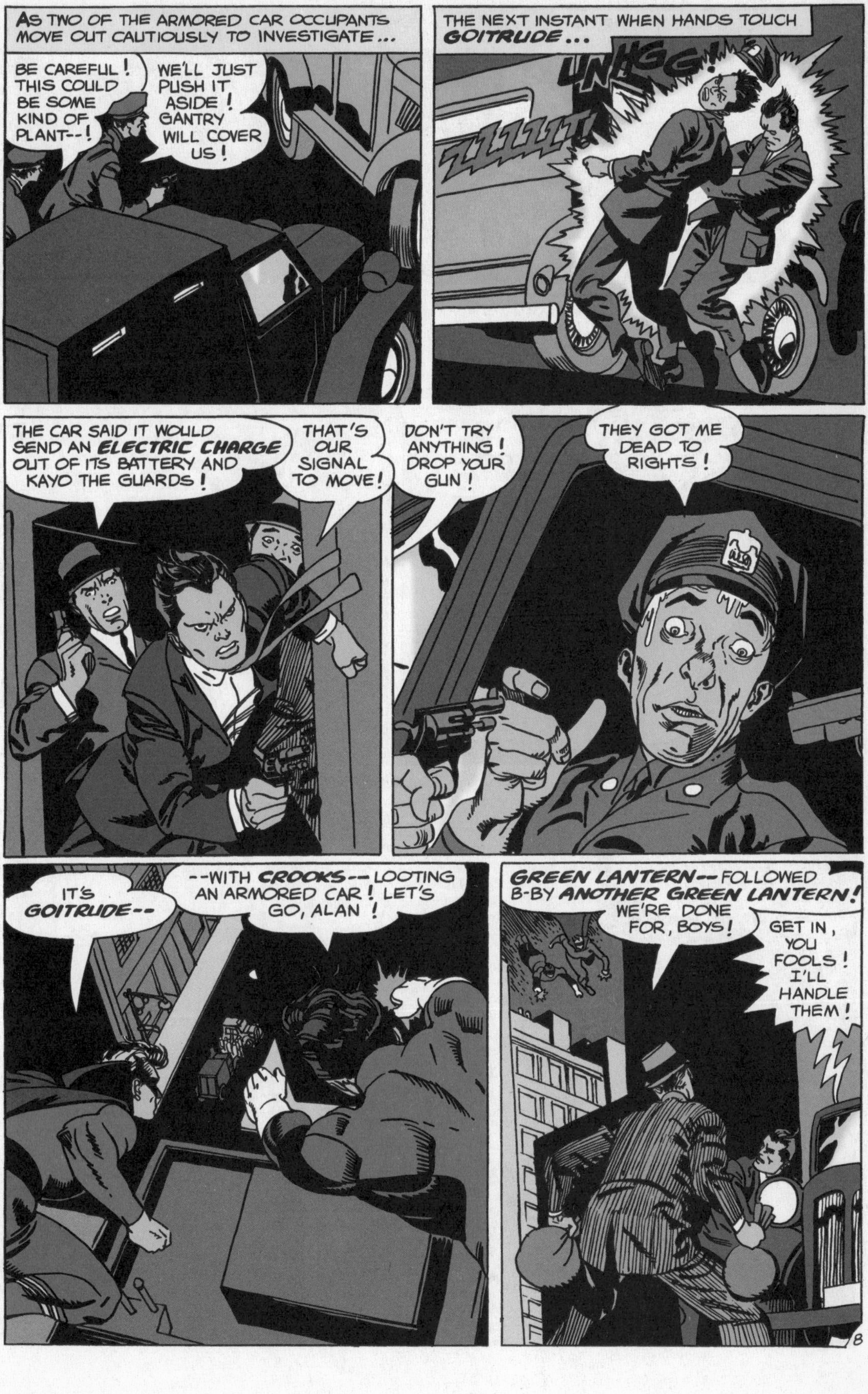
AS TWO OF THE ARMORED CAR OCCUPANTS MOVE OUT CAUTIOUSLY TO INVESTIGATE...
BE CAREFUL! THIS COULD BE SOME KIND OF PLANT--!
WE'LL JUST PUSH IT ASIDE! GANTRY WILL COVER US!
THE NEXT INSTANT WHEN HANDS TOUCH GOITRUDE...
UNHGG!
ZZZZZT!
THE CAR SAID IT WOULD SEND AN ELECTRIC CHARGE OUT OF ITS BATTERY AND KAYO THE GUARDS!
THAT'S OUR SIGNAL TO MOVE!
DON'T TRY ANYTHING! DROP YOUR GUN!
THEY GOT ME DEAD TO RIGHTS!
IT'S GOITRUDE--
--WITH CROOKS--LOOTING AN ARMORED CAR! LET'S GO, ALAN!
GREEN LANTERN--FOLLOWED B-BY ANOTHER GREEN LANTERN! WE'RE DONE FOR, BOYS!
GET IN, YOU FOOLS! I'LL HANDLE THEM!
8

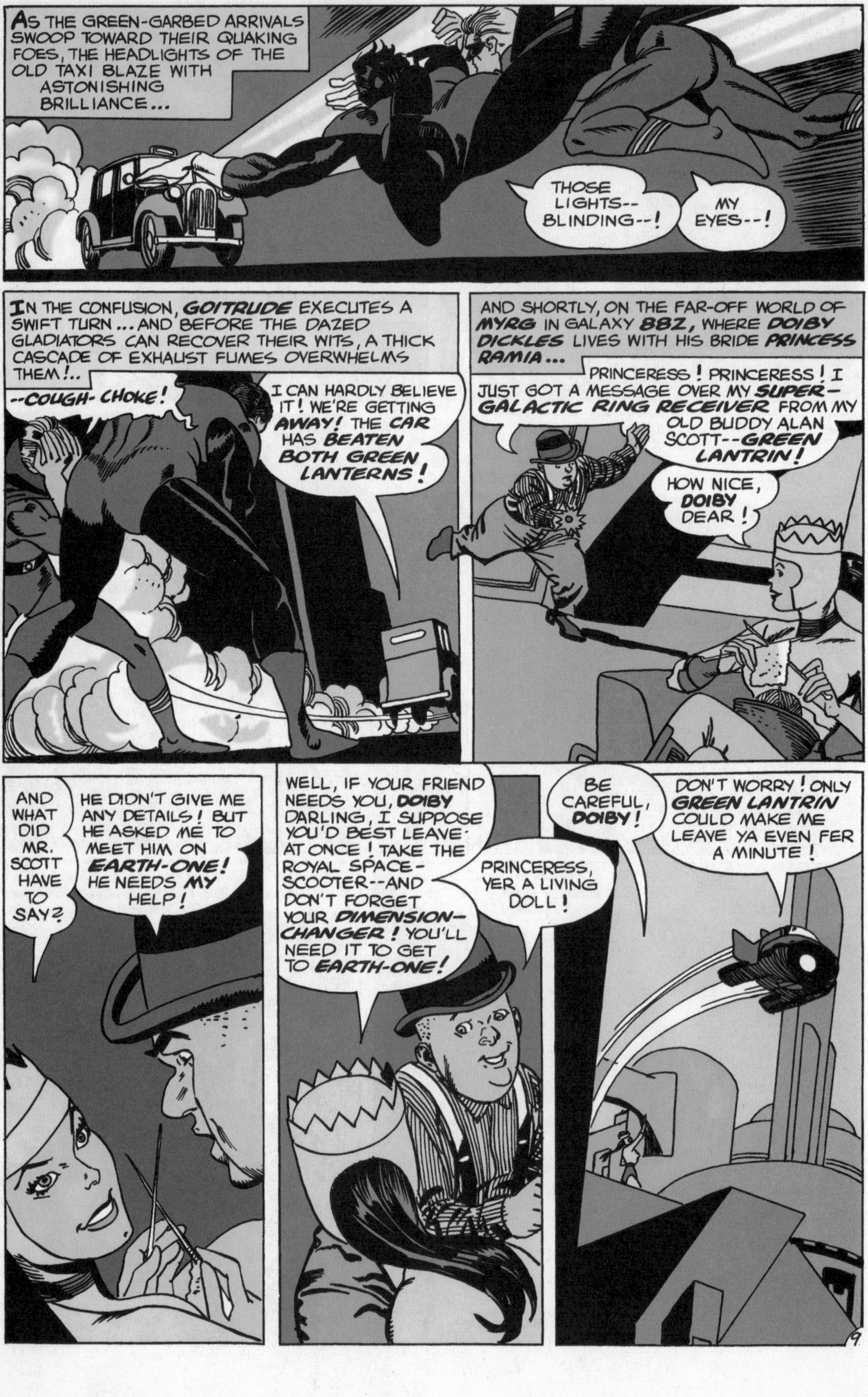
AS THE GREEN-GARBED ARRIVALS SWOOP TOWARD THEIR QUAKING FOES, THE HEADLIGHTS OF THE OLD TAXI BLAZE WITH ASTONISHING BRILLIANCE...
THOSE LIGHTS-- BLINDING--!
MY EYES--!
IN THE CONFUSION, GOITRUDE EXECUTES A SWIFT TURN ... AND BEFORE THE DAZED GLADIATORS CAN RECOVER THEIR WITS, A THICK CASCADE OF EXHAUST FUMES OVERWHELMS THEM!..
--COUGH- CHOKE!
I CAN HARDLY BELIEVE IT! WE'RE GETTING AWAY! THE CAR HAS BEATEN BOTH GREEN LANTERNS!
AND SHORTLY, ON THE FAR-OFF WORLD OF MYRG IN GALAXY 88Z, WHERE DOIBY DICKLES LIVES WITH HIS BRIDE PRINCESS RAMIA...
PRINCERESS! PRINCERESS! I JUST GOT A MESSAGE OVER MY SUPER-GALACTIC RING RECEIVER FROM MY OLD BUDDY ALAN SCOTT--GREEN LANTRIN!
HOW NICE, DOIBY DEAR!
AND WHAT DID MR. SCOTT HAVE TO SAY?
HE DIDN'T GIVE ME ANY DETAILS! BUT HE ASKED ME TO MEET HIM ON EARTH-ONE! HE NEEDS MY HELP!
WELL, IF YOUR FRIEND NEEDS YOU, DOIBY DARLING, I SUPPOSE YOU'D BEST LEAVE AT ONCE! TAKE THE ROYAL SPACE-SCOOTER--AND DON'T FORGET YOUR DIMENSION-CHANGER! YOU'LL NEED IT TO GET TO EARTH-ONE!
PRINCERESS, YER A LIVING DOLL!
BE CAREFUL, DOIBY!
DON'T WORRY! ONLY GREEN LANTRIN COULD MAKE ME LEAVE YA EVEN FER A MINUTE!
9

As the royal consort of **MYRG** settles down to his starry journey...

ALAN GAVE ME THIS RING IN CASE I NEEDED TO CONTACT **HIM**! WE DIDN'T REALIZE IT WOULD BE USED BECAUSE HE NEEDED **MY** HELP! AND THAT MAKES ME WONDER...

...WHAT COULD BE WRONG? **HOW** CAN **I** HELP **GREEN LANTRIN**? SURE SEEMS STRANGE FOR ME TO BE GOIN' TO **HIS** ASSISTANCE! BUT I'LL FIND OUT **SOON** WHAT'S UP! THIS ROYAL SCOOTER REALLY HIGH-TAILS ALONG!

On **EARTH-ONE** where an outshooting **GREEN BEAM** has guided the lone spaceman...

HERE HE COMES!

IT'S ALAN-- AND HAL-- **GREEN LANTRIN**!

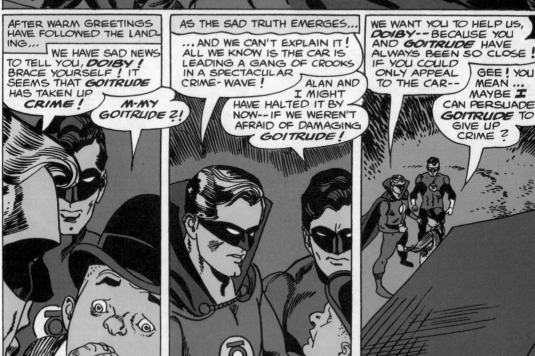

After warm greetings have followed the landing...

WE HAVE SAD NEWS TO TELL YOU, **DOIBY**! BRACE YOURSELF! IT SEEMS THAT **GOITRUDE** HAS TAKEN UP **CRIME**!

M-MY GOITRUDE?!

As the sad truth emerges...

...AND WE CAN'T EXPLAIN IT! ALL WE KNOW IS THE CAR IS LEADING A GANG OF CROOKS IN A SPECTACULAR CRIME-WAVE!

ALAN AND I MIGHT HAVE HALTED IT BY NOW-- IF WE WEREN'T AFRAID OF DAMAGING **GOITRUDE**!

WE WANT YOU TO HELP US, **DOIBY**-- BECAUSE YOU AND **GOITRUDE** HAVE ALWAYS BEEN SO CLOSE! IF YOU COULD ONLY APPEAL TO THE CAR--

GEE! YOU MEAN... MAYBE **I** CAN PERSUADE **GOITRUDE** TO GIVE UP CRIME?

10.

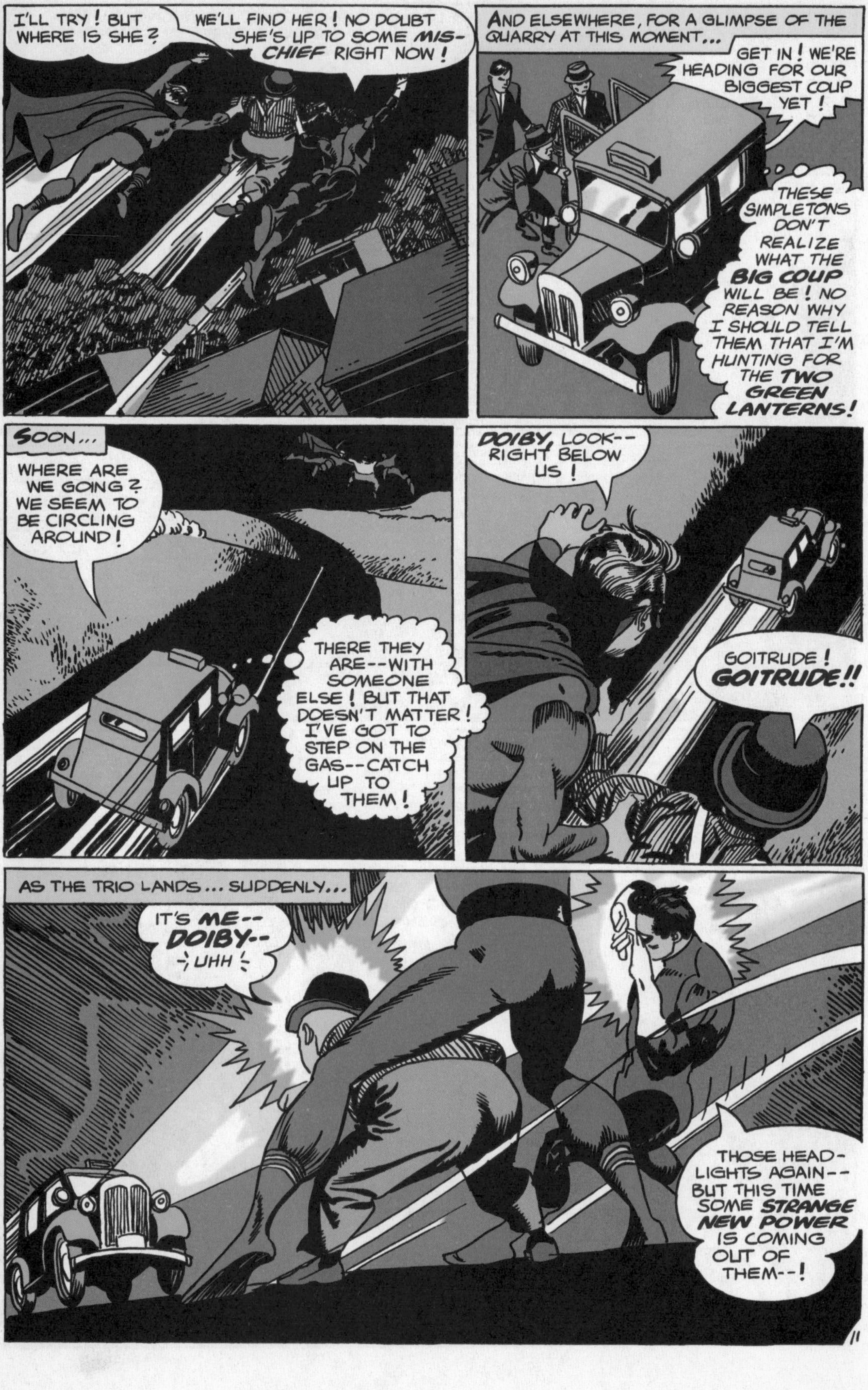
I'LL TRY! BUT WHERE IS SHE?
WE'LL FIND HER! NO DOUBT SHE'S UP TO SOME MIS-CHIEF RIGHT NOW!
AND ELSEWHERE, FOR A GLIMPSE OF THE QUARRY AT THIS MOMENT...
GET IN! WE'RE HEADING FOR OUR BIGGEST COUP YET!
THESE SIMPLETONS DON'T REALIZE WHAT THE BIG COUP WILL BE! NO REASON WHY I SHOULD TELL THEM THAT I'M HUNTING FOR THE TWO GREEN LANTERNS!
SOON...
WHERE ARE WE GOING? WE SEEM TO BE CIRCLING AROUND!
THERE THEY ARE--WITH SOMEONE ELSE! BUT THAT DOESN'T MATTER! I'VE GOT TO STEP ON THE GAS--CATCH UP TO THEM!
DOIBY, LOOK--RIGHT BELOW US!
GOITRUDE! GOITRUDE!!
AS THE TRIO LANDS... SUDDENLY...
IT'S ME--DOIBY-- -UHH-
THOSE HEAD-LIGHTS AGAIN--BUT THIS TIME SOME STRANGE NEW POWER IS COMING OUT OF THEM--!
11

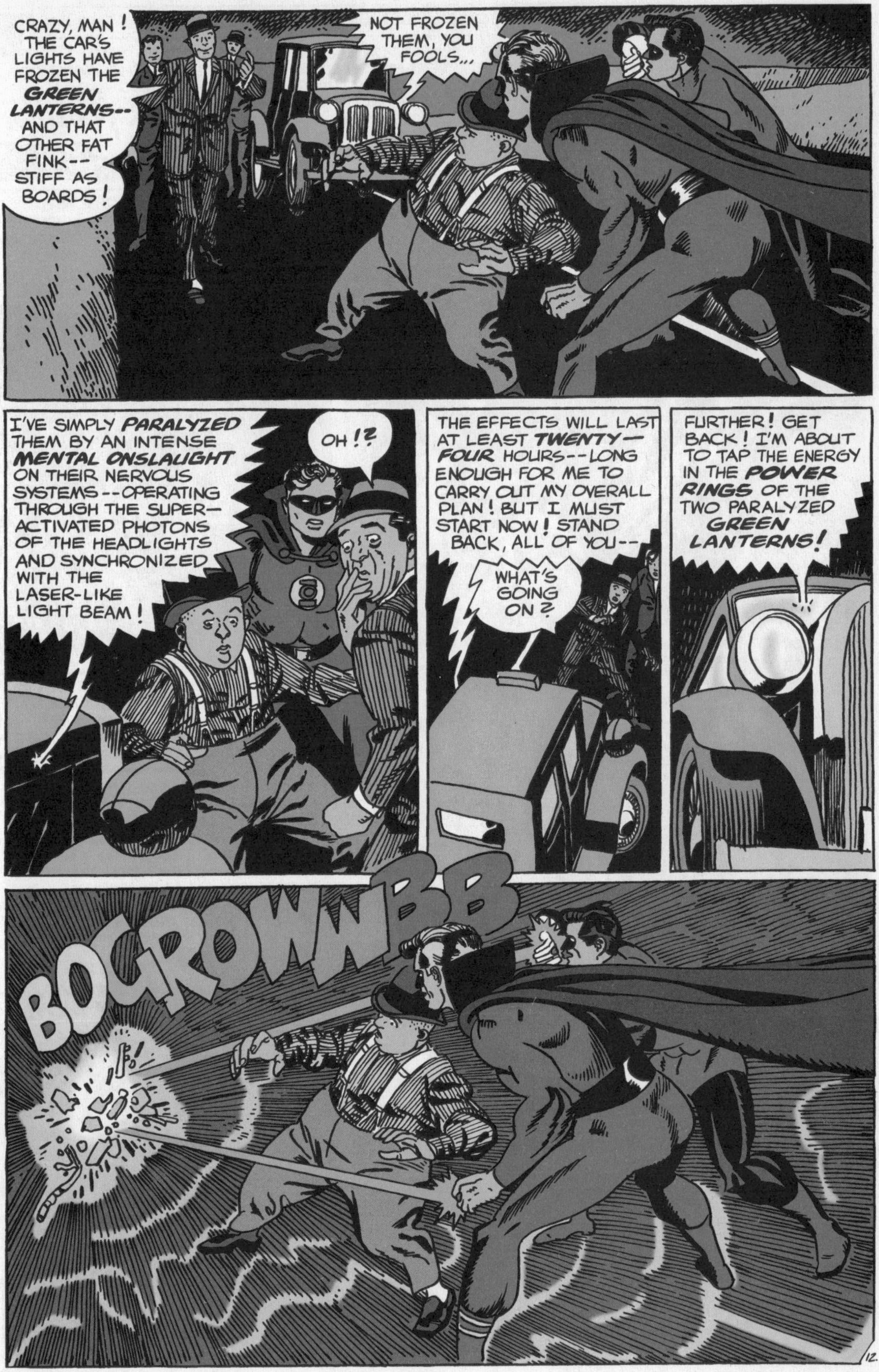
CRAZY, MAN! THE CAR'S LIGHTS HAVE FROZEN THE GREEN LANTERNS-- AND THAT OTHER FAT FINK-- STIFF AS BOARDS!
NOT FROZEN THEM, YOU FOOLS...
I'VE SIMPLY PARALYZED THEM BY AN INTENSE MENTAL ONSLAUGHT ON THEIR NERVOUS SYSTEMS--OPERATING THROUGH THE SUPER-ACTIVATED PHOTONS OF THE HEADLIGHTS AND SYNCHRONIZED WITH THE LASER-LIKE LIGHT BEAM!
OH!?
THE EFFECTS WILL LAST AT LEAST TWENTY-FOUR HOURS--LONG ENOUGH FOR ME TO CARRY OUT MY OVERALL PLAN! BUT I MUST START NOW! STAND BACK, ALL OF YOU--
WHAT'S GOING ON?
FURTHER! GET BACK! I'M ABOUT TO TAP THE ENERGY IN THE POWER RINGS OF THE TWO PARALYZED GREEN LANTERNS!
BOGROWWBB
12.

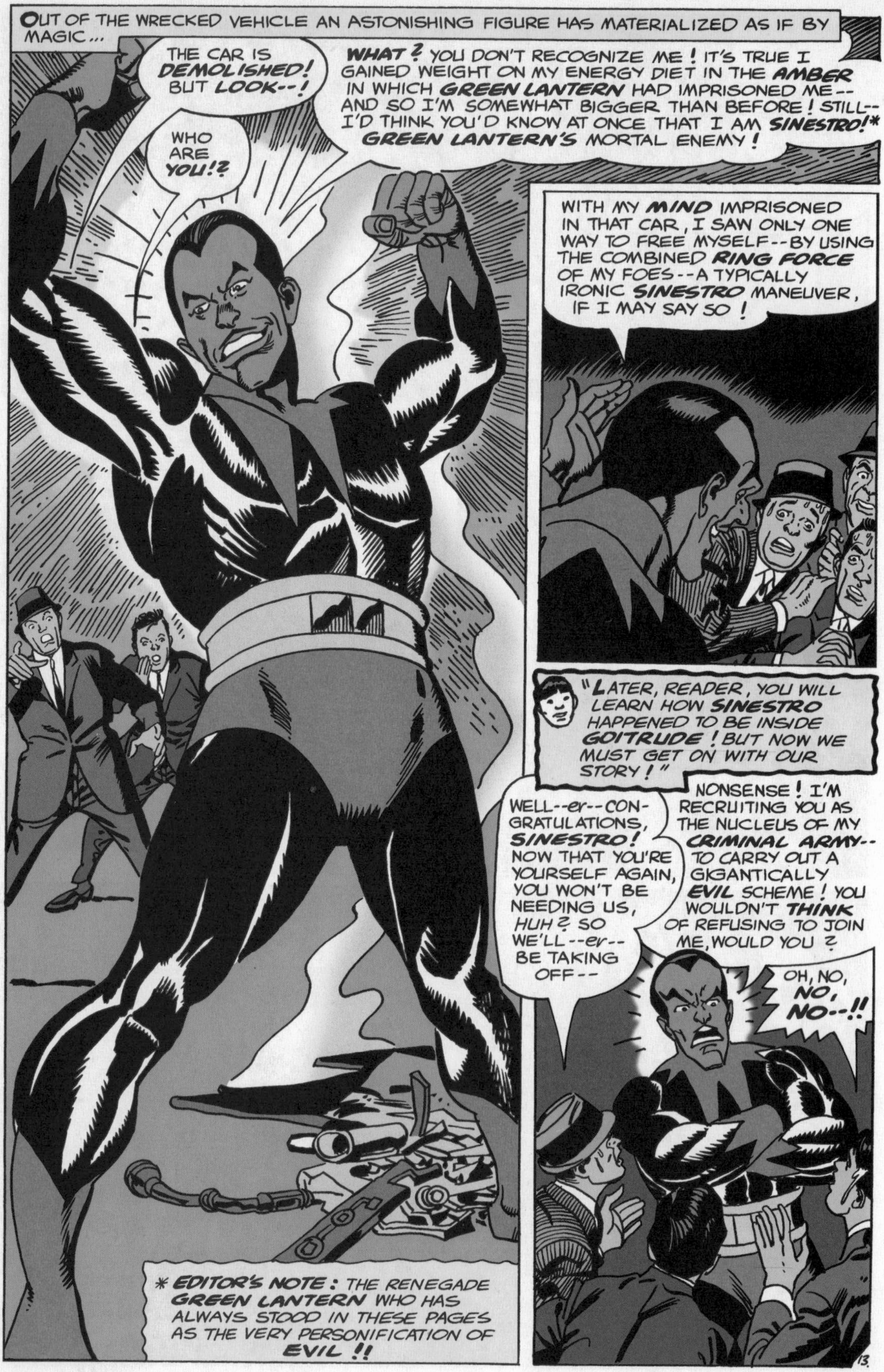
OUT OF THE WRECKED VEHICLE AN ASTONISHING FIGURE HAS MATERIALIZED AS IF BY MAGIC...
THE CAR IS DEMOLISHED! BUT LOOK--!
WHO ARE YOU!?
WHAT? YOU DON'T RECOGNIZE ME! IT'S TRUE I GAINED WEIGHT ON MY ENERGY DIET IN THE AMBER IN WHICH GREEN LANTERN HAD IMPRISONED ME-- AND SO I'M SOMEWHAT BIGGER THAN BEFORE! STILL-- I'D THINK YOU'D KNOW AT ONCE THAT I AM SINESTRO!* GREEN LANTERN'S MORTAL ENEMY!
* EDITOR'S NOTE: THE RENEGADE GREEN LANTERN WHO HAS ALWAYS STOOD IN THESE PAGES AS THE VERY PERSONIFICATION OF EVIL!!
WITH MY MIND IMPRISONED IN THAT CAR, I SAW ONLY ONE WAY TO FREE MYSELF--BY USING THE COMBINED RING FORCE OF MY FOES--A TYPICALLY IRONIC SINESTRO MANEUVER, IF I MAY SAY SO!
"LATER, READER, YOU WILL LEARN HOW SINESTRO HAPPENED TO BE INSIDE GOITRUDE! BUT NOW WE MUST GET ON WITH OUR STORY!"
WELL--er--CONGRATULATIONS, SINESTRO! NOW THAT YOU'RE YOURSELF AGAIN, YOU WON'T BE NEEDING US, HUH? SO WE'LL--er--BE TAKING OFF--
NONSENSE! I'M RECRUITING YOU AS THE NUCLEUS OF MY CRIMINAL ARMY-- TO CARRY OUT A GIGANTICALLY EVIL SCHEME! YOU WOULDN'T THINK OF REFUSING TO JOIN ME, WOULD YOU?
OH, NO, NO, NO--!!
13.

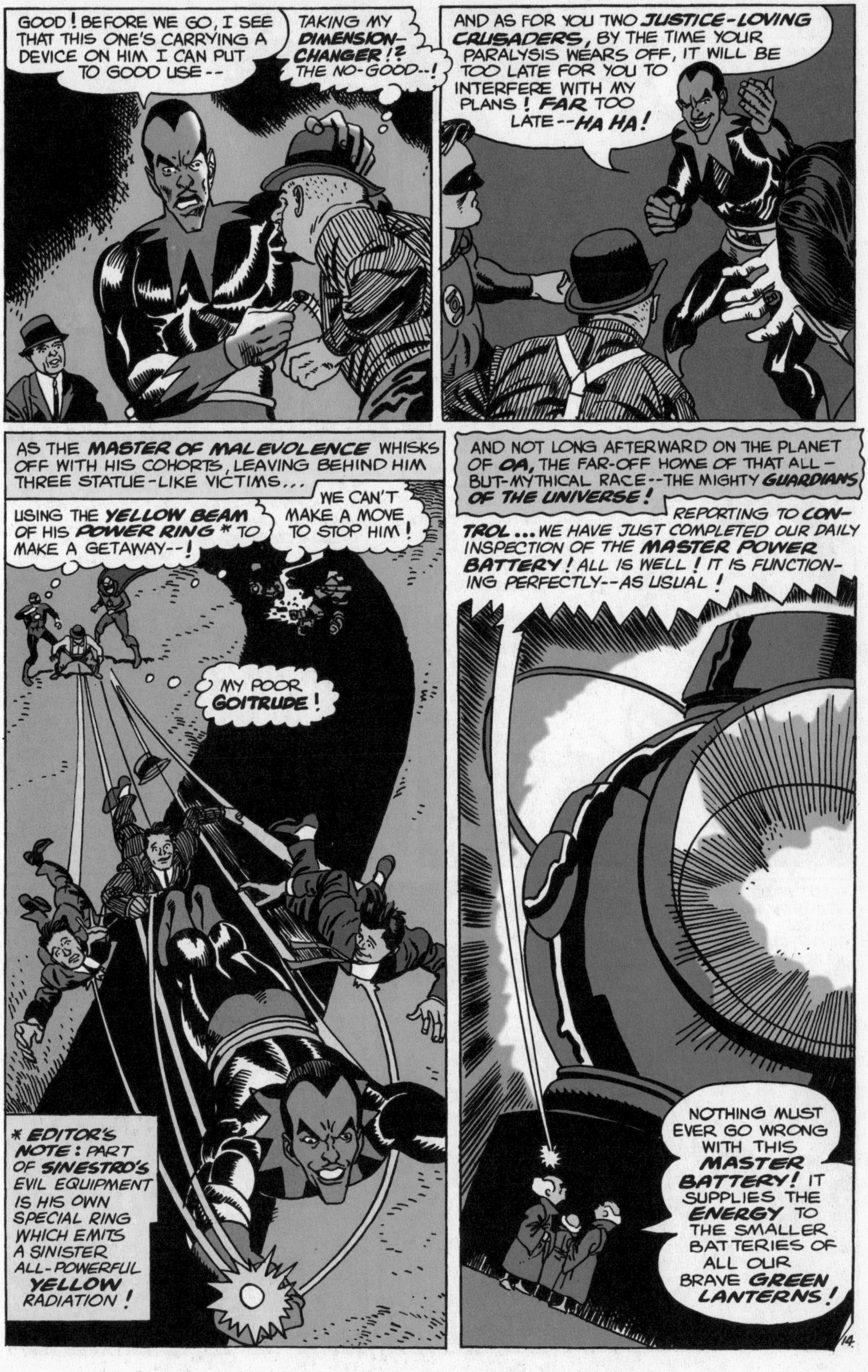
GOOD! BEFORE WE GO, I SEE THAT THIS ONE'S CARRYING A DEVICE ON HIM I CAN PUT TO GOOD USE--
TAKING MY DIMENSION-CHANGER!? THE NO-GOOD--!
AND AS FOR YOU TWO JUSTICE-LOVING CRUSADERS, BY THE TIME YOUR PARALYSIS WEARS OFF, IT WILL BE TOO LATE FOR YOU TO INTERFERE WITH MY PLANS! FAR TOO LATE--HA HA!
AS THE MASTER OF MALEVOLENCE WHISKS OFF WITH HIS COHORTS, LEAVING BEHIND HIM THREE STATUE-LIKE VICTIMS...
USING THE YELLOW BEAM OF HIS POWER RING * TO MAKE A GETAWAY--!
WE CAN'T MAKE A MOVE TO STOP HIM!
MY POOR GOITRUDE!
* EDITOR'S NOTE: PART OF SINESTRO'S EVIL EQUIPMENT IS HIS OWN SPECIAL RING WHICH EMITS A SINISTER ALL-POWERFUL YELLOW RADIATION!
AND NOT LONG AFTERWARD ON THE PLANET OF OA, THE FAR-OFF HOME OF THAT ALL-BUT-MYTHICAL RACE--THE MIGHTY GUARDIANS OF THE UNIVERSE!
REPORTING TO CONTROL... WE HAVE JUST COMPLETED OUR DAILY INSPECTION OF THE MASTER POWER BATTERY! ALL IS WELL! IT IS FUNCTIONING PERFECTLY--AS USUAL!
NOTHING MUST EVER GO WRONG WITH THIS MASTER BATTERY! IT SUPPLIES THE ENERGY TO THE SMALLER BATTERIES OF ALL OUR BRAVE GREEN LANTERNS!
14.

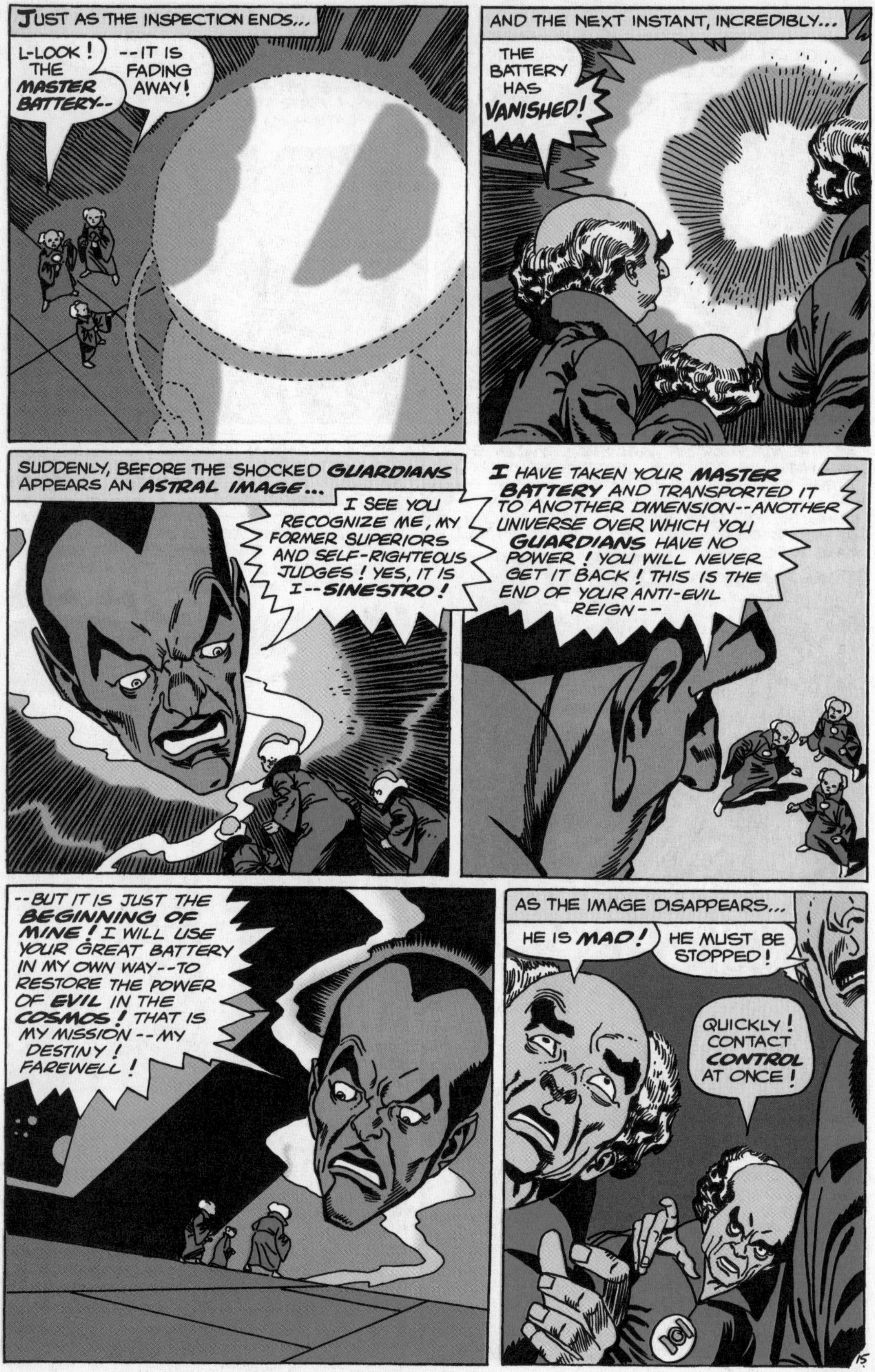
JUST AS THE INSPECTION ENDS...
L-LOOK! THE MASTER BATTERY--
--IT IS FADING AWAY!
AND THE NEXT INSTANT, INCREDIBLY...
THE BATTERY HAS VANISHED!
SUDDENLY, BEFORE THE SHOCKED GUARDIANS APPEARS AN ASTRAL IMAGE...
I SEE YOU RECOGNIZE ME, MY FORMER SUPERIORS AND SELF-RIGHTEOUS JUDGES! YES, IT IS I--SINESTRO!
I HAVE TAKEN YOUR MASTER BATTERY AND TRANSPORTED IT TO ANOTHER DIMENSION--ANOTHER UNIVERSE OVER WHICH YOU GUARDIANS HAVE NO POWER! YOU WILL NEVER GET IT BACK! THIS IS THE END OF YOUR ANTI-EVIL REIGN--
--BUT IT IS JUST THE BEGINNING OF MINE! I WILL USE YOUR GREAT BATTERY IN MY OWN WAY--TO RESTORE THE POWER OF EVIL IN THE COSMOS! THAT IS MY MISSION--MY DESTINY! FAREWELL!
AS THE IMAGE DISAPPEARS...
HE IS MAD!
HE MUST BE STOPPED!
QUICKLY! CONTACT CONTROL AT ONCE!
15

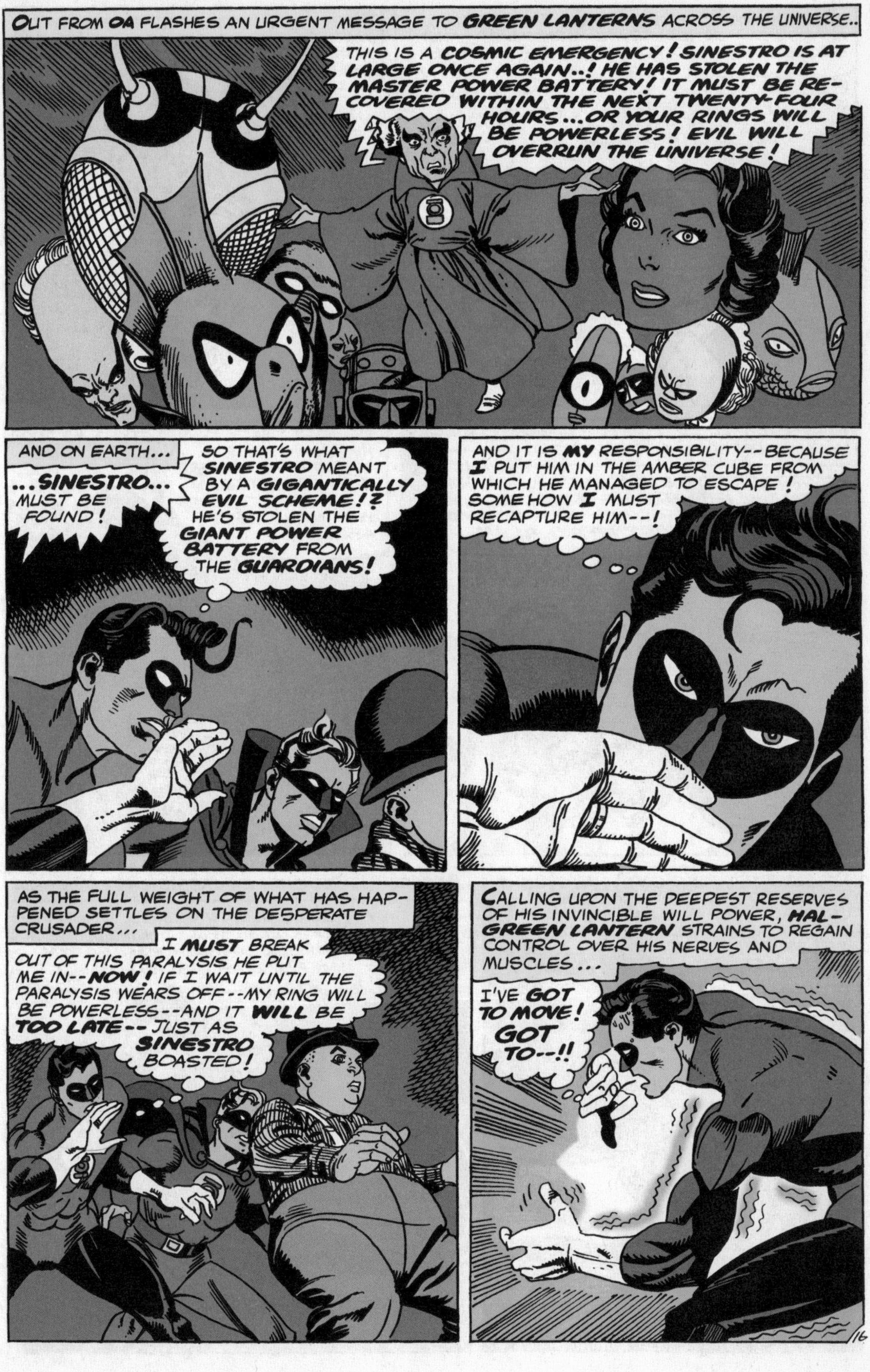

OUT FROM OA FLASHES AN URGENT MESSAGE TO GREEN LANTERNS ACROSS THE UNIVERSE..
THIS IS A COSMIC EMERGENCY! SINESTRO IS AT LARGE ONCE AGAIN..! HE HAS STOLEN THE MASTER POWER BATTERY! IT MUST BE RECOVERED WITHIN THE NEXT TWENTY-FOUR HOURS...OR YOUR RINGS WILL BE POWERLESS! EVIL WILL OVERRUN THE UNIVERSE!
AND ON EARTH...
...SINESTRO... MUST BE FOUND!
SO THAT'S WHAT SINESTRO MEANT BY A GIGANTICALLY EVIL SCHEME!? HE'S STOLEN THE GIANT POWER BATTERY FROM THE GUARDIANS!
AND IT IS MY RESPONSIBILITY--BECAUSE I PUT HIM IN THE AMBER CUBE FROM WHICH HE MANAGED TO ESCAPE! SOMEHOW I MUST RECAPTURE HIM--!
AS THE FULL WEIGHT OF WHAT HAS HAPPENED SETTLES ON THE DESPERATE CRUSADER...
I MUST BREAK OUT OF THIS PARALYSIS HE PUT ME IN--NOW! IF I WAIT UNTIL THE PARALYSIS WEARS OFF--MY RING WILL BE POWERLESS--AND IT WILL BE TOO LATE--JUST AS SINESTRO BOASTED!
CALLING UPON THE DEEPEST RESERVES OF HIS INVINCIBLE WILL POWER, HAL-GREEN LANTERN STRAINS TO REGAIN CONTROL OVER HIS NERVES AND MUSCLES...
I'VE GOT TO MOVE! GOT TO--!!
16

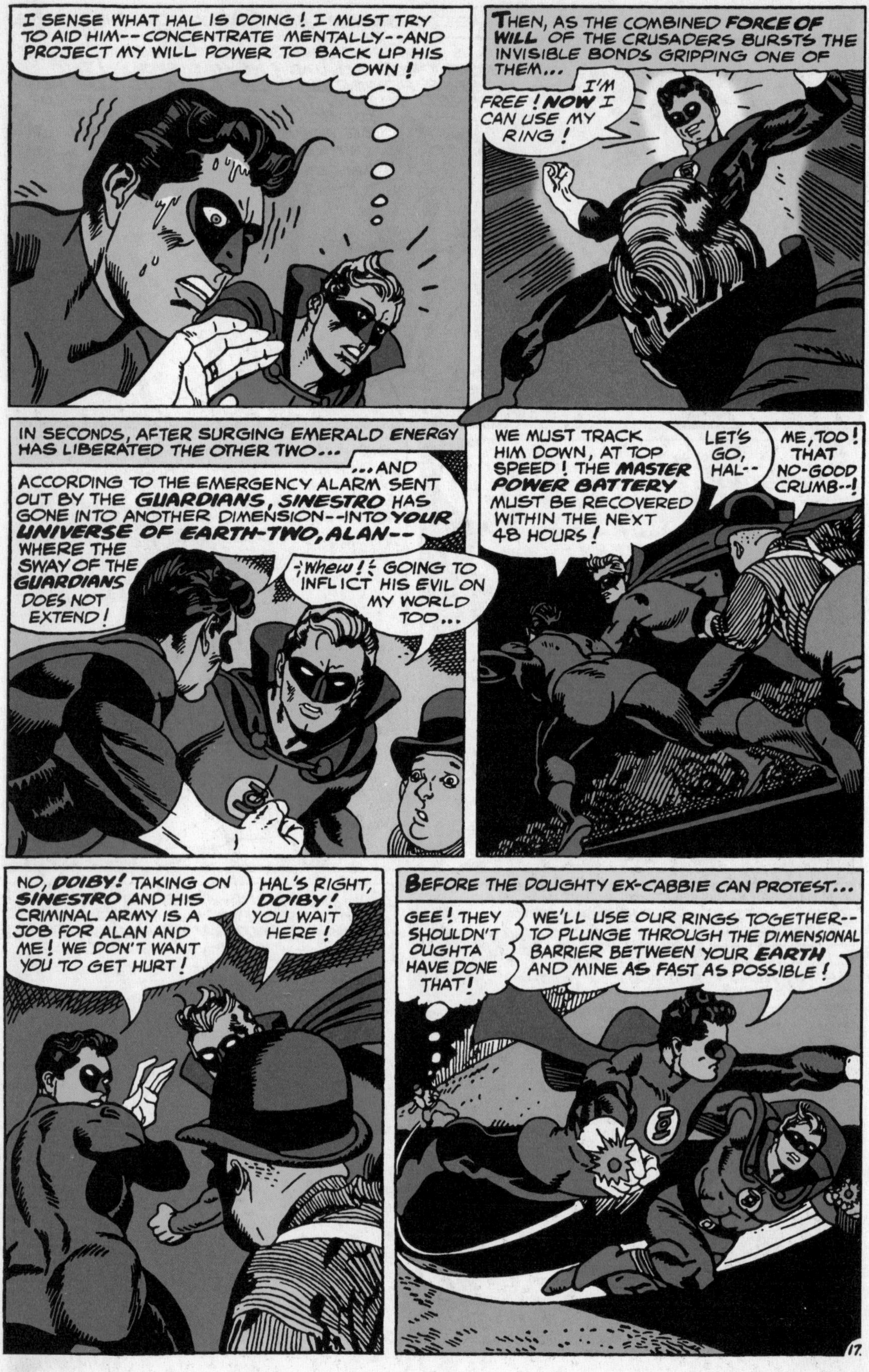
I SENSE WHAT HAL IS DOING! I MUST TRY TO AID HIM--CONCENTRATE MENTALLY--AND PROJECT MY WILL POWER TO BACK UP HIS OWN!
THEN, AS THE COMBINED FORCE OF WILL OF THE CRUSADERS BURSTS THE INVISIBLE BONDS GRIPPING ONE OF THEM...
I'M FREE! NOW I CAN USE MY RING!
IN SECONDS, AFTER SURGING EMERALD ENERGY HAS LIBERATED THE OTHER TWO...
...AND ACCORDING TO THE EMERGENCY ALARM SENT OUT BY THE GUARDIANS, SINESTRO HAS GONE INTO ANOTHER DIMENSION--INTO YOUR UNIVERSE OF EARTH-TWO, ALAN--WHERE THE SWAY OF THE GUARDIANS DOES NOT EXTEND!
Whew! GOING TO INFLICT HIS EVIL ON MY WORLD TOO...
WE MUST TRACK HIM DOWN, AT TOP SPEED! THE MASTER POWER BATTERY MUST BE RECOVERED WITHIN THE NEXT 48 HOURS!
LET'S GO, HAL--
ME, TOO! THAT NO-GOOD CRUMB--!
NO, DOIBY! TAKING ON SINESTRO AND HIS CRIMINAL ARMY IS A JOB FOR ALAN AND ME! WE DON'T WANT YOU TO GET HURT!
HAL'S RIGHT, DOIBY! YOU WAIT HERE!
BEFORE THE DOUGHTY EX-CABBIE CAN PROTEST...
GEE! THEY SHOULDN'T OUGHTA HAVE DONE THAT!
WE'LL USE OUR RINGS TOGETHER--TO PLUNGE THROUGH THE DIMENSIONAL BARRIER BETWEEN YOUR EARTH AND MINE AS FAST AS POSSIBLE!
17.

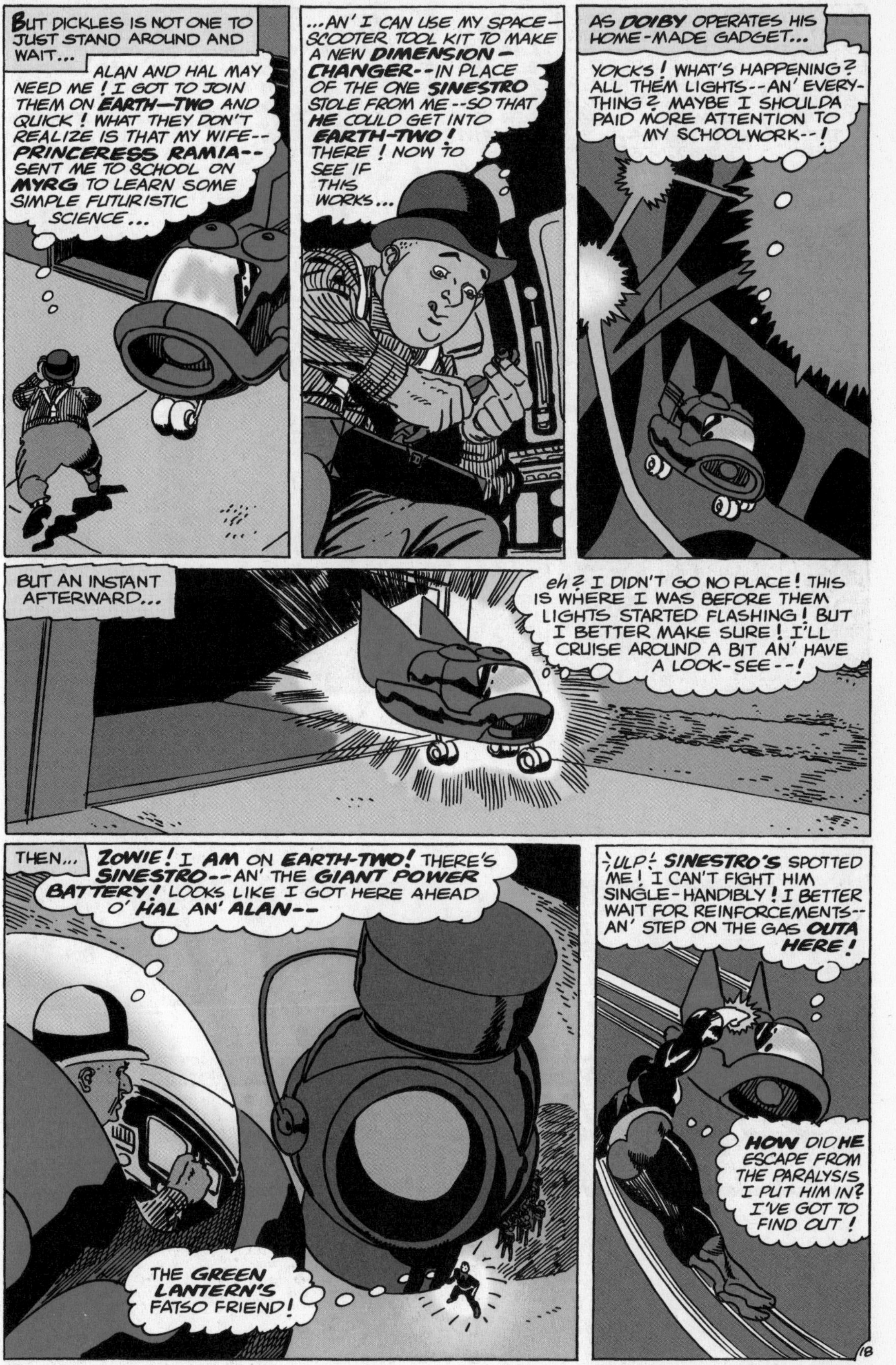
BUT DICKLES IS NOT ONE TO JUST STAND AROUND AND WAIT...
ALAN AND HAL MAY NEED ME! I GOT TO JOIN THEM ON EARTH-TWO AND QUICK! WHAT THEY DON'T REALIZE IS THAT MY WIFE-- PRINCERESS RAMIA-- SENT ME TO SCHOOL ON MYRG TO LEARN SOME SIMPLE FUTURISTIC SCIENCE...
...AN' I CAN USE MY SPACE-SCOOTER TOOL KIT TO MAKE A NEW DIMENSION-CHANGER--IN PLACE OF THE ONE SINESTRO STOLE FROM ME--SO THAT HE COULD GET INTO EARTH-TWO! THERE! NOW TO SEE IF THIS WORKS...
AS DOIBY OPERATES HIS HOME-MADE GADGET...
YOICKS! WHAT'S HAPPENING? ALL THEM LIGHTS--AN' EVERYTHING? MAYBE I SHOULDA PAID MORE ATTENTION TO MY SCHOOLWORK--!
BUT AN INSTANT AFTERWARD...
eh? I DIDN'T GO NO PLACE! THIS IS WHERE I WAS BEFORE THEM LIGHTS STARTED FLASHING! BUT I BETTER MAKE SURE! I'LL CRUISE AROUND A BIT AN' HAVE A LOOK-SEE--!
THEN...
ZOWIE! I AM ON EARTH-TWO! THERE'S SINESTRO--AN' THE GIANT POWER BATTERY! LOOKS LIKE I GOT HERE AHEAD O' HAL AN' ALAN--
THE GREEN LANTERN'S FATSO FRIEND!
ULP! SINESTRO'S SPOTTED ME! I CAN'T FIGHT HIM SINGLE-HANDIBLY! I BETTER WAIT FOR REINFORCEMENTS-- AN' STEP ON THE GAS OUTA HERE!
HOW DID HE ESCAPE FROM THE PARALYSIS I PUT HIM IN? I'VE GOT TO FIND OUT!
18

AND AS DOIBY WHISKS OFF, PURSUED BY THE AROUSED MASTER OF MALEVOLENCE ...
WE'VE BROKEN THROUGH THE DIMENSIONAL BARRIER, HAL!
RIGHT ON TARGET! THERE'S THE MASTER POWER BATTERY-- SURROUNDED BY SINESTRO'S MINIONS!
THE TWO GREEN LANTERNS!? BUT WE HAVE POWER RINGS NOW--MADE FOR US BY SINESTRO USING THE MASTER POWER BATTERY! AT THEM, ALL YOU EVIL GREEN LANTERNS!
EVIL GREEN LANTERNS?
THERE'S ONE STILL CHARGING HIS RING--!
IN BRIGHTEST DAY, IN BLACKEST NIGHT, NO JUSTICE SHALL ESCAPE MY SIGHT! LET THOSE WHO WORSHIP JUSTICE'S MIGHT-- BEWARE MY POWER-- EVIL GREEN LANTERN'S LIGHT!
19

CRISIS ON MULTIPLE EARTHS
THE TEAM UPS

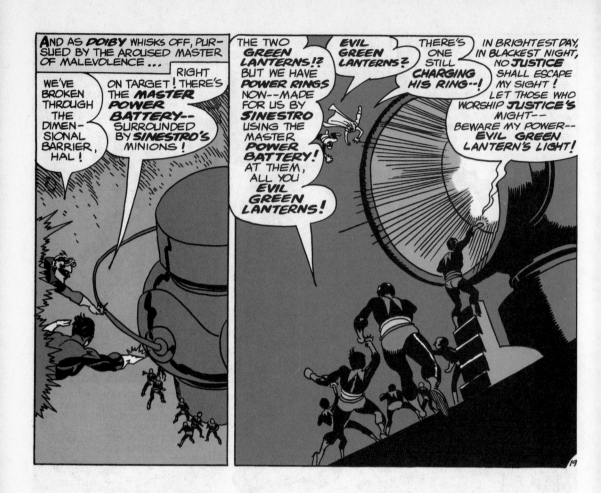

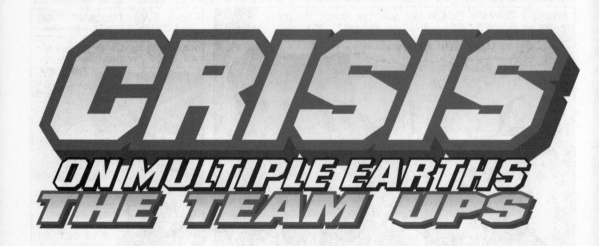

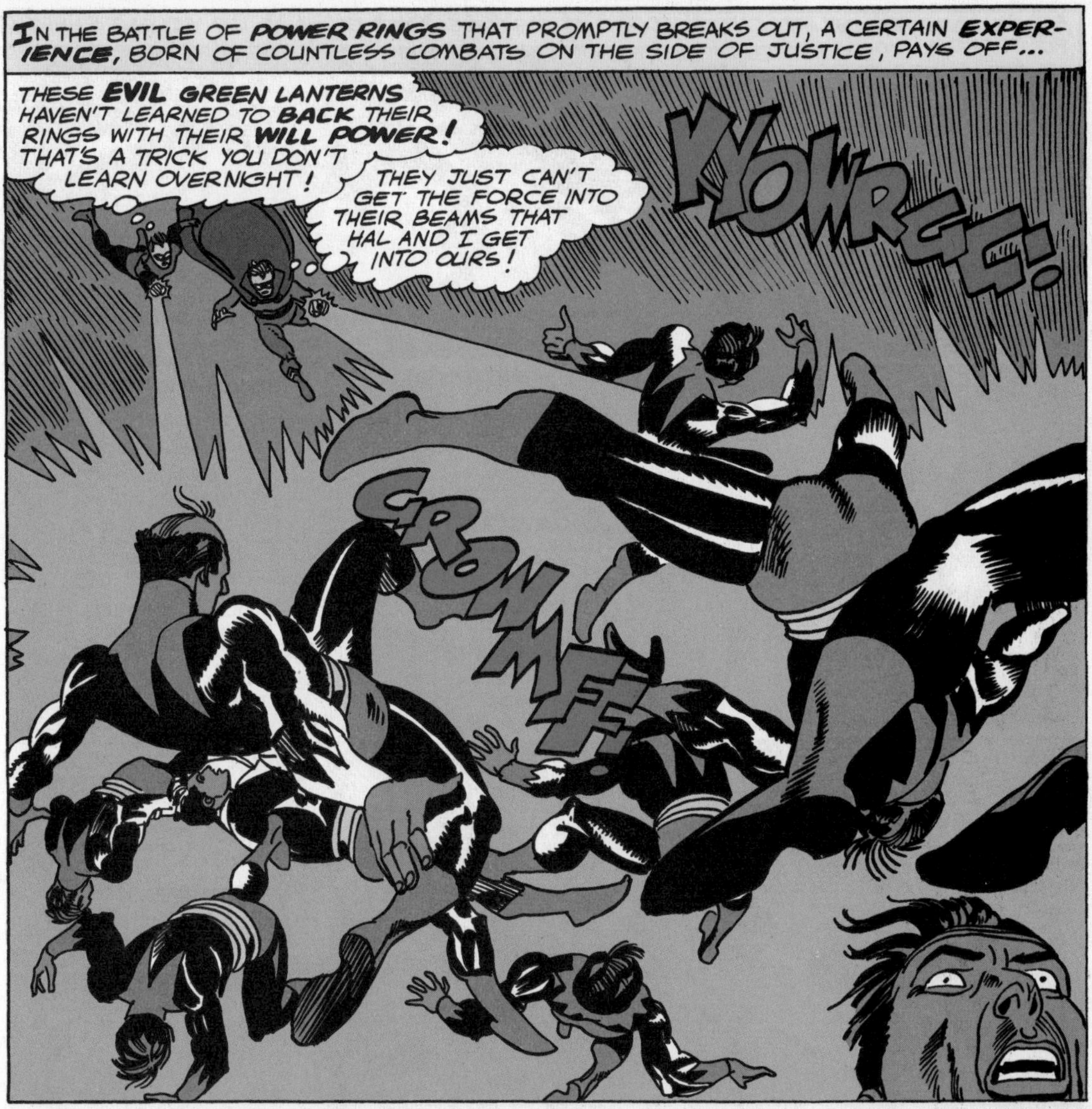
IN THE BATTLE OF POWER RINGS THAT PROMPTLY BREAKS OUT, A CERTAIN EXPERIENCE, BORN OF COUNTLESS COMBATS ON THE SIDE OF JUSTICE, PAYS OFF...
THESE EVIL GREEN LANTERNS HAVEN'T LEARNED TO BACK THEIR RINGS WITH THEIR WILL POWER! THAT'S A TRICK YOU DON'T LEARN OVERNIGHT!
THEY JUST CAN'T GET THE FORCE INTO THEIR BEAMS THAT HAL AND I GET INTO OURS!
KYOWRGG!
CROMMFF!

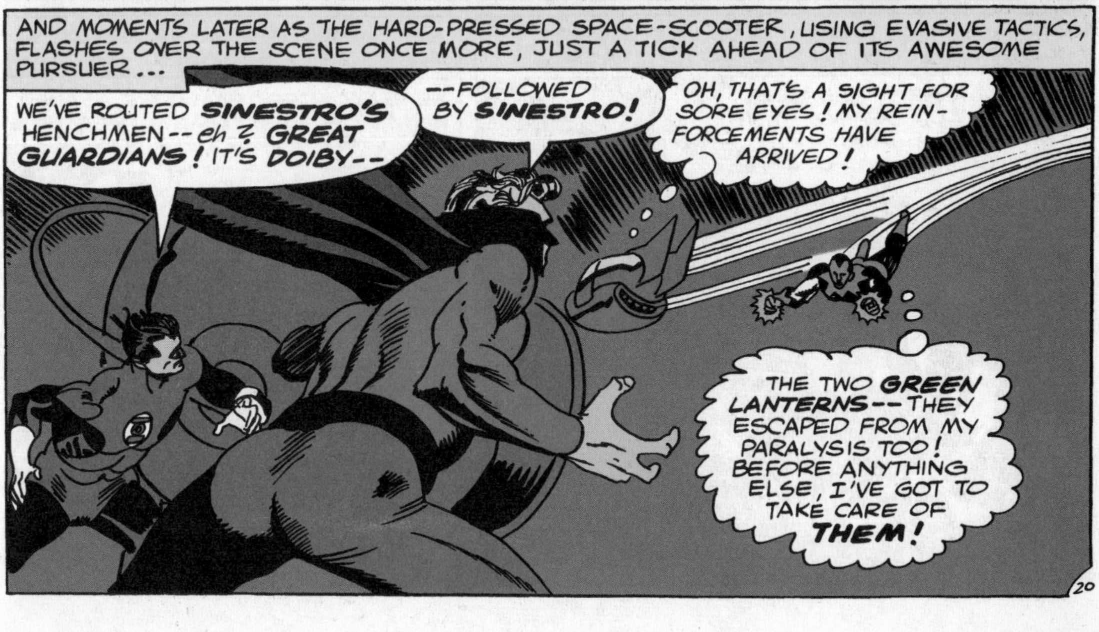
AND MOMENTS LATER AS THE HARD-PRESSED SPACE-SCOOTER, USING EVASIVE TACTICS, FLASHES OVER THE SCENE ONCE MORE, JUST A TICK AHEAD OF ITS AWESOME PURSUER...
WE'VE ROUTED SINESTRO'S HENCHMEN-- eh ? GREAT GUARDIANS! IT'S DOIBY--
--FOLLOWED BY SINESTRO!
OH, THAT'S A SIGHT FOR SORE EYES! MY REINFORCEMENTS HAVE ARRIVED!
THE TWO GREEN LANTERNS--THEY ESCAPED FROM MY PARALYSIS TOO! BEFORE ANYTHING ELSE, I'VE GOT TO TAKE CARE OF THEM!
20

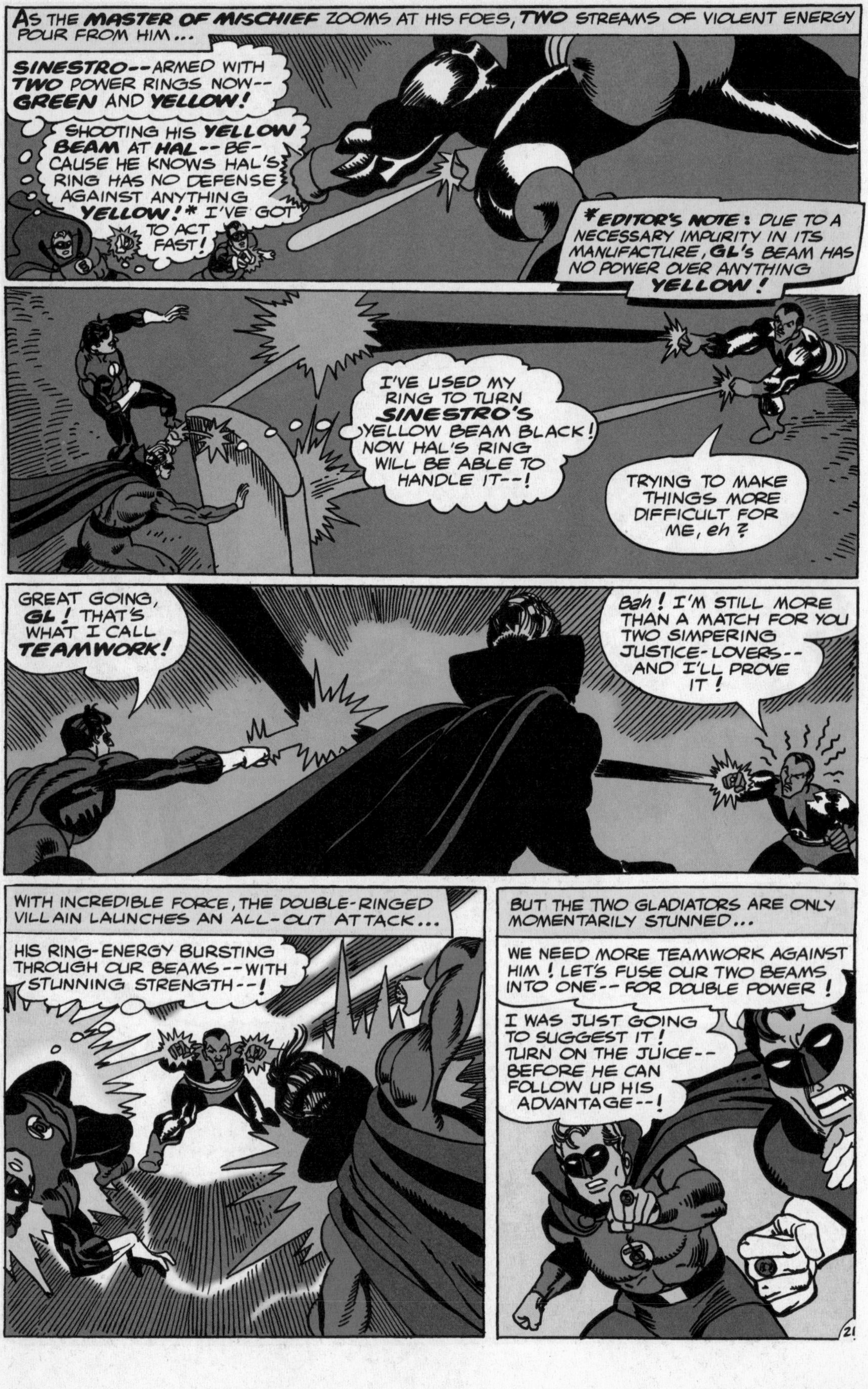

AS THE MASTER OF MISCHIEF ZOOMS AT HIS FOES, TWO STREAMS OF VIOLENT ENERGY POUR FROM HIM...
SINESTRO--ARMED WITH TWO POWER RINGS NOW--GREEN AND YELLOW!
SHOOTING HIS YELLOW BEAM AT HAL--BECAUSE HE KNOWS HAL'S RING HAS NO DEFENSE AGAINST ANYTHING YELLOW!* I'VE GOT TO ACT FAST!
*EDITOR'S NOTE: DUE TO A NECESSARY IMPURITY IN ITS MANUFACTURE, GL'S BEAM HAS NO POWER OVER ANYTHING YELLOW!
I'VE USED MY RING TO TURN SINESTRO'S YELLOW BEAM BLACK! NOW HAL'S RING WILL BE ABLE TO HANDLE IT--!
TRYING TO MAKE THINGS MORE DIFFICULT FOR ME, eh?
GREAT GOING, GL! THAT'S WHAT I CALL TEAMWORK!
Bah! I'M STILL MORE THAN A MATCH FOR YOU TWO SIMPERING JUSTICE-LOVERS--AND I'LL PROVE IT!
WITH INCREDIBLE FORCE, THE DOUBLE-RINGED VILLAIN LAUNCHES AN ALL-OUT ATTACK...
HIS RING-ENERGY BURSTING THROUGH OUR BEAMS--WITH STUNNING STRENGTH--!
BUT THE TWO GLADIATORS ARE ONLY MOMENTARILY STUNNED...
WE NEED MORE TEAMWORK AGAINST HIM! LET'S FUSE OUR TWO BEAMS INTO ONE--FOR DOUBLE POWER!
I WAS JUST GOING TO SUGGEST IT! TURN ON THE JUICE--BEFORE HE CAN FOLLOW UP HIS ADVANTAGE--!
21

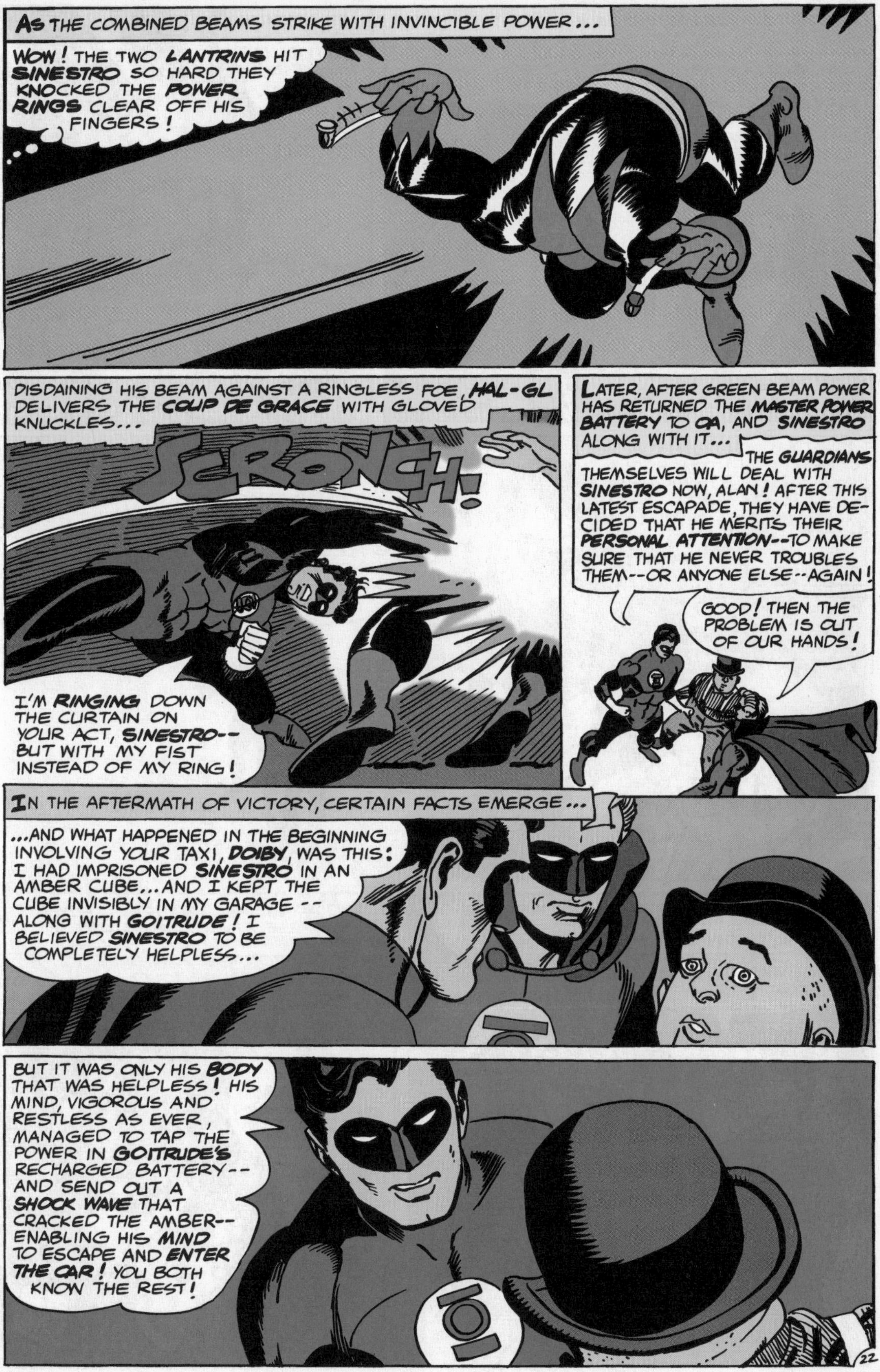
AS THE COMBINED BEAMS STRIKE WITH INVINCIBLE POWER...
WOW! THE TWO LANTRINS HIT SINESTRO SO HARD THEY KNOCKED THE POWER RINGS CLEAR OFF HIS FINGERS!
DISDAINING HIS BEAM AGAINST A RINGLESS FOE, HAL-GL DELIVERS THE COUP DE GRACE WITH GLOVED KNUCKLES...
SCRONCH!
I'M RINGING DOWN THE CURTAIN ON YOUR ACT, SINESTRO-- BUT WITH MY FIST INSTEAD OF MY RING!
LATER, AFTER GREEN BEAM POWER HAS RETURNED THE MASTER POWER BATTERY TO OA, AND SINESTRO ALONG WITH IT...
THE GUARDIANS THEMSELVES WILL DEAL WITH SINESTRO NOW, ALAN! AFTER THIS LATEST ESCAPADE, THEY HAVE DECIDED THAT HE MERITS THEIR PERSONAL ATTENTION--TO MAKE SURE THAT HE NEVER TROUBLES THEM--OR ANYONE ELSE--AGAIN!
GOOD! THEN THE PROBLEM IS OUT OF OUR HANDS!
IN THE AFTERMATH OF VICTORY, CERTAIN FACTS EMERGE...
...AND WHAT HAPPENED IN THE BEGINNING INVOLVING YOUR TAXI, DOIBY, WAS THIS: I HAD IMPRISONED SINESTRO IN AN AMBER CUBE...AND I KEPT THE CUBE INVISIBLY IN MY GARAGE -- ALONG WITH GOITRUDE! I BELIEVED SINESTRO TO BE COMPLETELY HELPLESS...
BUT IT WAS ONLY HIS BODY THAT WAS HELPLESS! HIS MIND, VIGOROUS AND RESTLESS AS EVER, MANAGED TO TAP THE POWER IN GOITRUDE'S RECHARGED BATTERY-- AND SEND OUT A SHOCK WAVE THAT CRACKED THE AMBER-- ENABLING HIS MIND TO ESCAPE AND ENTER THE CAR! YOU BOTH KNOW THE REST!
22

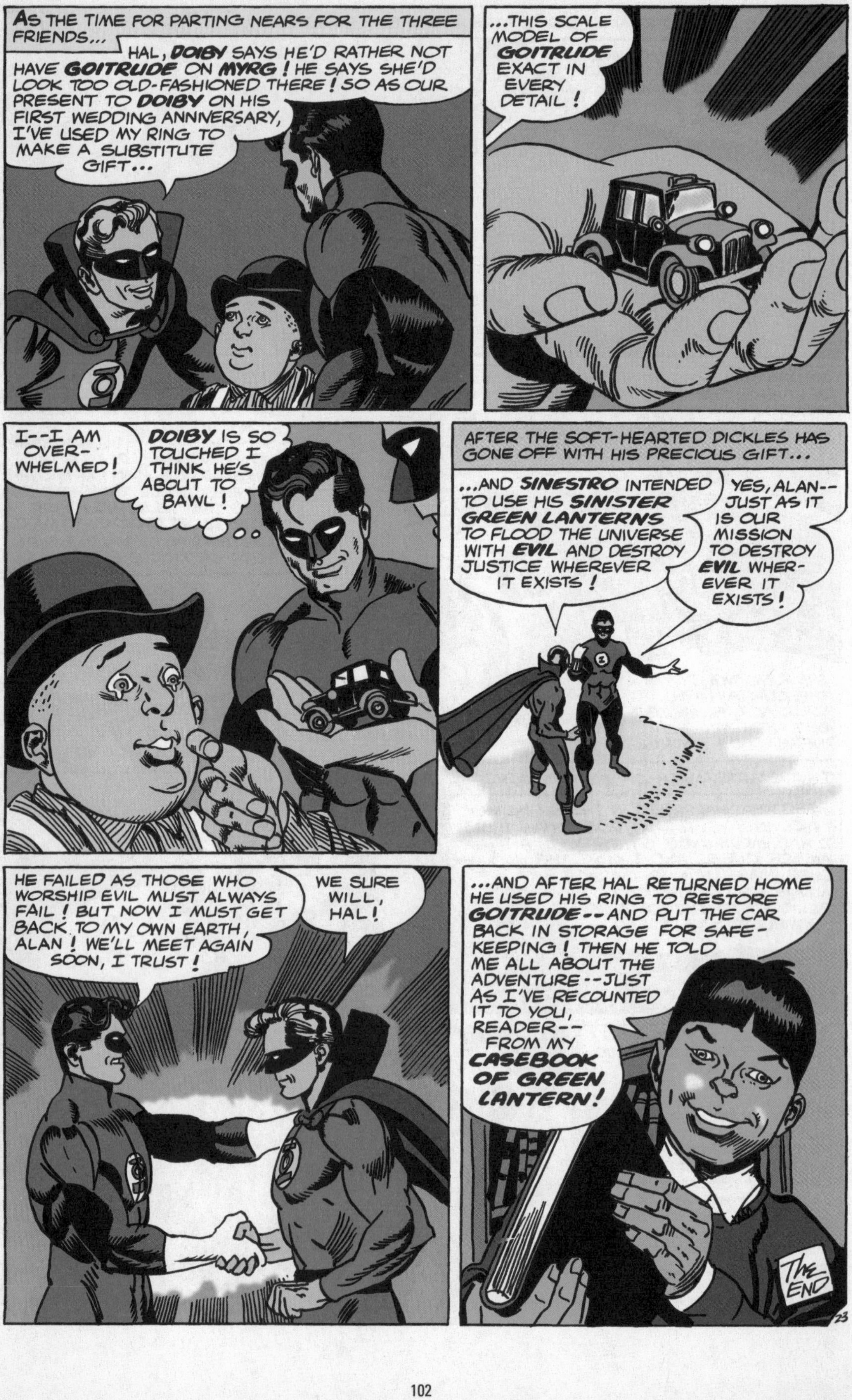
AS THE TIME FOR PARTING NEARS FOR THE THREE FRIENDS,...
HAL, DOIBY SAYS HE'D RATHER NOT HAVE GOITRUDE ON MYRG! HE SAYS SHE'D LOOK TOO OLD-FASHIONED THERE! SO AS OUR PRESENT TO DOIBY ON HIS FIRST WEDDING ANNIVERSARY, I'VE USED MY RING TO MAKE A SUBSTITUTE GIFT...
...THIS SCALE MODEL OF GOITRUDE EXACT IN EVERY DETAIL!
I--I AM OVER-WHELMED!
DOIBY IS SO TOUCHED I THINK HE'S ABOUT TO BAWL!
AFTER THE SOFT-HEARTED DICKLES HAS GONE OFF WITH HIS PRECIOUS GIFT...
...AND SINESTRO INTENDED TO USE HIS SINISTER GREEN LANTERNS TO FLOOD THE UNIVERSE WITH EVIL AND DESTROY JUSTICE WHEREVER IT EXISTS!
YES, ALAN--JUST AS IT IS OUR MISSION TO DESTROY EVIL WHER-EVER IT EXISTS!
HE FAILED AS THOSE WHO WORSHIP EVIL MUST ALWAYS FAIL! BUT NOW I MUST GET BACK TO MY OWN EARTH, ALAN! WE'LL MEET AGAIN SOON, I TRUST!
WE SURE WILL, HAL!
...AND AFTER HAL RETURNED HOME HE USED HIS RING TO RESTORE GOITRUDE--AND PUT THE CAR BACK IN STORAGE FOR SAFE-KEEPING! THEN HE TOLD ME ALL ABOUT THE ADVENTURE--JUST AS I'VE RECOUNTED IT TO YOU, READER--FROM MY CASEBOOK OF GREEN LANTERN!
THE END
23

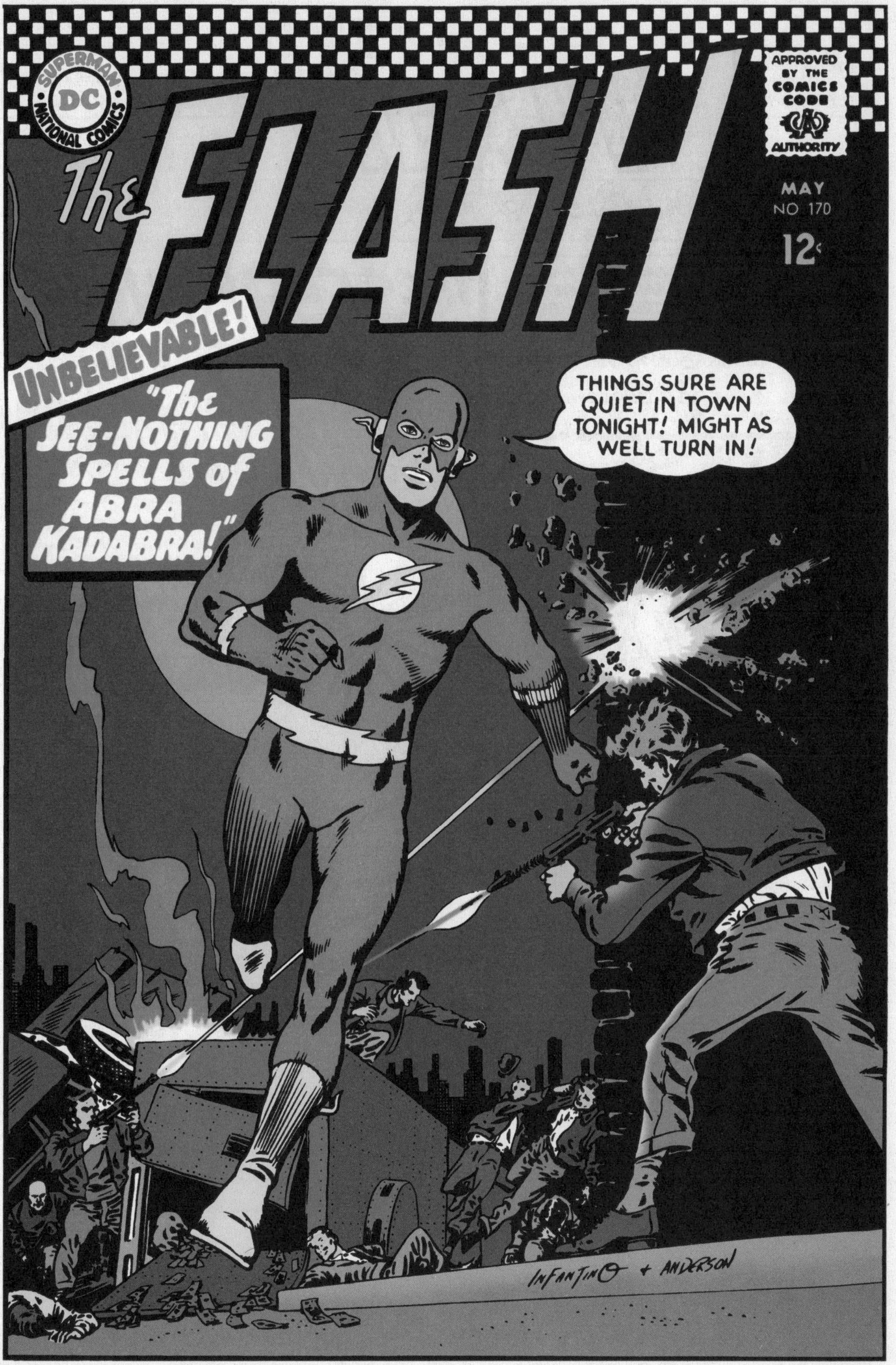
SUPERMAN
DC
NATIONAL COMICS
APPROVED BY THE COMICS CODE AUTHORITY
The FLASH
MAY
NO 170
12¢
UNBELIEVABLE!
"The SEE-NOTHING SPELLS of ABRA KADABRA!"
THINGS SURE ARE QUIET IN TOWN TONIGHT! MIGHT AS WELL TURN IN!
INFANTINO + ANDERSON

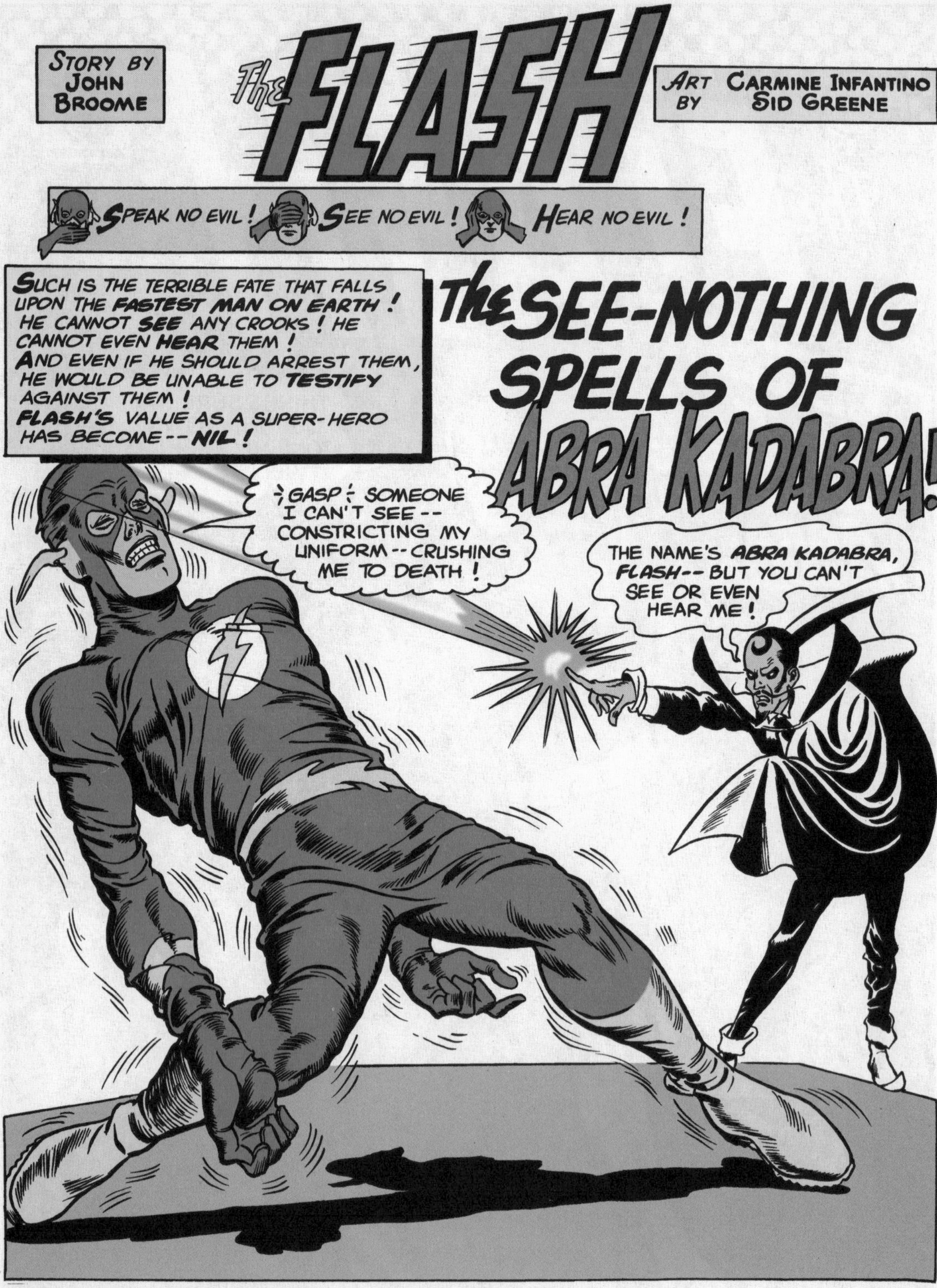

STORY BY JOHN BROOME
THE FLASH
ART BY CARMINE INFANTINO SID GREENE
SPEAK NO EVIL! SEE NO EVIL! HEAR NO EVIL!
SUCH IS THE TERRIBLE FATE THAT FALLS UPON THE FASTEST MAN ON EARTH! HE CANNOT SEE ANY CROOKS! HE CANNOT EVEN HEAR THEM! AND EVEN IF HE SHOULD ARREST THEM, HE WOULD BE UNABLE TO TESTIFY AGAINST THEM! FLASH'S VALUE AS A SUPER-HERO HAS BECOME--NIL!
THE SEE-NOTHING SPELLS OF ABRA KADABRA!
GASP SOMEONE I CAN'T SEE--CONSTRICTING MY UNIFORM--CRUSHING ME TO DEATH!
THE NAME'S ABRA KADABRA, FLASH--BUT YOU CAN'T SEE OR EVEN HEAR ME!

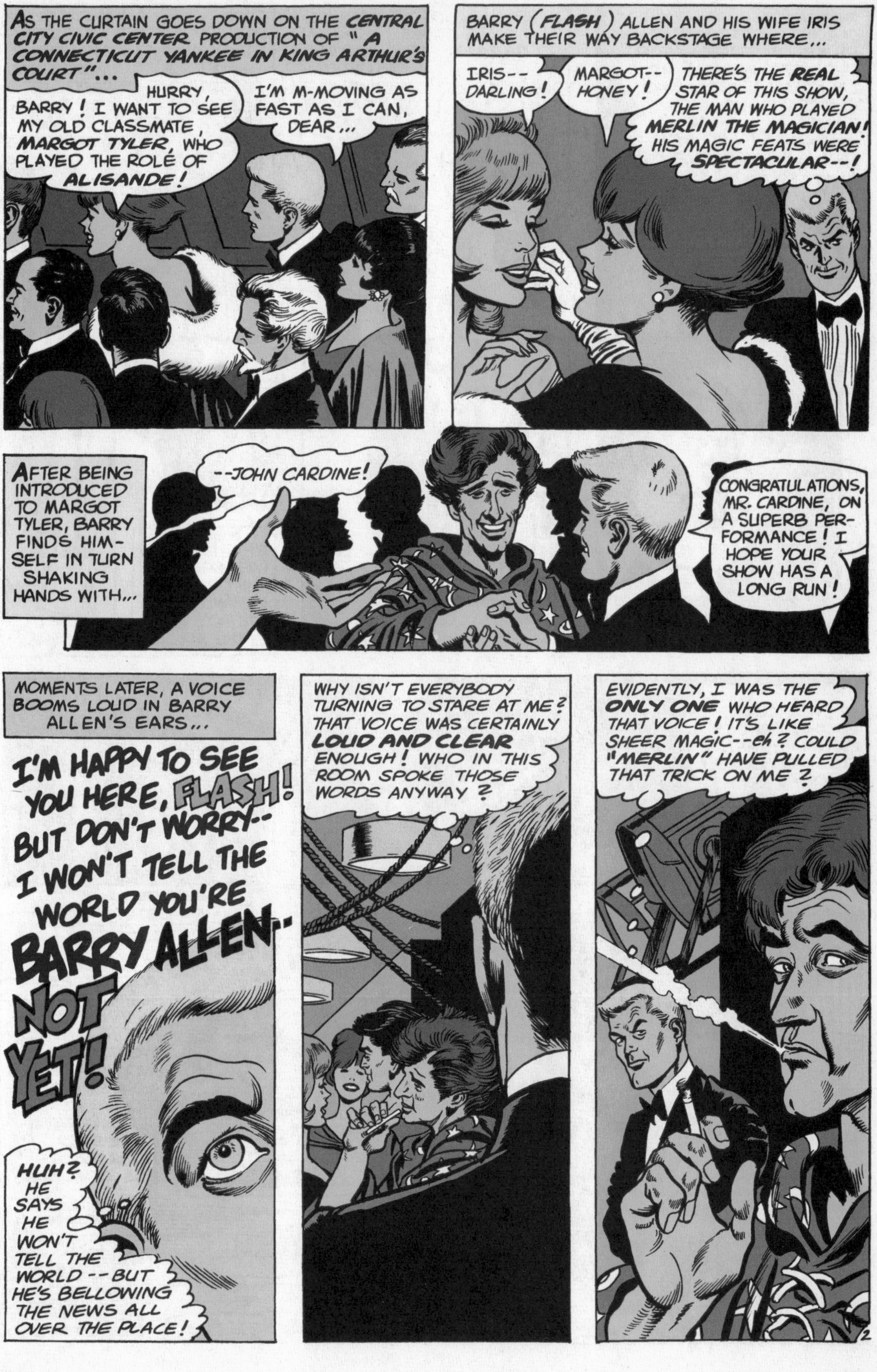

AS THE CURTAIN GOES DOWN ON THE CENTRAL CITY CIVIC CENTER PRODUCTION OF "A CONNECTICUT YANKEE IN KING ARTHUR'S COURT"...
HURRY, BARRY! I WANT TO SEE MY OLD CLASSMATE, MARGOT TYLER, WHO PLAYED THE ROLE OF ALISANDE!
I'M M-MOVING AS FAST AS I CAN, DEAR...
BARRY (FLASH) ALLEN AND HIS WIFE IRIS MAKE THEIR WAY BACKSTAGE WHERE,...
IRIS-- DARLING!
MARGOT-- HONEY!
THERE'S THE REAL STAR OF THIS SHOW, THE MAN WHO PLAYED MERLIN THE MAGICIAN! HIS MAGIC FEATS WERE SPECTACULAR--!
AFTER BEING INTRODUCED TO MARGOT TYLER, BARRY FINDS HIMSELF IN TURN SHAKING HANDS WITH,...
--JOHN CARDINE!
CONGRATULATIONS, MR. CARDINE, ON A SUPERB PERFORMANCE! I HOPE YOUR SHOW HAS A LONG RUN!
MOMENTS LATER, A VOICE BOOMS LOUD IN BARRY ALLEN'S EARS...
I'M HAPPY TO SEE YOU HERE, FLASH! BUT DON'T WORRY-- I WON'T TELL THE WORLD YOU'RE BARRY ALLEN-- NOT YET!
HUH? HE SAYS HE WON'T TELL THE WORLD--BUT HE'S BELLOWING THE NEWS ALL OVER THE PLACE!
WHY ISN'T EVERYBODY TURNING TO STARE AT ME? THAT VOICE WAS CERTAINLY LOUD AND CLEAR ENOUGH! WHO IN THIS ROOM SPOKE THOSE WORDS ANYWAY?
EVIDENTLY, I WAS THE ONLY ONE WHO HEARD THAT VOICE! IT'S LIKE SHEER MAGIC--eh? COULD "MERLIN" HAVE PULLED THAT TRICK ON ME?
2

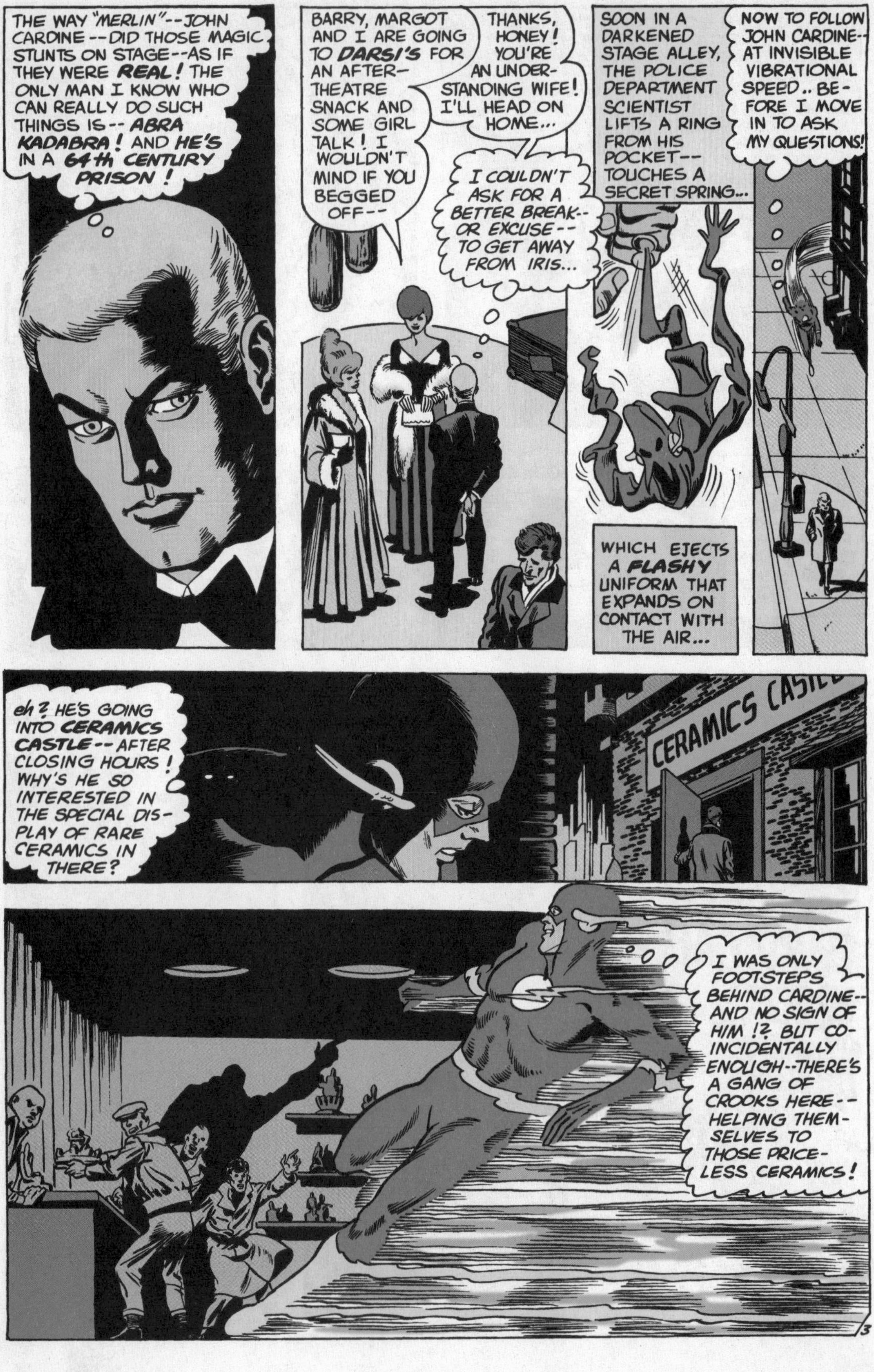

THE WAY "MERLIN"--JOHN CARDINE--DID THOSE MAGIC STUNTS ON STAGE--AS IF THEY WERE REAL! THE ONLY MAN I KNOW WHO CAN REALLY DO SUCH THINGS IS--ABRA KADABRA! AND HE'S IN A 64th CENTURY PRISON!
BARRY, MARGOT AND I ARE GOING TO DARSI'S FOR AN AFTER-THEATRE SNACK AND SOME GIRL TALK! I WOULDN'T MIND IF YOU BEGGED OFF--
THANKS, HONEY! YOU'RE AN UNDER-STANDING WIFE! I'LL HEAD ON HOME...
I COULDN'T ASK FOR A BETTER BREAK--OR EXCUSE--TO GET AWAY FROM IRIS...
SOON IN A DARKENED STAGE ALLEY, THE POLICE DEPARTMENT SCIENTIST LIFTS A RING FROM HIS POCKET--TOUCHES A SECRET SPRING...
WHICH EJECTS A FLASHY UNIFORM THAT EXPANDS ON CONTACT WITH THE AIR...
NOW TO FOLLOW JOHN CARDINE--AT INVISIBLE VIBRATIONAL SPEED.. BE-FORE I MOVE IN TO ASK MY QUESTIONS!
eh? HE'S GOING INTO CERAMICS CASTLE--AFTER CLOSING HOURS! WHY'S HE SO INTERESTED IN THE SPECIAL DIS-PLAY OF RARE CERAMICS IN THERE?
CERAMICS CASTLE
CERAMICS
I WAS ONLY FOOTSTEPS BEHIND CARDINE--AND NO SIGN OF HIM!? BUT CO-INCIDENTALLY ENOUGH--THERE'S A GANG OF CROOKS HERE--HELPING THEM-SELVES TO THOSE PRICE-LESS CERAMICS!
3

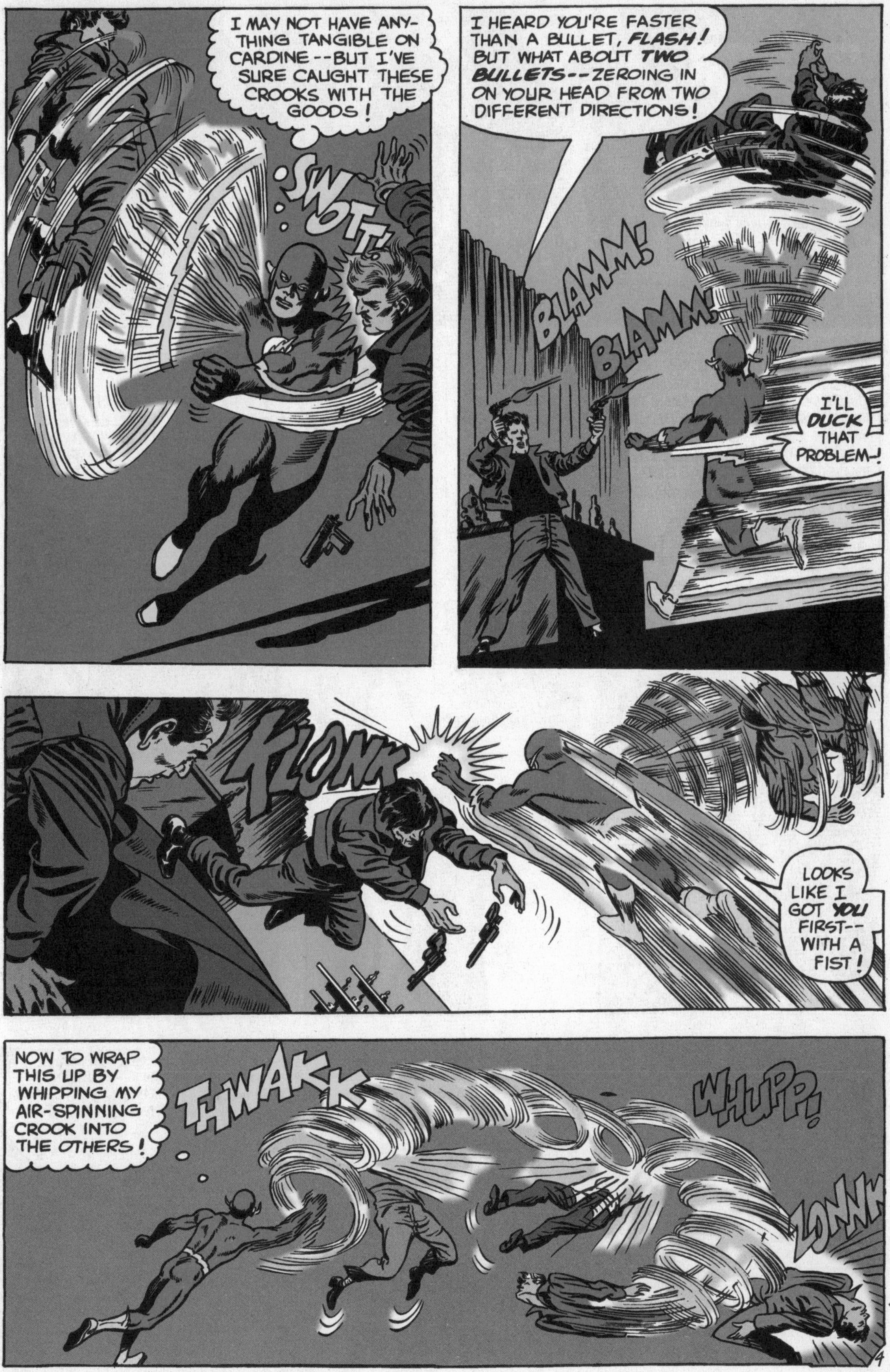
I MAY NOT HAVE ANYTHING TANGIBLE ON CARDINE--BUT I'VE SURE CAUGHT THESE CROOKS WITH THE GOODS!
SWOTT!
I HEARD YOU'RE FASTER THAN A BULLET, FLASH! BUT WHAT ABOUT TWO BULLETS--ZEROING IN ON YOUR HEAD FROM TWO DIFFERENT DIRECTIONS!
BLAMM!
BLAMM!
I'LL DUCK THAT PROBLEM--!
KLONK
LOOKS LIKE I GOT YOU FIRST--WITH A FIST!
NOW TO WRAP THIS UP BY WHIPPING MY AIR-SPINNING CROOK INTO THE OTHERS!
THWAKK
WHUPP!
ZONNK
4

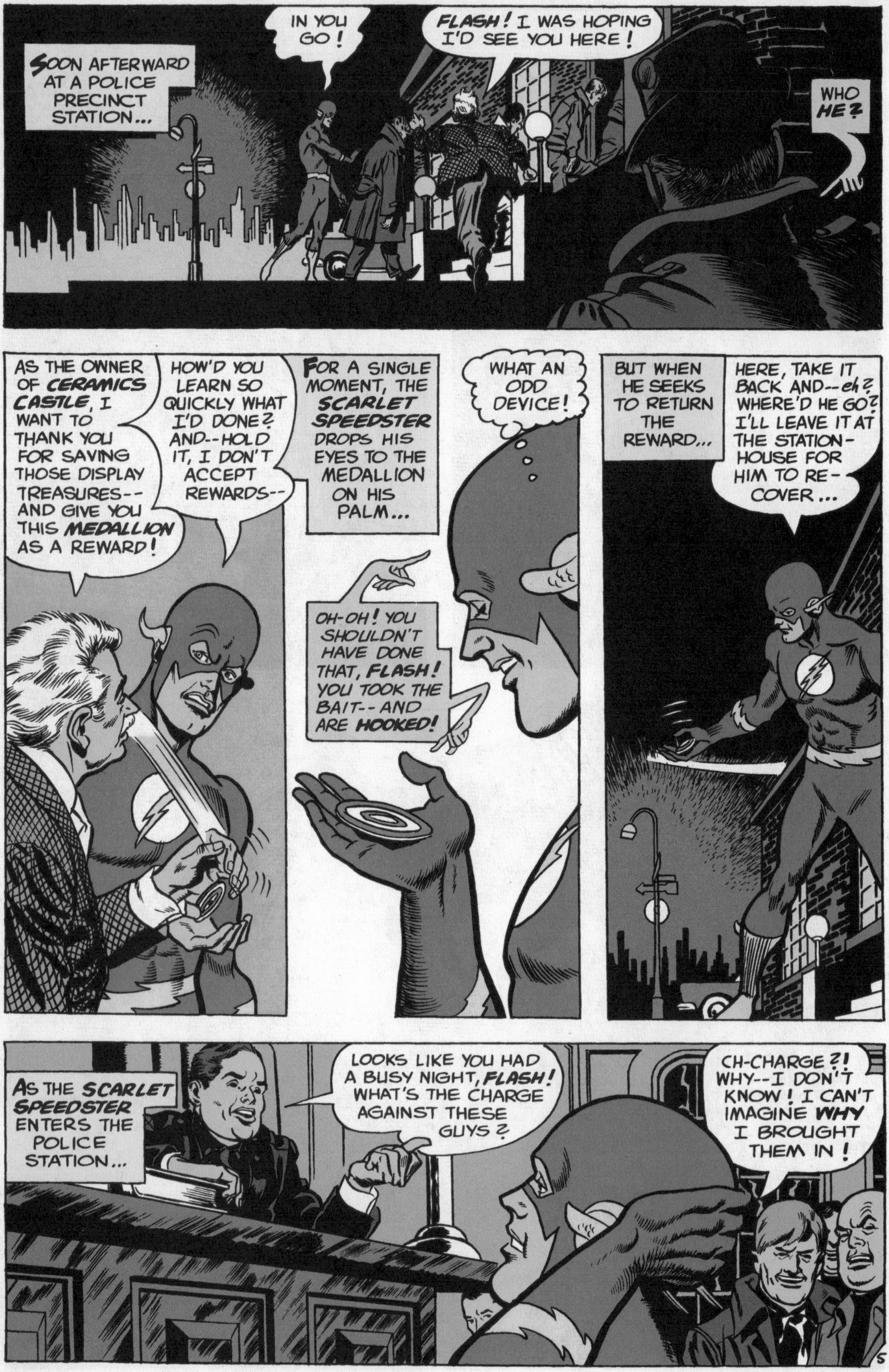
SOON AFTERWARD AT A POLICE PRECINCT STATION...
IN YOU GO!
FLASH! I WAS HOPING I'D SEE YOU HERE!
WHO HE?
AS THE OWNER OF CERAMICS CASTLE, I WANT TO THANK YOU FOR SAVING THOSE DISPLAY TREASURES-- AND GIVE YOU THIS MEDALLION AS A REWARD!
HOW'D YOU LEARN SO QUICKLY WHAT I'D DONE? AND--HOLD IT, I DON'T ACCEPT REWARDS--
FOR A SINGLE MOMENT, THE SCARLET SPEEDSTER DROPS HIS EYES TO THE MEDALLION ON HIS PALM...
WHAT AN ODD DEVICE!
OH-OH! YOU SHOULDN'T HAVE DONE THAT, FLASH! YOU TOOK THE BAIT-- AND ARE HOOKED!
BUT WHEN HE SEEKS TO RETURN THE REWARD...
HERE, TAKE IT BACK AND--eh? WHERE'D HE GO? I'LL LEAVE IT AT THE STATION-HOUSE FOR HIM TO RE-COVER...
AS THE SCARLET SPEEDSTER ENTERS THE POLICE STATION...
LOOKS LIKE YOU HAD A BUSY NIGHT, FLASH! WHAT'S THE CHARGE AGAINST THESE GUYS?
CH-CHARGE?! WHY--I DON'T KNOW! I CAN'T IMAGINE WHY I BROUGHT THEM IN!
5

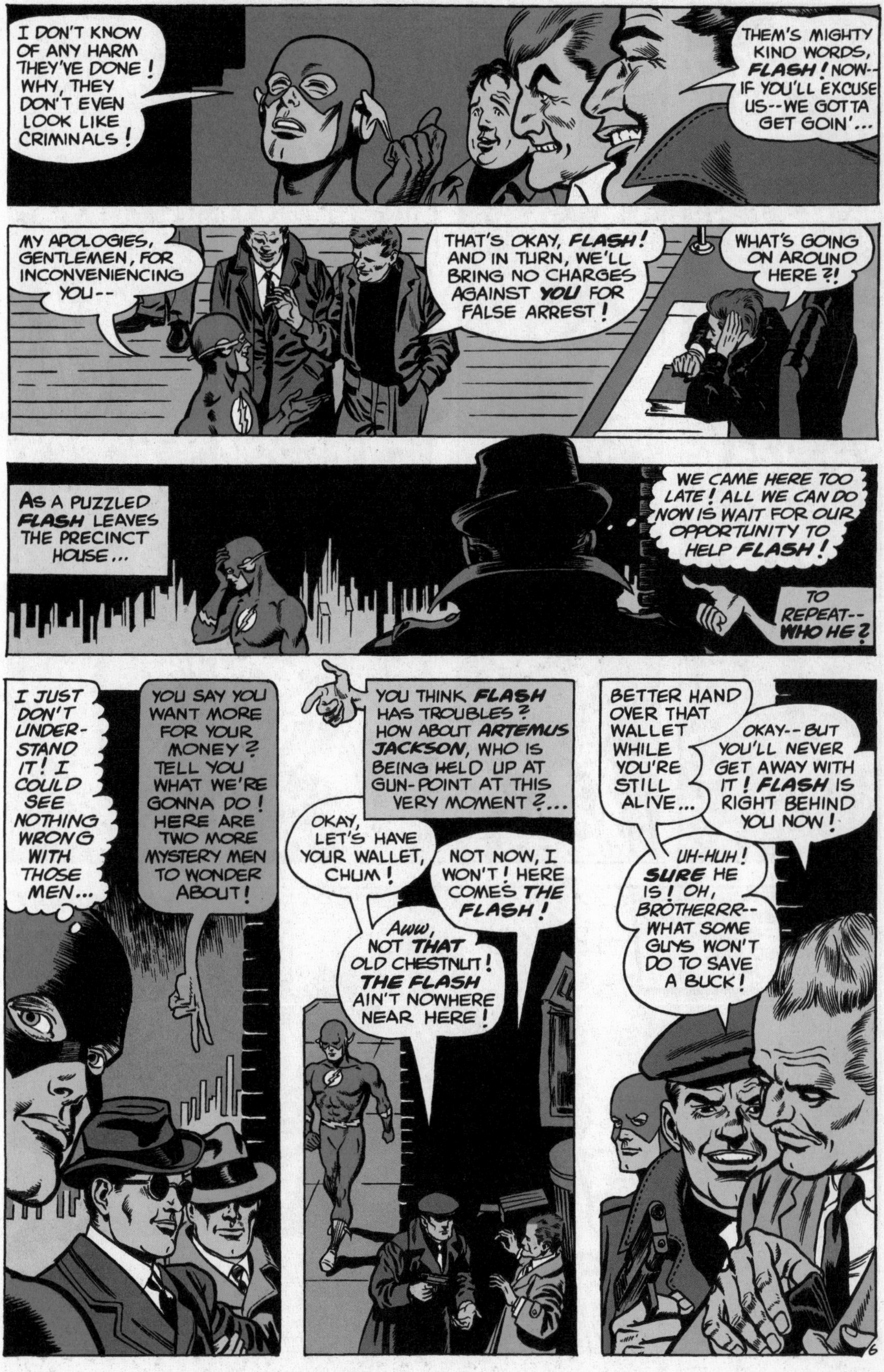
I DON'T KNOW OF ANY HARM THEY'VE DONE! WHY, THEY DON'T EVEN LOOK LIKE CRIMINALS!
THEM'S MIGHTY KIND WORDS, FLASH! NOW-- IF YOU'LL EXCUSE US--WE GOTTA GET GOIN'...
MY APOLOGIES, GENTLEMEN, FOR INCONVENIENCING YOU--
THAT'S OKAY, FLASH! AND IN TURN, WE'LL BRING NO CHARGES AGAINST YOU FOR FALSE ARREST!
WHAT'S GOING ON AROUND HERE ?!
AS A PUZZLED FLASH LEAVES THE PRECINCT HOUSE...
WE CAME HERE TOO LATE! ALL WE CAN DO NOW IS WAIT FOR OUR OPPORTUNITY TO HELP FLASH!
TO REPEAT-- WHO HE?
I JUST DON'T UNDER-STAND IT! I COULD SEE NOTHING WRONG WITH THOSE MEN...
YOU SAY YOU WANT MORE FOR YOUR MONEY? TELL YOU WHAT WE'RE GONNA DO! HERE ARE TWO MORE MYSTERY MEN TO WONDER ABOUT!
YOU THINK FLASH HAS TROUBLES? HOW ABOUT ARTEMUS JACKSON, WHO IS BEING HELD UP AT GUN-POINT AT THIS VERY MOMENT?...
OKAY, LET'S HAVE YOUR WALLET, CHUM!
NOT NOW, I WON'T! HERE COMES THE FLASH!
Aww, NOT THAT OLD CHESTNUT! THE FLASH AIN'T NOWHERE NEAR HERE!
BETTER HAND OVER THAT WALLET WHILE YOU'RE STILL ALIVE...
OKAY-- BUT YOU'LL NEVER GET AWAY WITH IT! FLASH IS RIGHT BEHIND YOU NOW!
UH-HUH! SURE HE IS! OH, BROTHERRR-- WHAT SOME GUYS WON'T DO TO SAVE A BUCK!
6

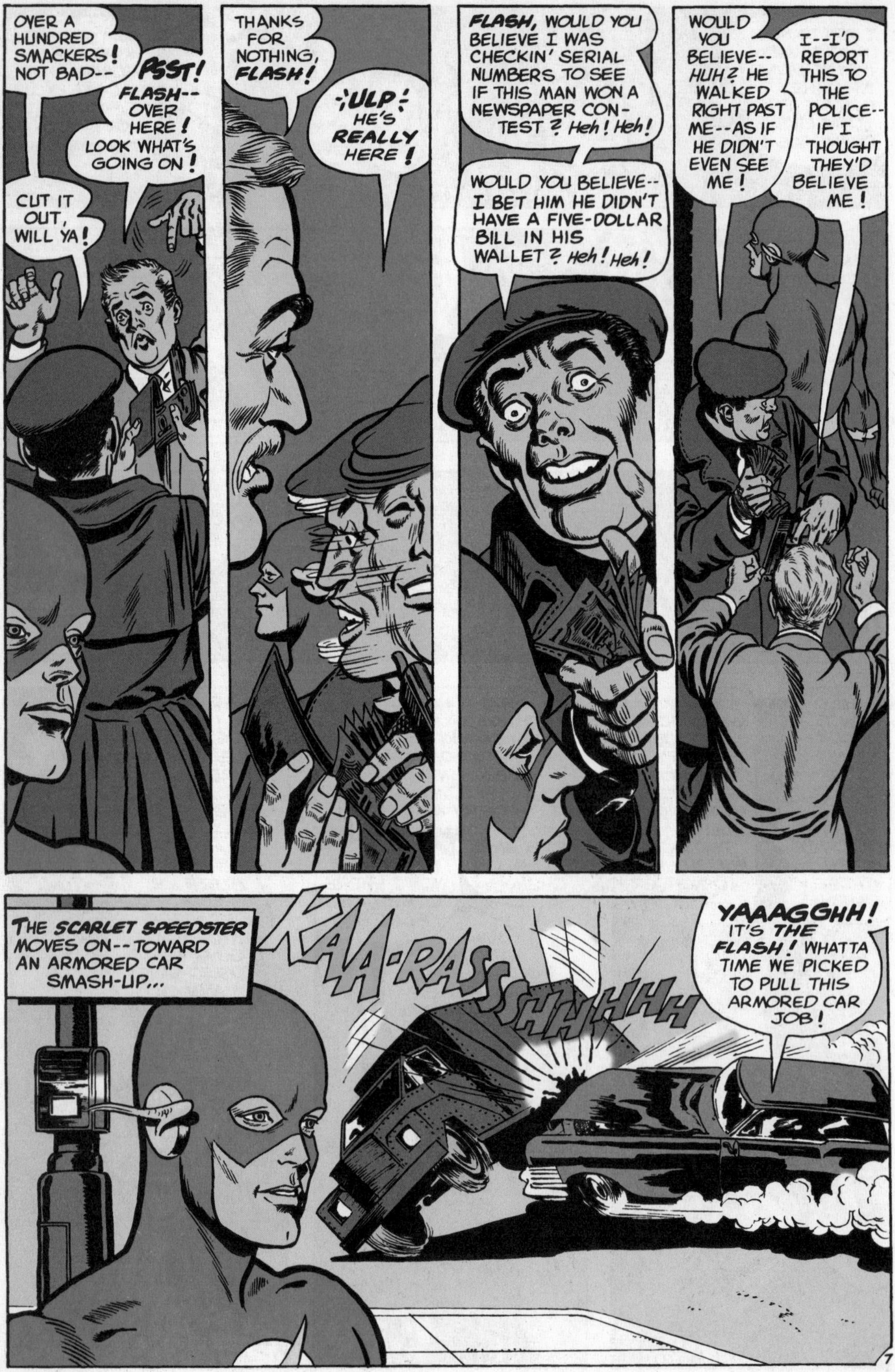
OVER A HUNDRED SMACKERS! NOT BAD--
PSST! FLASH-- OVER HERE! LOOK WHAT'S GOING ON!
CUT IT OUT, WILL YA!
THANKS FOR NOTHING, FLASH!
ULP! HE'S REALLY HERE!
FLASH, WOULD YOU BELIEVE I WAS CHECKIN' SERIAL NUMBERS TO SEE IF THIS MAN WON A NEWSPAPER CON-TEST? Heh! Heh!
WOULD YOU BELIEVE-- I BET HIM HE DIDN'T HAVE A FIVE-DOLLAR BILL IN HIS WALLET? Heh! Heh!
WOULD YOU BELIEVE-- HUH? HE WALKED RIGHT PAST ME--AS IF HE DIDN'T EVEN SEE ME!
I--I'D REPORT THIS TO THE POLICE-- IF I THOUGHT THEY'D BELIEVE ME!
THE SCARLET SPEEDSTER MOVES ON--TOWARD AN ARMORED CAR SMASH-UP...
KAA-RASSSHHHHHH
YAAAGGHH! IT'S THE FLASH! WHATTA TIME WE PICKED TO PULL THIS ARMORED CAR JOB!
7

HE DON'T SEE OR HEAR US! HOW LUCKY CAN A GUY GET?
MAYBE HE DOESN'T WORK OVERTIME! LET'S GRAB THE DOUGH AND RUN!
AGAIN THE NIGHT ERUPTS AROUND HIM AS TWO TOURING CARS BARREL DOWN CENTRAL BOULEVARD WITH RIVAL MOBSTERS TRIGGERING THEIR GUNS...
LOOK-- IT'S THE SCARLET SPEEDSTER HIMSELF!
WE BETTER CALL A TRUCE AND SETTLE THIS LATER!
RAT-TAT-!
BLAM!
BLAM!
HE AIN'T DOIN' NOTHING TO STOP US!
THEN KEEP ON SHOOTING!!
SCREEEEE
WOW!
IS CENTRAL CITY IN FOR TROUBLE! IF FLASH CAN NEITHER SEE NOR HEAR CRIMINALS--BUT READ WHAT HAPPENS AS THE STORY CONTINUES ON THE NEXT PAGE FOLLOWING!
8

CRISIS ON MULTIPLE EARTHS
THE TEAM UPS

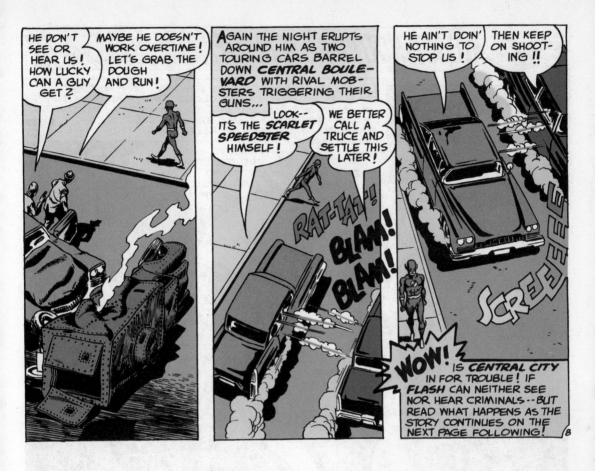

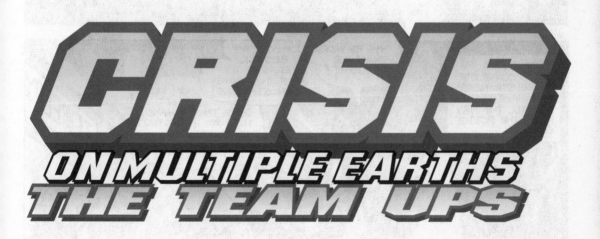

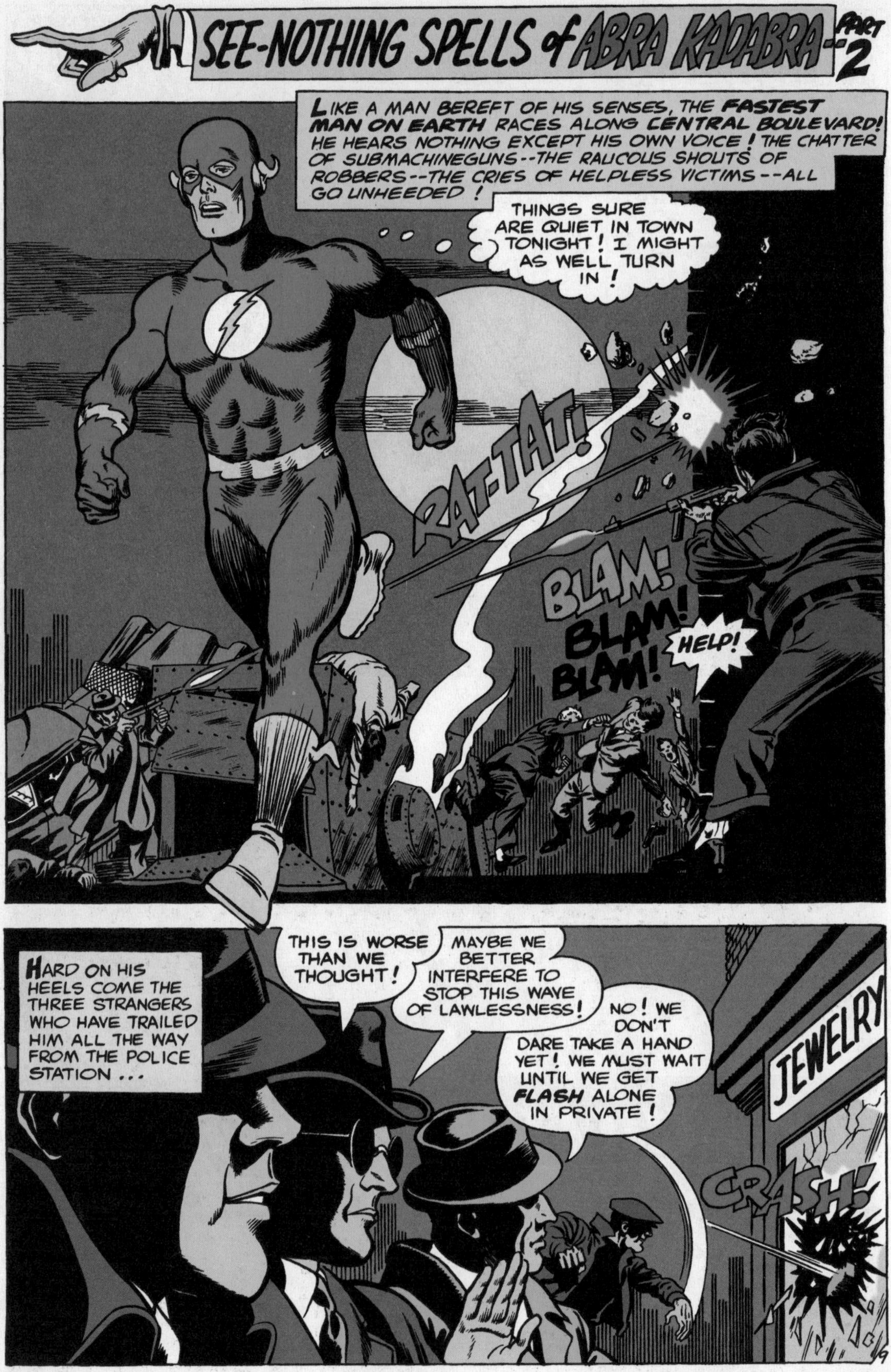
SEE-NOTHING SPELLS of ABRA KADABRA--PART 2
LIKE A MAN BEREFT OF HIS SENSES, THE FASTEST MAN ON EARTH RACES ALONG CENTRAL BOULEVARD! HE HEARS NOTHING EXCEPT HIS OWN VOICE! THE CHATTER OF SUBMACHINEGUNS--THE RAUCOUS SHOUTS OF ROBBERS--THE CRIES OF HELPLESS VICTIMS--ALL GO UNHEEDED!
THINGS SURE ARE QUIET IN TOWN TONIGHT! I MIGHT AS WELL TURN IN!
RAT-TAT!
BLAM! BLAM! BLAM!
HELP!
HARD ON HIS HEELS COME THE THREE STRANGERS WHO HAVE TRAILED HIM ALL THE WAY FROM THE POLICE STATION...
THIS IS WORSE THAN WE THOUGHT!
MAYBE WE BETTER INTERFERE TO STOP THIS WAVE OF LAWLESSNESS!
NO! WE DON'T DARE TAKE A HAND YET! WE MUST WAIT UNTIL WE GET FLASH ALONE IN PRIVATE!
JEWELRY
CRASH!

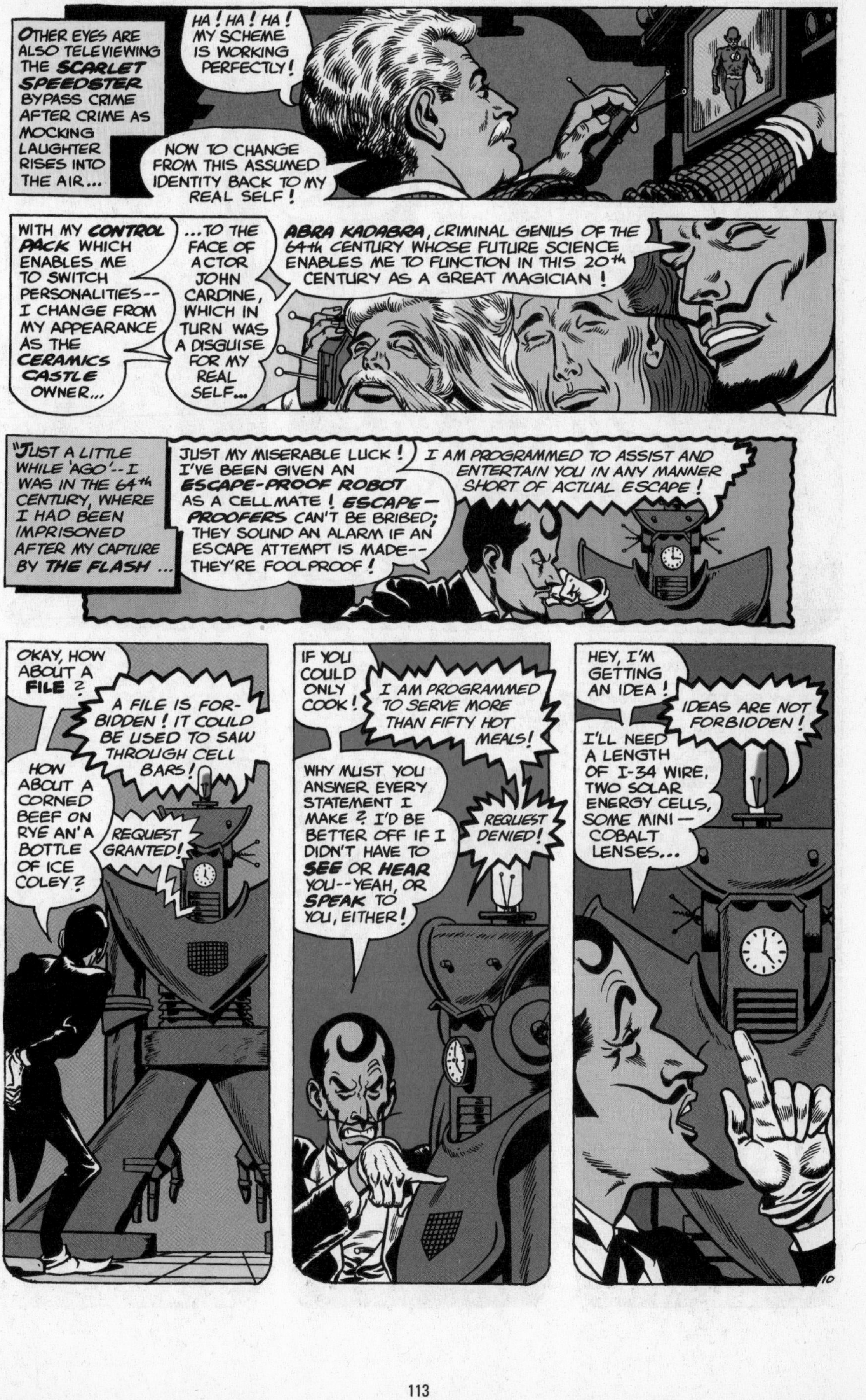
OTHER EYES ARE ALSO TELEVIEWING THE SCARLET SPEEDSTER BYPASS CRIME AFTER CRIME AS MOCKING LAUGHTER RISES INTO THE AIR...
HA! HA! HA! MY SCHEME IS WORKING PERFECTLY!
NOW TO CHANGE FROM THIS ASSUMED IDENTITY BACK TO MY REAL SELF!
WITH MY CONTROL PACK WHICH ENABLES ME TO SWITCH PERSONALITIES-- I CHANGE FROM MY APPEARANCE AS THE CERAMICS CASTLE OWNER...
...TO THE FACE OF ACTOR JOHN CARDINE, WHICH IN TURN WAS A DISGUISE FOR MY REAL SELF...
ABRA KADABRA, CRIMINAL GENIUS OF THE 64th CENTURY WHOSE FUTURE SCIENCE ENABLES ME TO FUNCTION IN THIS 20th CENTURY AS A GREAT MAGICIAN!
"JUST A LITTLE WHILE 'AGO'-- I WAS IN THE 64th CENTURY, WHERE I HAD BEEN IMPRISONED AFTER MY CAPTURE BY THE FLASH...
JUST MY MISERABLE LUCK! I'VE BEEN GIVEN AN ESCAPE-PROOF ROBOT AS A CELLMATE! ESCAPE-PROOFERS CAN'T BE BRIBED; THEY SOUND AN ALARM IF AN ESCAPE ATTEMPT IS MADE-- THEY'RE FOOLPROOF!
I AM PROGRAMMED TO ASSIST AND ENTERTAIN YOU IN ANY MANNER SHORT OF ACTUAL ESCAPE!
OKAY, HOW ABOUT A FILE?
A FILE IS FORBIDDEN! IT COULD BE USED TO SAW THROUGH CELL BARS!
HOW ABOUT A CORNED BEEF ON RYE AN' A BOTTLE OF ICE COLEY?
REQUEST GRANTED!
IF YOU COULD ONLY COOK!
I AM PROGRAMMED TO SERVE MORE THAN FIFTY HOT MEALS!
WHY MUST YOU ANSWER EVERY STATEMENT I MAKE? I'D BE BETTER OFF IF I DIDN'T HAVE TO SEE OR HEAR YOU--YEAH, OR SPEAK TO YOU, EITHER!
REQUEST DENIED!
HEY, I'M GETTING AN IDEA!
IDEAS ARE NOT FORBIDDEN!
I'LL NEED A LENGTH OF I-34 WIRE, TWO SOLAR ENERGY CELLS, SOME MINI-COBALT LENSES...
10

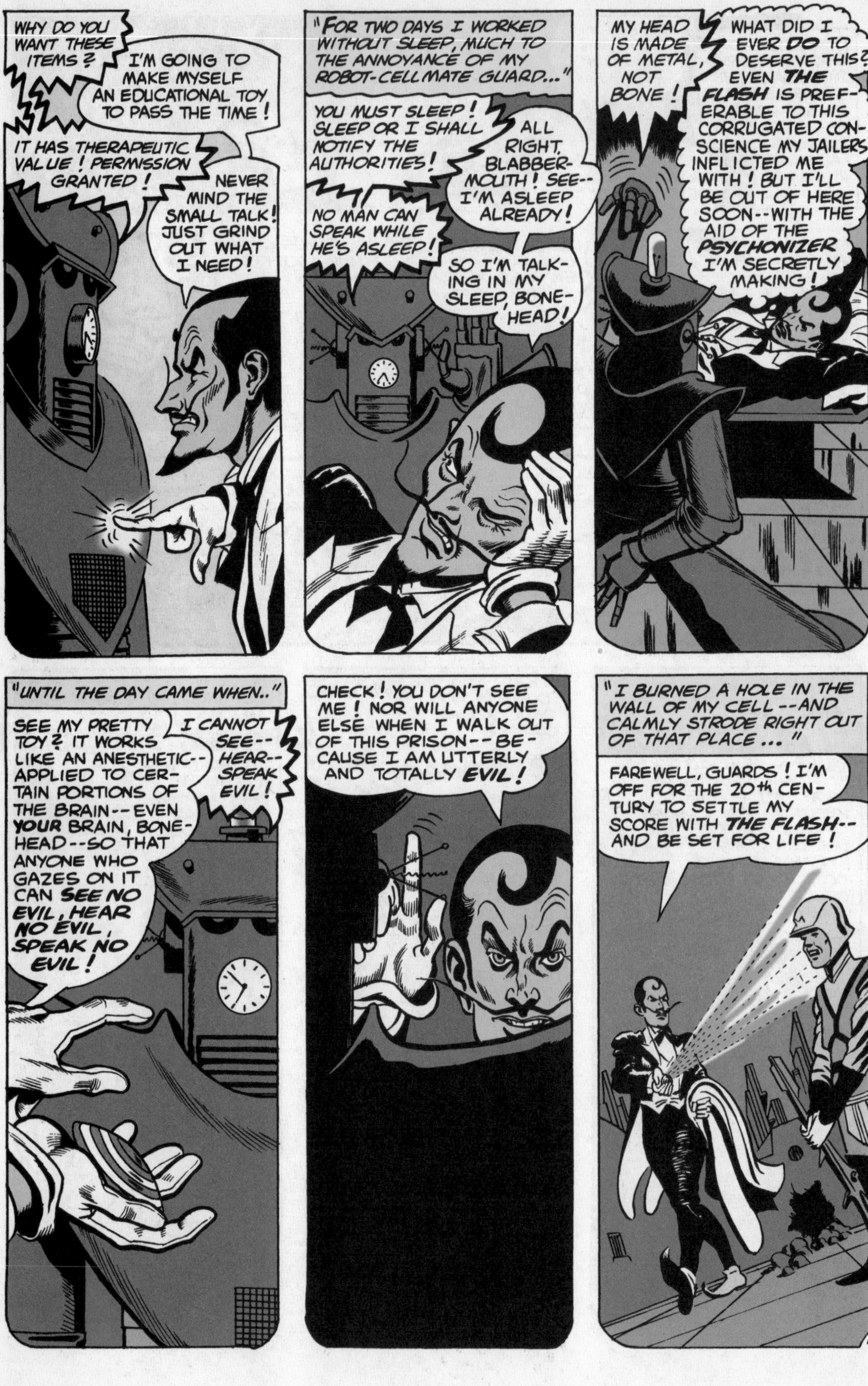
WHY DO YOU WANT THESE ITEMS?
I'M GOING TO MAKE MYSELF AN EDUCATIONAL TOY TO PASS THE TIME!
IT HAS THERAPEUTIC VALUE! PERMISSION GRANTED!
NEVER MIND THE SMALL TALK! JUST GRIND OUT WHAT I NEED!
"FOR TWO DAYS I WORKED WITHOUT SLEEP, MUCH TO THE ANNOYANCE OF MY ROBOT-CELLMATE GUARD..."
YOU MUST SLEEP! SLEEP OR I SHALL NOTIFY THE AUTHORITIES!
ALL RIGHT, BLABBERMOUTH! SEE-- I'M ASLEEP ALREADY!
NO MAN CAN SPEAK WHILE HE'S ASLEEP!
SO I'M TALKING IN MY SLEEP, BONEHEAD!
MY HEAD IS MADE OF METAL, NOT BONE!
WHAT DID I EVER DO TO DESERVE THIS? EVEN THE FLASH IS PREFERABLE TO THIS CORRUGATED CONSCIENCE MY JAILERS INFLICTED ME WITH! BUT I'LL BE OUT OF HERE SOON--WITH THE AID OF THE PSYCHONIZER I'M SECRETLY MAKING!
"UNTIL THE DAY CAME WHEN.."
SEE MY PRETTY TOY? IT WORKS LIKE AN ANESTHETIC--APPLIED TO CERTAIN PORTIONS OF THE BRAIN--EVEN YOUR BRAIN, BONEHEAD--SO THAT ANYONE WHO GAZES ON IT CAN SEE NO EVIL, HEAR NO EVIL, SPEAK NO EVIL!
I CANNOT SEE-- HEAR-- SPEAK EVIL!
CHECK! YOU DON'T SEE ME! NOR WILL ANYONE ELSE WHEN I WALK OUT OF THIS PRISON--BECAUSE I AM UTTERLY AND TOTALLY EVIL!
"I BURNED A HOLE IN THE WALL OF MY CELL--AND CALMLY STRODE RIGHT OUT OF THAT PLACE..."
FAREWELL, GUARDS! I'M OFF FOR THE 20th CENTURY TO SETTLE MY SCORE WITH THE FLASH--AND BE SET FOR LIFE!
11

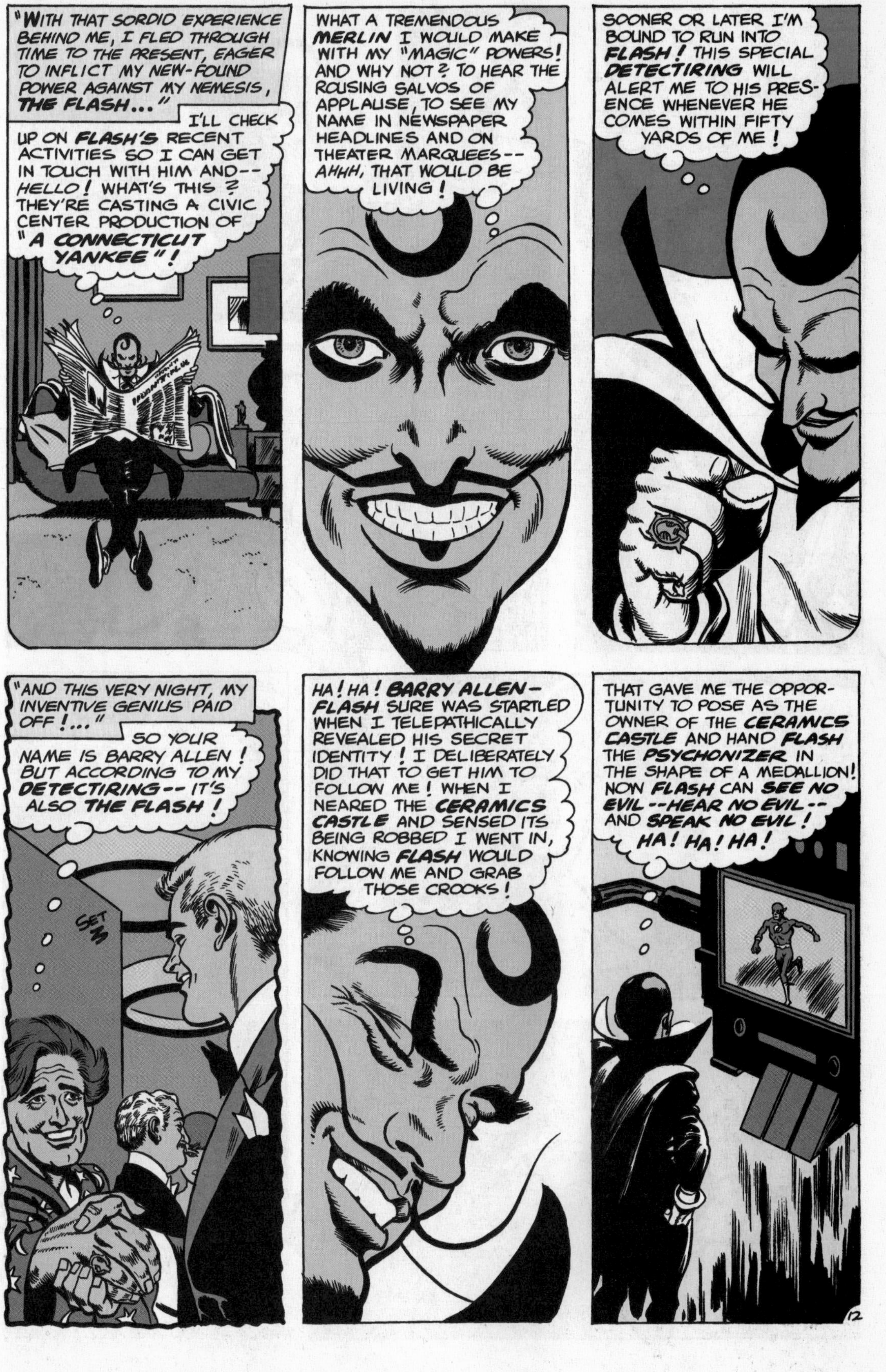
"WITH THAT SORDID EXPERIENCE BEHIND ME, I FLED THROUGH TIME TO THE PRESENT, EAGER TO INFLICT MY NEW-FOUND POWER AGAINST MY NEMESIS, THE FLASH..."
I'LL CHECK UP ON FLASH'S RECENT ACTIVITIES SO I CAN GET IN TOUCH WITH HIM AND-- HELLO! WHAT'S THIS? THEY'RE CASTING A CIVIC CENTER PRODUCTION OF "A CONNECTICUT YANKEE"!
WHAT A TREMENDOUS MERLIN I WOULD MAKE WITH MY "MAGIC" POWERS! AND WHY NOT? TO HEAR THE ROUSING SALVOS OF APPLAUSE, TO SEE MY NAME IN NEWSPAPER HEADLINES AND ON THEATER MARQUEES-- AHHH, THAT WOULD BE LIVING!
SOONER OR LATER I'M BOUND TO RUN INTO FLASH! THIS SPECIAL DETECTIRING WILL ALERT ME TO HIS PRESENCE WHENEVER HE COMES WITHIN FIFTY YARDS OF ME!
"AND THIS VERY NIGHT, MY INVENTIVE GENIUS PAID OFF!..."
SO YOUR NAME IS BARRY ALLEN! BUT ACCORDING TO MY DETECTIRING-- IT'S ALSO THE FLASH!
SET 3
HA! HA! BARRY ALLEN-FLASH SURE WAS STARTLED WHEN I TELEPATHICALLY REVEALED HIS SECRET IDENTITY! I DELIBERATELY DID THAT TO GET HIM TO FOLLOW ME! WHEN I NEARED THE CERAMICS CASTLE AND SENSED ITS BEING ROBBED I WENT IN, KNOWING FLASH WOULD FOLLOW ME AND GRAB THOSE CROOKS!
THAT GAVE ME THE OPPORTUNITY TO POSE AS THE OWNER OF THE CERAMICS CASTLE AND HAND FLASH THE PSYCHONIZER IN THE SHAPE OF A MEDALLION! NOW FLASH CAN SEE NO EVIL--HEAR NO EVIL-- AND SPEAK NO EVIL! HA! HA! HA!
12

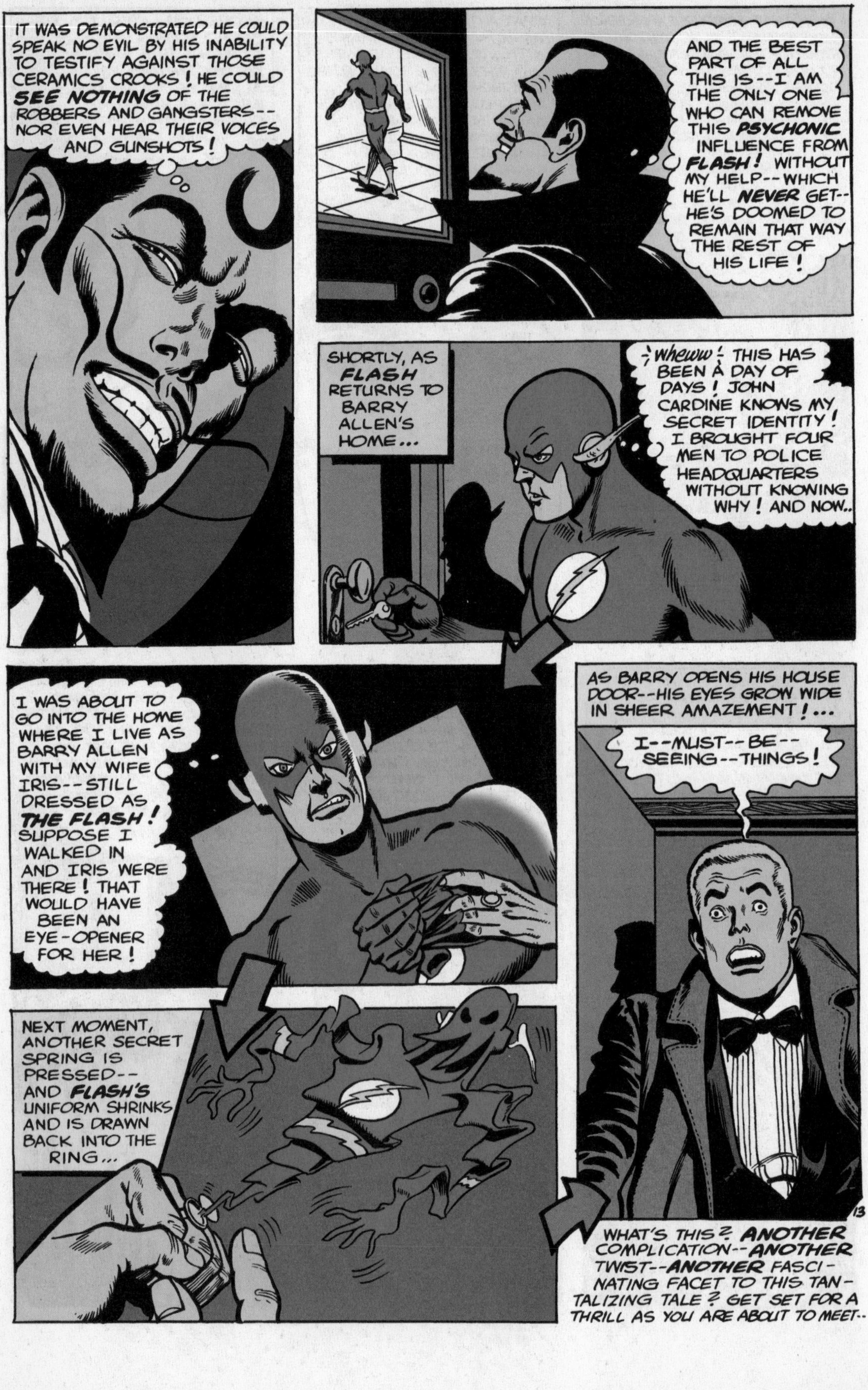

IT WAS DEMONSTRATED HE COULD SPEAK NO EVIL BY HIS INABILITY TO TESTIFY AGAINST THOSE CERAMICS CROOKS! HE COULD SEE NOTHING OF THE ROBBERS AND GANGSTERS--NOR EVEN HEAR THEIR VOICES AND GUNSHOTS!
AND THE BEST PART OF ALL THIS IS--I AM THE ONLY ONE WHO CAN REMOVE THIS PSYCHONIC INFLUENCE FROM FLASH! WITHOUT MY HELP--WHICH HE'LL NEVER GET--HE'S DOOMED TO REMAIN THAT WAY THE REST OF HIS LIFE!
SHORTLY, AS FLASH RETURNS TO BARRY ALLEN'S HOME...
WHEWW! THIS HAS BEEN A DAY OF DAYS! JOHN CARDINE KNOWS MY SECRET IDENTITY! I BROUGHT FOUR MEN TO POLICE HEADQUARTERS WITHOUT KNOWING WHY! AND NOW..
I WAS ABOUT TO GO INTO THE HOME WHERE I LIVE AS BARRY ALLEN WITH MY WIFE IRIS--STILL DRESSED AS THE FLASH! SUPPOSE I WALKED IN AND IRIS WERE THERE! THAT WOULD HAVE BEEN AN EYE-OPENER FOR HER!
NEXT MOMENT, ANOTHER SECRET SPRING IS PRESSED--AND FLASH'S UNIFORM SHRINKS AND IS DRAWN BACK INTO THE RING...
AS BARRY OPENS HIS HOUSE DOOR--HIS EYES GROW WIDE IN SHEER AMAZEMENT!...
I--MUST--BE--SEEING--THINGS!
13
WHAT'S THIS? ANOTHER COMPLICATION--ANOTHER TWIST--ANOTHER FASCINATING FACET TO THIS TANTALIZING TALE? GET SET FOR A THRILL AS YOU ARE ABOUT TO MEET--

DOCTOR FATE! FLASH OF EARTH-TWO! DOCTOR MID-NITE! WHAT BRINGS *YOU* HERE?

WE HAD TO SEE YOU ALONE, BARRY! SOMETHING TERRIBLE IS HAPPENING ON YOUR EARTH!

YES, THESE ARE A TRIO OF SUPER-HEROES FROM THAT *OTHER EARTH* WHICH IS A PARALLEL OF OUR OWN! ON THEIR WORLD THEY TRACK DOWN CRIME AND EVIL JUST AS THE *SCARLET SPEEDSTER* ON *EARTH-ONE!*...

BUT BEFORE WE GO INTO THAT, *FLASH*-- WHY DIDN'T YOU STOP ALL THOSE CRIMES BEING COMMITTED TONIGHT RIGHT UNDER YOUR NOSE?

CRIMES? WHAT CRIMES? IT WAS A REAL QUIET NIGHT IN *CENTRAL CITY!*

Hmmm! THEN LET ME TELL YOU WHAT YOU OVERLOOKED...

WHEN *DR. MID-NITE* RELATES WHAT TOOK PLACE AFTER *FLASH* LEFT THE POLICE STATION...

AND YOU SAY ALL THOSE THINGS HAPPENED-- WITHOUT MY BEING AWARE OF IT?!

THE ANSWER MUST TIE IN WITH *WHY* WE'RE HERE ON *EARTH-ONE!* LISTEN...

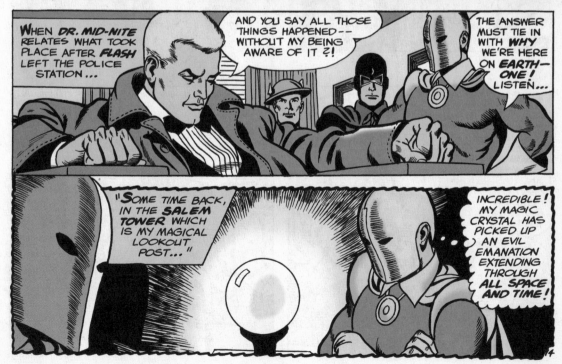

"SOME TIME BACK, IN THE *SALEM TOWER* WHICH IS MY MAGICAL LOOKOUT POST..."

INCREDIBLE! MY MAGIC CRYSTAL HAS PICKED UP AN EVIL EMANATION EXTENDING THROUGH *ALL SPACE AND TIME!*

"WITH THE AID OF THE SUPERNAL WISDOM AND EXTRATERRESTRIAL KNOWLEDGE WHICH WAS GIVEN TO ME BY **NABU THE WISE,** I TRACKED DOWN THAT EVIL-FILLED ENERGY..."

FAR IN THE FUTURE IT WAS BORN! THROUGH TIME AND SPACE IT HAS COME! IT TARRIES NOW IN **CENTRAL CITY** ON **EARTH-ONE!** -- BUT **THAT** IS WHERE **FLASH** LIVES!

"MY NEXT MOVE WAS TO PAY A VISIT TO JAY GARRICK -- **THE FLASH** OF MY WORLD, WHERE TO MY SURPRISE AND DELIGHT I FOUND..."

DOCTOR MID-NITE! HOW GOOD TO FIND YOU HERE TOO! THIS WILL INTEREST YOU, AS WELL AS **FLASH!**

"WHEN I TOLD OF MY DISCOVERY..."

YOU'RE RIGHT, **DOCTOR FATE!** WE MUST ALERT **FLASH OF EARTH-ONE** TO THIS THREAT! BUT WE MUST PROCEED CAREFULLY -- SAY, IN OUR **CIVILIAN IDENTITIES** -- TO AVOID POSSIBLE RECOGNITION AND DETECTION BY THE UNKNOWN EVIL MENACE...

TO PLAY IT EVEN SAFER, WE'LL CONTACT **FLASH** IN COMPLETE SECRECY!

HOLD ON! I'M COMING WITH YOU! LAST TIME I SAW **FLASH** HE TALKED ME OUT OF JOINING HIM ON A CASE!

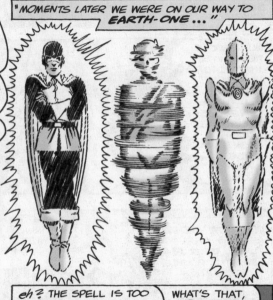

"MOMENTS LATER WE WERE ON OUR WAY TO **EARTH-ONE** ..."

AS **DOCTOR FATE** CONCLUDES HIS TALE...

FROM WHAT YOU'VE TOLD ME AND FROM WHAT'S ALREADY HAPPENED, I CAN ONLY CONCLUDE THAT **ABRA KADABRA** ESCAPED HIS 64th CENTURY JAIL AND HAS RETURNED TO **CENTRAL CITY!** MOREOVER -- HE'S PUT A **MAGIC** SPELL ON ME!

MAGIC SPELL? THAT'S **MY** DEPARTMENT! I'LL REMOVE IT...

eh? THE SPELL IS TOO POWERFUL FOR ME TO REMOVE! SOME FORCE BEYOND EVEN MY POWERS IS AT WORK HERE! BUT ONE THING I **CAN** DO...

WHAT'S THAT, **DOCTOR FATE?**

15

I CAN REVEAL ABRA KADABRA'S TARGET FOR TONIGHT!
LOOK--ALREADY THIEVES ARE THERE--STEALING THOSE GOLD ARTIFACTS!
I--I CAN'T SEE A THING!
I'M BEGINNING TO GET AN IDEA--A PLAN OF ACTION!
MOMENTS LATER--AFTER FLASH DONS HIS UNIFORM--THE QUARTET OF SUPER-HEROES RACES OUT ON THE TRAIL OF ABRA KADABRA...
IF I'M UNABLE TO SEE OR HEAR ANYTHING EVIL THAT'S GOING ON--HOW CAN I FIGHT IT?
HAVE NO FEARS ON THAT SCORE, FLASH!
WE AREN'T HERE AS WINDOW DRESSING!
WITH FLASH SENSELESS TO EVIL--WHAT CAN HE POSSIBLY DO AGAINST THE MASTER MAGE FROM THE FUTURE? WHAT PLAN HAS FLASH FROM EARTH-TWO WORKED OUT?
STORY CONTINUES ON THE PAGE FOLLOWING!
16

CRISIS ON MULTIPLE EARTHS
THE TEAM UPS

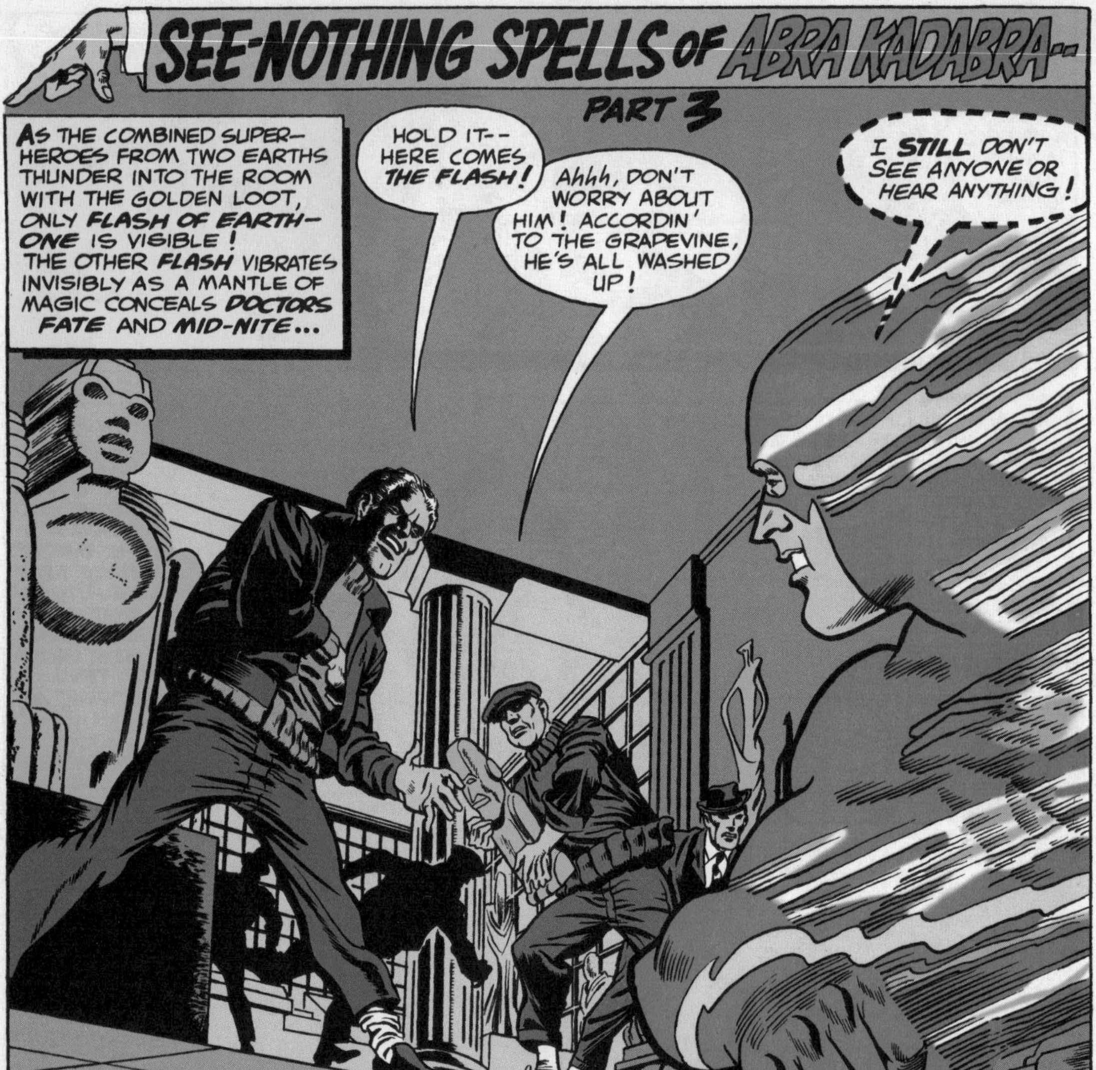
SEE-NOTHING SPELLS OF ABRA KADABRA--
PART 3
AS THE COMBINED SUPER-HEROES FROM TWO EARTHS THUNDER INTO THE ROOM WITH THE GOLDEN LOOT, ONLY FLASH OF EARTH-ONE IS VISIBLE! THE OTHER FLASH VIBRATES INVISIBLY AS A MANTLE OF MAGIC CONCEALS DOCTORS FATE AND MID-NITE...
HOLD IT-- HERE COMES THE FLASH!
Ahhh, DON'T WORRY ABOUT HIM! ACCORDIN' TO THE GRAPEVINE, HE'S ALL WASHED UP!
I STILL DON'T SEE ANYONE OR HEAR ANYTHING!

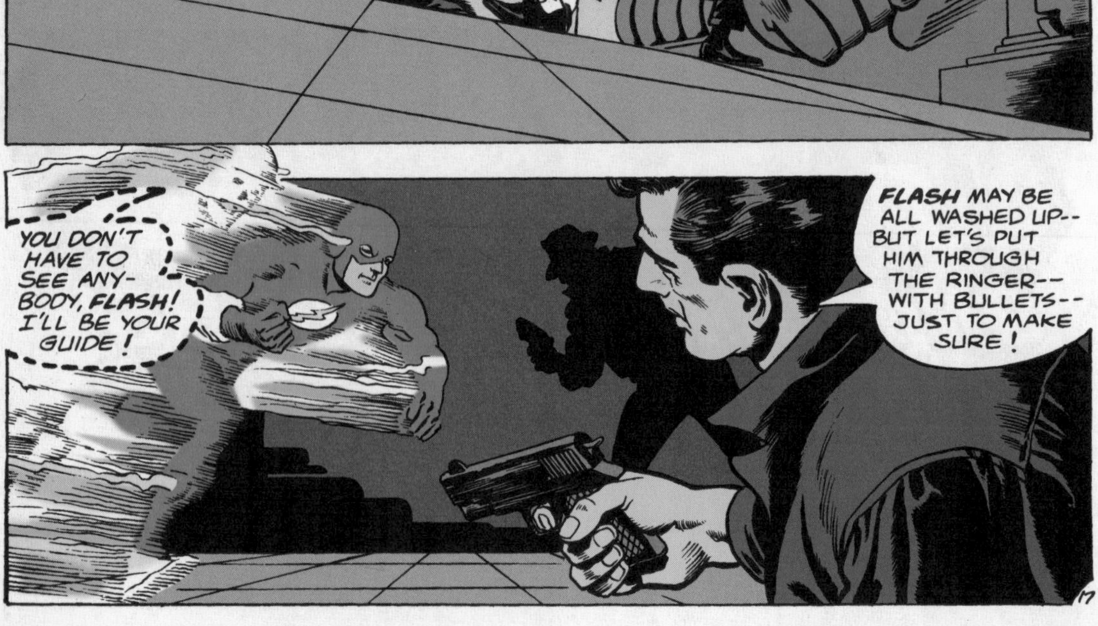
YOU DON'T HAVE TO SEE ANY-BODY, FLASH! I'LL BE YOUR GUIDE!
FLASH MAY BE ALL WASHED UP-- BUT LET'S PUT HIM THROUGH THE RINGER-- WITH BULLETS-- JUST TO MAKE SURE!
17

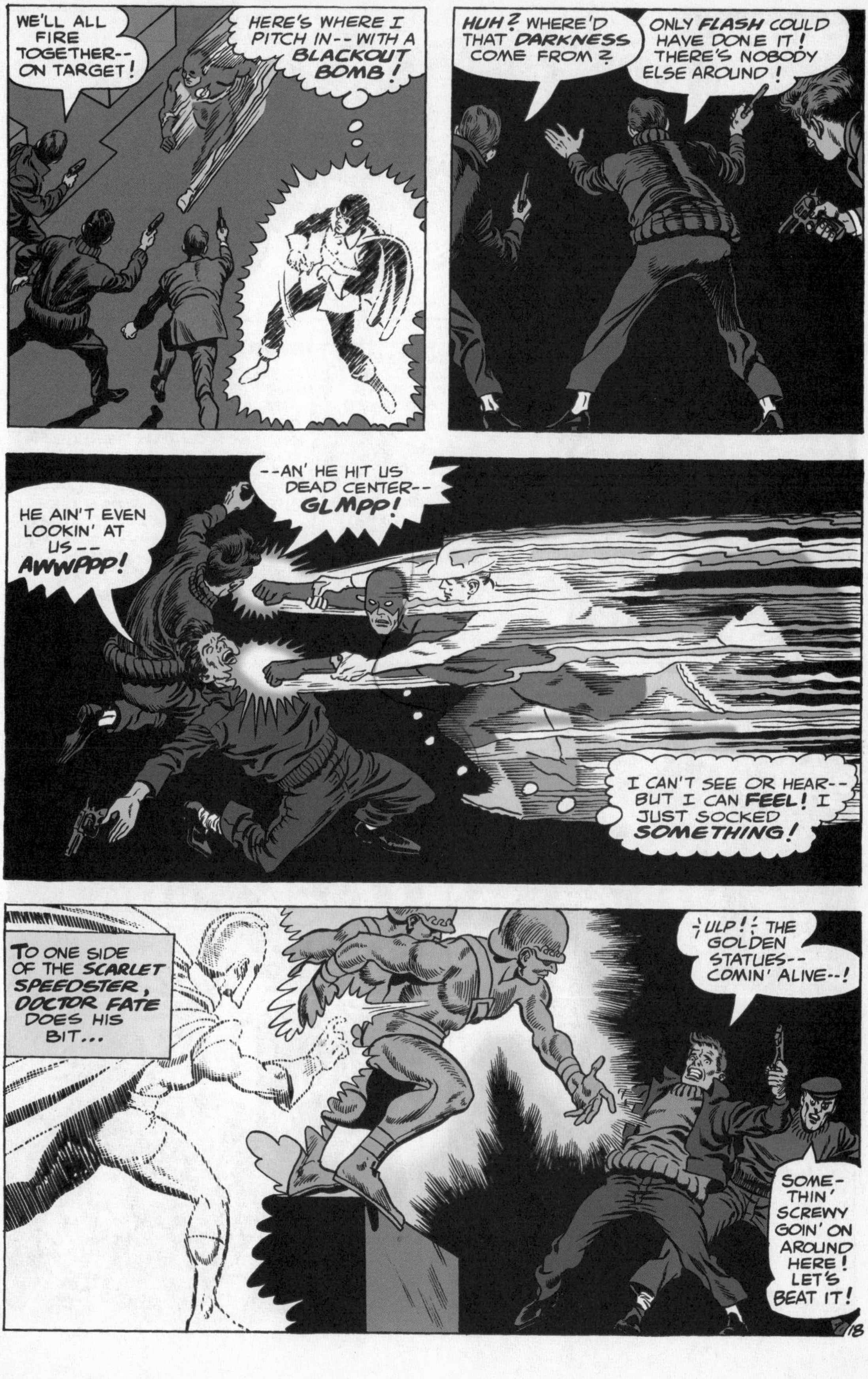
WE'LL ALL FIRE TOGETHER-- ON TARGET!
HERE'S WHERE I PITCH IN--WITH A BLACKOUT BOMB!
HUH? WHERE'D THAT DARKNESS COME FROM?
ONLY FLASH COULD HAVE DONE IT! THERE'S NOBODY ELSE AROUND!
--AN' HE HIT US DEAD CENTER-- GLMPP!
HE AIN'T EVEN LOOKIN' AT US -- AWWPPP!
I CAN'T SEE OR HEAR-- BUT I CAN FEEL! I JUST SOCKED SOMETHING!
TO ONE SIDE OF THE SCARLET SPEEDSTER, DOCTOR FATE DOES HIS BIT...
-ULP!- THE GOLDEN STATUES-- COMIN' ALIVE--!
SOME-THIN' SCREWY GOIN' ON AROUND HERE! LET'S BEAT IT!
18

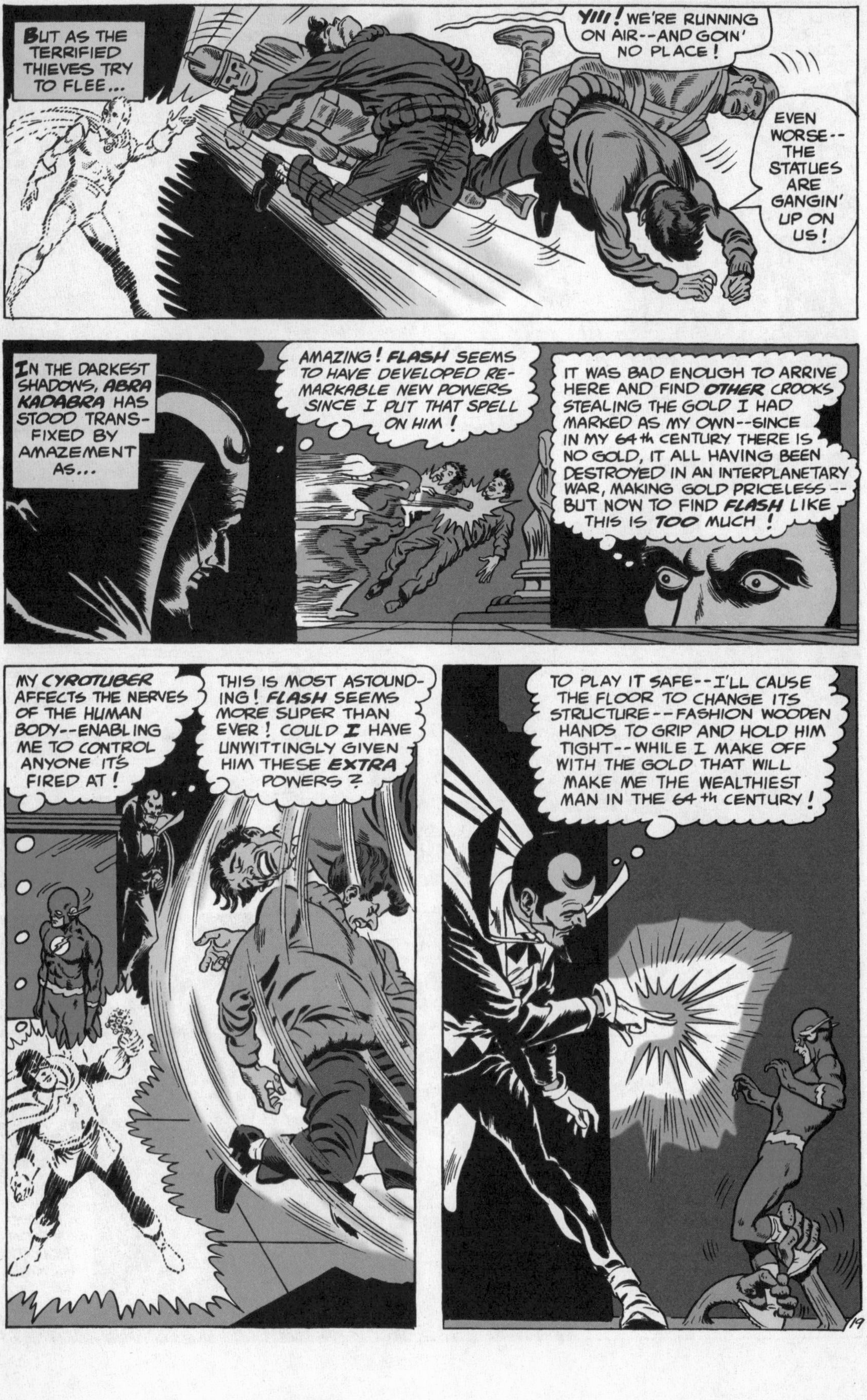
BUT AS THE TERRIFIED THIEVES TRY TO FLEE...
YIII! WE'RE RUNNING ON AIR--AND GOIN' NO PLACE!
EVEN WORSE--THE STATUES ARE GANGIN' UP ON US!
IN THE DARKEST SHADOWS, ABRA KADABRA HAS STOOD TRANSFIXED BY AMAZEMENT AS...
AMAZING! FLASH SEEMS TO HAVE DEVELOPED REMARKABLE NEW POWERS SINCE I PUT THAT SPELL ON HIM!
IT WAS BAD ENOUGH TO ARRIVE HERE AND FIND OTHER CROOKS STEALING THE GOLD I HAD MARKED AS MY OWN--SINCE IN MY 64th CENTURY THERE IS NO GOLD, IT ALL HAVING BEEN DESTROYED IN AN INTERPLANETARY WAR, MAKING GOLD PRICELESS--BUT NOW TO FIND FLASH LIKE THIS IS TOO MUCH!
MY CYROTUBER AFFECTS THE NERVES OF THE HUMAN BODY--ENABLING ME TO CONTROL ANYONE IT'S FIRED AT!
THIS IS MOST ASTOUNDING! FLASH SEEMS MORE SUPER THAN EVER! COULD I HAVE UNWITTINGLY GIVEN HIM THESE EXTRA POWERS?
TO PLAY IT SAFE--I'LL CAUSE THE FLOOR TO CHANGE ITS STRUCTURE--FASHION WOODEN HANDS TO GRIP AND HOLD HIM TIGHT--WHILE I MAKE OFF WITH THE GOLD THAT WILL MAKE ME THE WEALTHIEST MAN IN THE 64th CENTURY!
19

MOMENTS LATER, THE WOODEN HANDS LIFT *FLASH*-- SWING HIM 'ROUND AND 'ROUND...

eh? WHAT'S *THIS?* HOW CAN MY WOODEN HANDS ACT ON THEIR OWN?

THE ANSWER IS MAGIC À LA DR. FATE--BUT ABRA KADABRA DOESN'T KNOW THAT--AND NOW...

*L*IKE A LIVING BULLET THOSE HANDS HURL *THE FLASH*-- STRAIGHT ON TARGET...

A VICTIM OF MY OWN WOODEN HANDS-- *GNNGGG!!*

I'LL CUSHION THE BLOW FOR FLASH SO HE DOESN'T FEEL A THING!

ZWOPP

DRIVEN BACK INTO THE VERY GOLDEN HOARD HE SEEKS TO STEAL, THE *MASTER OF MAGIC* SNARLS IN FURY...

THERE'S ONLY ONE ANSWER! BY REMOVING YOUR ABILITY TO SEE, HEAR AND SPEAK EVIL--I'VE *INCREASED* YOUR POWERS! BUT YOU'RE STILL NO MATCH FOR ME, *FLASH!*

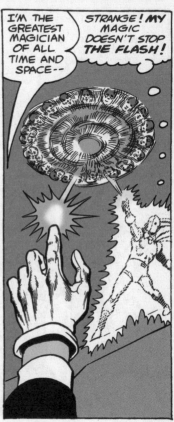

I'M THE GREATEST MAGICIAN OF ALL TIME AND SPACE--

STRANGE! MY MAGIC DOESN'T STOP *THE FLASH!*

HA! HA! THAT STOPS YOU-- *DEAD!*

FLASH IS STILL UNDER THE INFLUENCE OF MY *CYROTUBER*, DOCTOR FATE! HE WON'T BE HARMED!

I WASN'T ABLE TO STOP HIS SPINNING--BUT I CAN DO SOMETHING ELSE TO HELP HIM...

20

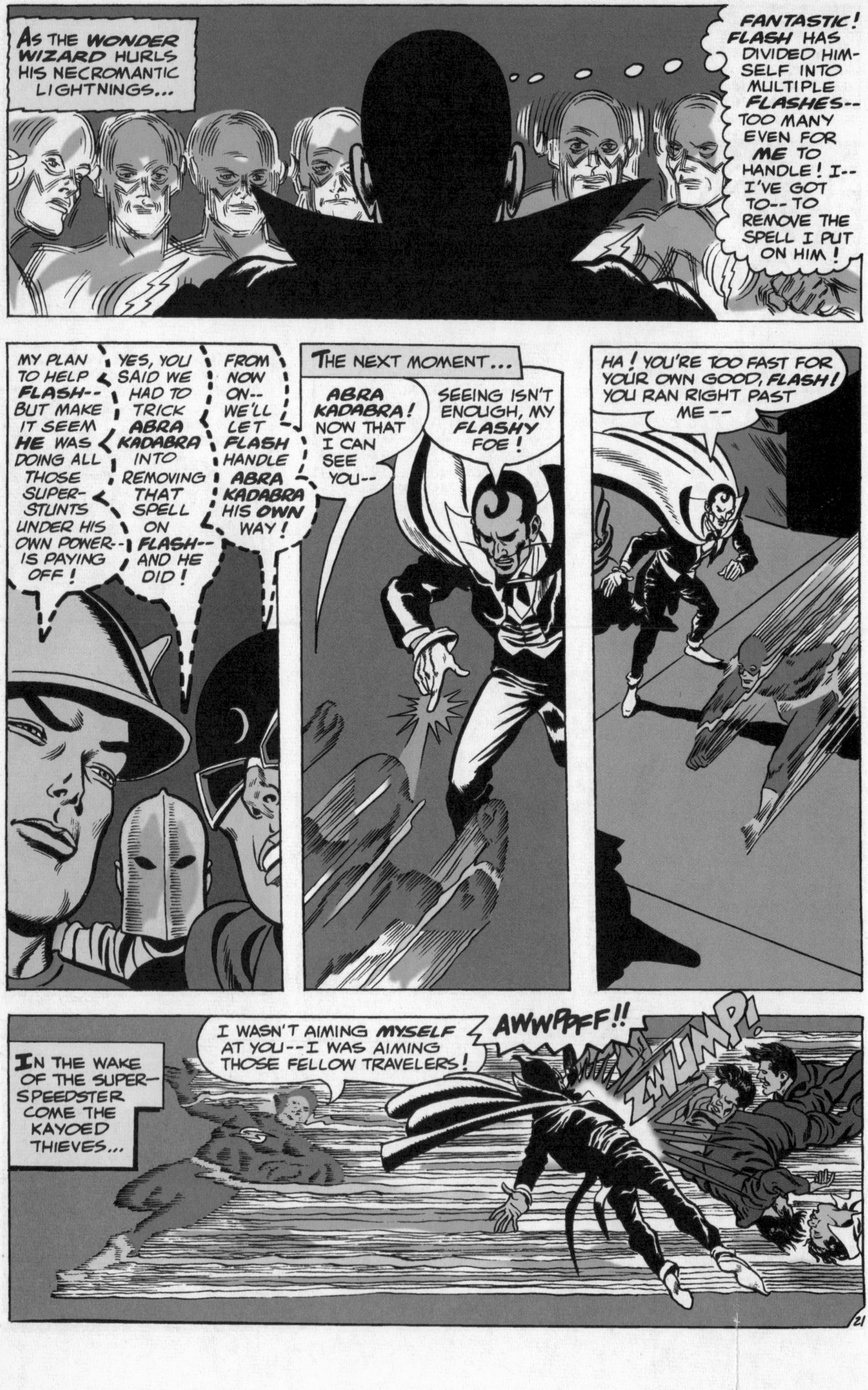
AS THE WONDER WIZARD HURLS HIS NECROMANTIC LIGHTNINGS...
FANTASTIC! FLASH HAS DIVIDED HIMSELF INTO MULTIPLE FLASHES-- TOO MANY EVEN FOR ME TO HANDLE! I-- I'VE GOT TO-- TO REMOVE THE SPELL I PUT ON HIM!
MY PLAN TO HELP FLASH-- BUT MAKE IT SEEM HE WAS DOING ALL THOSE SUPER-STUNTS UNDER HIS OWN POWER-- IS PAYING OFF!
YES, YOU SAID WE HAD TO TRICK ABRA KADABRA INTO REMOVING THAT SPELL ON FLASH-- AND HE DID!
FROM NOW ON-- WE'LL LET FLASH HANDLE ABRA KADABRA HIS OWN WAY!
THE NEXT MOMENT...
ABRA KADABRA! NOW THAT I CAN SEE YOU--
SEEING ISN'T ENOUGH, MY FLASHY FOE!
HA! YOU'RE TOO FAST FOR YOUR OWN GOOD, FLASH! YOU RAN RIGHT PAST ME--
IN THE WAKE OF THE SUPER-SPEEDSTER COME THE KAYOED THIEVES...
I WASN'T AIMING MYSELF AT YOU--I WAS AIMING THOSE FELLOW TRAVELERS!
AWWPPFF!!
ZWUMP!
21

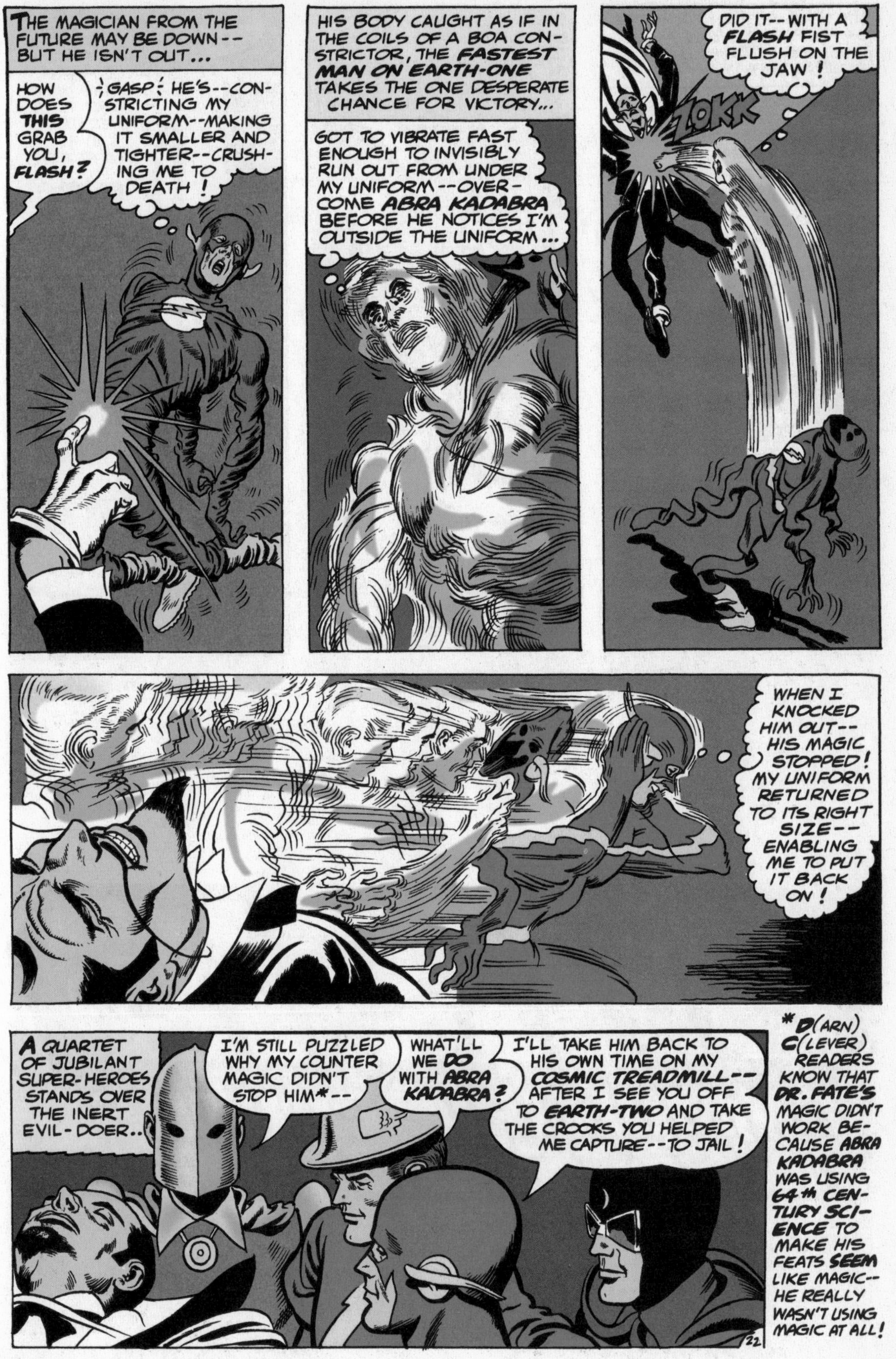
THE MAGICIAN FROM THE FUTURE MAY BE DOWN--BUT HE ISN'T OUT...
HOW DOES THIS GRAB YOU, FLASH?
GASP! HE'S--CONSTRICTING MY UNIFORM--MAKING IT SMALLER AND TIGHTER--CRUSHING ME TO DEATH!
HIS BODY CAUGHT AS IF IN THE COILS OF A BOA CONSTRICTOR, THE FASTEST MAN ON EARTH-ONE TAKES THE ONE DESPERATE CHANCE FOR VICTORY...
GOT TO VIBRATE FAST ENOUGH TO INVISIBLY RUN OUT FROM UNDER MY UNIFORM--OVERCOME ABRA KADABRA BEFORE HE NOTICES I'M OUTSIDE THE UNIFORM...
DID IT--WITH A FLASH FIST FLUSH ON THE JAW!
ZOKK
WHEN I KNOCKED HIM OUT--HIS MAGIC STOPPED! MY UNIFORM RETURNED TO ITS RIGHT SIZE--ENABLING ME TO PUT IT BACK ON!
A QUARTET OF JUBILANT SUPER-HEROES STANDS OVER THE INERT EVIL-DOER..
I'M STILL PUZZLED WHY MY COUNTER MAGIC DIDN'T STOP HIM*--
WHAT'LL WE DO WITH ABRA KADABRA?
I'LL TAKE HIM BACK TO HIS OWN TIME ON MY COSMIC TREADMILL--AFTER I SEE YOU OFF TO EARTH-TWO AND TAKE THE CROOKS YOU HELPED ME CAPTURE--TO JAIL!
22
*D(ARN) C(LEVER) READERS KNOW THAT DR. FATE'S MAGIC DIDN'T WORK BECAUSE ABRA KADABRA WAS USING 64th CENTURY SCIENCE TO MAKE HIS FEATS SEEM LIKE MAGIC--HE REALLY WASN'T USING MAGIC AT ALL!

UPON HIS RETURN FROM THE 64th CENTURY, FLASH CHANGES INTO HIS BARRY ALLEN IDENTITY AND...
I HOPE THAT FUTURE PRISON WILL HOLD ABRA KADABRA THIS TIME--
IRIS! YOU'RE GETTING HOME KIND OF LATE!
MARGOT AND I HAD SO MUCH TO TALK ABOUT! BUT HOW COME YOU'RE SO LATE?
I RAN INTO SOME-- er--OLD FRIENDS, TOO! THEY WERE IN TOWN FOR ONLY A SHORT TIME...
OH? I'D LIKE TO MEET THEM SOMETIME!
YOU WILL, DEAR-- YOU WILL!
ONCE I FINALLY MAKE UP MY MIND TO TELL HER THAT I'M -- THE FLASH!
THE END
23

CRISIS ON MULTIPLE EARTHS
THE TEAM UPS

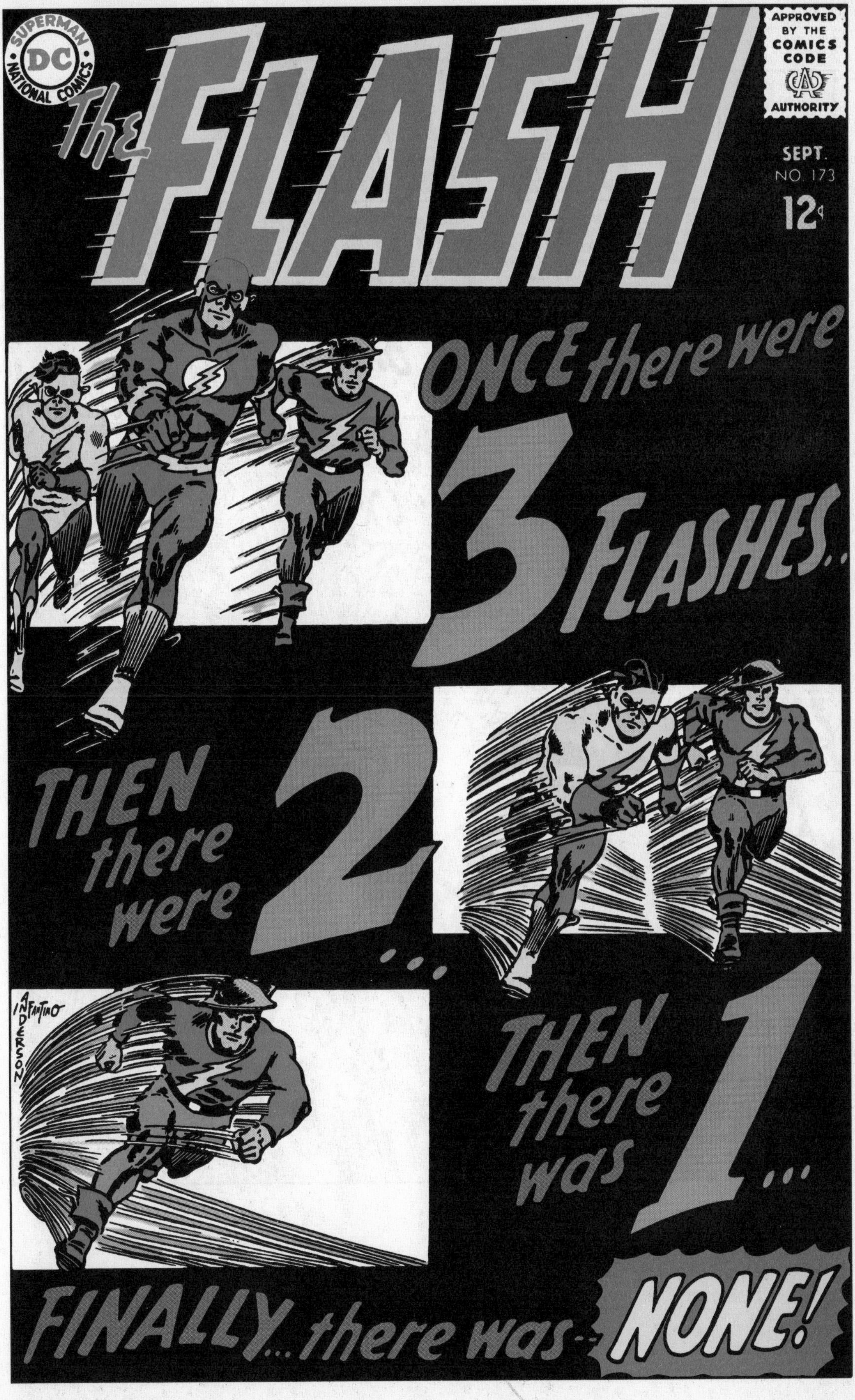
SUPERMAN
DC
NATIONAL COMICS
The FLASH
APPROVED BY THE COMICS CODE AUTHORITY
SEPT.
NO. 173
12¢
ONCE there were 3 FLASHES...
THEN there were 2...
INFANTINO ANDERSON
THEN there was 1...
FINALLY... there was-- NONE!

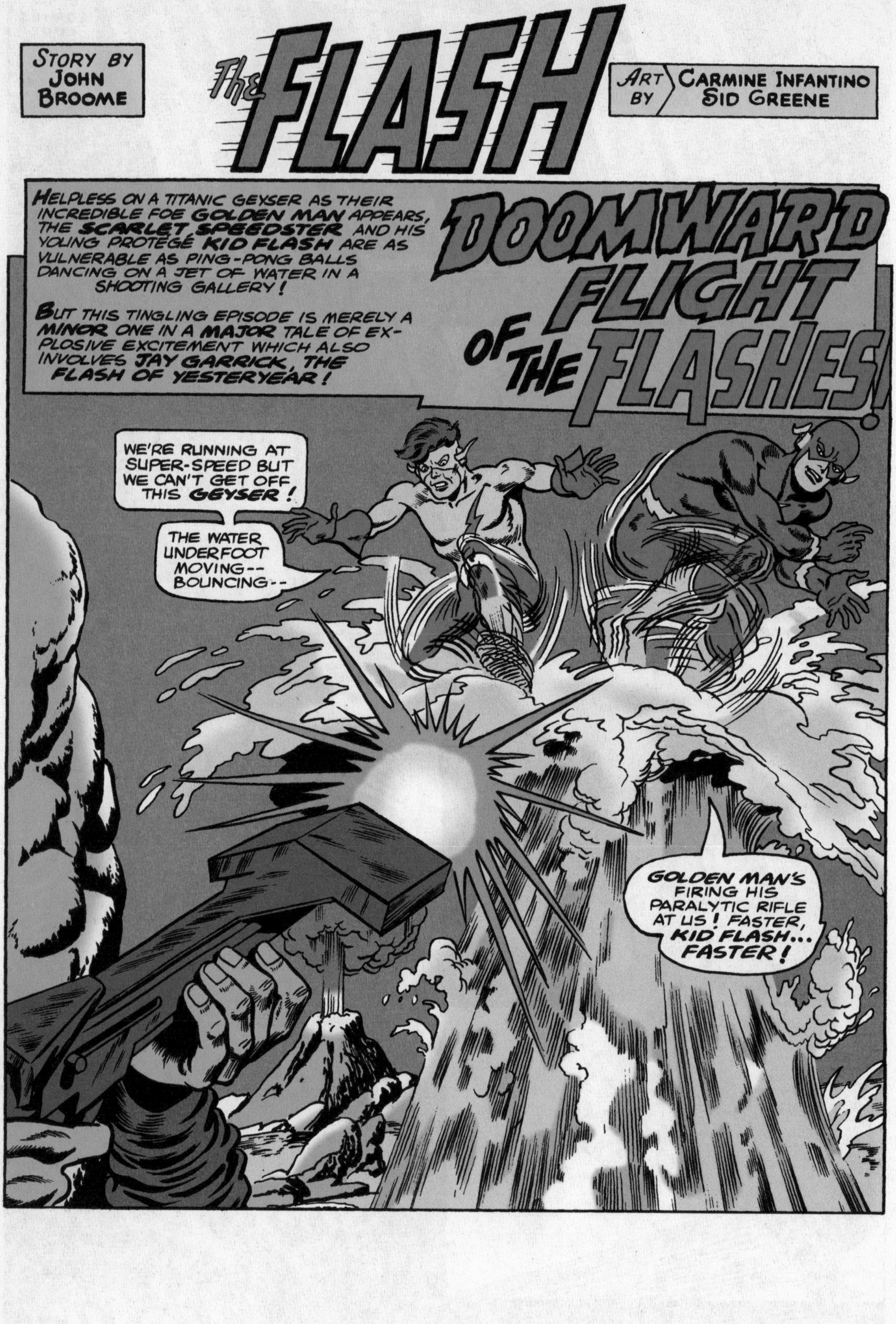

STORY BY JOHN BROOME
THE FLASH
ART BY CARMINE INFANTINO SID GREENE
HELPLESS ON A TITANIC GEYSER AS THEIR INCREDIBLE FOE GOLDEN MAN APPEARS, THE SCARLET SPEEDSTER AND HIS YOUNG PROTEGÉ KID FLASH ARE AS VULNERABLE AS PING-PONG BALLS DANCING ON A JET OF WATER IN A SHOOTING GALLERY!
BUT THIS TINGLING EPISODE IS MERELY A MINOR ONE IN A MAJOR TALE OF EXPLOSIVE EXCITEMENT WHICH ALSO INVOLVES JAY GARRICK, THE FLASH OF YESTERYEAR!
DOOMWARD FLIGHT OF THE FLASHES!
WE'RE RUNNING AT SUPER-SPEED BUT WE CAN'T GET OFF THIS GEYSER!
THE WATER UNDERFOOT MOVING-- BOUNCING--
GOLDEN MAN'S FIRING HIS PARALYTIC RIFLE AT US! FASTER, KID FLASH... FASTER!

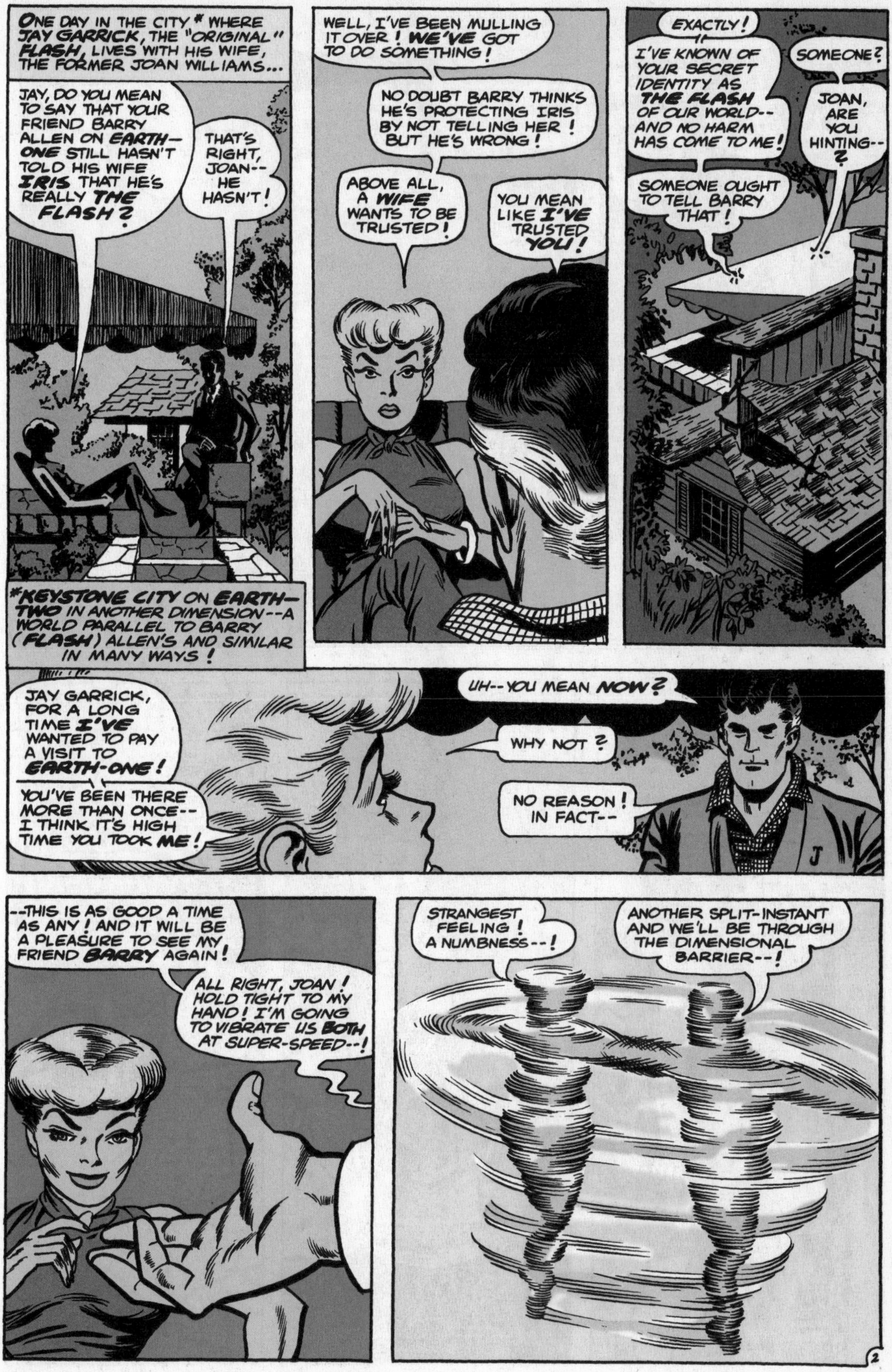

ONE DAY IN THE CITY* WHERE JAY GARRICK, THE "ORIGINAL" FLASH, LIVES WITH HIS WIFE, THE FORMER JOAN WILLIAMS...
JAY, DO YOU MEAN TO SAY THAT YOUR FRIEND BARRY ALLEN ON EARTH-ONE STILL HASN'T TOLD HIS WIFE IRIS THAT HE'S REALLY THE FLASH?
THAT'S RIGHT, JOAN-- HE HASN'T!
*KEYSTONE CITY ON EARTH-TWO IN ANOTHER DIMENSION--A WORLD PARALLEL TO BARRY (FLASH) ALLEN'S AND SIMILAR IN MANY WAYS!
WELL, I'VE BEEN MULLING IT OVER! WE'VE GOT TO DO SOMETHING!
NO DOUBT BARRY THINKS HE'S PROTECTING IRIS BY NOT TELLING HER! BUT HE'S WRONG!
ABOVE ALL, A WIFE WANTS TO BE TRUSTED!
YOU MEAN LIKE I'VE TRUSTED YOU!
EXACTLY!
I'VE KNOWN OF YOUR SECRET IDENTITY AS THE FLASH OF OUR WORLD-- AND NO HARM HAS COME TO ME!
SOMEONE OUGHT TO TELL BARRY THAT!
SOMEONE?
JOAN, ARE YOU HINTING--?
JAY GARRICK, FOR A LONG TIME I'VE WANTED TO PAY A VISIT TO EARTH-ONE!
YOU'VE BEEN THERE MORE THAN ONCE-- I THINK IT'S HIGH TIME YOU TOOK ME!
UH--YOU MEAN NOW?
WHY NOT?
NO REASON! IN FACT--
--THIS IS AS GOOD A TIME AS ANY! AND IT WILL BE A PLEASURE TO SEE MY FRIEND BARRY AGAIN!
ALL RIGHT, JOAN! HOLD TIGHT TO MY HAND! I'M GOING TO VIBRATE US BOTH AT SUPER-SPEED--!
STRANGEST FEELING! A NUMBNESS--!
ANOTHER SPLIT-INSTANT AND WE'LL BE THROUGH THE DIMENSIONAL BARRIER--!
2

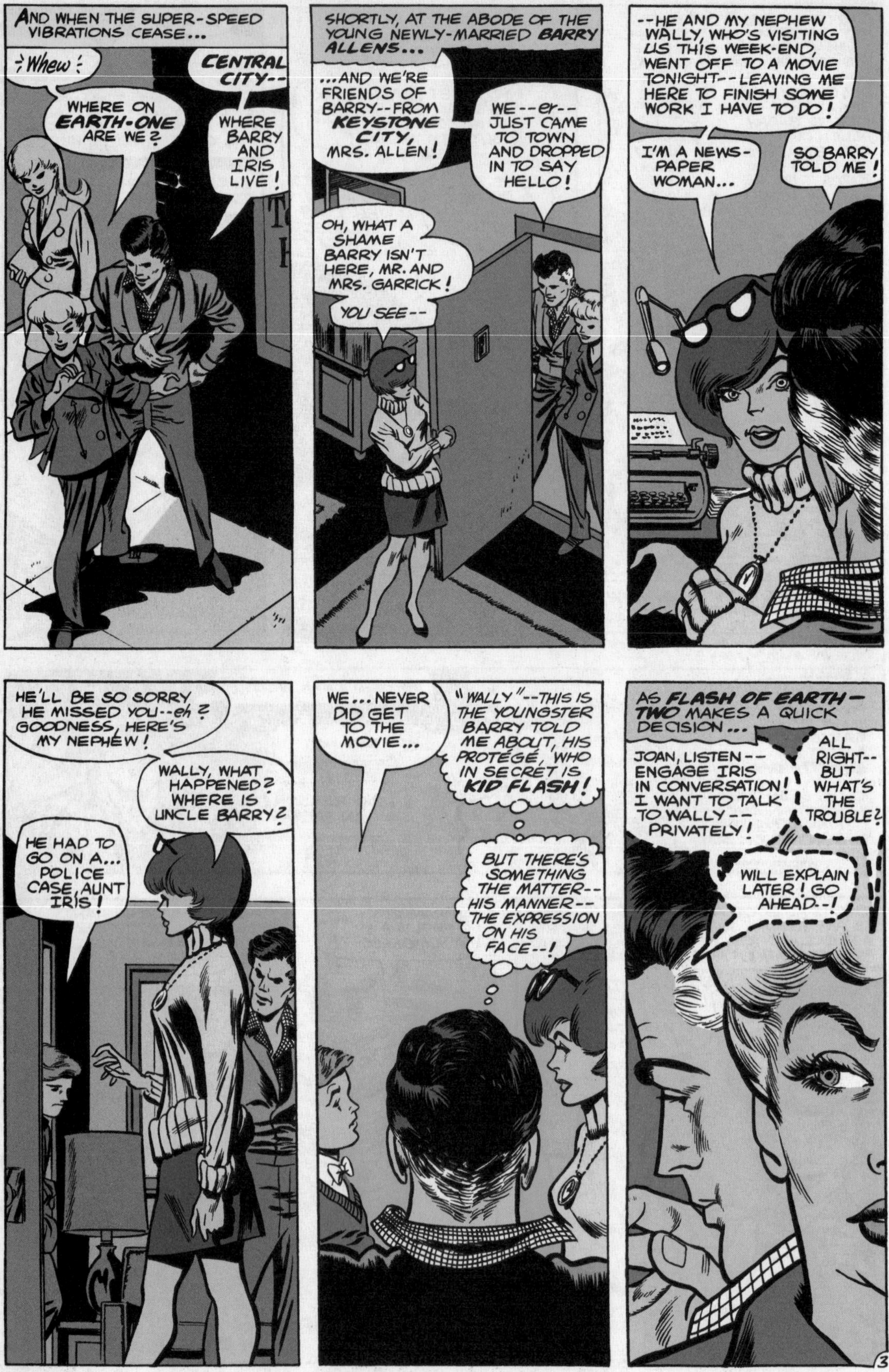
AND WHEN THE SUPER-SPEED VIBRATIONS CEASE...
Whew
CENTRAL CITY--
WHERE ON EARTH-ONE ARE WE?
WHERE BARRY AND IRIS LIVE!
SHORTLY, AT THE ABODE OF THE YOUNG NEWLY-MARRIED BARRY ALLENS...
...AND WE'RE FRIENDS OF BARRY--FROM KEYSTONE CITY, MRS. ALLEN!
WE--er--JUST CAME TO TOWN AND DROPPED IN TO SAY HELLO!
OH, WHAT A SHAME BARRY ISN'T HERE, MR. AND MRS. GARRICK!
YOU SEE--
--HE AND MY NEPHEW WALLY, WHO'S VISITING US THIS WEEK-END, WENT OFF TO A MOVIE TONIGHT--LEAVING ME HERE TO FINISH SOME WORK I HAVE TO DO!
I'M A NEWS-PAPER WOMAN...
SO BARRY TOLD ME!
HE'LL BE SO SORRY HE MISSED YOU--eh? GOODNESS, HERE'S MY NEPHEW!
WALLY, WHAT HAPPENED? WHERE IS UNCLE BARRY?
HE HAD TO GO ON A... POLICE CASE, AUNT IRIS!
WE... NEVER DID GET TO THE MOVIE...
"WALLY"--THIS IS THE YOUNGSTER BARRY TOLD ME ABOUT, HIS PROTÉGÉ, WHO IN SECRET IS KID FLASH!
BUT THERE'S SOMETHING THE MATTER--HIS MANNER--THE EXPRESSION ON HIS FACE--!
AS FLASH OF EARTH-TWO MAKES A QUICK DECISION...
JOAN, LISTEN--ENGAGE IRIS IN CONVERSATION! I WANT TO TALK TO WALLY--PRIVATELY!
ALL RIGHT--BUT WHAT'S THE TROUBLE?
WILL EXPLAIN LATER! GO AHEAD--!
3

IRIS--WILL YOU TELL ME ABOUT YOUR NEWSPAPER WORK?

OF COURSE JOAN--I'LL BE HAPPY TO!

WALLY...ACT AS IF NOTHING IS HAPPENING!

WALK OUT WITH ME TO THE TERRACE...

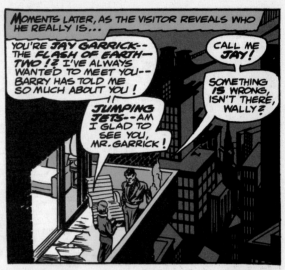

MOMENTS LATER, AS THE VISITOR REVEALS WHO HE REALLY IS...

YOU'RE JAY GARRICK-- THE FLASH OF EARTH-TWO!? I'VE ALWAYS WANTED TO MEET YOU-- BARRY HAS TOLD ME SO MUCH ABOUT YOU!

CALL ME JAY!

SOMETHING IS WRONG, ISN'T THERE, WALLY?

JUMPING JETS-- AM I GLAD TO SEE YOU, MR. GARRICK!

THERE SURE IS! I'LL TELL YOU WHAT HAPPENED TONIGHT, JAY-- WHAT I COULDN'T TELL AUNT IRIS...

BARRY AND I DID START OUT TO GO TO A MOVIE-- THAT PART IS TRUE!

BUT WE DIDN'T GET VERY FAR, BECAUSE ON THE WAY--

"--WE RAN INTO A SPECTACULAR CRIME RIGHT ON MAIN STREET!..."

THE DOMINO GANG-- LOOTING THAT MONEY EXCHANGE!

THIS MUST BE MY LUCKY EVENING! I'VE BEEN AFTER THAT GANG FOR THE PAST MONTH!

READY FOR A BIT OF SUPER-SPEED ACTION, WALLY?

LET'S JET UP AND GO, UNCLE BARRY!

MONEY CHANGED FOREIGN EXCHANGE

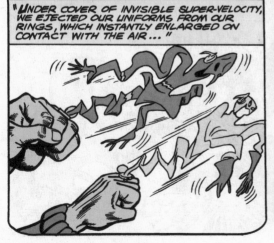

"UNDER COVER OF INVISIBLE SUPER-VELOCITY, WE EJECTED OUR UNIFORMS FROM OUR RINGS, WHICH INSTANTLY ENLARGED ON CONTACT WITH THE AIR..."

"AND AN EYE-BLINK LATER..."

FLASH!?

AND KID FLASH--?!

4

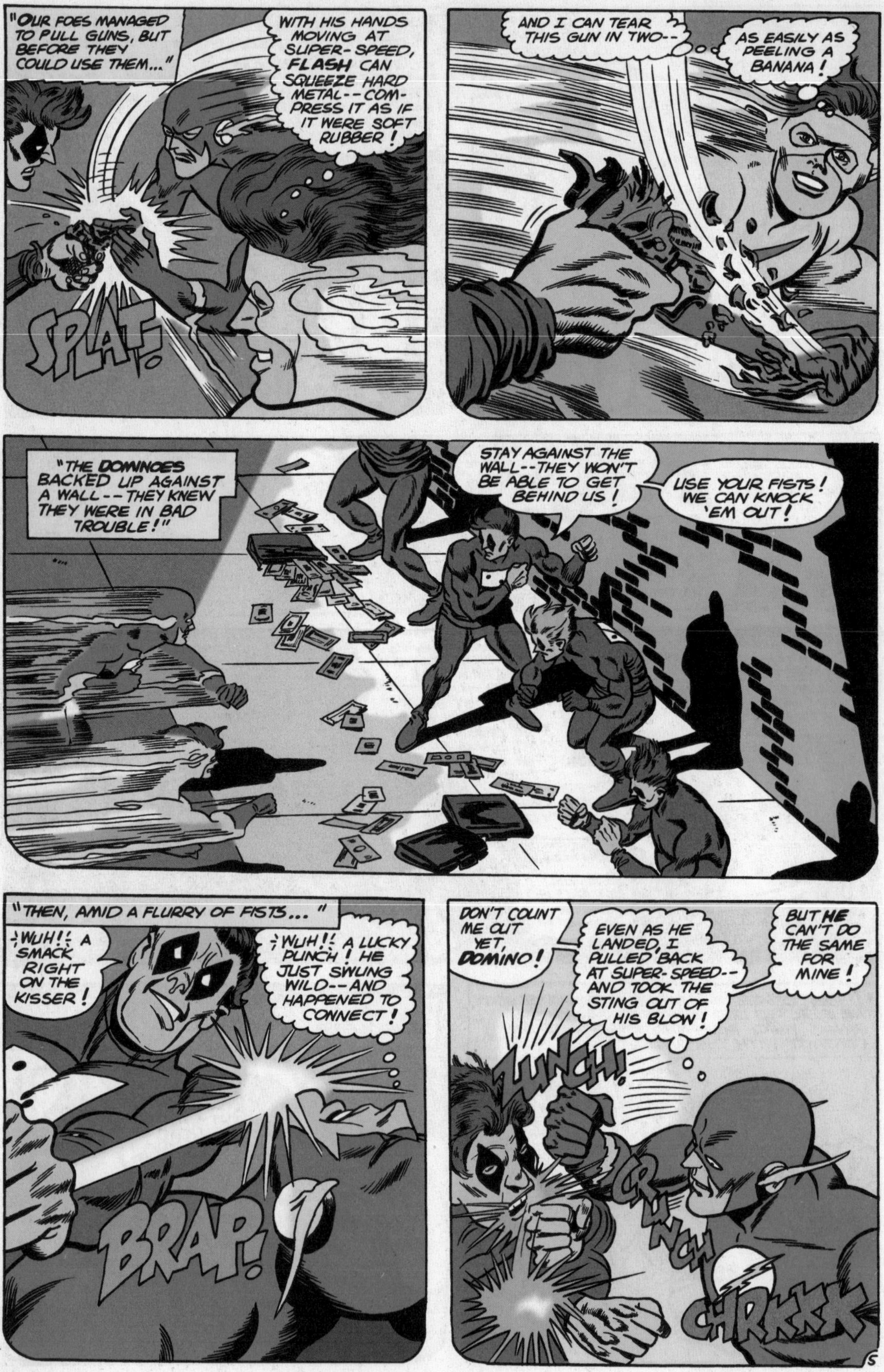
"OUR FOES MANAGED TO PULL GUNS, BUT BEFORE THEY COULD USE THEM..."
WITH HIS HANDS MOVING AT SUPER-SPEED, FLASH CAN SQUEEZE HARD METAL--COMPRESS IT AS IF IT WERE SOFT RUBBER!
SPLAT!
AND I CAN TEAR THIS GUN IN TWO--
AS EASILY AS PEELING A BANANA!
"THE DOMINOES BACKED UP AGAINST A WALL--THEY KNEW THEY WERE IN BAD TROUBLE!"
STAY AGAINST THE WALL--THEY WON'T BE ABLE TO GET BEHIND US!
USE YOUR FISTS! WE CAN KNOCK 'EM OUT!
"THEN, AMID A FLURRY OF FISTS..."
WUH!! A SMACK RIGHT ON THE KISSER!
WUH!! A LUCKY PUNCH! HE JUST SWUNG WILD--AND HAPPENED TO CONNECT!
BRAP!
DON'T COUNT ME OUT YET, DOMINO!
EVEN AS HE LANDED, I PULLED BACK AT SUPER-SPEED--AND TOOK THE STING OUT OF HIS BLOW!
BUT HE CAN'T DO THE SAME FOR MINE!
ZUNCH!
CRUNCH
CHRKKK
5

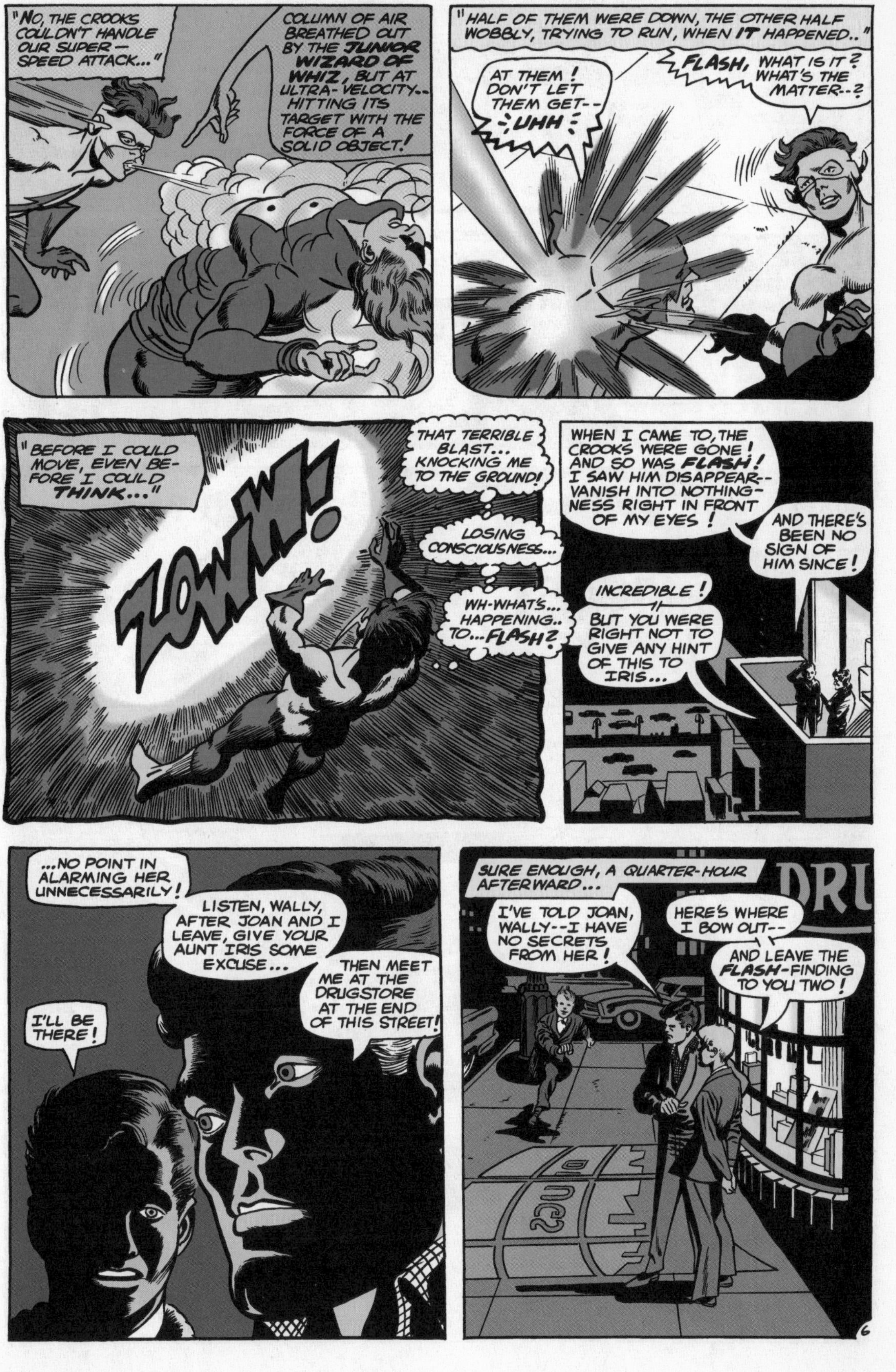
"NO, THE CROOKS COULDN'T HANDLE OUR SUPER-SPEED ATTACK..."
COLUMN OF AIR BREATHED OUT BY THE JUNIOR WIZARD OF WHIZ, BUT AT ULTRA-VELOCITY.. HITTING ITS TARGET WITH THE FORCE OF A SOLID OBJECT!
"HALF OF THEM WERE DOWN, THE OTHER HALF WOBBLY, TRYING TO RUN, WHEN IT HAPPENED.."
AT THEM! DON'T LET THEM GET-- UHH
FLASH, WHAT IS IT? WHAT'S THE MATTER--?
"BEFORE I COULD MOVE, EVEN BEFORE I COULD THINK..."
ZOWW!
THAT TERRIBLE BLAST... KNOCKING ME TO THE GROUND!
LOSING CONSCIOUSNESS...
WH-WHAT'S... HAPPENING.. TO...FLASH?
WHEN I CAME TO, THE CROOKS WERE GONE! AND SO WAS FLASH! I SAW HIM DISAPPEAR--VANISH INTO NOTHINGNESS RIGHT IN FRONT OF MY EYES!
AND THERE'S BEEN NO SIGN OF HIM SINCE!
INCREDIBLE!
BUT YOU WERE RIGHT NOT TO GIVE ANY HINT OF THIS TO IRIS...
...NO POINT IN ALARMING HER UNNECESSARILY!
LISTEN, WALLY, AFTER JOAN AND I LEAVE, GIVE YOUR AUNT IRIS SOME EXCUSE...
THEN MEET ME AT THE DRUGSTORE AT THE END OF THIS STREET!
I'LL BE THERE!
SURE ENOUGH, A QUARTER-HOUR AFTERWARD...
DRU
I'VE TOLD JOAN, WALLY--I HAVE NO SECRETS FROM HER!
HERE'S WHERE I BOW OUT--
AND LEAVE THE FLASH-FINDING TO YOU TWO!
6

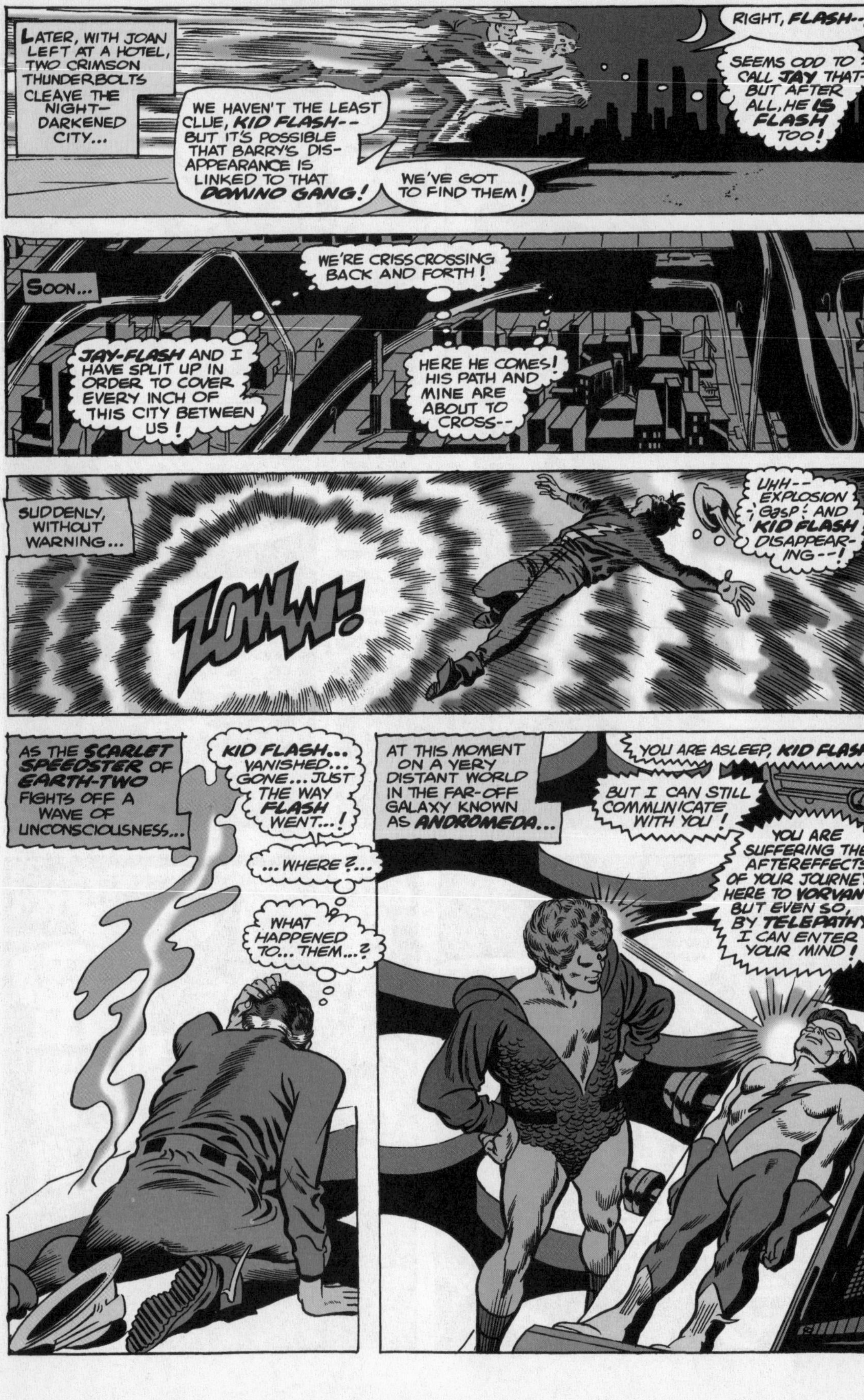
LATER, WITH JOAN LEFT AT A HOTEL, TWO CRIMSON THUNDERBOLTS CLEAVE THE NIGHT-DARKENED CITY...
WE HAVEN'T THE LEAST CLUE, KID FLASH-- BUT IT'S POSSIBLE THAT BARRY'S DIS-APPEARANCE IS LINKED TO THAT DOMINO GANG!
WE'VE GOT TO FIND THEM!
RIGHT, FLASH--!
SEEMS ODD TO CALL JAY THAT-- BUT AFTER ALL, HE IS FLASH TOO!
SOON...
WE'RE CRISSCROSSING BACK AND FORTH!
JAY-FLASH AND I HAVE SPLIT UP IN ORDER TO COVER EVERY INCH OF THIS CITY BETWEEN US!
HERE HE COMES! HIS PATH AND MINE ARE ABOUT TO CROSS--
SUDDENLY, WITHOUT WARNING...
ZOWW!
UHH-- EXPLOSION -gasp- AND KID FLASH DISAPPEARING--!
AS THE SCARLET SPEEDSTER OF EARTH-TWO FIGHTS OFF A WAVE OF UNCONSCIOUSNESS...
KID FLASH... VANISHED... GONE... JUST THE WAY FLASH WENT...!
...WHERE?...
WHAT HAPPENED TO... THEM...?
AT THIS MOMENT ON A VERY DISTANT WORLD IN THE FAR-OFF GALAXY KNOWN AS ANDROMEDA...
YOU ARE ASLEEP, KID FLASH--
BUT I CAN STILL COMMUNICATE WITH YOU!
YOU ARE SUFFERING THE AFTEREFFECTS OF YOUR JOURNEY HERE TO VORVAN-- BUT EVEN SO, BY TELEPATHY I CAN ENTER YOUR MIND!
7

WHEN YOU AWAKEN YOU **MUST** BE IN FULL POSSESSION OF ALL YOUR FACULTIES!

THEREFORE IT IS NECESSARY FOR YOU TO UNDERSTAND WHY--AND **HOW**--YOU WERE BROUGHT HERE!

TO BEGIN WITH--I AM CALLED--

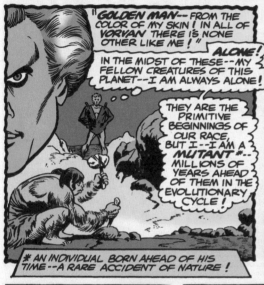

"**GOLDEN MAN**-- FROM THE COLOR OF MY SKIN! IN ALL OF **VORVAN** THERE IS NONE OTHER LIKE ME!"

ALONE! IN THE MIDST OF THESE--MY FELLOW CREATURES OF THIS PLANET--I AM ALWAYS ALONE!

THEY ARE THE PRIMITIVE BEGINNINGS OF OUR RACE, BUT I--I AM A **MUTANT** #-- MILLIONS OF YEARS AHEAD OF THEM IN THE EVOLUTIONARY CYCLE!

MY MENTAL CAPACITY IS GIGANTIC!

WITH IT, ALONE, I BUILT **VORVAN CITY**! BUT ONLY I LIVE IN IT!

THE OTHERS ALL LIVE IN CAVES-- WHICH THEY PREFER--AND WHICH SUITS THEM BETTER!

AN INDIVIDUAL BORN AHEAD OF HIS TIME--A RARE ACCIDENT OF NATURE!

...BUT DESPITE MY GIANT INTELLECT, MY LIFE BECAME IRKSOME--BORING!

HUNTING HAD ALWAYS BEEN MY PASSION--BUT EVEN THAT BECAME TIRESOME BECAUSE NO PREY ON **VORVAN** COULD ESCAPE ME! IN DESPERATION I TURNED TO **OTHER WORLDS** FOR **WORTHY GAME!**

AND THAT IS WHERE **YOU** COME IN, **KID FLASH**...

YOU WERE BROUGHT HERE-- LIKE YOUR MENTOR **FLASH**-- BY MY **TELEPORTATION** DEVICE WHICH ACTS INSTANTLY OVER ANY DISTANCE!

TO HUNT A QUARRY-- EQUIPPED WITH EXTRA-ORDINARY SPEED!

YOU TWO WERE SINGLED OUT BECAUSE OF ALL THE BEINGS ON ALL THE WORLDS I EXAMINED, YOU TWO PROMISED TO AFFORD ME A RARE THRILL--

YOUR MENTOR **FLASH** IS ALSO ASLEEP! WHEN YOU BOTH AWAKEN YOU WILL FIND YOURSELVES OUTSIDE **VORVAN CITY**-- TELEPORTED BY MY DEVICE! YOU WILL BE IN FULL POSSESSION OF ALL YOUR POWERS!

AND AT THAT MOMENT **THE HUNT WILL BEGIN!**

8

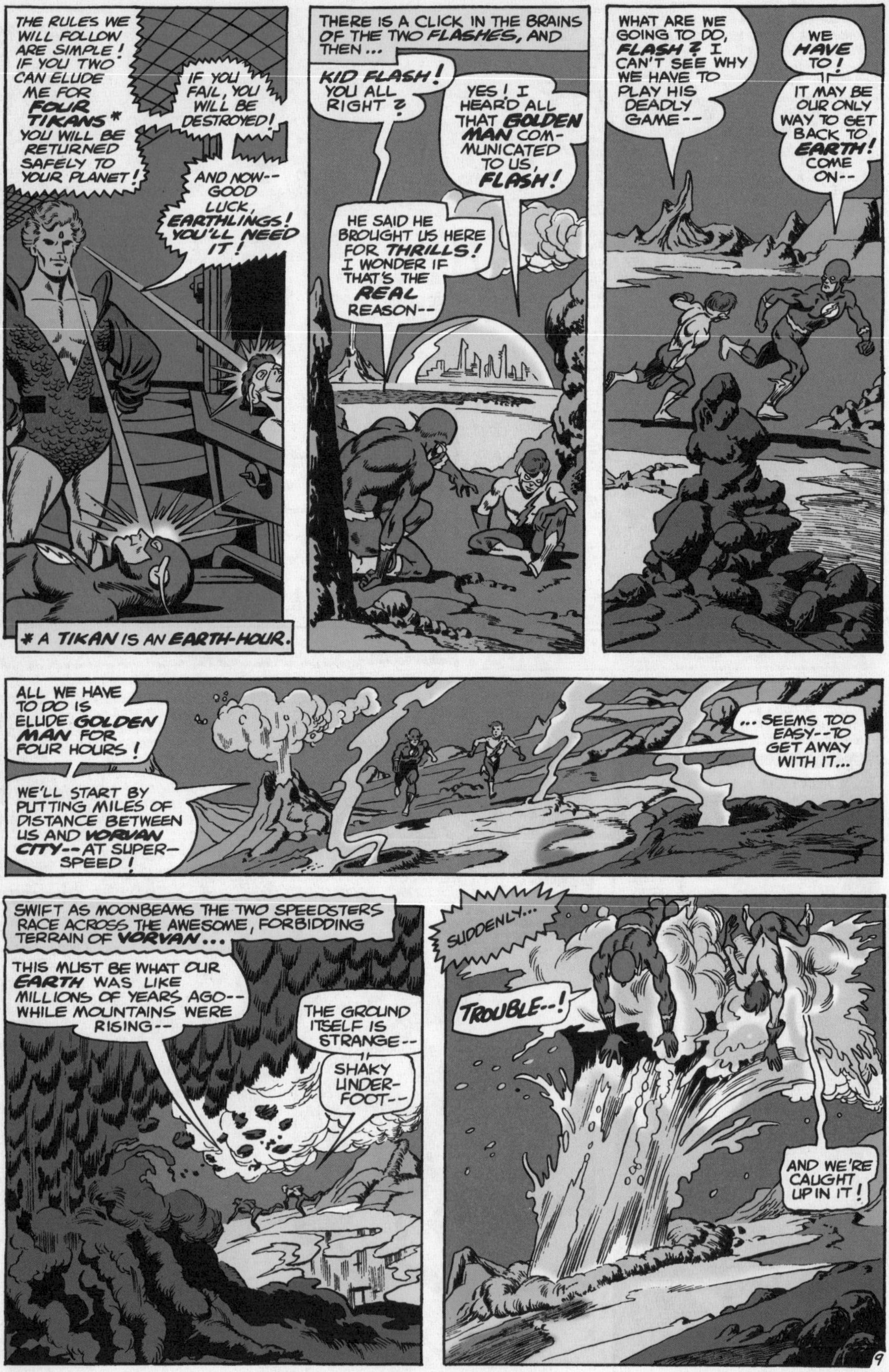
THE RULES WE WILL FOLLOW ARE SIMPLE! IF YOU TWO CAN ELUDE ME FOR FOUR TIKANS* YOU WILL BE RETURNED SAFELY TO YOUR PLANET!
IF YOU FAIL, YOU WILL BE DESTROYED!
AND NOW--GOOD LUCK, EARTHLINGS! YOU'LL NEED IT!
* A TIKAN IS AN EARTH-HOUR.
THERE IS A CLICK IN THE BRAINS OF THE TWO FLASHES, AND THEN...
KID FLASH! YOU ALL RIGHT?
YES! I HEAR'D ALL THAT GOLDEN MAN COMMUNICATED TO US, FLASH!
HE SAID HE BROUGHT US HERE FOR THRILLS! I WONDER IF THAT'S THE REAL REASON--
WHAT ARE WE GOING TO DO, FLASH? I CAN'T SEE WHY WE HAVE TO PLAY HIS DEADLY GAME--
WE HAVE TO!
IT MAY BE OUR ONLY WAY TO GET BACK TO EARTH! COME ON--
ALL WE HAVE TO DO IS ELUDE GOLDEN MAN FOR FOUR HOURS!
WE'LL START BY PUTTING MILES OF DISTANCE BETWEEN US AND VORVAN CITY--AT SUPER-SPEED!
...SEEMS TOO EASY--TO GET AWAY WITH IT...
SWIFT AS MOONBEAMS THE TWO SPEEDSTERS RACE ACROSS THE AWESOME, FORBIDDING TERRAIN OF VORVAN...
THIS MUST BE WHAT OUR EARTH WAS LIKE MILLIONS OF YEARS AGO--WHILE MOUNTAINS WERE RISING--
THE GROUND ITSELF IS STRANGE--
SHAKY UNDERFOOT--
SUDDENLY...
TROUBLE--!
AND WE'RE CAUGHT UP IN IT!
9

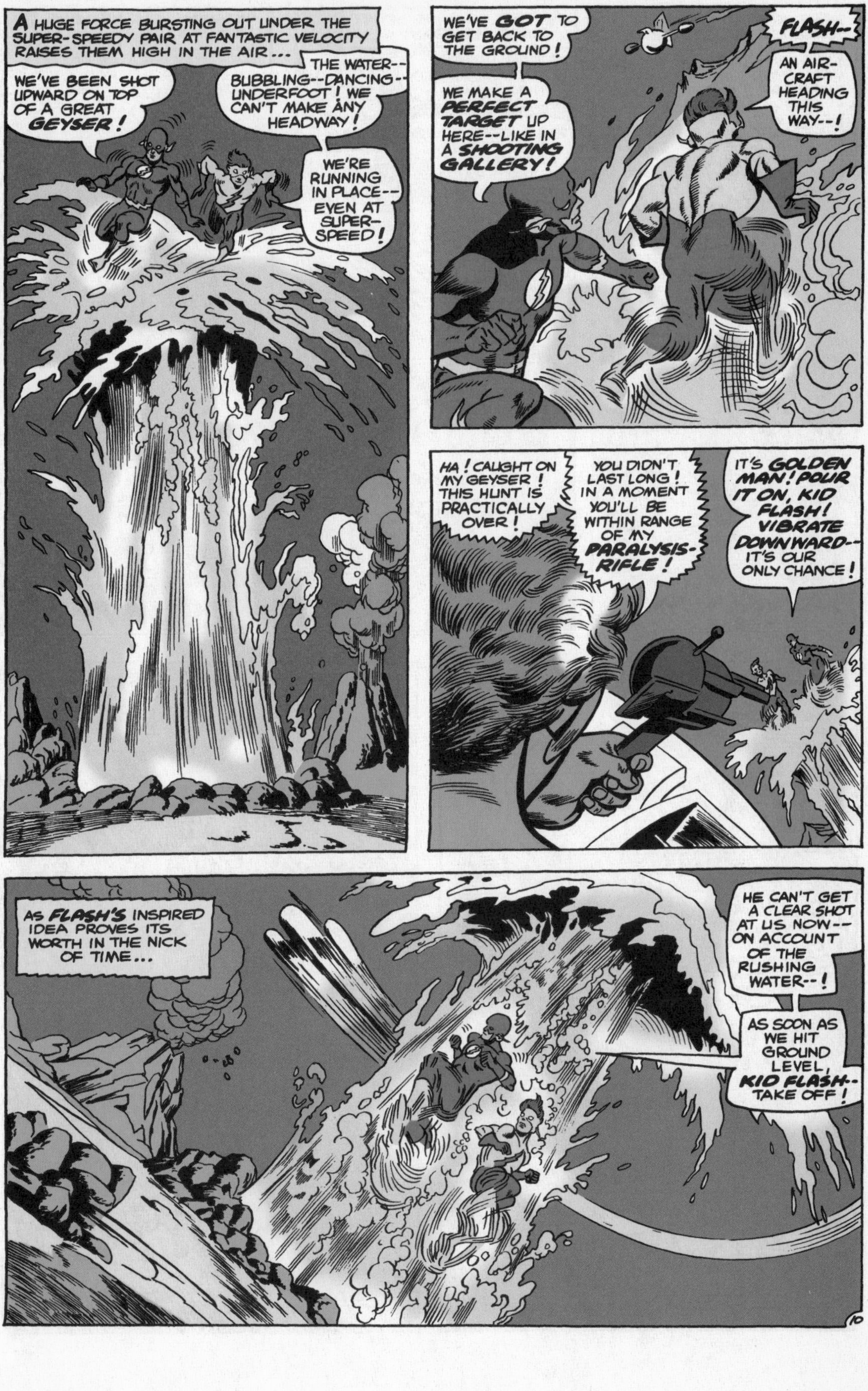
A HUGE FORCE BURSTING OUT UNDER THE SUPER-SPEEDY PAIR AT FANTASTIC VELOCITY RAISES THEM HIGH IN THE AIR...
WE'VE BEEN SHOT UPWARD ON TOP OF A GREAT GEYSER!
THE WATER-- BUBBLING--DANCING-- UNDERFOOT! WE CAN'T MAKE ANY HEADWAY!
WE'RE RUNNING IN PLACE-- EVEN AT SUPER-SPEED!
WE'VE GOT TO GET BACK TO THE GROUND!
WE MAKE A PERFECT TARGET UP HERE--LIKE IN A SHOOTING GALLERY!
FLASH--
AN AIR-CRAFT HEADING THIS WAY--!
HA! CAUGHT ON MY GEYSER! THIS HUNT IS PRACTICALLY OVER!
YOU DIDN'T LAST LONG! IN A MOMENT YOU'LL BE WITHIN RANGE OF MY PARALYSIS-RIFLE!
IT'S GOLDEN MAN! POUR IT ON, KID FLASH! VIBRATE DOWNWARD-- IT'S OUR ONLY CHANCE!
AS FLASH'S INSPIRED IDEA PROVES ITS WORTH IN THE NICK OF TIME...
HE CAN'T GET A CLEAR SHOT AT US NOW-- ON ACCOUNT OF THE RUSHING WATER--!
AS SOON AS WE HIT GROUND LEVEL, KID FLASH-- TAKE OFF!
10

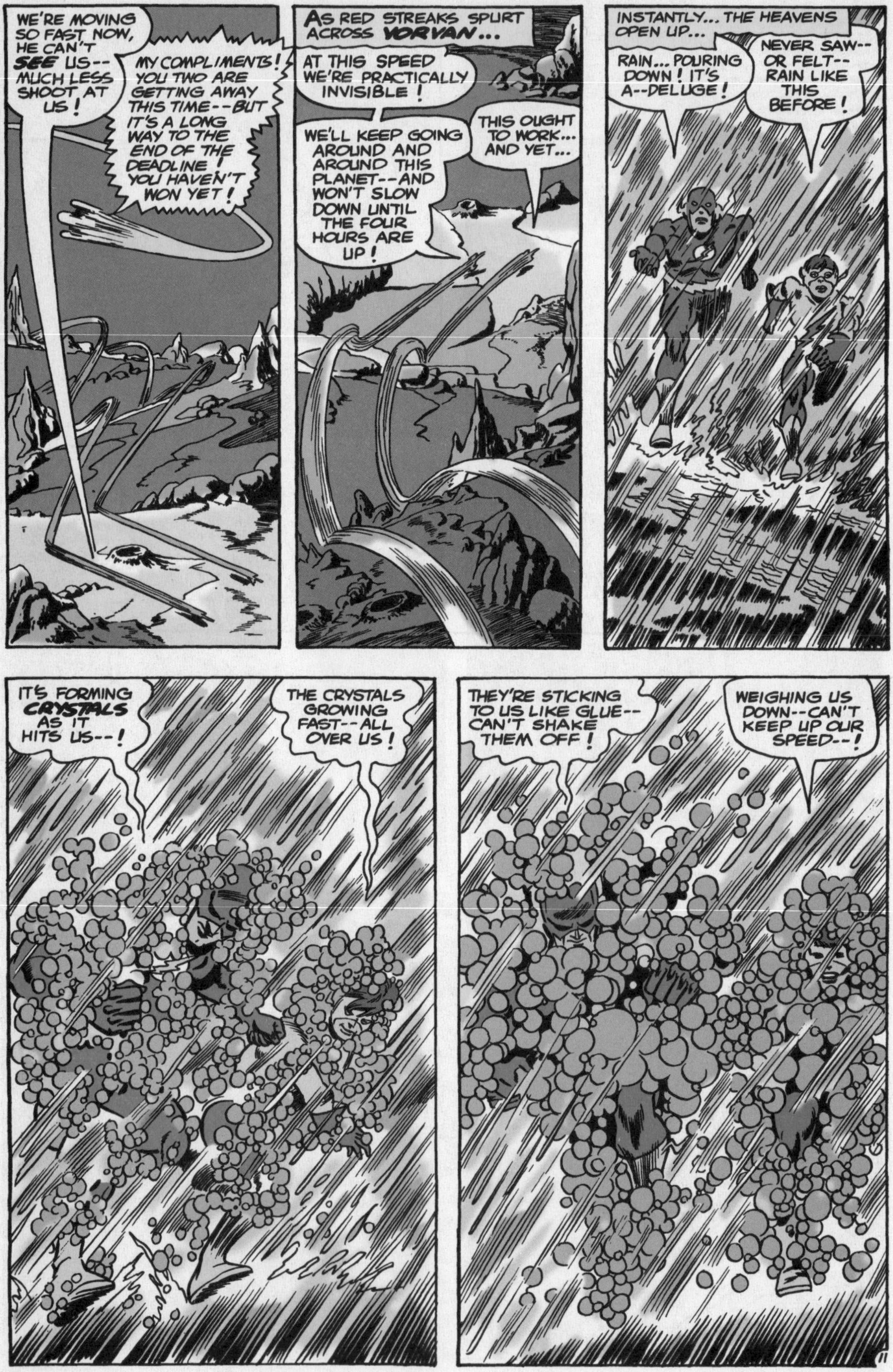
WE'RE MOVING SO FAST NOW, HE CAN'T SEE US--MUCH LESS SHOOT AT US!
MY COMPLIMENTS! YOU TWO ARE GETTING AWAY THIS TIME--BUT IT'S A LONG WAY TO THE END OF THE DEADLINE! YOU HAVEN'T WON YET!
AS RED STREAKS SPURT ACROSS VORVAN...
AT THIS SPEED WE'RE PRACTICALLY INVISIBLE!
WE'LL KEEP GOING AROUND AND AROUND THIS PLANET--AND WON'T SLOW DOWN UNTIL THE FOUR HOURS ARE UP!
THIS OUGHT TO WORK... AND YET...
INSTANTLY... THE HEAVENS OPEN UP...
RAIN... POURING DOWN! IT'S A--DELUGE!
NEVER SAW--OR FELT--RAIN LIKE THIS BEFORE!
IT'S FORMING CRYSTALS AS IT HITS US--!
THE CRYSTALS GROWING FAST--ALL OVER US!
THEY'RE STICKING TO US LIKE GLUE--CAN'T SHAKE THEM OFF!
WEIGHING US DOWN--CAN'T KEEP UP OUR SPEED--!
11

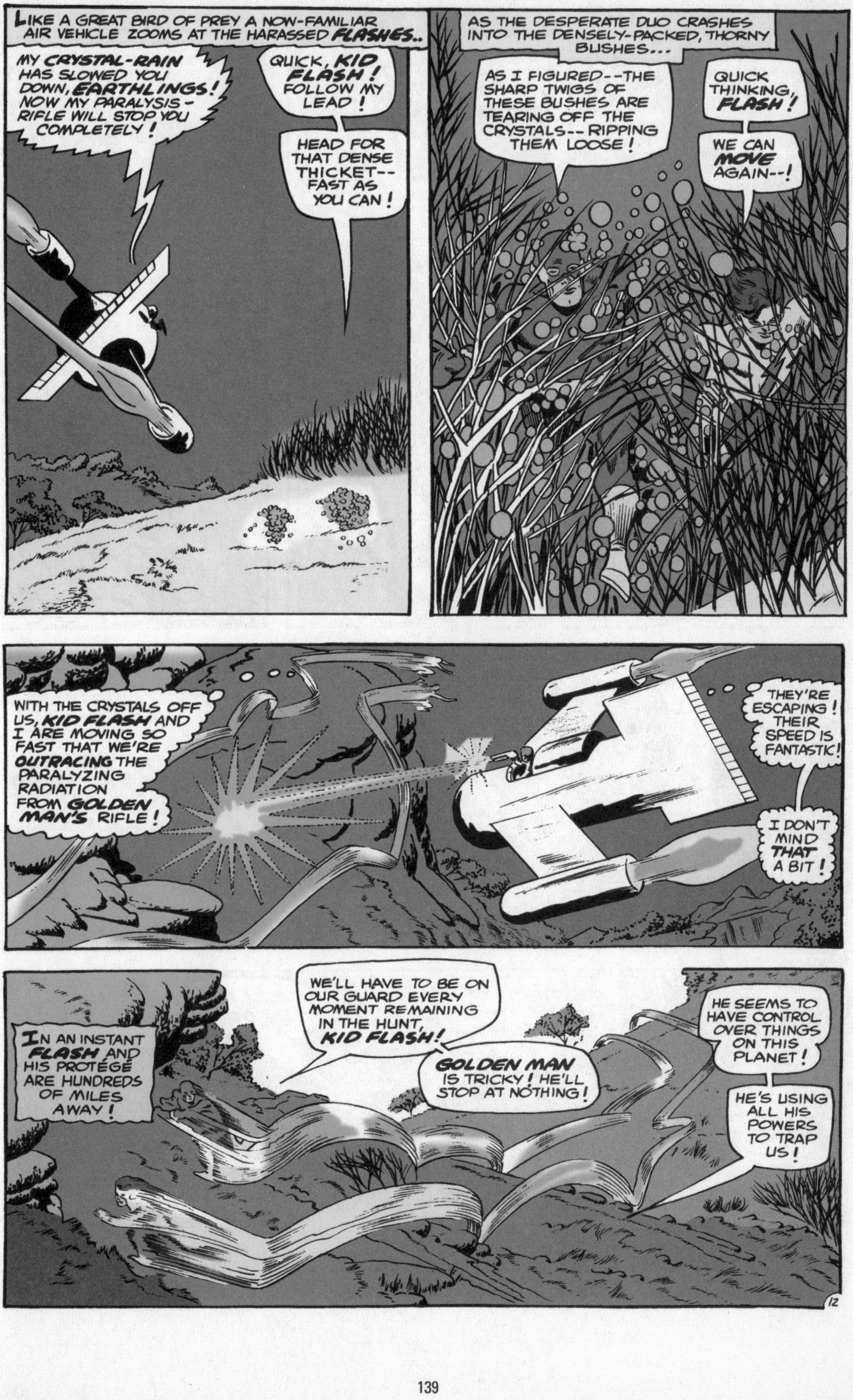
LIKE A GREAT BIRD OF PREY A NOW-FAMILIAR AIR VEHICLE ZOOMS AT THE HARASSED FLASHES..
MY CRYSTAL-RAIN HAS SLOWED YOU DOWN, EARTHLINGS! NOW MY PARALYSIS-RIFLE WILL STOP YOU COMPLETELY!
QUICK, KID FLASH! FOLLOW MY LEAD!
HEAD FOR THAT DENSE THICKET--FAST AS YOU CAN!
AS THE DESPERATE DUO CRASHES INTO THE DENSELY-PACKED, THORNY BUSHES...
AS I FIGURED--THE SHARP TWIGS OF THESE BUSHES ARE TEARING OFF THE CRYSTALS--RIPPING THEM LOOSE!
QUICK THINKING, FLASH!
WE CAN MOVE AGAIN--!
WITH THE CRYSTALS OFF US, KID FLASH AND I ARE MOVING SO FAST THAT WE'RE OUTRACING THE PARALYZING RADIATION FROM GOLDEN MAN'S RIFLE!
THEY'RE ESCAPING! THEIR SPEED IS FANTASTIC!
I DON'T MIND THAT A BIT!
IN AN INSTANT FLASH AND HIS PROTÉGÉ ARE HUNDREDS OF MILES AWAY!
WE'LL HAVE TO BE ON OUR GUARD EVERY MOMENT REMAINING IN THE HUNT, KID FLASH!
GOLDEN MAN IS TRICKY! HE'LL STOP AT NOTHING!
HE SEEMS TO HAVE CONTROL OVER THINGS ON THIS PLANET!
HE'S USING ALL HIS POWERS TO TRAP US!
12

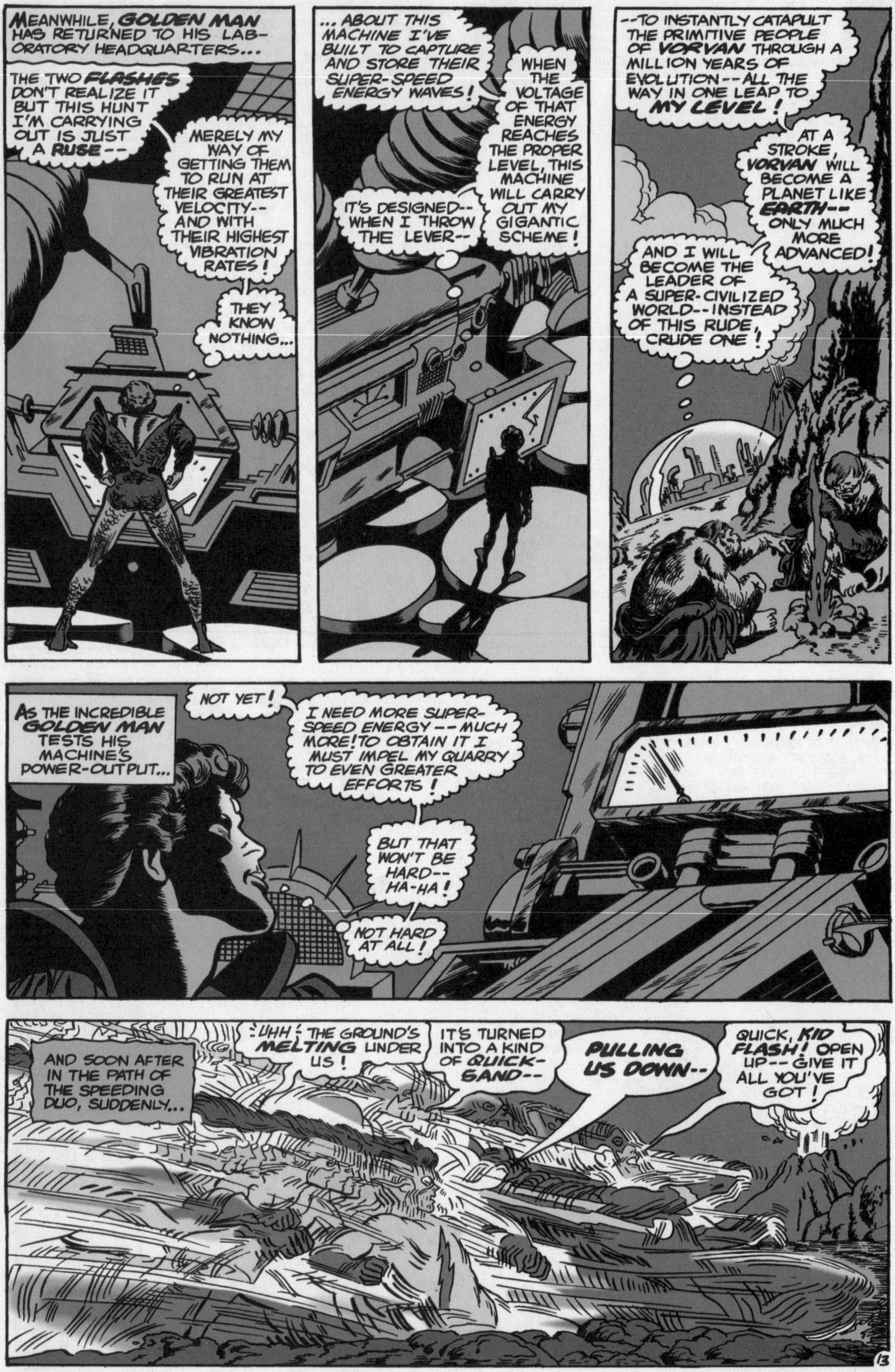
MEANWHILE, GOLDEN MAN HAS RETURNED TO HIS LABORATORY HEADQUARTERS...
THE TWO FLASHES DON'T REALIZE IT BUT THIS HUNT I'M CARRYING OUT IS JUST A RUSE--
MERELY MY WAY OF GETTING THEM TO RUN AT THEIR GREATEST VELOCITY--AND WITH THEIR HIGHEST VIBRATION RATES!
THEY KNOW NOTHING...
...ABOUT THIS MACHINE I'VE BUILT TO CAPTURE AND STORE THEIR SUPER-SPEED ENERGY WAVES!
WHEN THE VOLTAGE OF THAT ENERGY REACHES THE PROPER LEVEL, THIS MACHINE WILL CARRY OUT MY GIGANTIC SCHEME!
IT'S DESIGNED--WHEN I THROW THE LEVER--
--TO INSTANTLY CATAPULT THE PRIMITIVE PEOPLE OF VORVAN THROUGH A MILLION YEARS OF EVOLUTION--ALL THE WAY IN ONE LEAP TO MY LEVEL!
AT A STROKE, VORVAN WILL BECOME A PLANET LIKE EARTH--ONLY MUCH MORE ADVANCED!
AND I WILL BECOME THE LEADER OF A SUPER-CIVILIZED WORLD--INSTEAD OF THIS RUDE, CRUDE ONE!
AS THE INCREDIBLE GOLDEN MAN TESTS HIS MACHINE'S POWER-OUTPUT...
NOT YET!
I NEED MORE SUPER-SPEED ENERGY--MUCH MORE! TO OBTAIN IT I MUST IMPEL MY QUARRY TO EVEN GREATER EFFORTS!
BUT THAT WON'T BE HARD--HA-HA!
NOT HARD AT ALL!
AND SOON AFTER IN THE PATH OF THE SPEEDING DUO, SUDDENLY...
UHH! THE GROUND'S MELTING UNDER US!
IT'S TURNED INTO A KIND OF QUICK-SAND--
PULLING US DOWN--
QUICK, KID FLASH! OPEN UP--GIVE IT ALL YOU'VE GOT!
13

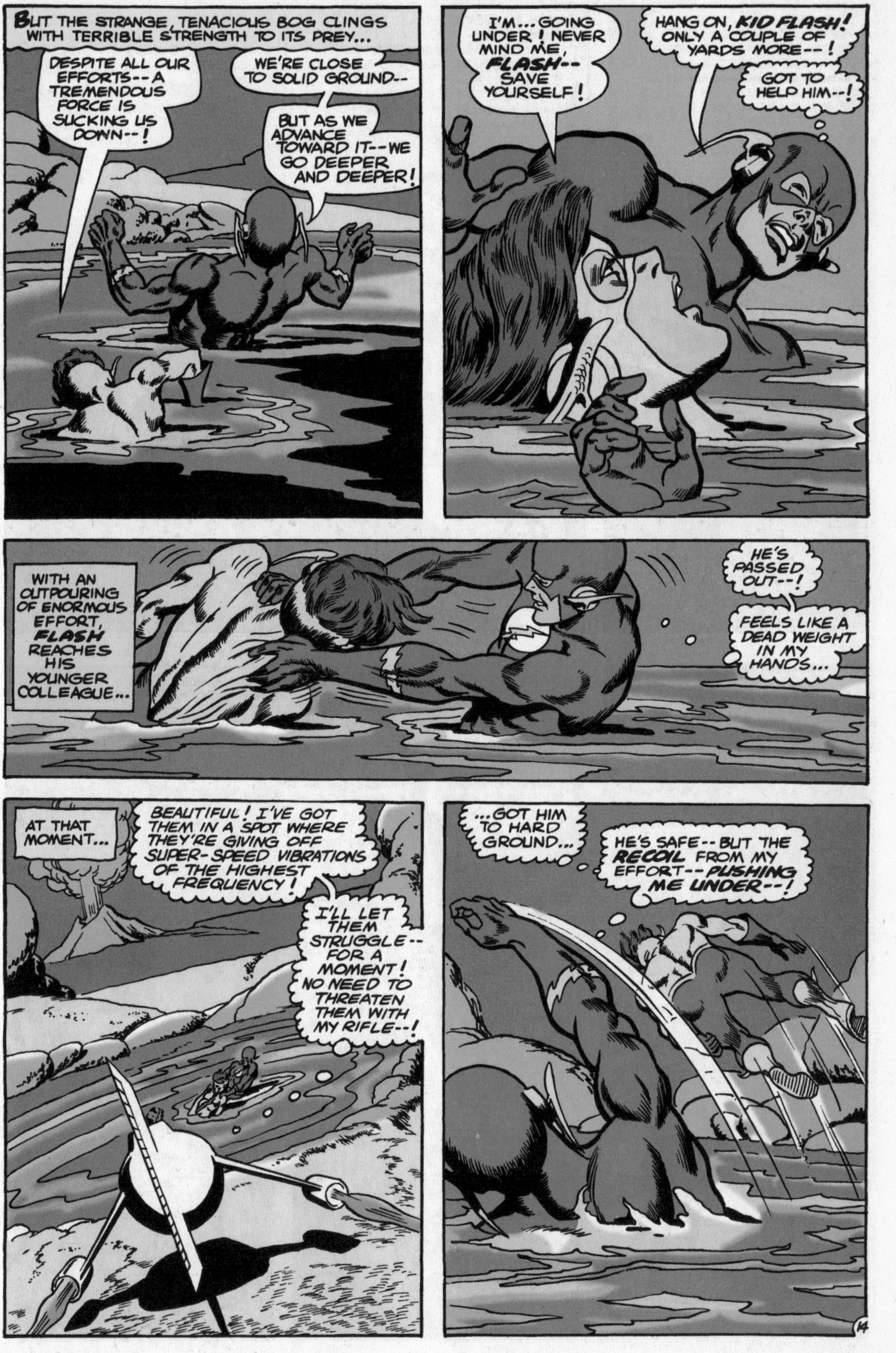
BUT THE STRANGE, TENACIOUS BOG CLINGS WITH TERRIBLE STRENGTH TO ITS PREY...
DESPITE ALL OUR EFFORTS-- A TREMENDOUS FORCE IS SUCKING US DOWN--!
WE'RE CLOSE TO SOLID GROUND--
BUT AS WE ADVANCE TOWARD IT--WE GO DEEPER AND DEEPER!
I'M... GOING UNDER! NEVER MIND ME, FLASH-- SAVE YOURSELF!
HANG ON, KID FLASH! ONLY A COUPLE OF YARDS MORE--!
GOT TO HELP HIM--!
WITH AN OUTPOURING OF ENORMOUS EFFORT, FLASH REACHES HIS YOUNGER COLLEAGUE...
HE'S PASSED OUT--!
FEELS LIKE A DEAD WEIGHT IN MY HANDS...
AT THAT MOMENT...
BEAUTIFUL! I'VE GOT THEM IN A SPOT WHERE THEY'RE GIVING OFF SUPER-SPEED VIBRATIONS OF THE HIGHEST FREQUENCY!
I'LL LET THEM STRUGGLE-- FOR A MOMENT! NO NEED TO THREATEN THEM WITH MY RIFLE--!
...GOT HIM TO HARD GROUND...
HE'S SAFE--BUT THE RECOIL FROM MY EFFORT--PUSHING ME UNDER--!
14

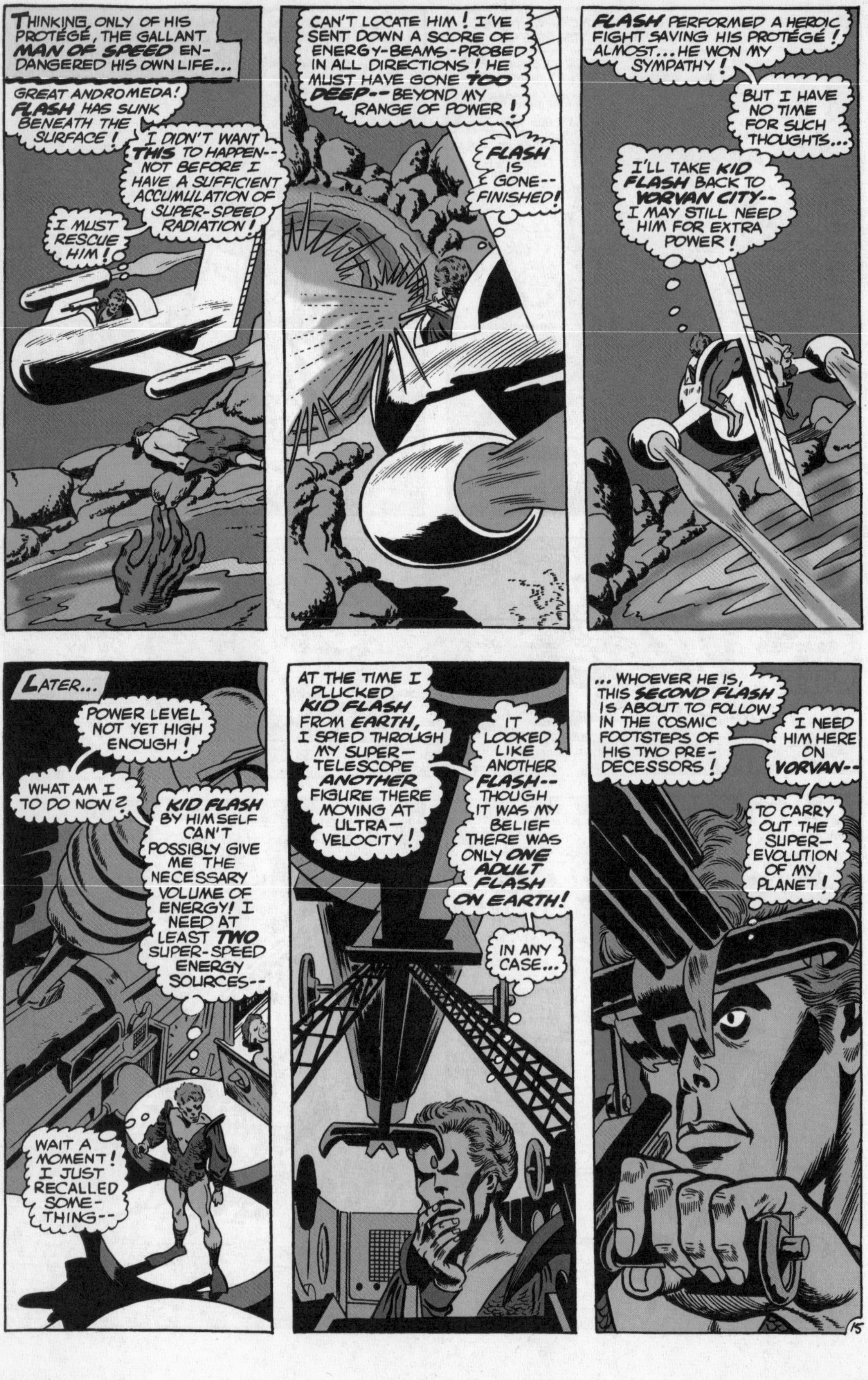
THINKING ONLY OF HIS PROTÉGÉ, THE GALLANT MAN OF SPEED ENDANGERED HIS OWN LIFE...
GREAT ANDROMEDA! FLASH HAS SUNK BENEATH THE SURFACE!
I DIDN'T WANT THIS TO HAPPEN-- NOT BEFORE I HAVE A SUFFICIENT ACCUMULATION OF SUPER-SPEED RADIATION!
I MUST RESCUE HIM!
CAN'T LOCATE HIM! I'VE SENT DOWN A SCORE OF ENERGY-BEAMS-PROBED IN ALL DIRECTIONS! HE MUST HAVE GONE TOO DEEP-- BEYOND MY RANGE OF POWER!
FLASH IS GONE-- FINISHED!
FLASH PERFORMED A HEROIC FIGHT SAVING HIS PROTÉGÉ! ALMOST... HE WON MY SYMPATHY!
BUT I HAVE NO TIME FOR SUCH THOUGHTS...
I'LL TAKE KID FLASH BACK TO VORVAN CITY-- I MAY STILL NEED HIM FOR EXTRA POWER!
LATER...
POWER LEVEL NOT YET HIGH ENOUGH!
WHAT AM I TO DO NOW?
KID FLASH BY HIMSELF CAN'T POSSIBLY GIVE ME THE NECESSARY VOLUME OF ENERGY! I NEED AT LEAST TWO SUPER-SPEED ENERGY SOURCES--
WAIT A MOMENT! I JUST RECALLED SOME-THING--
AT THE TIME I PLUCKED KID FLASH FROM EARTH, I SPIED THROUGH MY SUPER-TELESCOPE ANOTHER FIGURE THERE MOVING AT ULTRA-VELOCITY!
IT LOOKED LIKE ANOTHER FLASH-- THOUGH IT WAS MY BELIEF THERE WAS ONLY ONE ADULT FLASH ON EARTH!
IN ANY CASE...
... WHOEVER HE IS, THIS SECOND FLASH IS ABOUT TO FOLLOW IN THE COSMIC FOOTSTEPS OF HIS TWO PREDECESSORS!
I NEED HIM HERE ON VORVAN--
TO CARRY OUT THE SUPER-EVOLUTION OF MY PLANET!
15

MEANWHILE, AS THE *SCARLET SPEEDSTER* OF *EARTH-TWO* SEEKS HIS MISSING FRIENDS...

NO CLUE--OR TRACE--OF THEIR WHERE-ABOUTS--OR OF THE MYSTERIOUS FORCE THAT SEIZED THEM--

MAYBE IF I SLOW DOWN A BIT--MAKE IT EASY FOR THAT FORCE TO *FIND* ME...

IT WILL SEIZE ME TOO!

WHATEVER THE DANGER-- I MUST RISK IT!

THEN... WITH BLINDING OVERPOWERING IMPACT...

EARTH DIS-APPEARING AROUND ME--A FORCE LIKE A THOUSAND LIGHTNING BOLTS PICKING ME UP--

THIS IS IT!

FIRST *FLASH*... THEN *KID FLASH*... NOW ME!

KRONGG!

16

CRISIS
ON MULTIPLE EARTHS
THE TEAM UPS

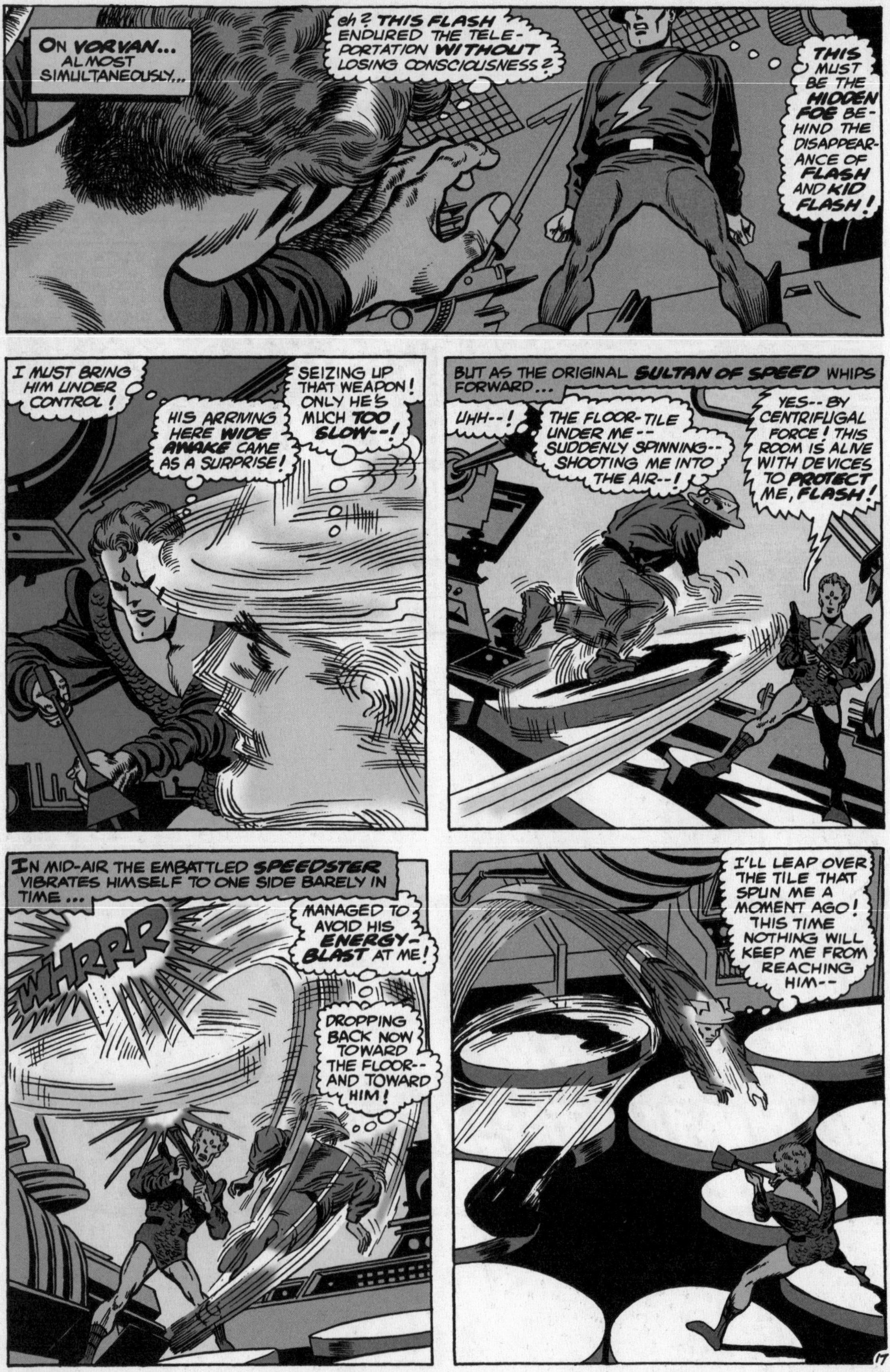

ON VORVAN... ALMOST SIMULTANEOUSLY...
eh? THIS FLASH ENDURED THE TELE-PORTATION WITHOUT LOSING CONSCIOUSNESS?
THIS MUST BE THE HIDDEN FOE BE-HIND THE DISAPPEAR-ANCE OF FLASH AND KID FLASH!
I MUST BRING HIM UNDER CONTROL!
HIS ARRIVING HERE WIDE AWAKE CAME AS A SURPRISE!
SEIZING UP THAT WEAPON! ONLY HE'S MUCH TOO SLOW--!
BUT AS THE ORIGINAL SULTAN OF SPEED WHIPS FORWARD...
UHH--!
THE FLOOR-TILE UNDER ME--SUDDENLY SPINNING--SHOOTING ME INTO THE AIR--!
YES--BY CENTRIFUGAL FORCE! THIS ROOM IS ALIVE WITH DEVICES TO PROTECT ME, FLASH!
IN MID-AIR THE EMBATTLED SPEEDSTER VIBRATES HIMSELF TO ONE SIDE BARELY IN TIME...
WHRRR
MANAGED TO AVOID HIS ENERGY-BLAST AT ME!
DROPPING BACK NOW TOWARD THE FLOOR--AND TOWARD HIM!
I'LL LEAP OVER THE TILE THAT SPUN ME A MOMENT AGO! THIS TIME NOTHING WILL KEEP ME FROM REACHING HIM--
17

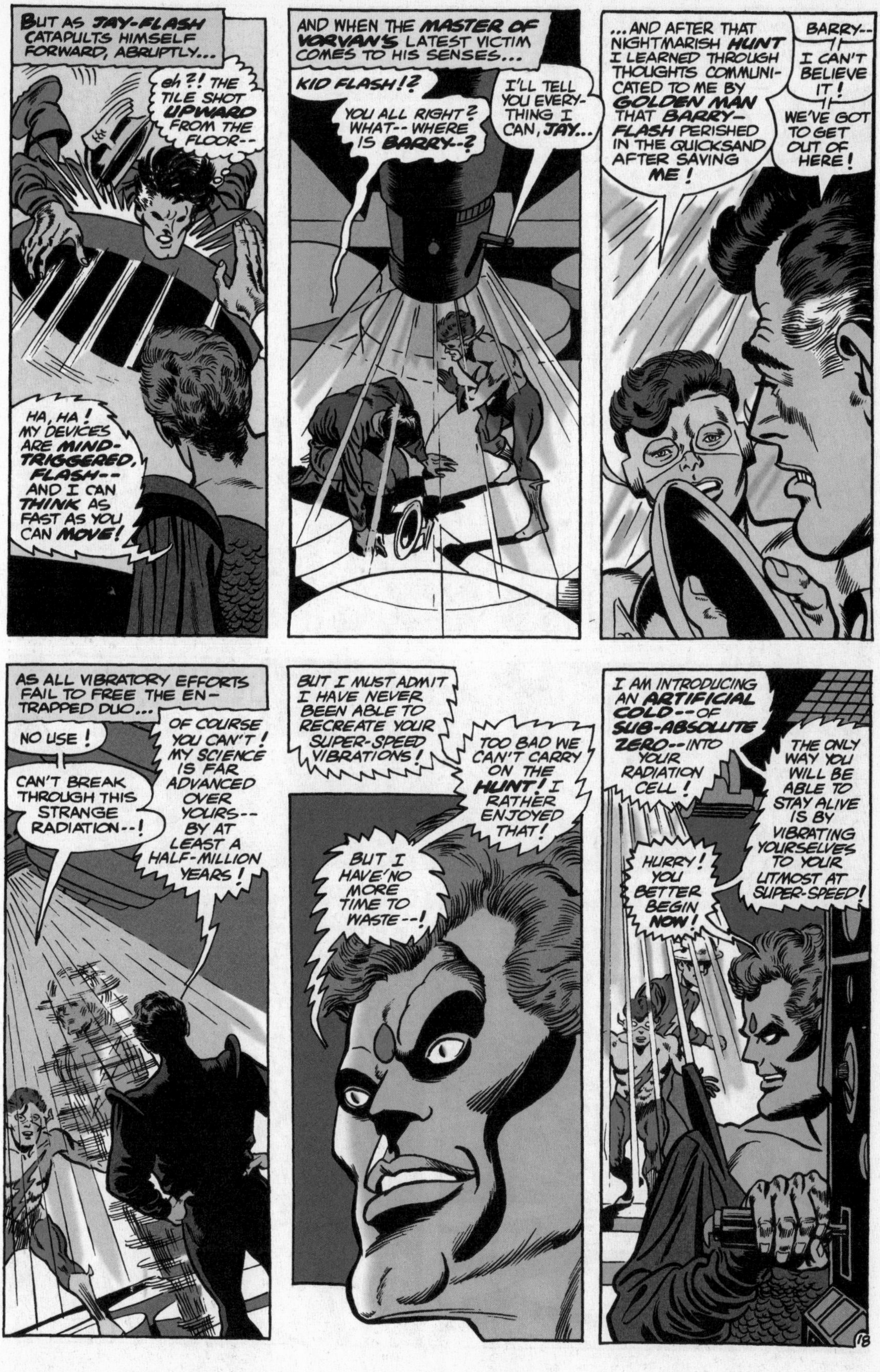

BUT AS JAY-FLASH CATAPULTS HIMSELF FORWARD, ABRUPTLY...
eh?! THE TILE SHOT UPWARD FROM THE FLOOR--
HA, HA! MY DEVICES ARE MIND-TRIGGERED, FLASH-- AND I CAN THINK AS FAST AS YOU CAN MOVE!
AND WHEN THE MASTER OF VORVAN'S LATEST VICTIM COMES TO HIS SENSES...
KID FLASH!?
YOU ALL RIGHT? WHAT-- WHERE IS BARRY--?
I'LL TELL YOU EVERYTHING I CAN, JAY...
...AND AFTER THAT NIGHTMARISH HUNT I LEARNED THROUGH THOUGHTS COMMUNICATED TO ME BY GOLDEN MAN THAT BARRY-FLASH PERISHED IN THE QUICKSAND AFTER SAVING ME!
BARRY--
I CAN'T BELIEVE IT!
WE'VE GOT TO GET OUT OF HERE!
AS ALL VIBRATORY EFFORTS FAIL TO FREE THE ENTRAPPED DUO...
NO USE!
CAN'T BREAK THROUGH THIS STRANGE RADIATION--!
OF COURSE YOU CAN'T! MY SCIENCE IS FAR ADVANCED OVER YOURS-- BY AT LEAST A HALF-MILLION YEARS!
BUT I MUST ADMIT I HAVE NEVER BEEN ABLE TO RECREATE YOUR SUPER-SPEED VIBRATIONS!
TOO BAD WE CAN'T CARRY ON THE HUNT! I RATHER ENJOYED THAT!
BUT I HAVE NO MORE TIME TO WASTE--!
I AM INTRODUCING AN ARTIFICIAL COLD--OF SUB-ABSOLUTE ZERO--INTO YOUR RADIATION CELL!
THE ONLY WAY YOU WILL BE ABLE TO STAY ALIVE IS BY VIBRATING YOURSELVES TO YOUR UTMOST AT SUPER-SPEED!
HURRY! YOU BETTER BEGIN NOW!
18

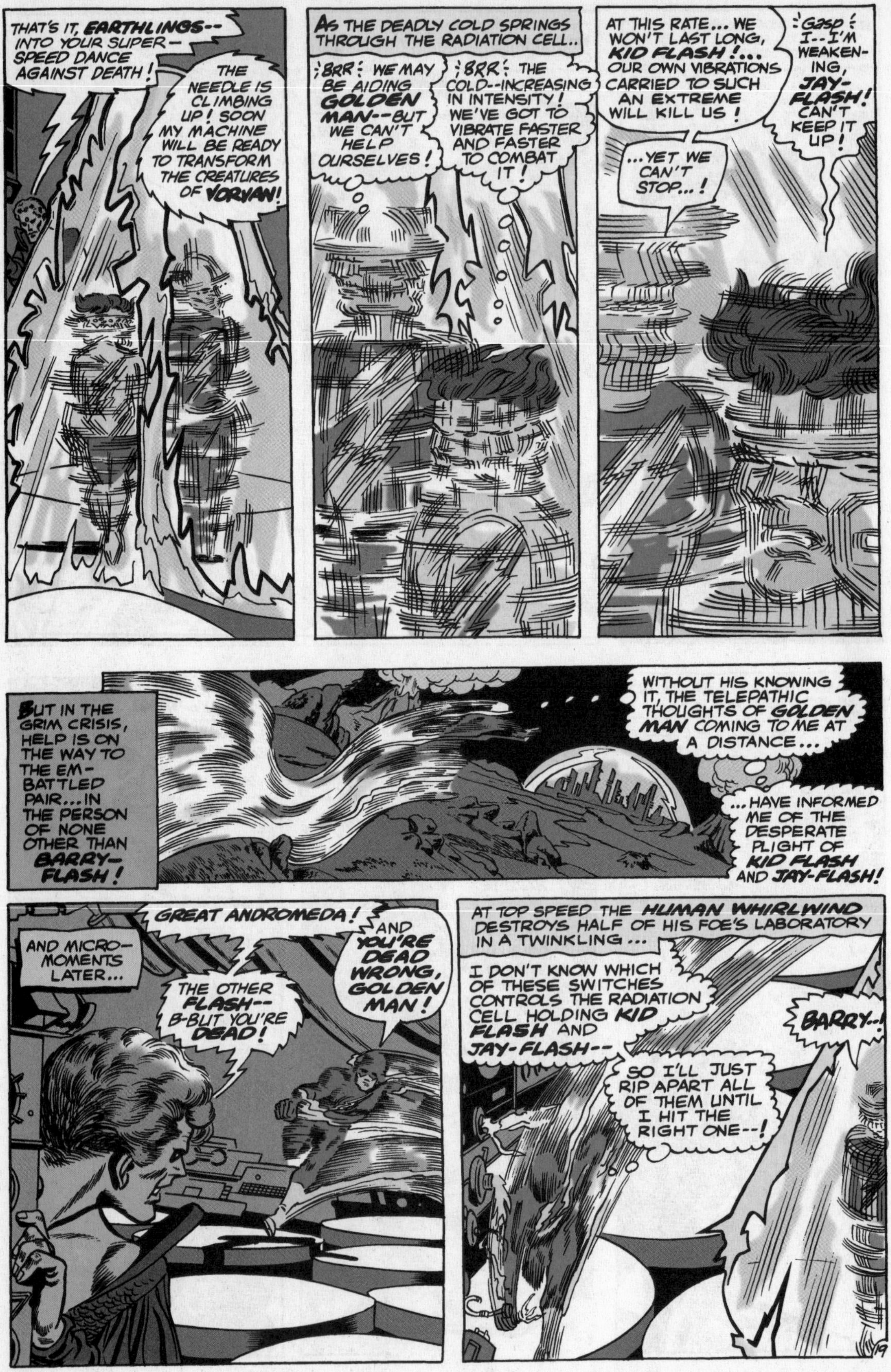
THAT'S IT, EARTHLINGS-- INTO YOUR SUPER-SPEED DANCE AGAINST DEATH!
THE NEEDLE IS CLIMBING UP! SOON MY MACHINE WILL BE READY TO TRANSFORM THE CREATURES OF VORVAN!
AS THE DEADLY COLD SPRINGS THROUGH THE RADIATION CELL..
BRR! WE MAY BE AIDING GOLDEN MAN--BUT WE CAN'T HELP OURSELVES!
BRR! THE COLD--INCREASING IN INTENSITY! WE'VE GOT TO VIBRATE FASTER AND FASTER TO COMBAT IT!
AT THIS RATE... WE WON'T LAST LONG, KID FLASH!... OUR OWN VIBRATIONS CARRIED TO SUCH AN EXTREME WILL KILL US!
...YET WE CAN'T STOP...!
Gasp! I--I'M WEAKENING, JAY-FLASH! CAN'T KEEP IT UP!
BUT IN THE GRIM CRISIS, HELP IS ON THE WAY TO THE EMBATTLED PAIR... IN THE PERSON OF NONE OTHER THAN BARRY-FLASH!
WITHOUT HIS KNOWING IT, THE TELEPATHIC THOUGHTS OF GOLDEN MAN COMING TO ME AT A DISTANCE...
...HAVE INFORMED ME OF THE DESPERATE PLIGHT OF KID FLASH AND JAY-FLASH!
AND MICRO-MOMENTS LATER...
GREAT ANDROMEDA!
THE OTHER FLASH-- B-BUT YOU'RE DEAD!
AND YOU'RE DEAD WRONG, GOLDEN MAN!
AT TOP SPEED THE HUMAN WHIRLWIND DESTROYS HALF OF HIS FOE'S LABORATORY IN A TWINKLING...
I DON'T KNOW WHICH OF THESE SWITCHES CONTROLS THE RADIATION CELL HOLDING KID FLASH AND JAY-FLASH--
SO I'LL JUST RIP APART ALL OF THEM UNTIL I HIT THE RIGHT ONE--!
BARRY--!
19

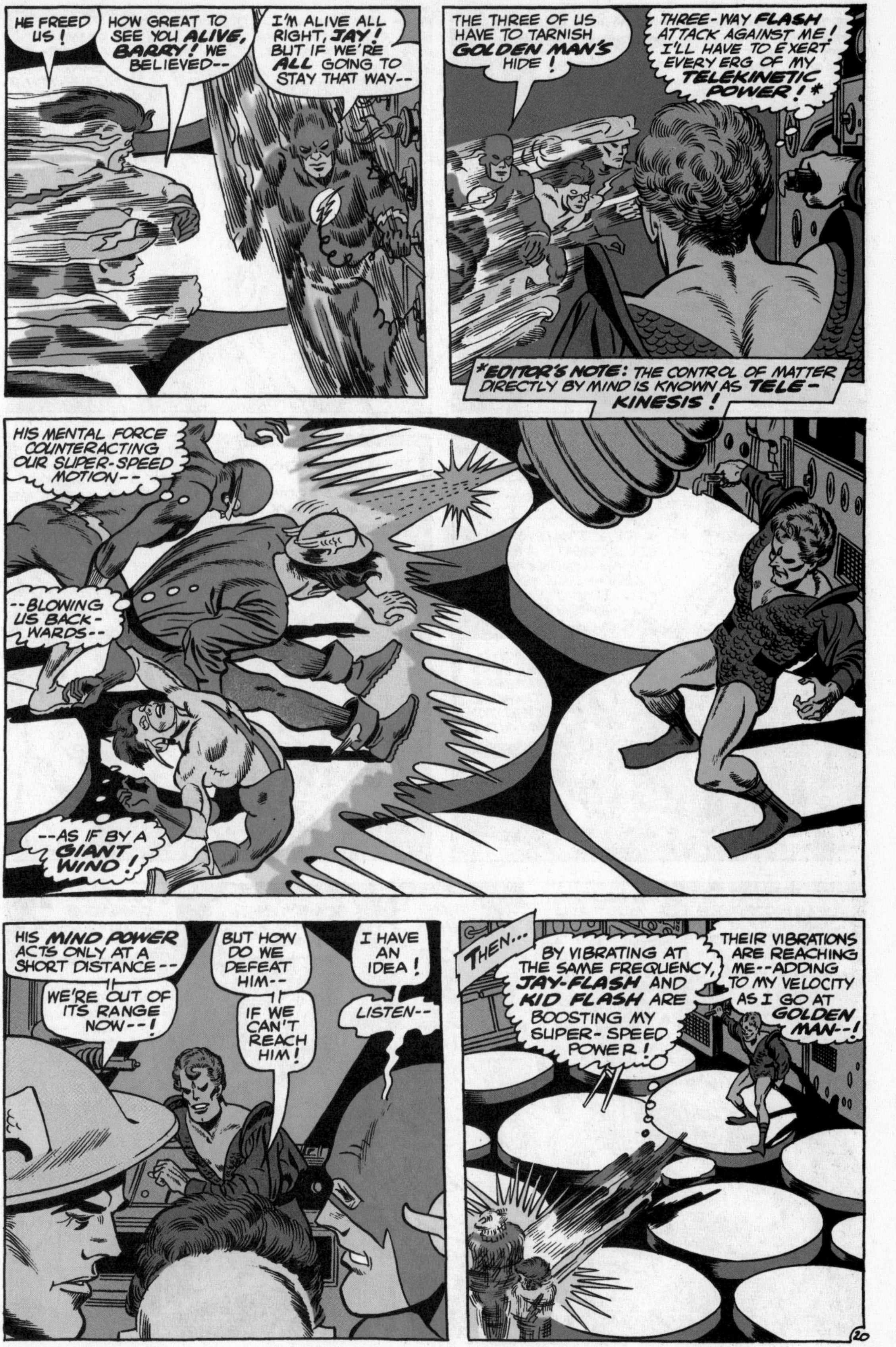
HE FREED US!
HOW GREAT TO SEE YOU ALIVE, BARRY! WE BELIEVED--
I'M ALIVE ALL RIGHT, JAY! BUT IF WE'RE ALL GOING TO STAY THAT WAY--
THE THREE OF US HAVE TO TARNISH GOLDEN MAN'S HIDE!
THREE-WAY FLASH ATTACK AGAINST ME! I'LL HAVE TO EXERT EVERY ERG OF MY TELEKINETIC POWER!*
*EDITOR'S NOTE: THE CONTROL OF MATTER DIRECTLY BY MIND IS KNOWN AS TELE-KINESIS!
HIS MENTAL FORCE COUNTERACTING OUR SUPER-SPEED MOTION--
--BLOWING US BACK-WARDS--
--AS IF BY A GIANT WIND!
HIS MIND POWER ACTS ONLY AT A SHORT DISTANCE--
WE'RE OUT OF ITS RANGE NOW--!
BUT HOW DO WE DEFEAT HIM--
IF WE CAN'T REACH HIM!
I HAVE AN IDEA!
LISTEN--
THEN...
BY VIBRATING AT THE SAME FREQUENCY, JAY-FLASH AND KID FLASH ARE BOOSTING MY SUPER-SPEED POWER!
THEIR VIBRATIONS ARE REACHING ME--ADDING TO MY VELOCITY AS I GO AT GOLDEN MAN--!
20

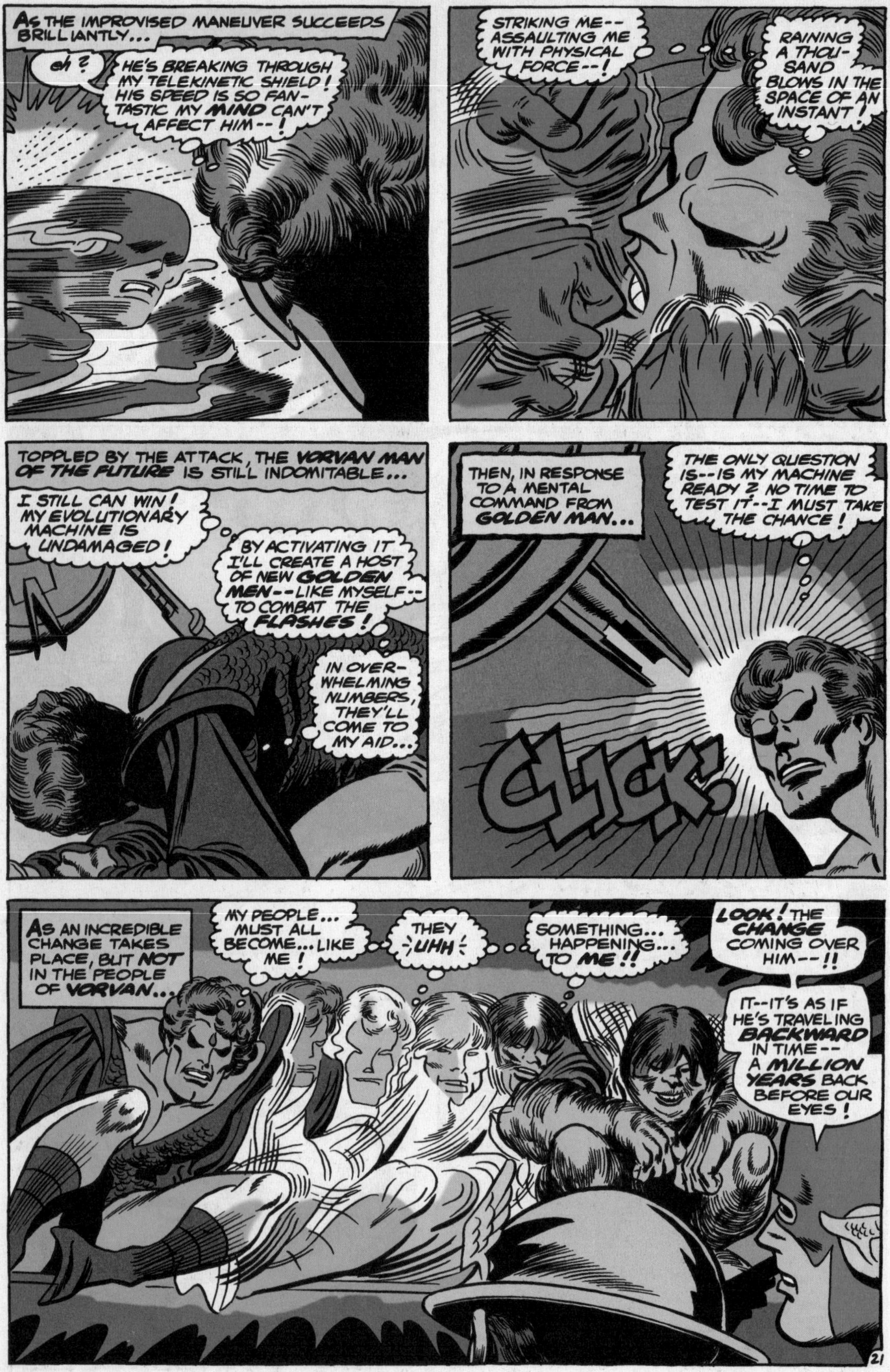

AS THE IMPROVISED MANEUVER SUCCEEDS BRILLIANTLY...
eh ?
HE'S BREAKING THROUGH MY TELEKINETIC SHIELD! HIS SPEED IS SO FANTASTIC MY MIND CAN'T AFFECT HIM--!
STRIKING ME--ASSAULTING ME WITH PHYSICAL FORCE--!
RAINING A THOUSAND BLOWS IN THE SPACE OF AN INSTANT!
TOPPLED BY THE ATTACK, THE VORVAN MAN OF THE FUTURE IS STILL INDOMITABLE...
I STILL CAN WIN! MY EVOLUTIONARY MACHINE IS UNDAMAGED!
BY ACTIVATING IT I'LL CREATE A HOST OF NEW GOLDEN MEN--LIKE MYSELF--TO COMBAT THE FLASHES!
IN OVERWHELMING NUMBERS, THEY'LL COME TO MY AID...
THEN, IN RESPONSE TO A MENTAL COMMAND FROM GOLDEN MAN...
THE ONLY QUESTION IS--IS MY MACHINE READY? NO TIME TO TEST IT--I MUST TAKE THE CHANCE!
CLICK!
AS AN INCREDIBLE CHANGE TAKES PLACE, BUT NOT IN THE PEOPLE OF VORVAN...
MY PEOPLE... MUST ALL BECOME... LIKE ME!
THEY UHH
SOMETHING... HAPPENING... TO ME!!
LOOK! THE CHANGE COMING OVER HIM--!!
IT--IT'S AS IF HE'S TRAVELING BACKWARD IN TIME--A MILLION YEARS BACK BEFORE OUR EYES!
21

AS THE CHANGE IS COMPLETED AND THE MACHINE STOPS...

HE'S BECOME JUST LIKE THE OTHER PRIMITIVES HERE!

INCREDIBLE! HIS MENTAL FORCE IS GONE--I CAN FEEL IT!

HE'S NO MENACE TO US NOW!

HE WAS OUT OF PLACE HERE-- FAR AHEAD OF THE PLANET'S EVOLUTION!

NOW VOR-VAN CAN PROGRESS NATURALLY TOWARD CIVILI-ZATION-- IN EONS OF TIME! HE TRIED TO RUSH THINGS-- BUT HIS FUTURISTIC SCIENCE BOOMERANGED ON HIMSELF!

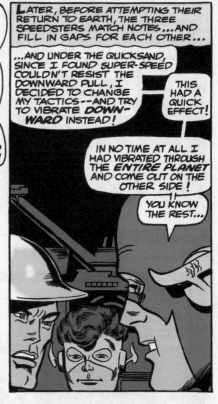

LATER, BEFORE ATTEMPTING THEIR RETURN TO EARTH, THE THREE SPEEDSTERS MATCH NOTES...AND FILL IN GAPS FOR EACH OTHER...

...AND UNDER THE QUICKSAND, SINCE I FOUND SUPER-SPEED COULDN'T RESIST THE DOWNWARD PULL, I DECIDED TO CHANGE MY TACTICS--AND TRY TO VIBRATE DOWN-WARD INSTEAD!

THIS HAD A QUICK EFFECT!

IN NO TIME AT ALL I HAD VIBRATED THROUGH THE ENTIRE PLANET AND COME OUT ON THE OTHER SIDE!

YOU KNOW THE REST...

YOU SURE HAD US SCARED FLASH!

WE WERE AFRAID YOU WERE REALLY DONE FOR!

I GAVE GOLDEN MAN A SCARE BY LANDING HERE CON-SCIOUS! I'VE FIGURED OUT WHAT HAPPENED--

YOU KNOW, AS FLASH I ALWAYS MAINTAIN AN INNER VIBRATION...

...WHICH CAUSES MY FACIAL FEATURES TO BLUR A LITTLE--AND THAT'S WHY I DON'T HAVE TO WEAR A MASK!

WHEN I'M THE FLASH NO ONE CAN RECOGNIZE ME AS JAY GARRICK!

AND IT WAS THAT VIBRATION WHICH MADE ME IMMUNE TO THE SHOCK OF TELE-PORTATION!

FINALLY, THE LAST REMAINING PROBLEM IS TACKLED...

WE'RE FINISHED!

WORKING AT SUPER SPEED WE'VE MANAGED TO REVERSE THE CIRCUITS ON GOLDEN MAN'S TELEPORTATION DEVICE!

WHEN IT'S TURNED ON IT SHOULD RETURN US TO EARTH!

And sure enough, only split-moments after the machine has been activated...

CENTRAL CITY! FLASH, WE MADE IT!

I'LL BET THE GIRLS WILL BE GLAD TO SEE US!

YES--BUT BEFORE WE CHANGE TO OUR CIVILIAN IDENTITIES, JAY, I HAVE AN IDEA...

A day later--after the FLASH trio has banded together to capture the rampaging DOMINO GANG--a farewell...

GOODBY, BARRY AND IRIS! GOODBY, WALLY!

JOAN SPOKE TO BARRY PRIVATELY--AND HE HAS PROMISED TO REVEAL HIS SECRET IDENTITY TO IRIS FOR THEIR ANNIVERSARY-- WHICH COMES UP NEXT MONTH!

HEADING HOMEWARD TOO IS YOUNG WALLY WEST...

HERE'S BLUE VALLEY!

WHEW!! WHAT WOULD THE KIDS IN SCHOOL SAY IF I TOLD THEM ABOUT THE ADVENTURE I'VE JUST HAD WITH MY FRIENDS THE TWO FLASHES?

ONE THING IS SURE...I WON'T EVER FORGET OUR ENCOUNTER WITH GOLDEN MAN!

The End

23

CRISIS
ON MULTIPLE EARTHS
THE TEAM UPS

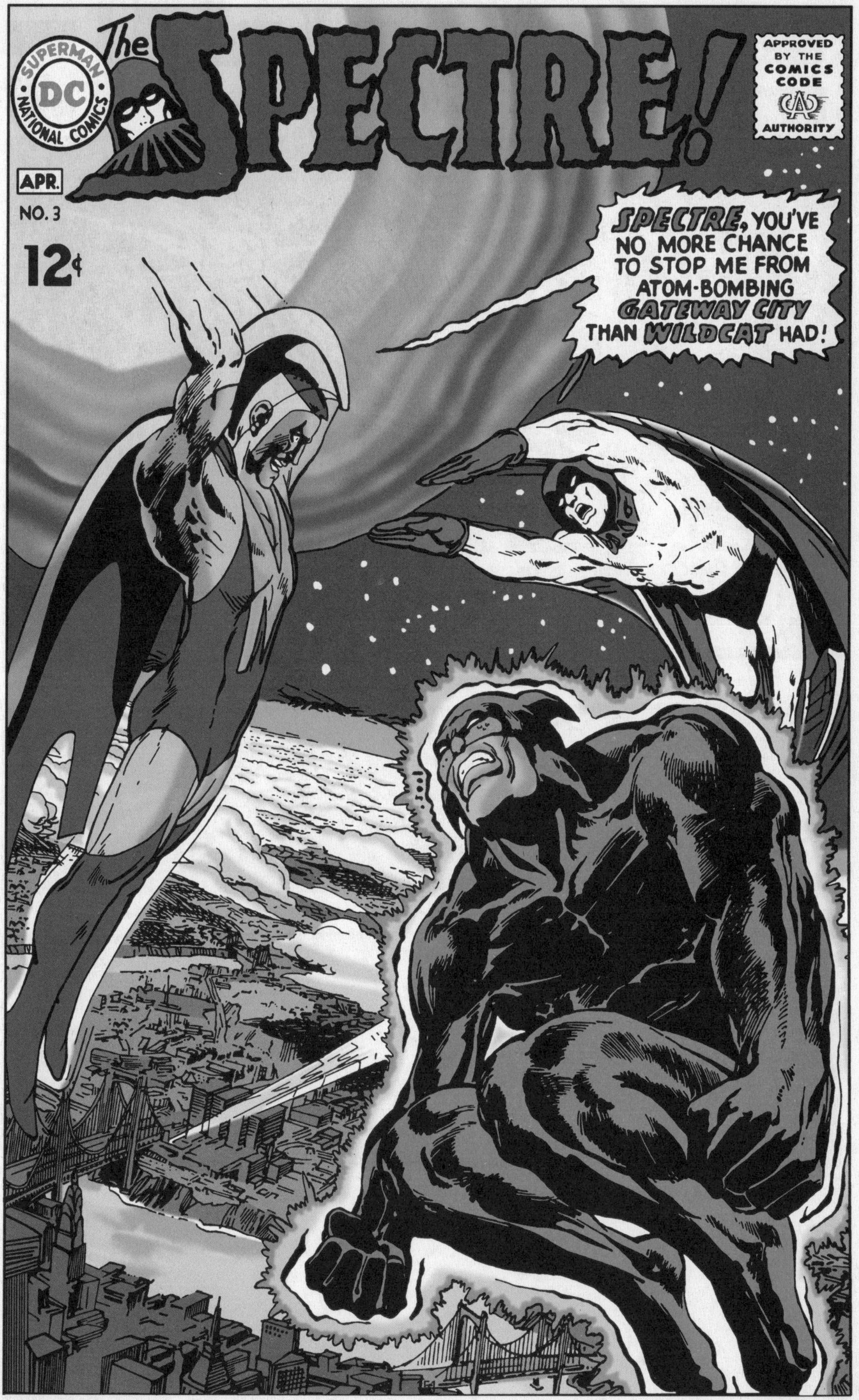
The SPECTRE!
SUPERMAN DC NATIONAL COMICS
APR.
NO. 3
12¢
APPROVED BY THE COMICS CODE AUTHORITY
SPECTRE, YOU'VE NO MORE CHANCE TO STOP ME FROM ATOM-BOMBING GATEWAY CITY THAN WILDCAT HAD!

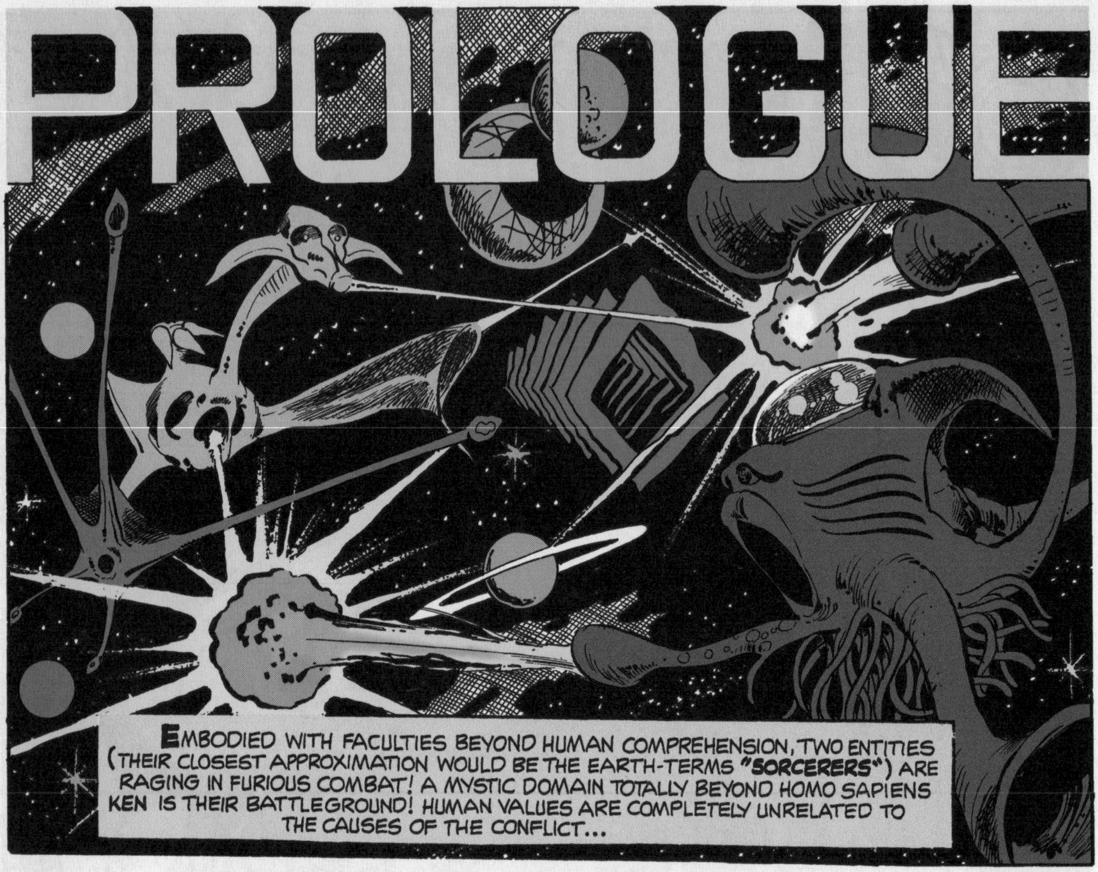
PROLOGUE
EMBODIED WITH FACULTIES BEYOND HUMAN COMPREHENSION, TWO ENTITIES (THEIR CLOSEST APPROXIMATION WOULD BE THE EARTH-TERMS "SORCERERS") ARE RAGING IN FURIOUS COMBAT! A MYSTIC DOMAIN TOTALLY BEYOND HOMO SAPIENS KEN IS THEIR BATTLEGROUND! HUMAN VALUES ARE COMPLETELY UNRELATED TO THE CAUSES OF THE CONFLICT...

SIMULTANEOUSLY, SINISTER SPELL-BOLTS SHOOT OUT...

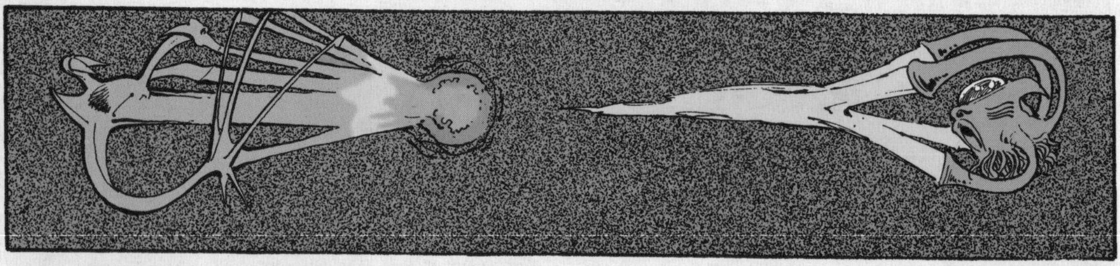

COLLIDING WITH FORCE UNIMAGINABLE, THEY FLARE OUT IN AN OVERWHELMING HOLOCAUST...

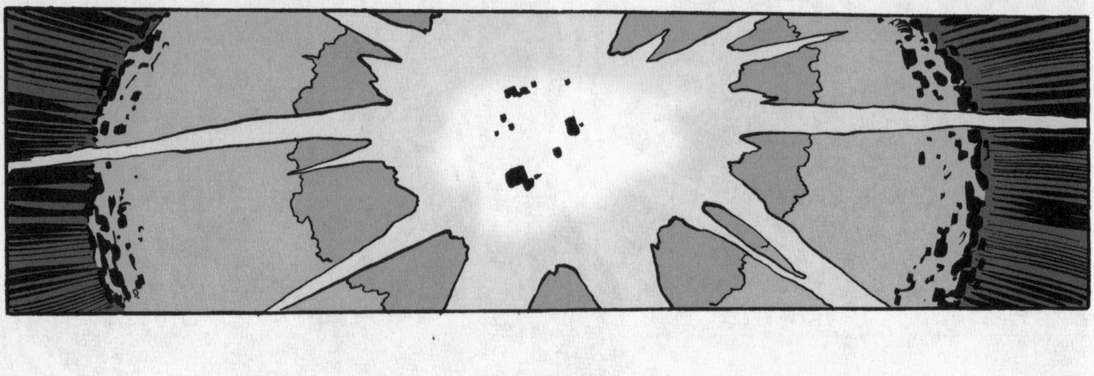

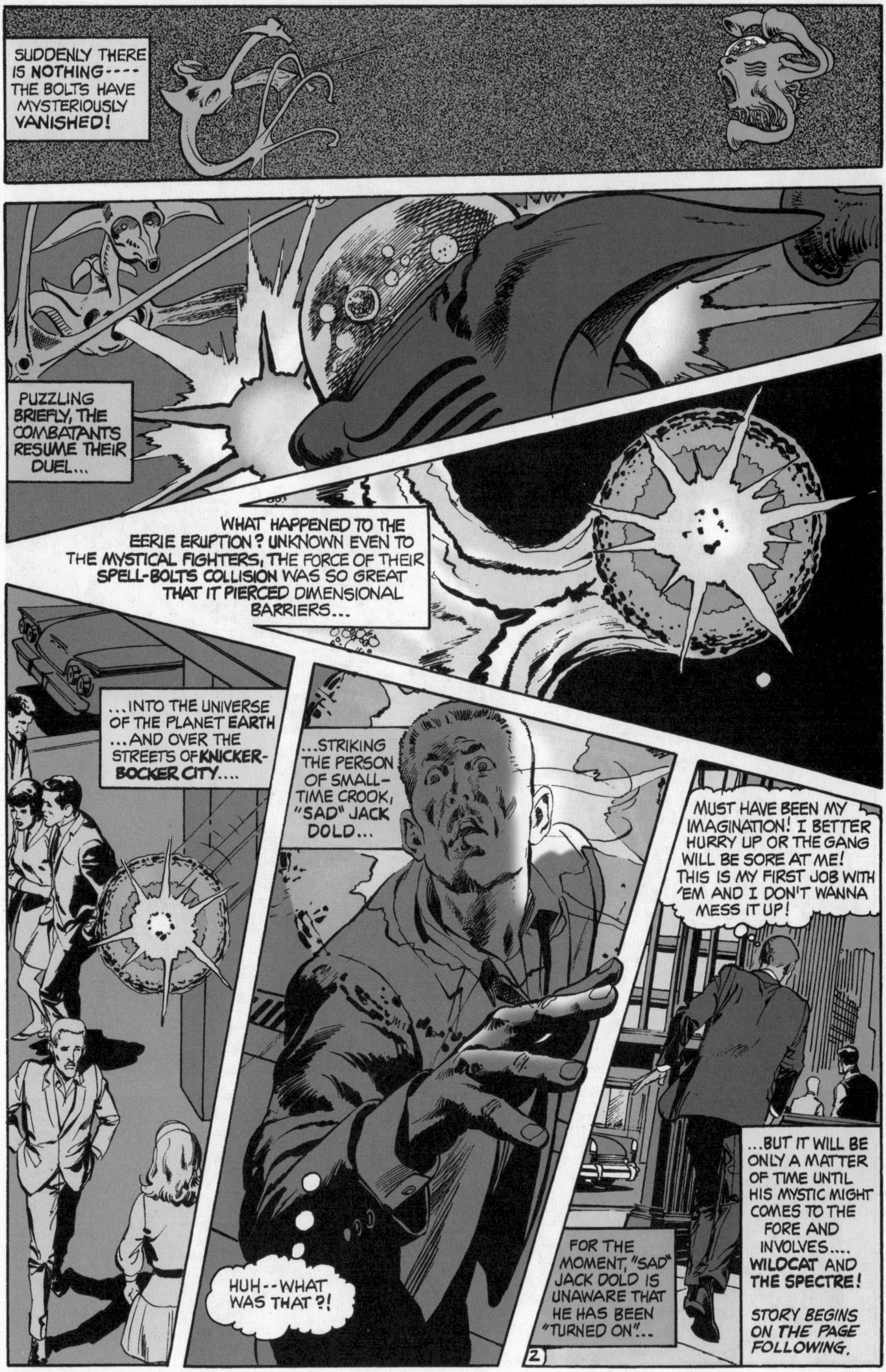
SUDDENLY THERE IS NOTHING---- THE BOLTS HAVE MYSTERIOUSLY VANISHED!
PUZZLING BRIEFLY, THE COMBATANTS RESUME THEIR DUEL...
WHAT HAPPENED TO THE EERIE ERUPTION? UNKNOWN EVEN TO THE MYSTICAL FIGHTERS, THE FORCE OF THEIR SPELL-BOLTS COLLISION WAS SO GREAT THAT IT PIERCED DIMENSIONAL BARRIERS...
...INTO THE UNIVERSE OF THE PLANET EARTH ...AND OVER THE STREETS OF KNICKER-BOCKER CITY....
...STRIKING THE PERSON OF SMALL-TIME CROOK, "SAD" JACK DOLD...
HUH--WHAT WAS THAT?!
MUST HAVE BEEN MY IMAGINATION! I BETTER HURRY UP OR THE GANG WILL BE SORE AT ME! THIS IS MY FIRST JOB WITH 'EM AND I DON'T WANNA MESS IT UP!
FOR THE MOMENT, "SAD" JACK DOLD IS UNAWARE THAT HE HAS BEEN "TURNED ON"...
...BUT IT WILL BE ONLY A MATTER OF TIME UNTIL HIS MYSTIC MIGHT COMES TO THE FORE AND INVOLVES.... WILDCAT AND THE SPECTRE!
STORY BEGINS ON THE PAGE FOLLOWING.
2

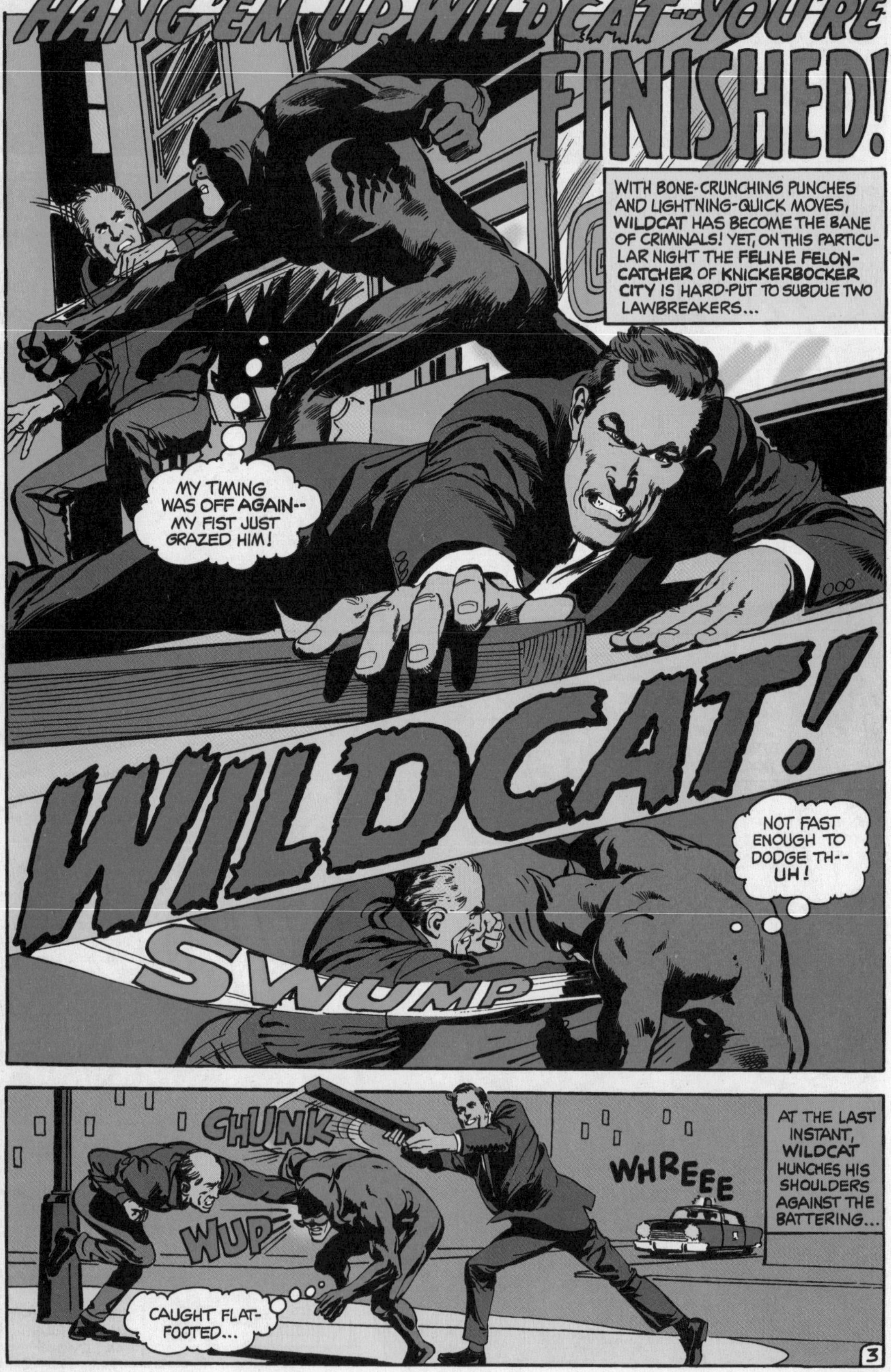
HANG 'EM UP, WILDCAT--YOU'RE FINISHED!
WITH BONE-CRUNCHING PUNCHES AND LIGHTNING-QUICK MOVES, WILDCAT HAS BECOME THE BANE OF CRIMINALS! YET, ON THIS PARTICULAR NIGHT THE FELINE FELON-CATCHER OF KNICKERBOCKER CITY IS HARD-PUT TO SUBDUE TWO LAWBREAKERS...
MY TIMING WAS OFF AGAIN-- MY FIST JUST GRAZED HIM!
WILDCAT!
NOT FAST ENOUGH TO DODGE TH-- UH!
SWUMP
AT THE LAST INSTANT, WILDCAT HUNCHES HIS SHOULDERS AGAINST THE BATTERING...
CHUNK
WHREEE
WUP
CAUGHT FLAT-FOOTED...
3

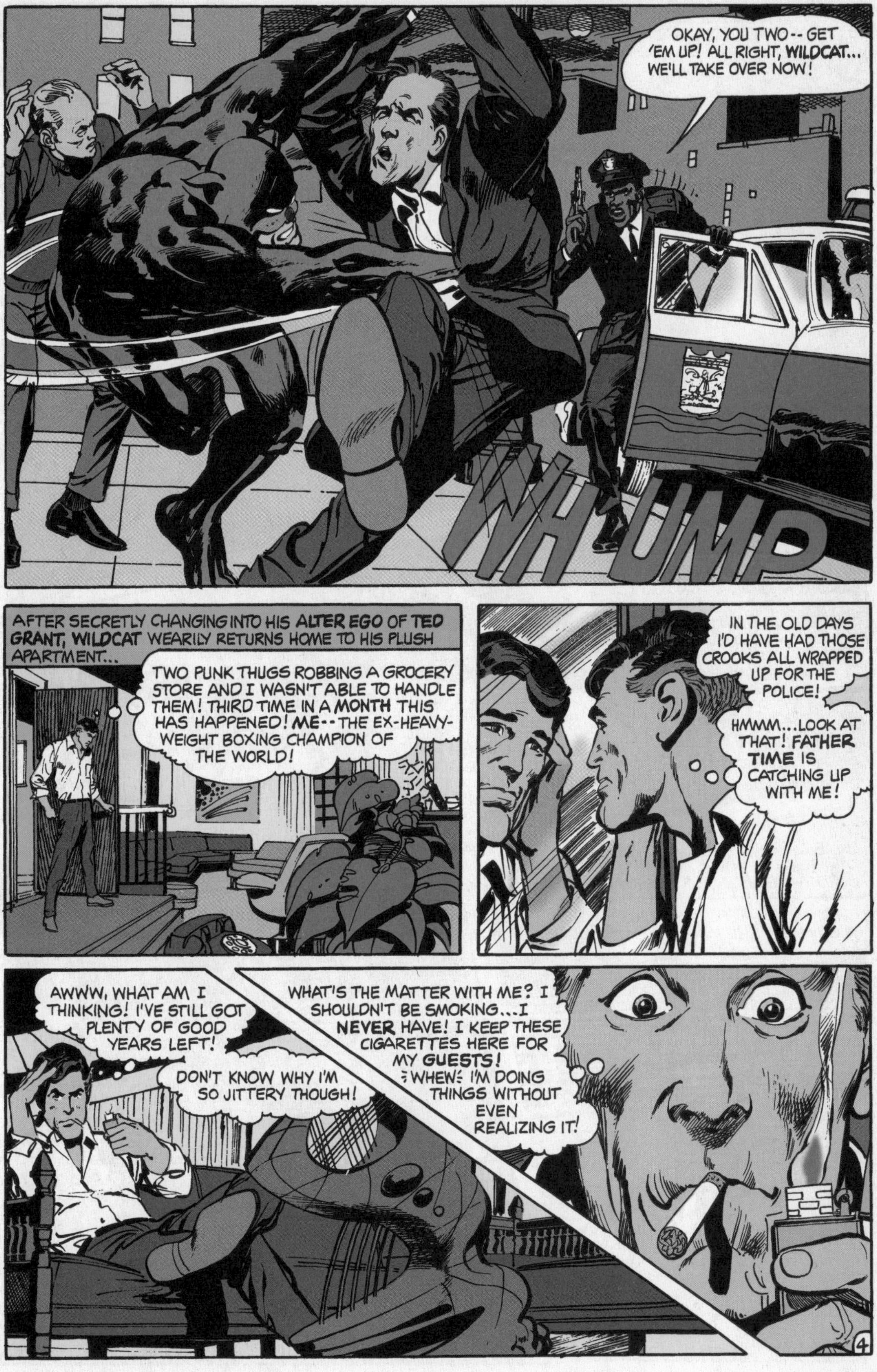
OKAY, YOU TWO-- GET 'EM UP! ALL RIGHT, WILDCAT... WE'LL TAKE OVER NOW!
WHUMP
AFTER SECRETLY CHANGING INTO HIS ALTER EGO OF TED GRANT, WILDCAT WEARILY RETURNS HOME TO HIS PLUSH APARTMENT...
TWO PUNK THUGS ROBBING A GROCERY STORE AND I WASN'T ABLE TO HANDLE THEM! THIRD TIME IN A MONTH THIS HAS HAPPENED! ME-- THE EX-HEAVY-WEIGHT BOXING CHAMPION OF THE WORLD!
IN THE OLD DAYS I'D HAVE HAD THOSE CROOKS ALL WRAPPED UP FOR THE POLICE!
HMMM... LOOK AT THAT! FATHER TIME IS CATCHING UP WITH ME!
AWWW, WHAT AM I THINKING! I'VE STILL GOT PLENTY OF GOOD YEARS LEFT!
DON'T KNOW WHY I'M SO JITTERY THOUGH!
WHAT'S THE MATTER WITH ME? I SHOULDN'T BE SMOKING... I NEVER HAVE! I KEEP THESE CIGARETTES HERE FOR MY GUESTS! WHEW! I'M DOING THINGS WITHOUT EVEN REALIZING IT!
4

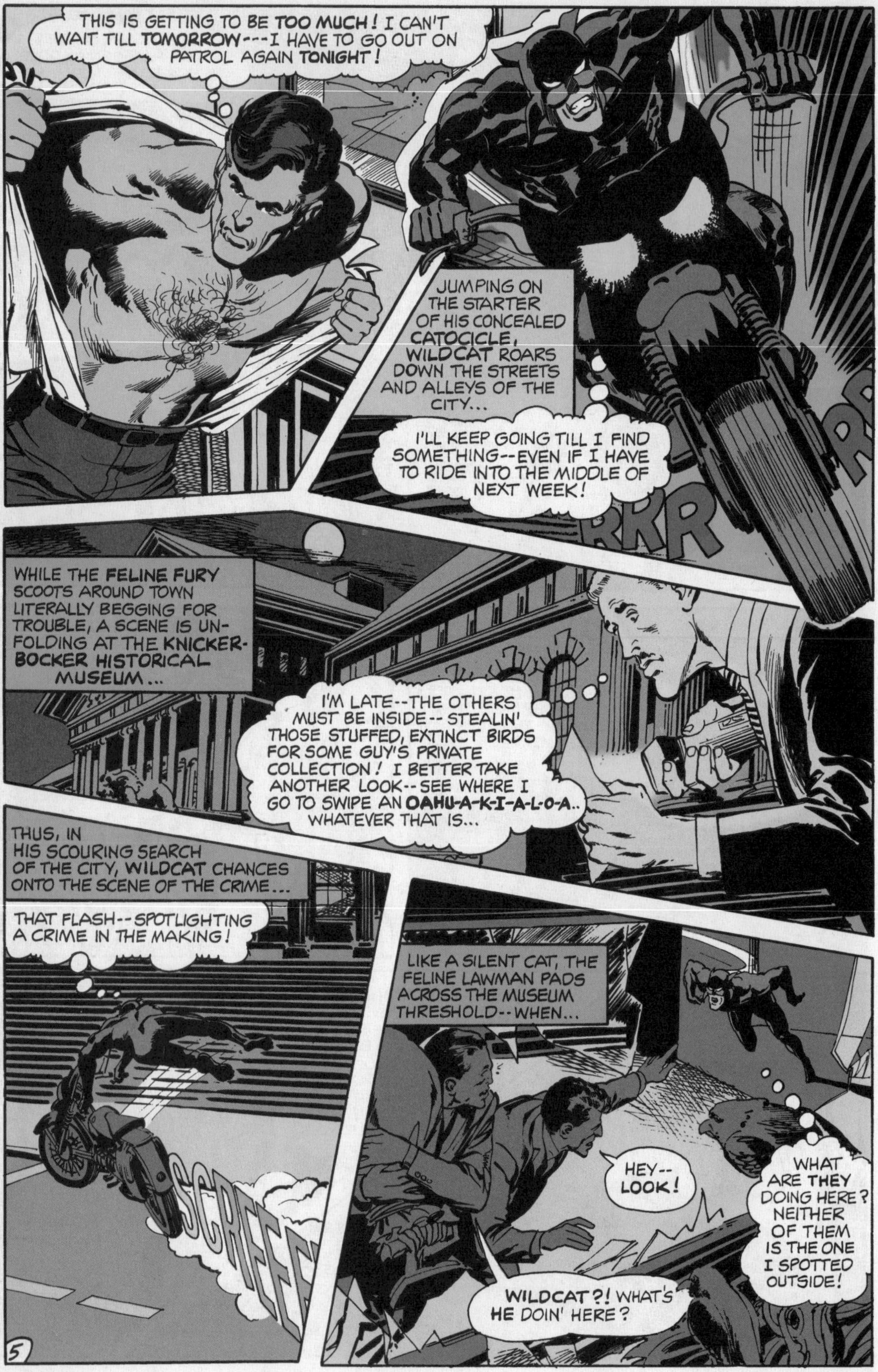
THIS IS GETTING TO BE TOO MUCH! I CAN'T WAIT TILL TOMORROW---I HAVE TO GO OUT ON PATROL AGAIN TONIGHT!
JUMPING ON THE STARTER OF HIS CONCEALED CATOCICLE, WILDCAT ROARS DOWN THE STREETS AND ALLEYS OF THE CITY...
I'LL KEEP GOING TILL I FIND SOMETHING--EVEN IF I HAVE TO RIDE INTO THE MIDDLE OF NEXT WEEK!
RRRRR
WHILE THE FELINE FURY SCOOTS AROUND TOWN LITERALLY BEGGING FOR TROUBLE, A SCENE IS UNFOLDING AT THE KNICKERBOCKER HISTORICAL MUSEUM...
I'M LATE--THE OTHERS MUST BE INSIDE--STEALIN' THOSE STUFFED, EXTINCT BIRDS FOR SOME GUY'S PRIVATE COLLECTION! I BETTER TAKE ANOTHER LOOK--SEE WHERE I GO TO SWIPE AN OAHU-A-K-I-A-L-O-A.. WHATEVER THAT IS...
THUS, IN HIS SCOURING SEARCH OF THE CITY, WILDCAT CHANCES ONTO THE SCENE OF THE CRIME...
THAT FLASH--SPOTLIGHTING A CRIME IN THE MAKING!
SCREEE
5
LIKE A SILENT CAT, THE FELINE LAWMAN PADS ACROSS THE MUSEUM THRESHOLD--WHEN...
HEY-- LOOK!
WILDCAT?! WHAT'S HE DOIN' HERE?
WHAT ARE THEY DOING HERE? NEITHER OF THEM IS THE ONE I SPOTTED OUTSIDE!

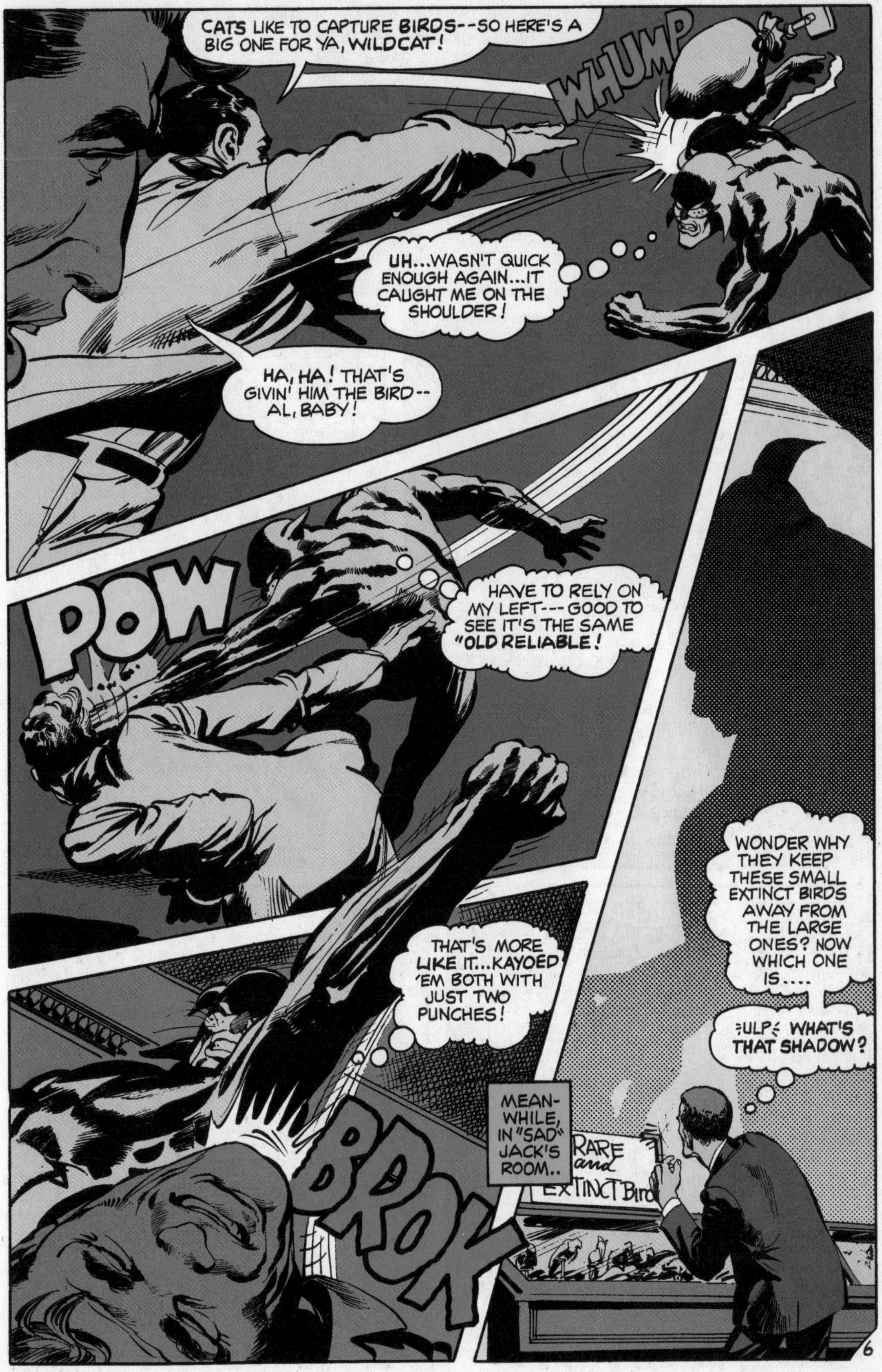
CATS LIKE TO CAPTURE BIRDS--SO HERE'S A BIG ONE FOR YA, WILDCAT!
WHUMP
UH...WASN'T QUICK ENOUGH AGAIN...IT CAUGHT ME ON THE SHOULDER!
HA, HA! THAT'S GIVIN' HIM THE BIRD--AL, BABY!
POW
HAVE TO RELY ON MY LEFT---GOOD TO SEE IT'S THE SAME "OLD RELIABLE!
THAT'S MORE LIKE IT...KAYOED 'EM BOTH WITH JUST TWO PUNCHES!
BROK
MEAN-WHILE, IN "SAD" JACK'S ROOM..
RARE and EXTINCT Bir
WONDER WHY THEY KEEP THESE SMALL EXTINCT BIRDS AWAY FROM THE LARGE ONES? NOW WHICH ONE IS....
ULP WHAT'S THAT SHADOW?
6

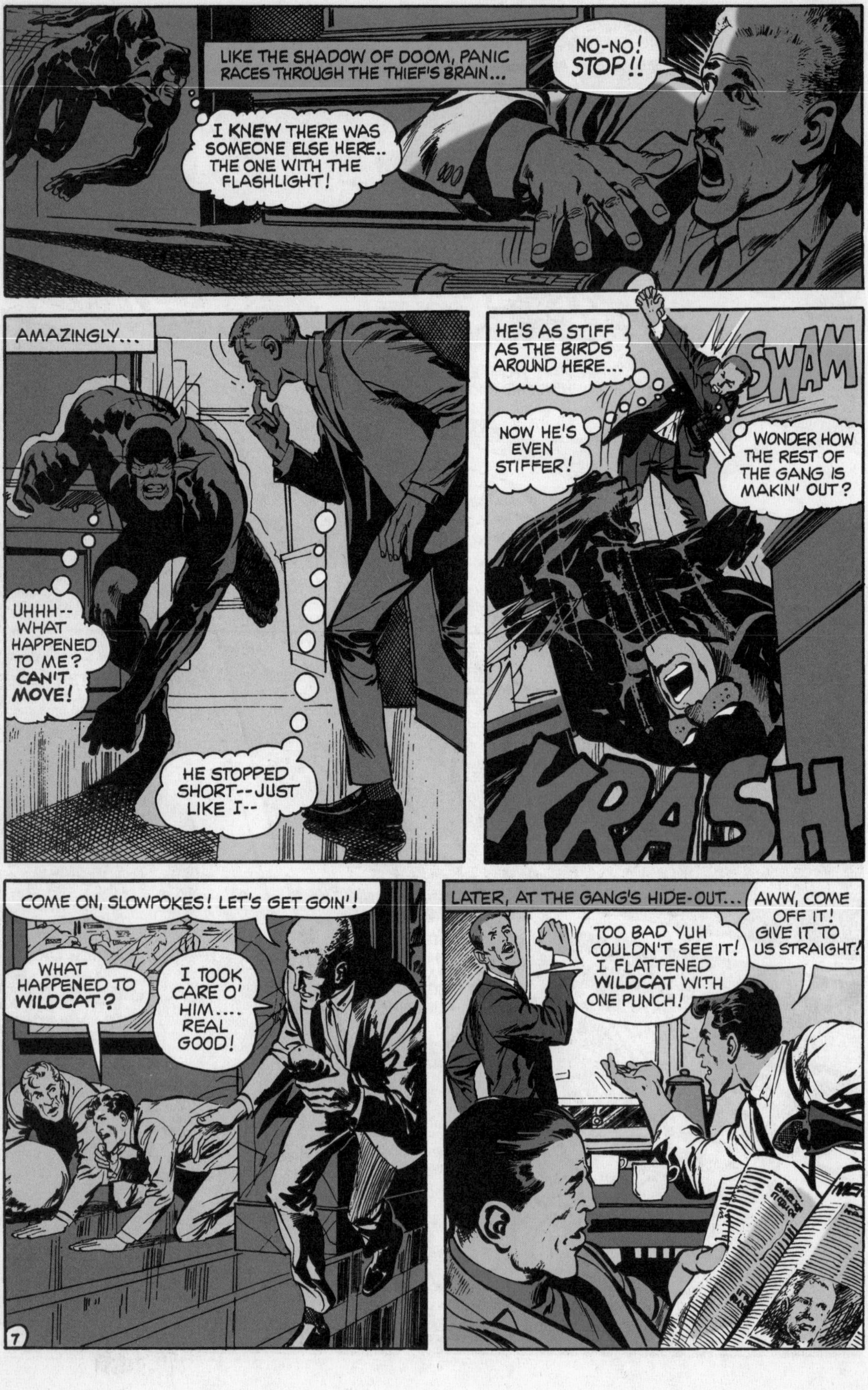

LIKE THE SHADOW OF DOOM, PANIC RACES THROUGH THE THIEF'S BRAIN...
NO-NO! STOP!!
I KNEW THERE WAS SOMEONE ELSE HERE.. THE ONE WITH THE FLASHLIGHT!
AMAZINGLY...
UHHH-- WHAT HAPPENED TO ME? CAN'T MOVE!
HE STOPPED SHORT--JUST LIKE I--
HE'S AS STIFF AS THE BIRDS AROUND HERE...
SWAM
NOW HE'S EVEN STIFFER!
WONDER HOW THE REST OF THE GANG IS MAKIN' OUT?
KRASH
COME ON, SLOWPOKES! LET'S GET GOIN'!
WHAT HAPPENED TO WILDCAT?
I TOOK CARE O' HIM..... REAL GOOD!
7
LATER, AT THE GANG'S HIDE-OUT...
TOO BAD YUH COULDN'T SEE IT! I FLATTENED WILDCAT WITH ONE PUNCH!
AWW, COME OFF IT! GIVE IT TO US STRAIGHT!

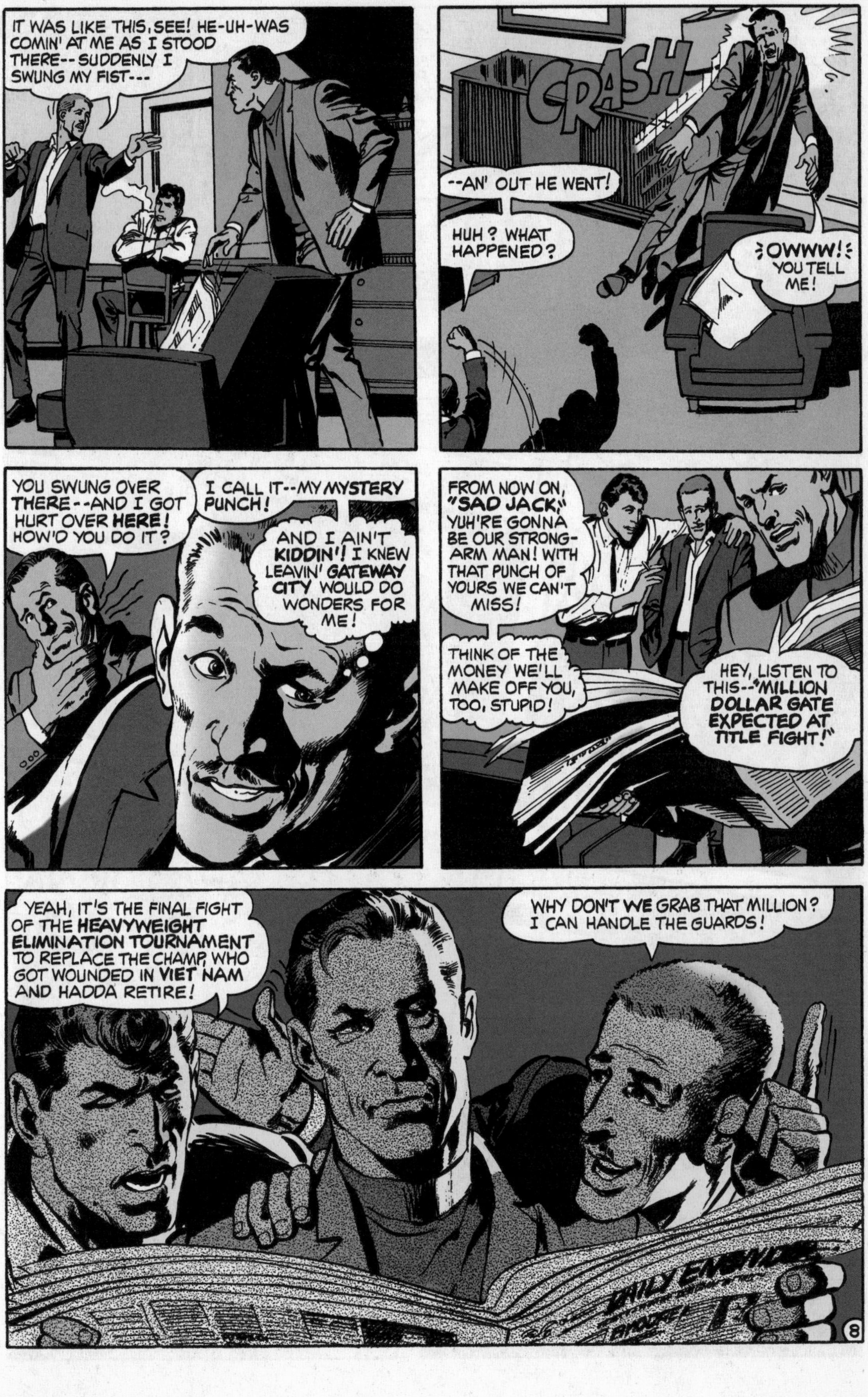

IT WAS LIKE THIS, SEE! HE-UH-WAS COMIN' AT ME AS I STOOD THERE--SUDDENLY I SWUNG MY FIST---
CRASH
--AN' OUT HE WENT!
HUH? WHAT HAPPENED?
OWWW! YOU TELL ME!
YOU SWUNG OVER THERE--AND I GOT HURT OVER HERE! HOW'D YOU DO IT?
I CALL IT--MY MYSTERY PUNCH!
AND I AIN'T KIDDIN'! I KNEW LEAVIN' GATEWAY CITY WOULD DO WONDERS FOR ME!
FROM NOW ON, "SAD JACK," YUH'RE GONNA BE OUR STRONG-ARM MAN! WITH THAT PUNCH OF YOURS WE CAN'T MISS!
THINK OF THE MONEY WE'LL MAKE OFF YOU, TOO, STUPID!
HEY, LISTEN TO THIS--"MILLION DOLLAR GATE EXPECTED AT TITLE FIGHT!"
YEAH, IT'S THE FINAL FIGHT OF THE HEAVYWEIGHT ELIMINATION TOURNAMENT TO REPLACE THE CHAMP, WHO GOT WOUNDED IN VIET NAM AND HADDA RETIRE!
WHY DON'T WE GRAB THAT MILLION? I CAN HANDLE THE GUARDS!
DAILY EMBALMER
8

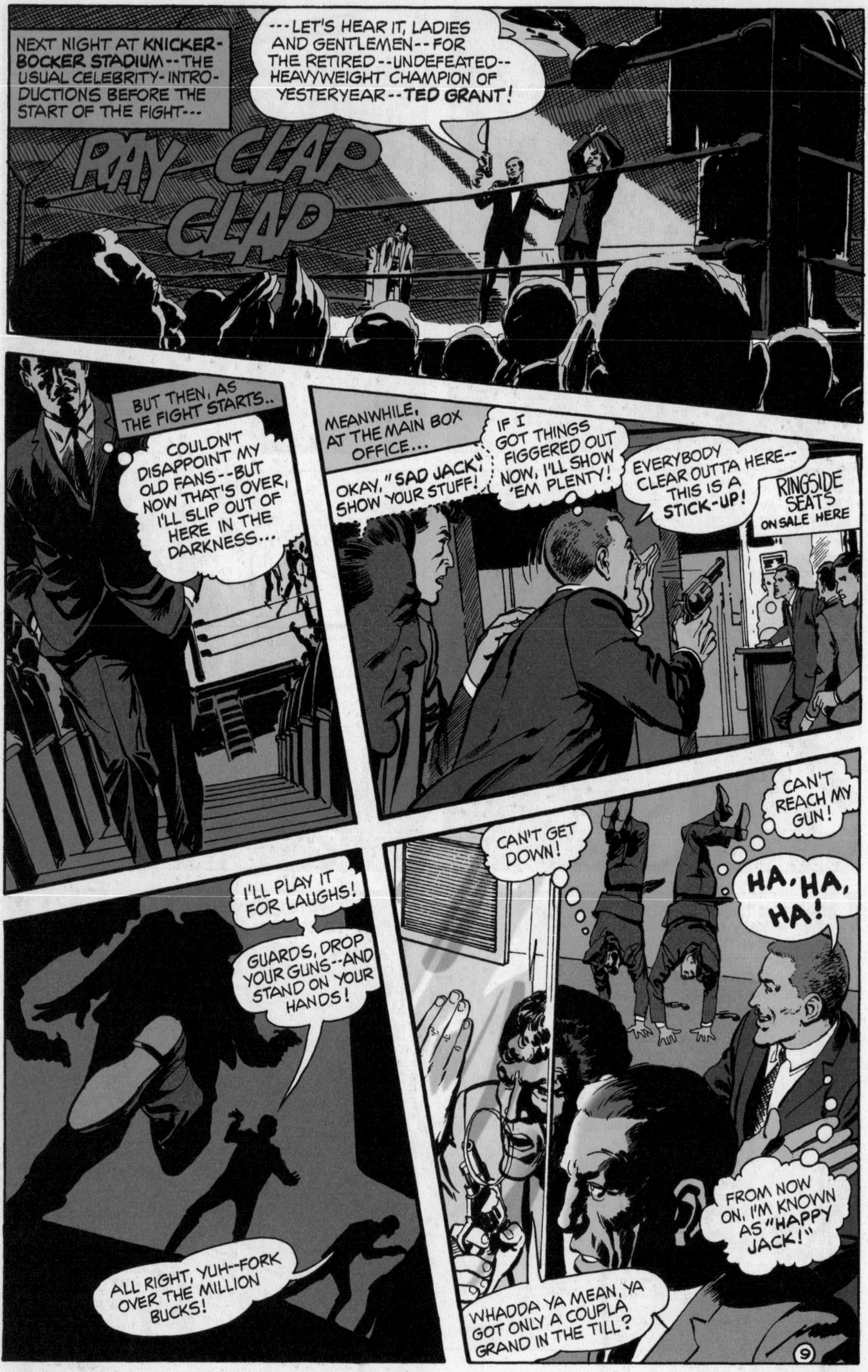
NEXT NIGHT AT KNICKERBOCKER STADIUM--THE USUAL CELEBRITY-INTRODUCTIONS BEFORE THE START OF THE FIGHT---
---LET'S HEAR IT, LADIES AND GENTLEMEN--FOR THE RETIRED--UNDEFEATED--HEAVYWEIGHT CHAMPION OF YESTERYEAR--TED GRANT!
RAY CLAP CLAP CLAP
BUT THEN, AS THE FIGHT STARTS..
COULDN'T DISAPPOINT MY OLD FANS--BUT NOW THAT'S OVER, I'LL SLIP OUT OF HERE IN THE DARKNESS...
MEANWHILE, AT THE MAIN BOX OFFICE...
OKAY, "SAD JACK," SHOW YOUR STUFF!
IF I GOT THINGS FIGGERED OUT NOW, I'LL SHOW 'EM PLENTY!
EVERYBODY CLEAR OUTTA HERE--THIS IS A STICK-UP!
RINGSIDE SEATS ON SALE HERE
I'LL PLAY IT FOR LAUGHS!
GUARDS, DROP YOUR GUNS--AND STAND ON YOUR HANDS!
ALL RIGHT, YUH--FORK OVER THE MILLION BUCKS!
CAN'T GET DOWN!
CAN'T REACH MY GUN!
HA, HA, HA!
FROM NOW ON, I'M KNOWN AS "HAPPY JACK!"
WHADDA YA MEAN, YA GOT ONLY A COUPLA GRAND IN THE TILL?
9

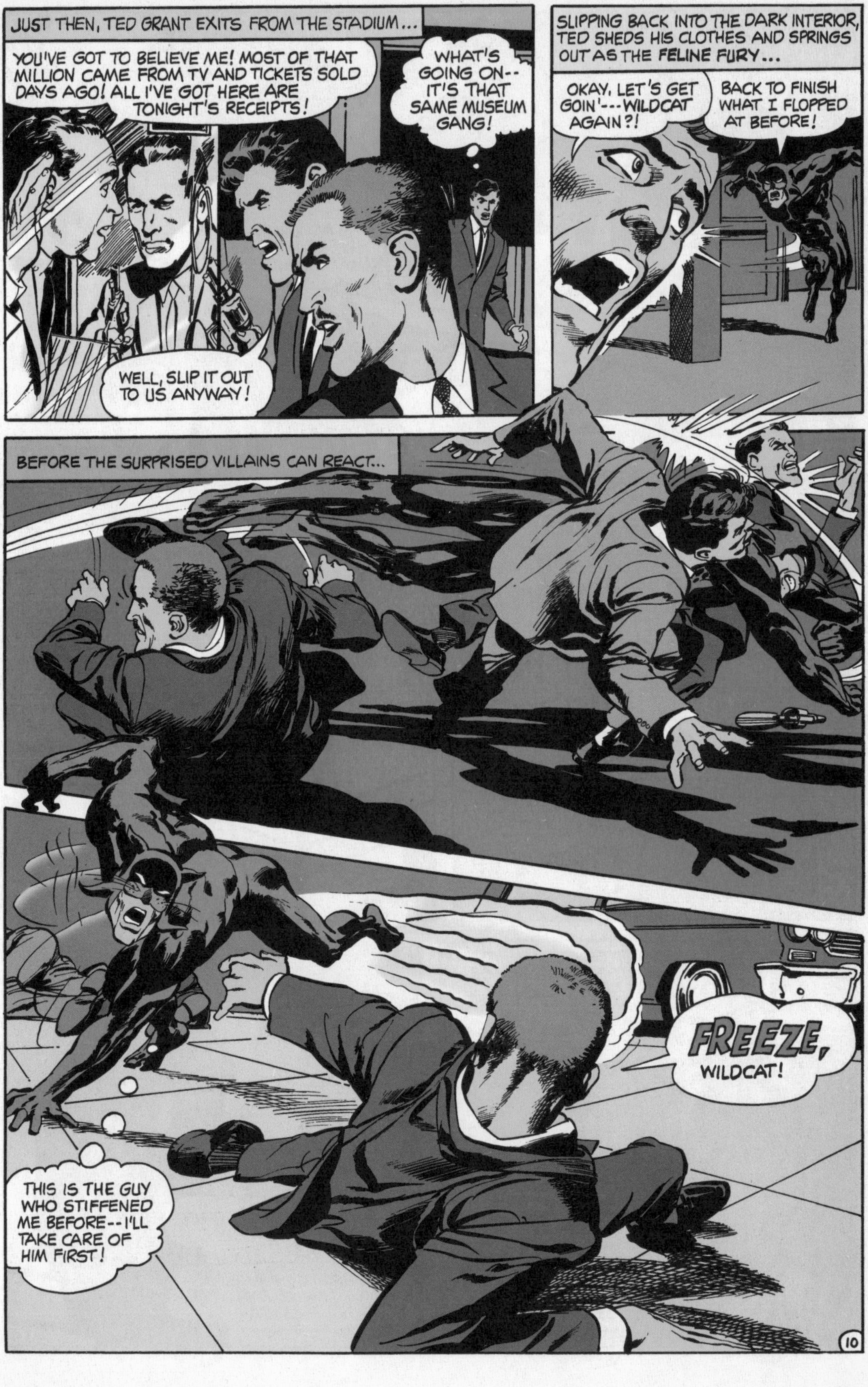

JUST THEN, TED GRANT EXITS FROM THE STADIUM...
YOU'VE GOT TO BELIEVE ME! MOST OF THAT MILLION CAME FROM TV AND TICKETS SOLD DAYS AGO! ALL I'VE GOT HERE ARE TONIGHT'S RECEIPTS!
WHAT'S GOING ON-- IT'S THAT SAME MUSEUM GANG!
WELL, SLIP IT OUT TO US ANYWAY!
SLIPPING BACK INTO THE DARK INTERIOR, TED SHEDS HIS CLOTHES AND SPRINGS OUT AS THE FELINE FURY...
OKAY, LET'S GET GOIN'---WILDCAT AGAIN?!
BACK TO FINISH WHAT I FLOPPED AT BEFORE!
BEFORE THE SURPRISED VILLAINS CAN REACT...
FREEZE, WILDCAT!
THIS IS THE GUY WHO STIFFENED ME BEFORE--I'LL TAKE CARE OF HIM FIRST!
10

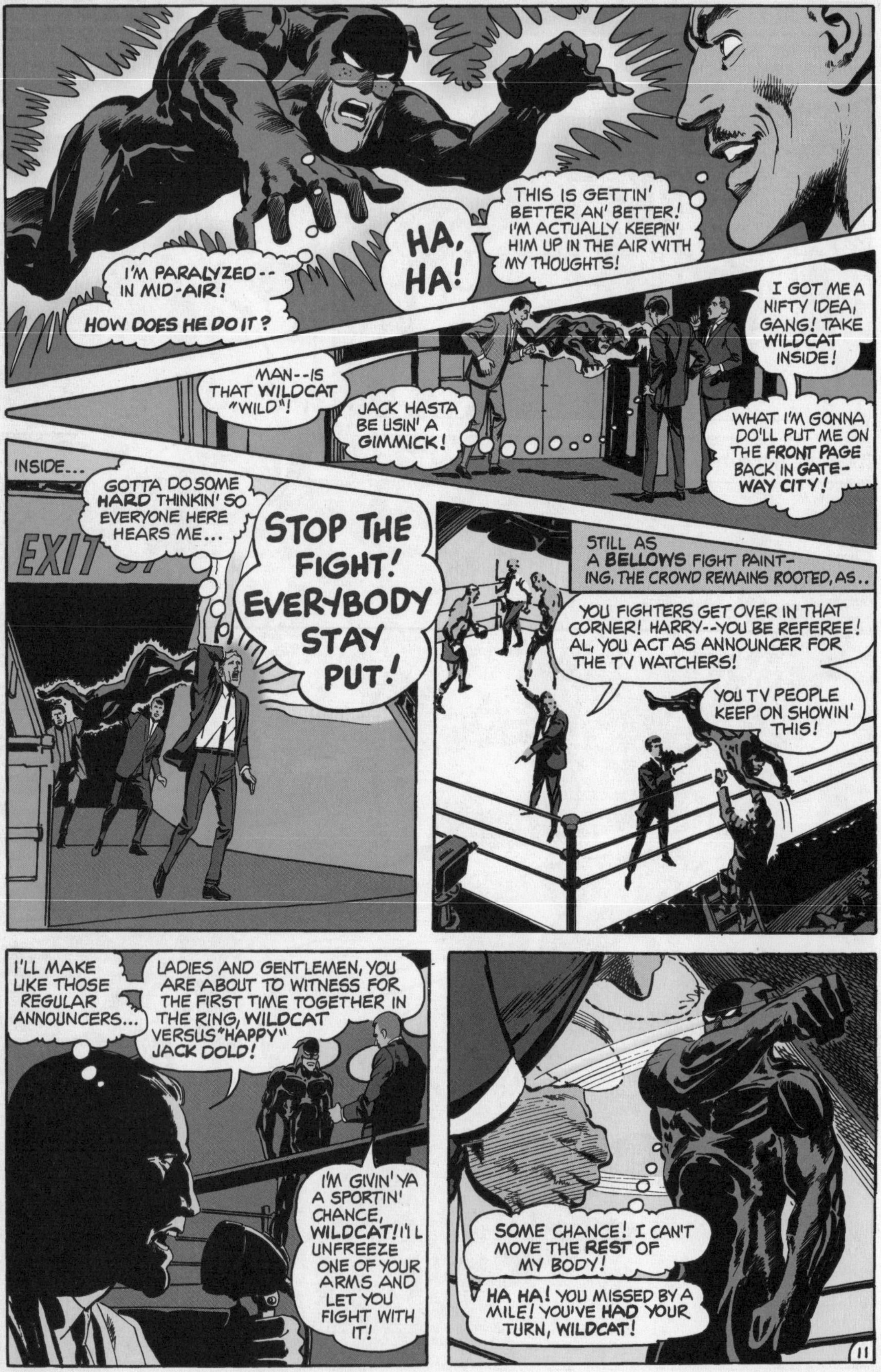
I'M PARALYZED-- IN MID-AIR! HOW DOES HE DO IT?
HA, HA!
THIS IS GETTIN' BETTER AN' BETTER! I'M ACTUALLY KEEPIN' HIM UP IN THE AIR WITH MY THOUGHTS!
MAN--IS THAT WILDCAT "WILD"!
JACK HASTA BE USIN' A GIMMICK!
I GOT ME A NIFTY IDEA, GANG! TAKE WILDCAT INSIDE!
WHAT I'M GONNA DO'LL PUT ME ON THE FRONT PAGE BACK IN GATEWAY CITY!
INSIDE...
GOTTA DO SOME HARD THINKIN' SO EVERYONE HERE HEARS ME...
STOP THE FIGHT! EVERYBODY STAY PUT!
EXIT
STILL AS A BELLOWS FIGHT PAINTING, THE CROWD REMAINS ROOTED, AS..
YOU FIGHTERS GET OVER IN THAT CORNER! HARRY--YOU BE REFEREE! AL, YOU ACT AS ANNOUNCER FOR THE TV WATCHERS!
YOU TV PEOPLE KEEP ON SHOWIN' THIS!
I'LL MAKE LIKE THOSE REGULAR ANNOUNCERS...
LADIES AND GENTLEMEN, YOU ARE ABOUT TO WITNESS FOR THE FIRST TIME TOGETHER IN THE RING, WILDCAT VERSUS "HAPPY" JACK DOLD!
I'M GIVIN' YA A SPORTIN' CHANCE, WILDCAT! I'LL UNFREEZE ONE OF YOUR ARMS AND LET YOU FIGHT WITH IT!
SOME CHANCE! I CAN'T MOVE THE REST OF MY BODY!
HA HA! YOU MISSED BY A MILE! YOU'VE HAD YOUR TURN, WILDCAT!
11

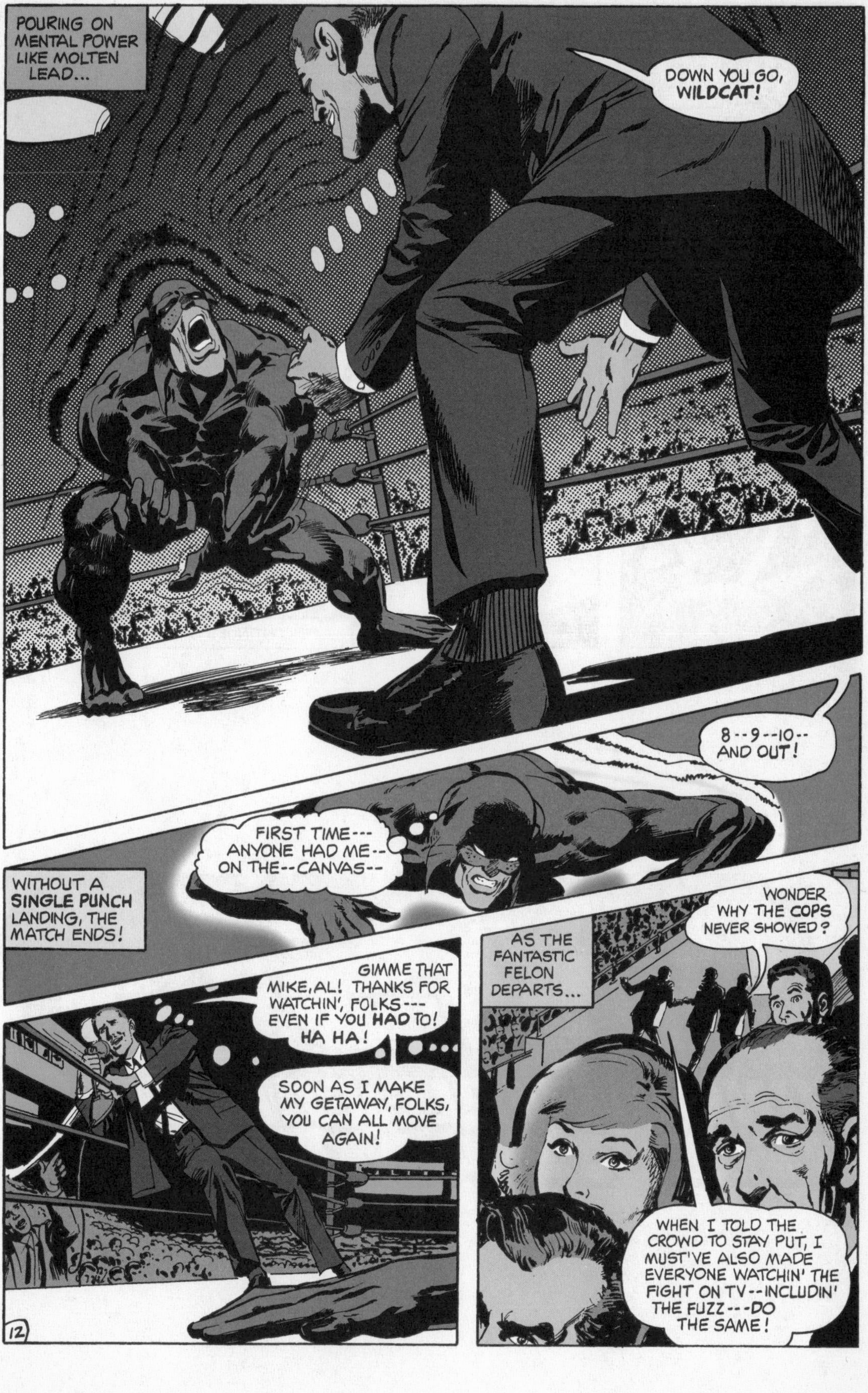

POURING ON MENTAL POWER LIKE MOLTEN LEAD...
DOWN YOU GO, WILDCAT!
8--9--10-- AND OUT!
FIRST TIME--- ANYONE HAD ME-- ON THE--CANVAS--
WITHOUT A SINGLE PUNCH LANDING, THE MATCH ENDS!
GIMME THAT MIKE, AL! THANKS FOR WATCHIN', FOLKS--- EVEN IF YOU HAD TO! HA HA!
SOON AS I MAKE MY GETAWAY, FOLKS, YOU CAN ALL MOVE AGAIN!
12
AS THE FANTASTIC FELON DEPARTS...
WONDER WHY THE COPS NEVER SHOWED?
WHEN I TOLD THE CROWD TO STAY PUT, I MUST'VE ALSO MADE EVERYONE WATCHIN' THE FIGHT ON TV--INCLUDIN' THE FUZZ---DO THE SAME!

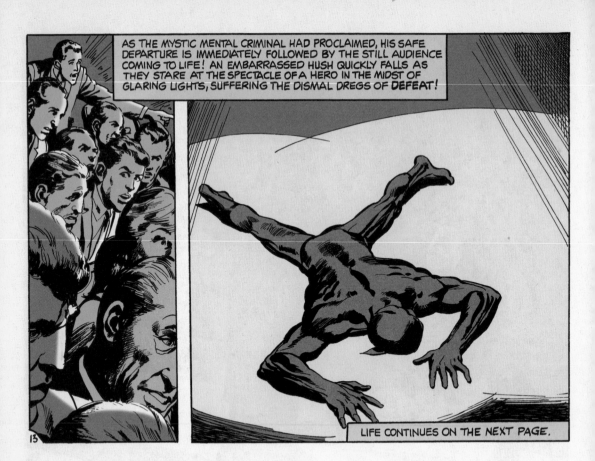

AS THE MYSTIC MENTAL CRIMINAL HAD PROCLAIMED, HIS SAFE DEPARTURE IS IMMEDIATELY FOLLOWED BY THE STILL AUDIENCE COMING TO LIFE! AN EMBARRASSED HUSH QUICKLY FALLS AS THEY STARE AT THE SPECTACLE OF A HERO IN THE MIDST OF GLARING LIGHTS, SUFFERING THE DISMAL DREGS OF DEFEAT!
LIFE CONTINUES ON THE NEXT PAGE.
13

CRISIS
ON MULTIPLE EARTHS
THE TEAM UPS

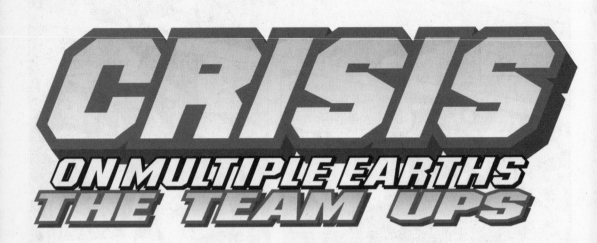

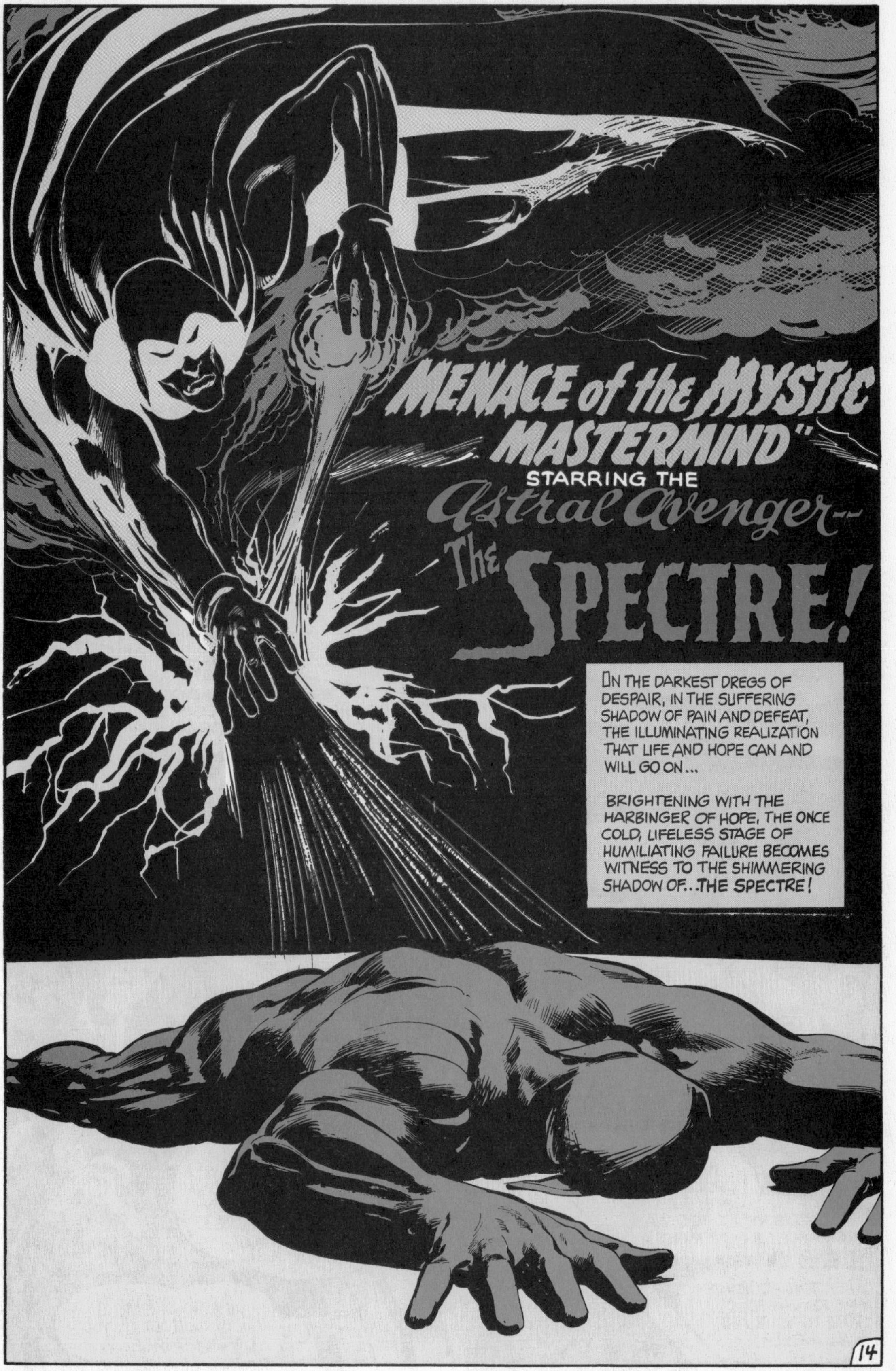
"MENACE of the MYSTIC MASTERMIND"
STARRING THE
Astral Avenger--
The SPECTRE!
ON THE DARKEST DREGS OF DESPAIR, IN THE SUFFERING SHADOW OF PAIN AND DEFEAT, THE ILLUMINATING REALIZATION THAT LIFE AND HOPE CAN AND WILL GO ON...
BRIGHTENING WITH THE HARBINGER OF HOPE, THE ONCE COLD, LIFELESS STAGE OF HUMILIATING FAILURE BECOMES WITNESS TO THE SHIMMERING SHADOW OF.. THE SPECTRE!
14

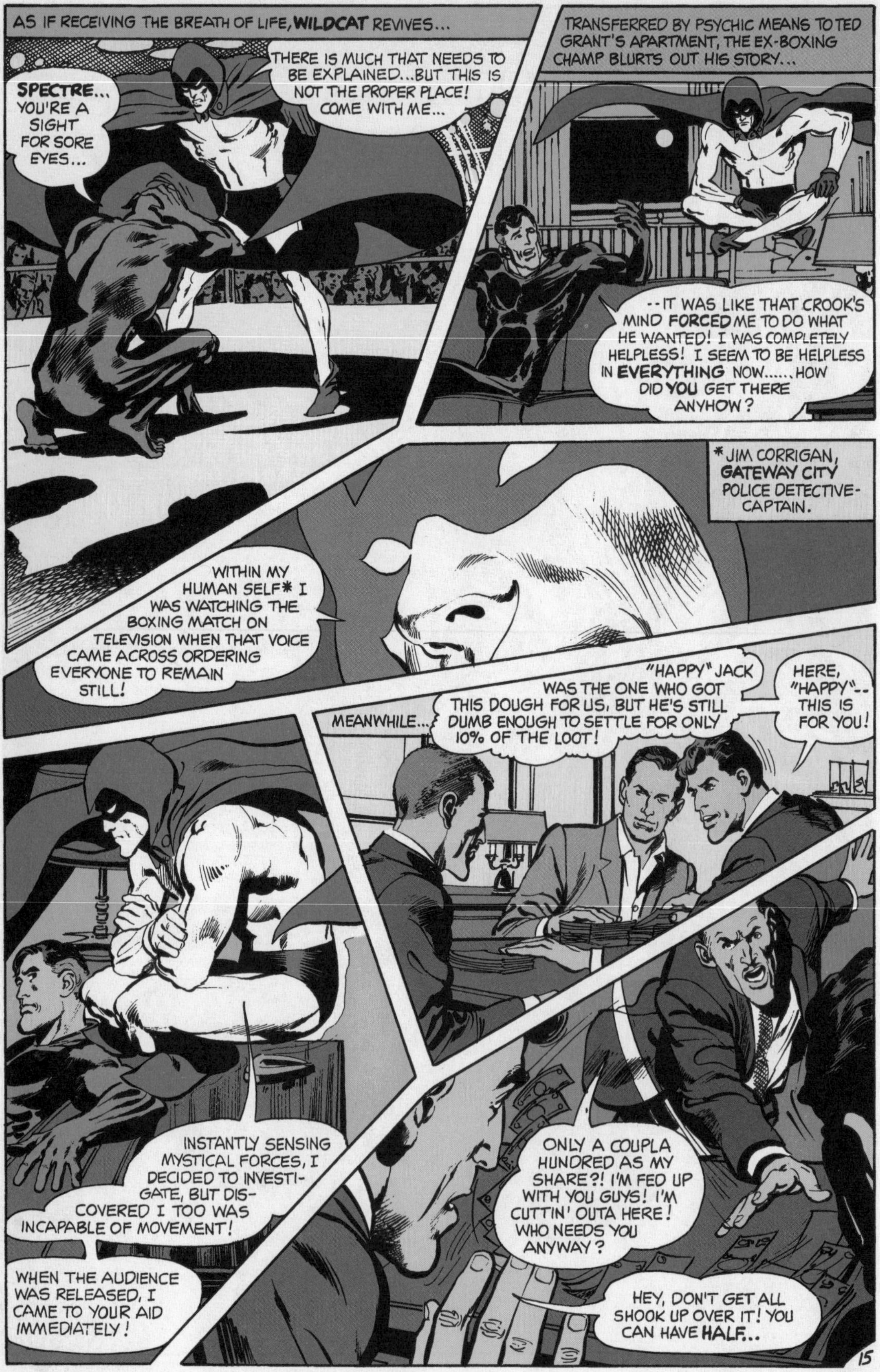

AS IF RECEIVING THE BREATH OF LIFE, WILDCAT REVIVES...
SPECTRE... YOU'RE A SIGHT FOR SORE EYES...
THERE IS MUCH THAT NEEDS TO BE EXPLAINED...BUT THIS IS NOT THE PROPER PLACE! COME WITH ME...
TRANSFERRED BY PSYCHIC MEANS TO TED GRANT'S APARTMENT, THE EX-BOXING CHAMP BLURTS OUT HIS STORY...
--IT WAS LIKE THAT CROOK'S MIND FORCED ME TO DO WHAT HE WANTED! I WAS COMPLETELY HELPLESS! I SEEM TO BE HELPLESS IN EVERYTHING NOW...... HOW DID YOU GET THERE ANYHOW?
WITHIN MY HUMAN SELF* I WAS WATCHING THE BOXING MATCH ON TELEVISION WHEN THAT VOICE CAME ACROSS ORDERING EVERYONE TO REMAIN STILL!
*JIM CORRIGAN, GATEWAY CITY POLICE DETECTIVE-CAPTAIN.
INSTANTLY SENSING MYSTICAL FORCES, I DECIDED TO INVESTI-GATE, BUT DIS-COVERED I TOO WAS INCAPABLE OF MOVEMENT!
WHEN THE AUDIENCE WAS RELEASED, I CAME TO YOUR AID IMMEDIATELY!
MEANWHILE...
"HAPPY" JACK WAS THE ONE WHO GOT THIS DOUGH FOR US, BUT HE'S STILL DUMB ENOUGH TO SETTLE FOR ONLY 10% OF THE LOOT!
HERE, "HAPPY"-- THIS IS FOR YOU!
ONLY A COUPLA HUNDRED AS MY SHARE?! I'M FED UP WITH YOU GUYS! I'M CUTTIN' OUTA HERE! WHO NEEDS YOU ANYWAY?
HEY, DON'T GET ALL SHOOK UP OVER IT! YOU CAN HAVE HALF...
15

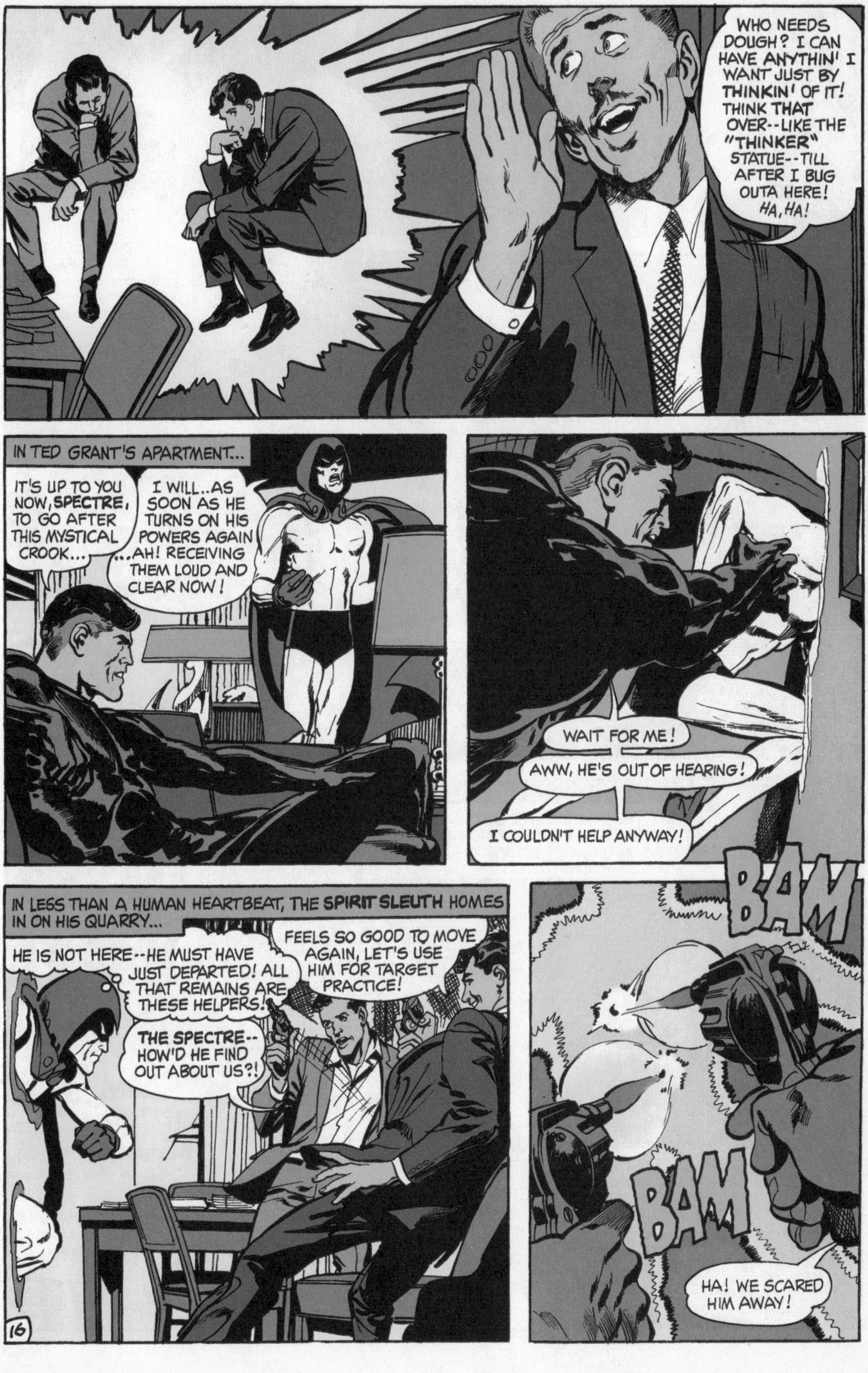
WHO NEEDS DOUGH? I CAN HAVE ANYTHIN' I WANT JUST BY THINKIN' OF IT! THINK THAT OVER--LIKE THE "THINKER" STATUE--TILL AFTER I BUG OUTA HERE! HA, HA!
IN TED GRANT'S APARTMENT...
IT'S UP TO YOU NOW, SPECTRE, TO GO AFTER THIS MYSTICAL CROOK...
I WILL..AS SOON AS HE TURNS ON HIS POWERS AGAIN ...AH! RECEIVING THEM LOUD AND CLEAR NOW!
WAIT FOR ME!
AWW, HE'S OUT OF HEARING!
I COULDN'T HELP ANYWAY!
IN LESS THAN A HUMAN HEARTBEAT, THE SPIRIT SLEUTH HOMES IN ON HIS QUARRY...
HE IS NOT HERE--HE MUST HAVE JUST DEPARTED! ALL THAT REMAINS ARE THESE HELPERS!
FEELS SO GOOD TO MOVE AGAIN, LET'S USE HIM FOR TARGET PRACTICE!
THE SPECTRE--HOW'D HE FIND OUT ABOUT US?!
16
BAM
BAM
HA! WE SCARED HIM AWAY!

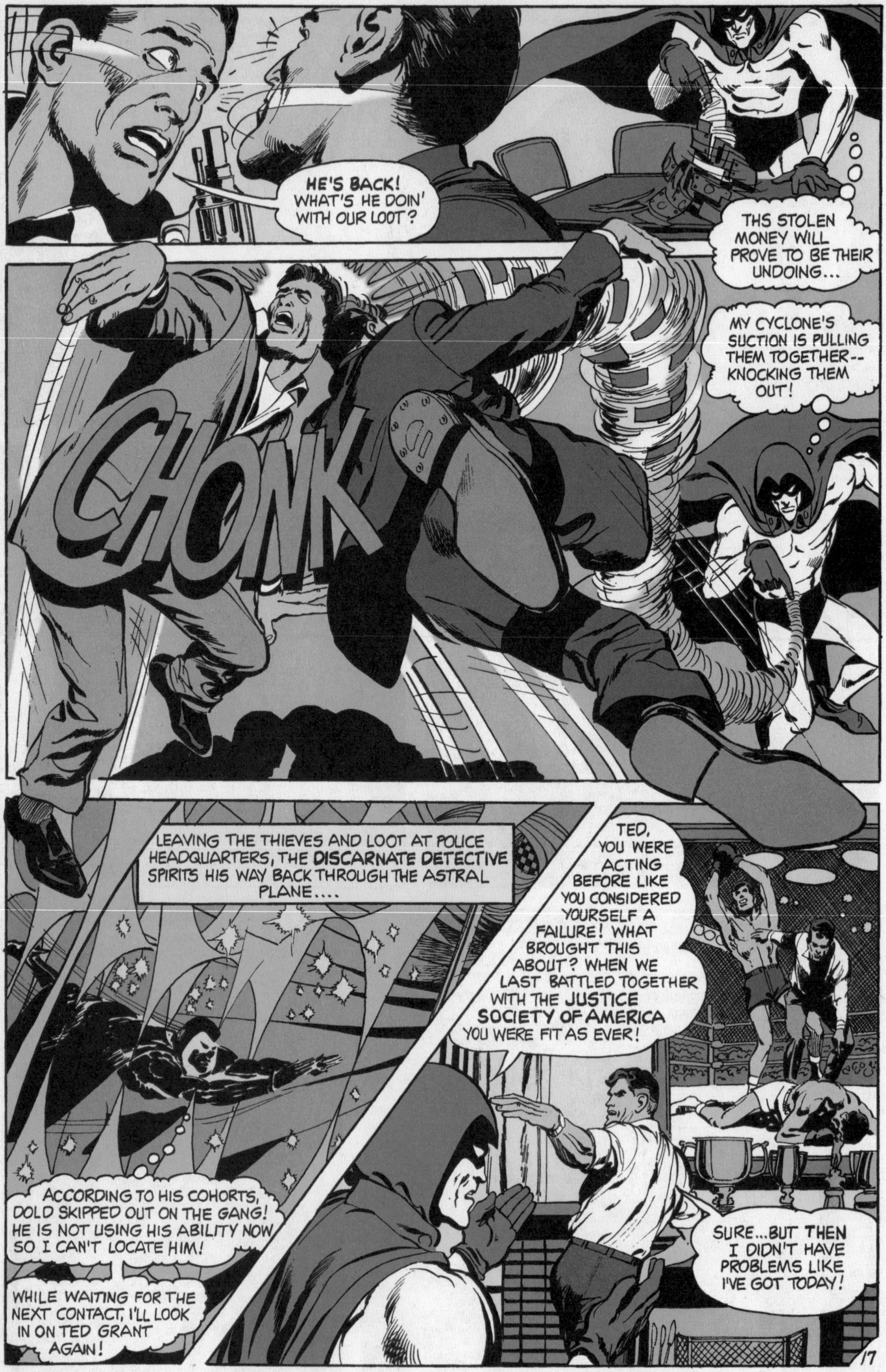

HE'S BACK! WHAT'S HE DOIN' WITH OUR LOOT?
THS STOLEN MONEY WILL PROVE TO BE THEIR UNDOING...
MY CYCLONE'S SUCTION IS PULLING THEM TOGETHER-- KNOCKING THEM OUT!
CHONK
LEAVING THE THIEVES AND LOOT AT POLICE HEADQUARTERS, THE DISCARNATE DETECTIVE SPIRITS HIS WAY BACK THROUGH THE ASTRAL PLANE....
ACCORDING TO HIS COHORTS, DOLD SKIPPED OUT ON THE GANG! HE IS NOT USING HIS ABILITY NOW SO I CAN'T LOCATE HIM!
WHILE WAITING FOR THE NEXT CONTACT, I'LL LOOK IN ON TED GRANT AGAIN!
TED, YOU WERE ACTING BEFORE LIKE YOU CONSIDERED YOURSELF A FAILURE! WHAT BROUGHT THIS ABOUT? WHEN WE LAST BATTLED TOGETHER WITH THE JUSTICE SOCIETY OF AMERICA YOU WERE FIT AS EVER!
SURE...BUT THEN I DIDN'T HAVE PROBLEMS LIKE I'VE GOT TODAY!
17

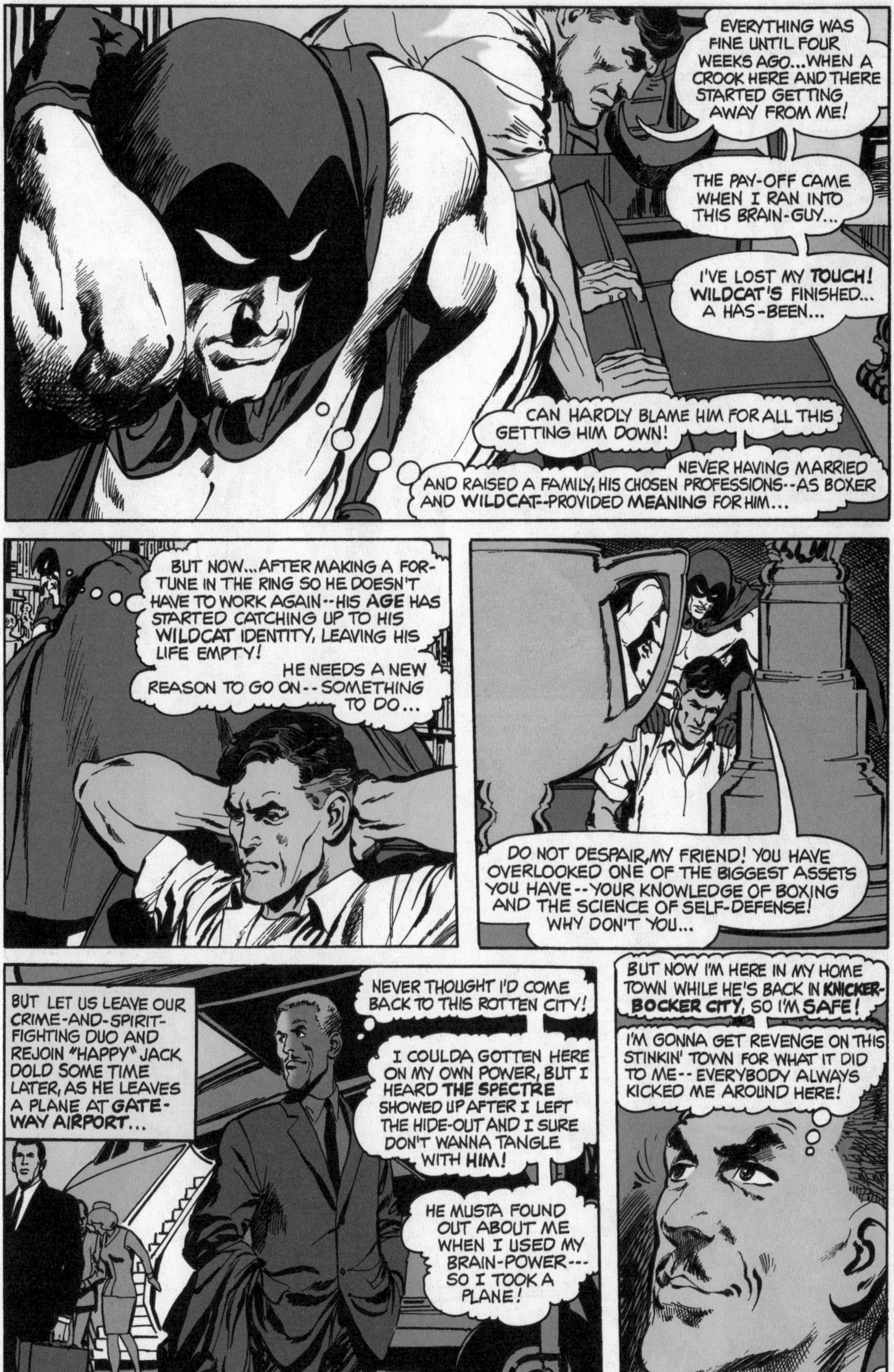
EVERYTHING WAS FINE UNTIL FOUR WEEKS AGO...WHEN A CROOK HERE AND THERE STARTED GETTING AWAY FROM ME!
THE PAY-OFF CAME WHEN I RAN INTO THIS BRAIN-GUY...
I'VE LOST MY TOUCH! WILDCAT'S FINISHED... A HAS-BEEN...
CAN HARDLY BLAME HIM FOR ALL THIS GETTING HIM DOWN!
NEVER HAVING MARRIED AND RAISED A FAMILY, HIS CHOSEN PROFESSIONS--AS BOXER AND WILDCAT--PROVIDED MEANING FOR HIM...
BUT NOW...AFTER MAKING A FORTUNE IN THE RING SO HE DOESN'T HAVE TO WORK AGAIN--HIS AGE HAS STARTED CATCHING UP TO HIS WILDCAT IDENTITY, LEAVING HIS LIFE EMPTY!
HE NEEDS A NEW REASON TO GO ON--SOMETHING TO DO...
DO NOT DESPAIR, MY FRIEND! YOU HAVE OVERLOOKED ONE OF THE BIGGEST ASSETS YOU HAVE--YOUR KNOWLEDGE OF BOXING AND THE SCIENCE OF SELF-DEFENSE! WHY DON'T YOU...
BUT LET US LEAVE OUR CRIME-AND-SPIRIT-FIGHTING DUO AND REJOIN "HAPPY" JACK DOLD SOME TIME LATER, AS HE LEAVES A PLANE AT GATEWAY AIRPORT...
NEVER THOUGHT I'D COME BACK TO THIS ROTTEN CITY!
I COULDA GOTTEN HERE ON MY OWN POWER, BUT I HEARD THE SPECTRE SHOWED UP AFTER I LEFT THE HIDE-OUT AND I SURE DON'T WANNA TANGLE WITH HIM!
HE MUSTA FOUND OUT ABOUT ME WHEN I USED MY BRAIN-POWER--- SO I TOOK A PLANE!
BUT NOW I'M HERE IN MY HOME TOWN WHILE HE'S BACK IN KNICKERBOCKER CITY, SO I'M SAFE!
I'M GONNA GET REVENGE ON THIS STINKIN' TOWN FOR WHAT IT DID TO ME--EVERYBODY ALWAYS KICKED ME AROUND HERE!
18

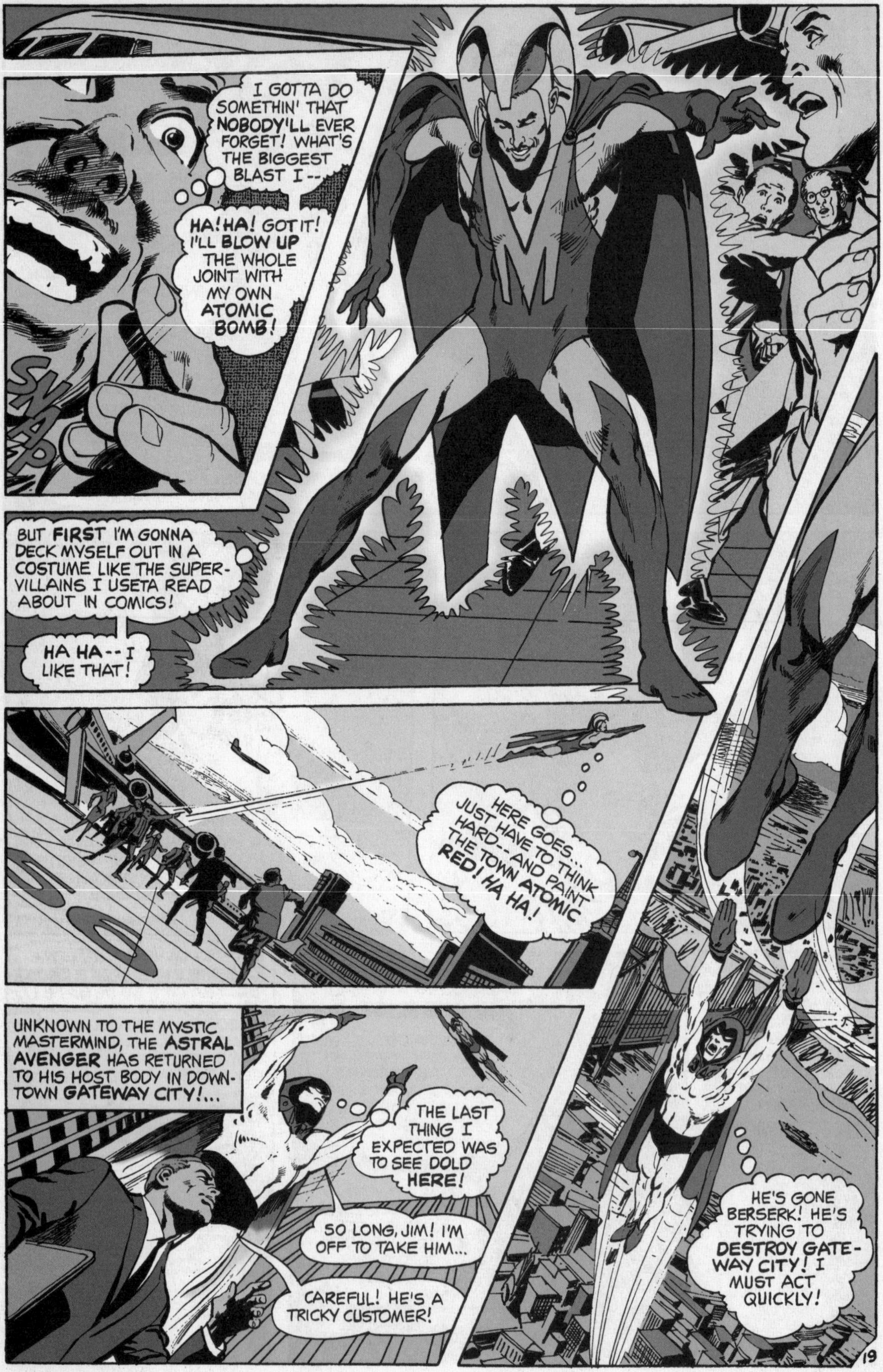
I GOTTA DO SOMETHIN' THAT NOBODY'LL EVER FORGET! WHAT'S THE BIGGEST BLAST I--
HA! HA! GOT IT! I'LL BLOW UP THE WHOLE JOINT WITH MY OWN ATOMIC BOMB!
SNAP
BUT FIRST I'M GONNA DECK MYSELF OUT IN A COSTUME LIKE THE SUPER-VILLAINS I USETA READ ABOUT IN COMICS!
HA HA-- I LIKE THAT!
HERE GOES... JUST HAVE TO THINK HARD--AND PAINT THE TOWN ATOMIC RED! HA HA!
UNKNOWN TO THE MYSTIC MASTERMIND, THE ASTRAL AVENGER HAS RETURNED TO HIS HOST BODY IN DOWN-TOWN GATEWAY CITY!...
THE LAST THING I EXPECTED WAS TO SEE DOLD HERE!
SO LONG, JIM! I'M OFF TO TAKE HIM...
CAREFUL! HE'S A TRICKY CUSTOMER!
HE'S GONE BERSERK! HE'S TRYING TO DESTROY GATE-WAY CITY! I MUST ACT QUICKLY!
19

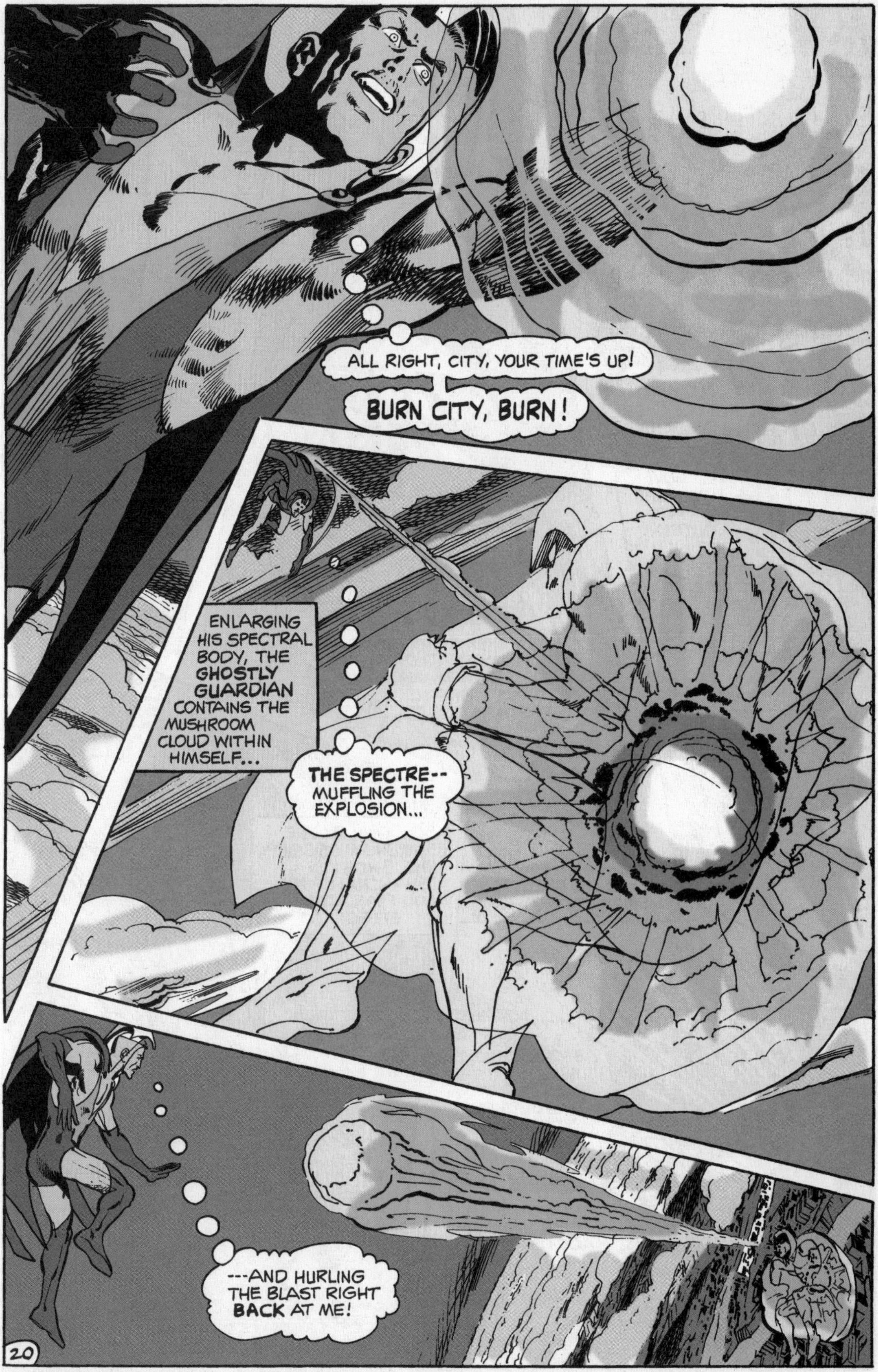
ALL RIGHT, CITY, YOUR TIME'S UP!
BURN CITY, BURN!
ENLARGING HIS SPECTRAL BODY, THE GHOSTLY GUARDIAN CONTAINS THE MUSHROOM CLOUD WITHIN HIMSELF...
THE SPECTRE-- MUFFLING THE EXPLOSION...
---AND HURLING THE BLAST RIGHT BACK AT ME!
20

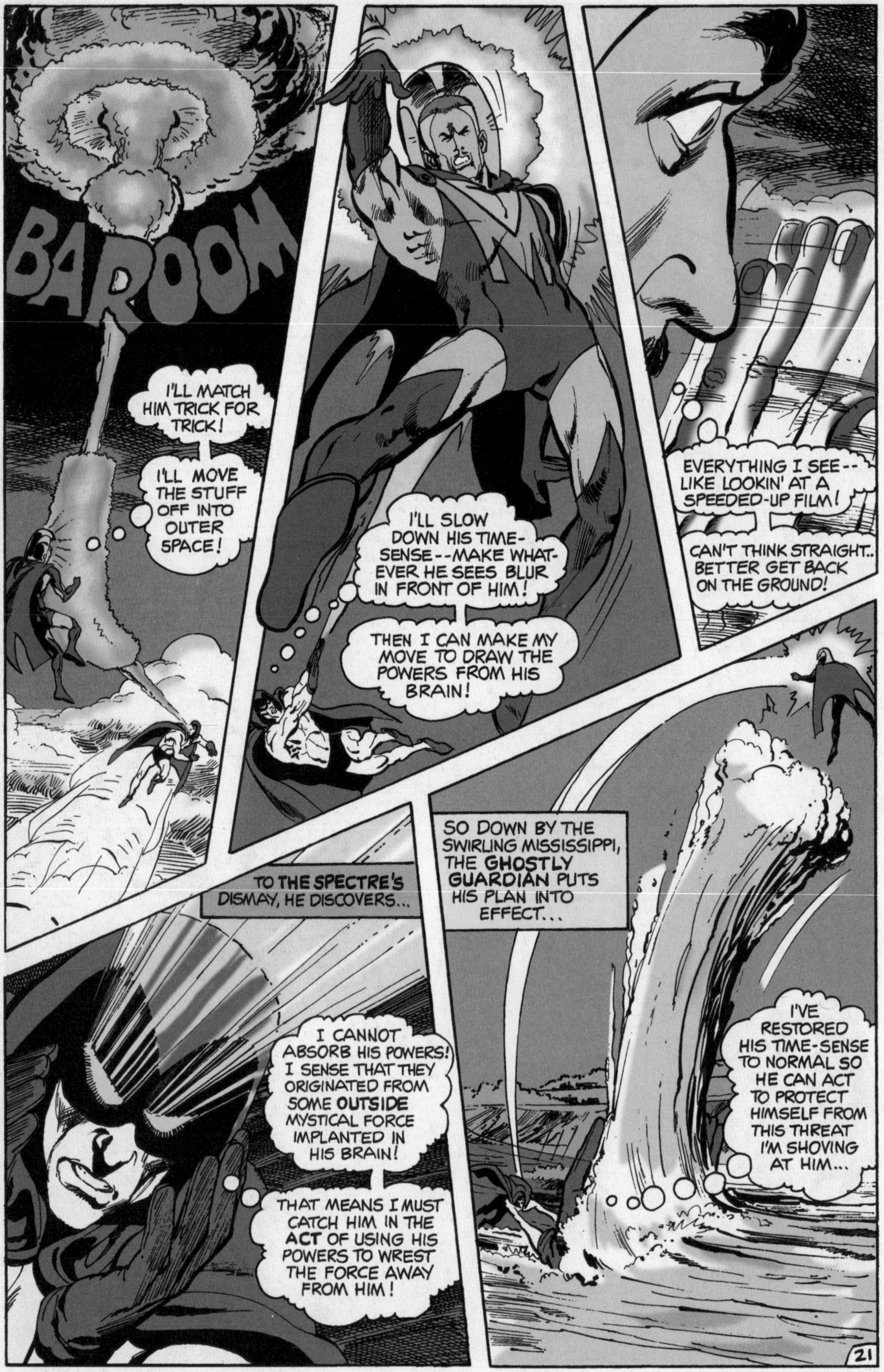
BAROOM
I'LL MATCH HIM TRICK FOR TRICK!
I'LL MOVE THE STUFF OFF INTO OUTER SPACE!
I'LL SLOW DOWN HIS TIME-SENSE--MAKE WHAT-EVER HE SEES BLUR IN FRONT OF HIM!
THEN I CAN MAKE MY MOVE TO DRAW THE POWERS FROM HIS BRAIN!
EVERYTHING I SEE--LIKE LOOKIN' AT A SPEEDED-UP FILM!
CAN'T THINK STRAIGHT.. BETTER GET BACK ON THE GROUND!
TO THE SPECTRE'S DISMAY, HE DISCOVERS...
I CANNOT ABSORB HIS POWERS! I SENSE THAT THEY ORIGINATED FROM SOME OUTSIDE MYSTICAL FORCE IMPLANTED IN HIS BRAIN!
THAT MEANS I MUST CATCH HIM IN THE ACT OF USING HIS POWERS TO WREST THE FORCE AWAY FROM HIM!
SO DOWN BY THE SWIRLING MISSISSIPPI, THE GHOSTLY GUARDIAN PUTS HIS PLAN INTO EFFECT...
I'VE RESTORED HIS TIME-SENSE TO NORMAL SO HE CAN ACT TO PROTECT HIMSELF FROM THIS THREAT I'M SHOVING AT HIM...
21

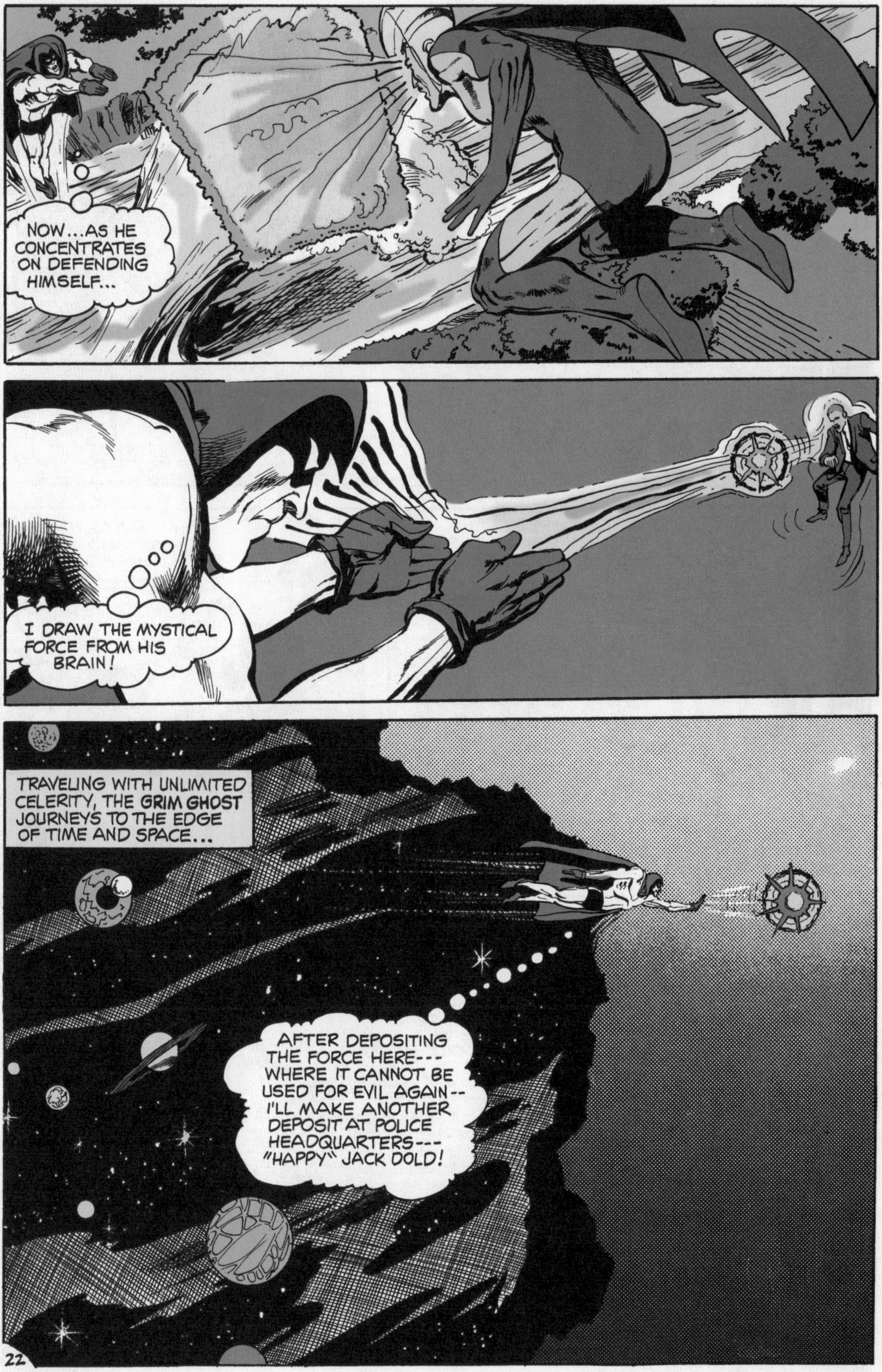
NOW...AS HE CONCENTRATES ON DEFENDING HIMSELF...
I DRAW THE MYSTICAL FORCE FROM HIS BRAIN!
TRAVELING WITH UNLIMITED CELERITY, THE GRIM GHOST JOURNEYS TO THE EDGE OF TIME AND SPACE...
AFTER DEPOSITING THE FORCE HERE--- WHERE IT CANNOT BE USED FOR EVIL AGAIN-- I'LL MAKE ANOTHER DEPOSIT AT POLICE HEADQUARTERS--- "HAPPY" JACK DOLD!
22

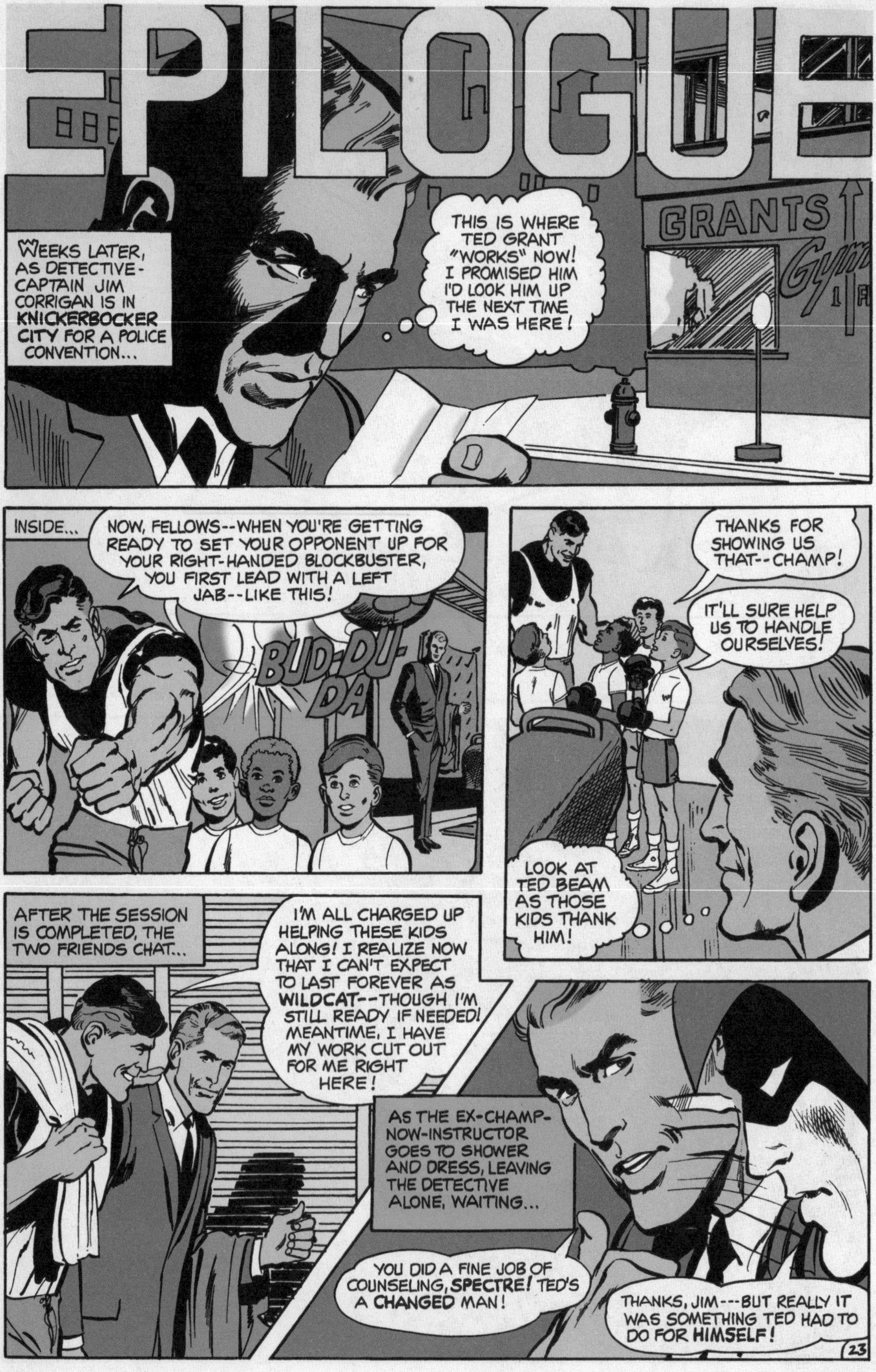
EPILOGUE
WEEKS LATER, AS DETECTIVE-CAPTAIN JIM CORRIGAN IS IN KNICKERBOCKER CITY FOR A POLICE CONVENTION...
THIS IS WHERE TED GRANT "WORKS" NOW! I PROMISED HIM I'D LOOK HIM UP THE NEXT TIME I WAS HERE!
GRANTS
Gym
INSIDE...
NOW, FELLOWS--WHEN YOU'RE GETTING READY TO SET YOUR OPPONENT UP FOR YOUR RIGHT-HANDED BLOCKBUSTER, YOU FIRST LEAD WITH A LEFT JAB--LIKE THIS!
BUD-DU-DA
THANKS FOR SHOWING US THAT--CHAMP!
IT'LL SURE HELP US TO HANDLE OURSELVES!
LOOK AT TED BEAM AS THOSE KIDS THANK HIM!
AFTER THE SESSION IS COMPLETED, THE TWO FRIENDS CHAT...
I'M ALL CHARGED UP HELPING THESE KIDS ALONG! I REALIZE NOW THAT I CAN'T EXPECT TO LAST FOREVER AS WILDCAT--THOUGH I'M STILL READY IF NEEDED! MEANTIME, I HAVE MY WORK CUT OUT FOR ME RIGHT HERE!
AS THE EX-CHAMP-NOW-INSTRUCTOR GOES TO SHOWER AND DRESS, LEAVING THE DETECTIVE ALONE, WAITING...
YOU DID A FINE JOB OF COUNSELING, SPECTRE! TED'S A CHANGED MAN!
THANKS, JIM---BUT REALLY IT WAS SOMETHING TED HAD TO DO FOR HIMSELF!
23

TED HAD SPENT HIS LIFE COMPLETELY IMMERSED IN HIS **WORK,** WHICH AS A WAY OF LIFE CAN EASILY COLLAPSE, AS IT DID IN HIS CASE...
I MERELY SUGGESTED THAT HE SHIFT HIS INTEREST TO **PEOPLE,** USING HIS GIFTED ABILITIES TO HELP THOSE HE MEETS AND WORKS WITH, TO **LIVE** MORE FULLY IN SOME WAY...
WHETHER BY TEACHING YOUNGSTERS HOW TO BOX, OR HELPING SOCIETY CAPTURE LAW-BREAKERS, OR JUST BRIGHTENING A FRIEND'S DAY BY GREETING HIM WITH A SMILE...
NEAL ADAMS
WE'D BETTER QUIT WHILE WE'RE AHEAD, BEFORE AUTHOR **MIKE FRIEDRICH** GETS CARRIED AWAY WITH PHILOSOPHICAL RAMBLINGS! **THE END.**
24

CRISIS ON MULTIPLE EARTHS THE TEAM UPS

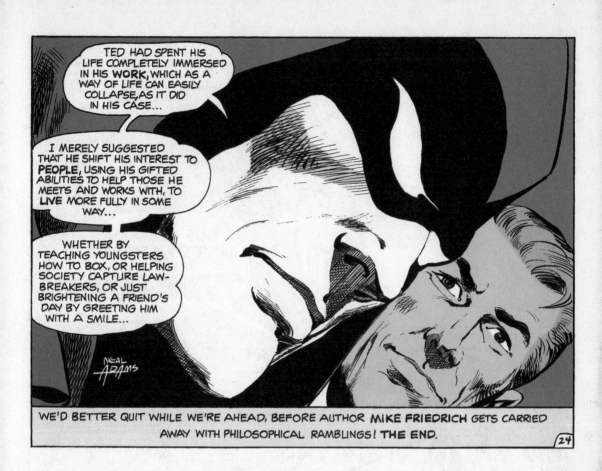

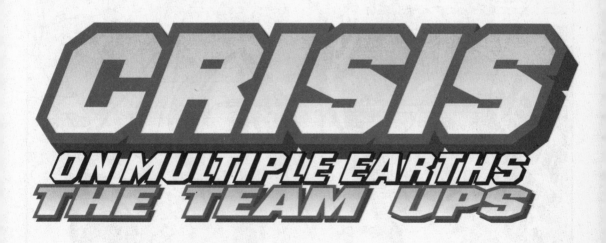

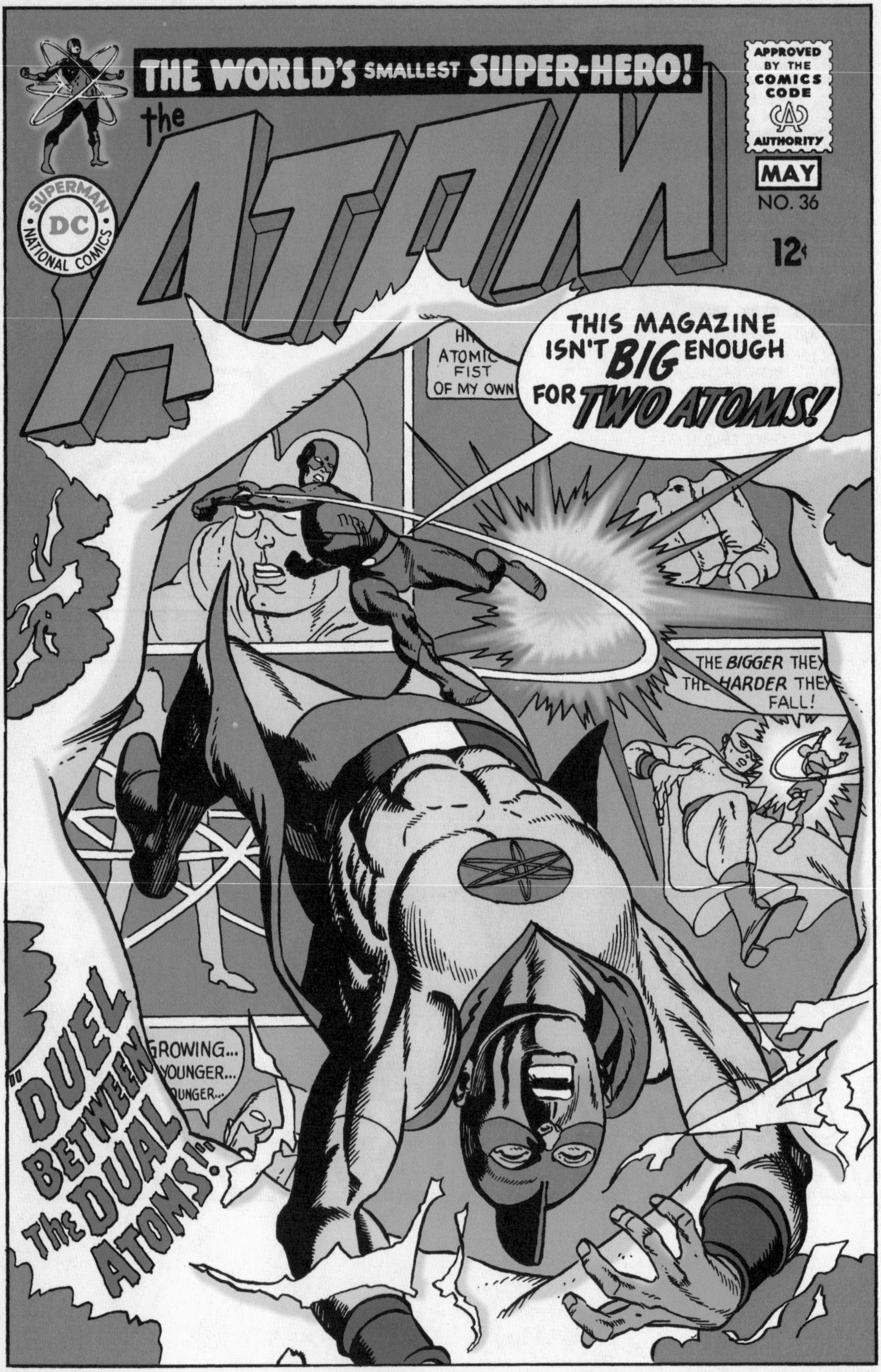
THE WORLD'S SMALLEST SUPER-HERO!
the ATOM
SUPERMAN DC NATIONAL COMICS
APPROVED BY THE COMICS CODE AUTHORITY
MAY
NO. 36
12¢
THIS MAGAZINE ISN'T BIG ENOUGH FOR TWO ATOMS!
HIT ATOMIC FIST OF MY OWN
THE BIGGER THEY THE HARDER THEY FALL!
GROWING... YOUNGER... YOUNGER...
"DUEL BETWEEN The DUAL ATOMS!"

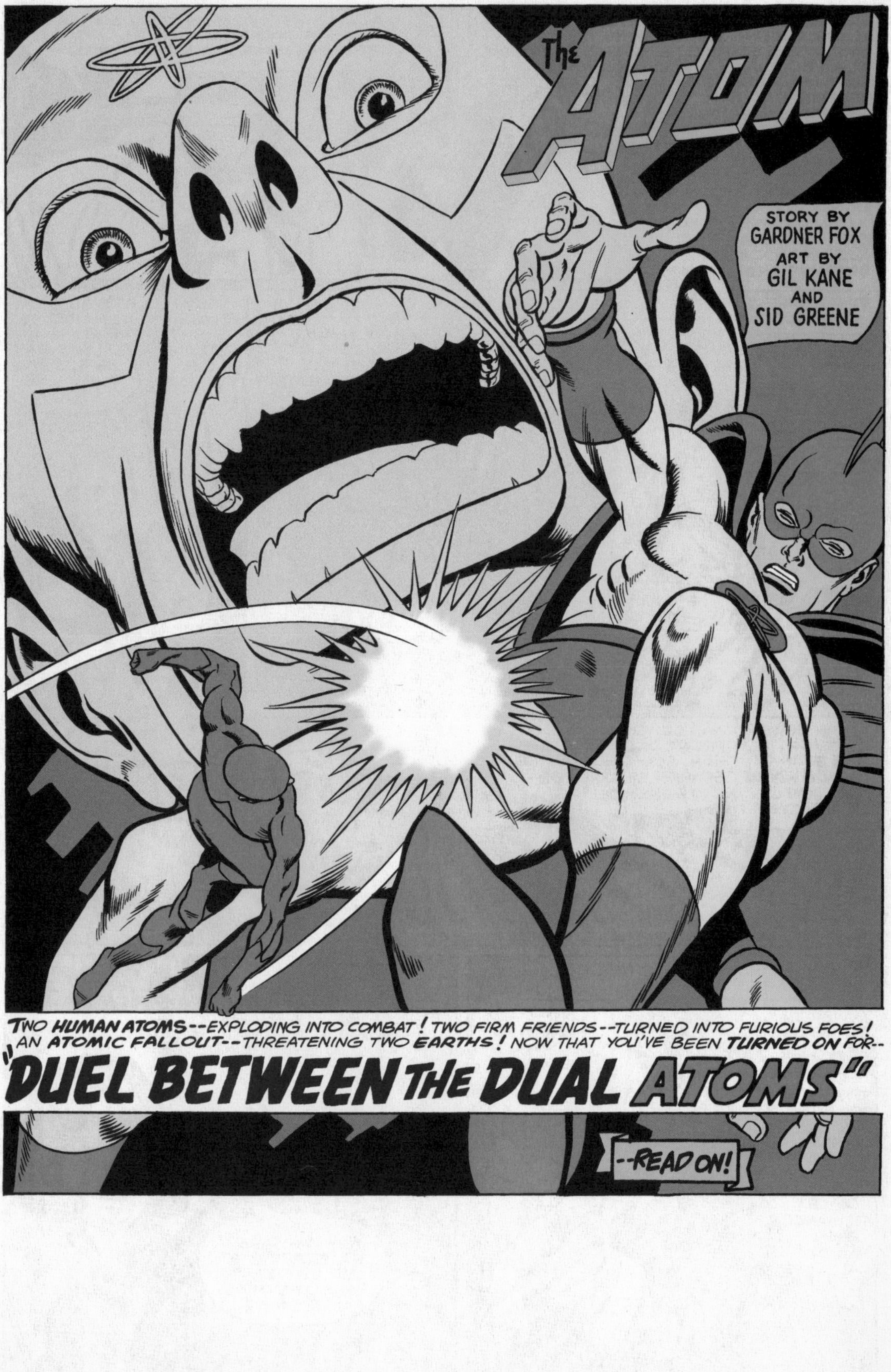

The ATOM
STORY BY GARDNER FOX
ART BY GIL KANE AND SID GREENE
TWO HUMAN ATOMS--EXPLODING INTO COMBAT! TWO FIRM FRIENDS--TURNED INTO FURIOUS FOES! AN ATOMIC FALLOUT--THREATENING TWO EARTHS! NOW THAT YOU'VE BEEN TURNED ON FOR--
"DUEL BETWEEN THE DUAL ATOMS"
--READ ON!

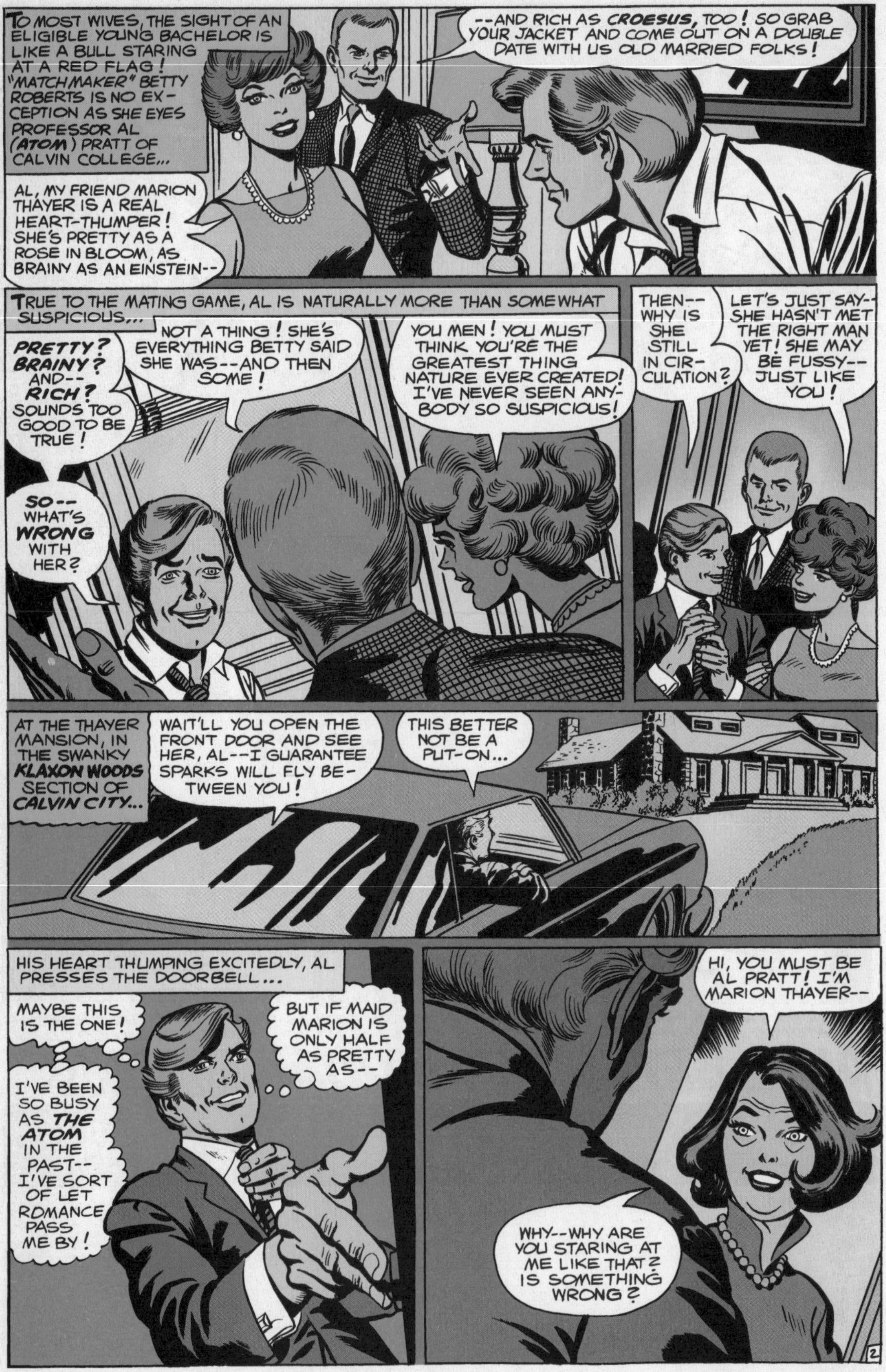

TO MOST WIVES, THE SIGHT OF AN ELIGIBLE YOUNG BACHELOR IS LIKE A BULL STARING AT A RED FLAG! "MATCHMAKER" BETTY ROBERTS IS NO EXCEPTION AS SHE EYES PROFESSOR AL (ATOM) PRATT OF CALVIN COLLEGE...
AL, MY FRIEND MARION THAYER IS A REAL HEART-THUMPER! SHE'S PRETTY AS A ROSE IN BLOOM, AS BRAINY AS AN EINSTEIN--
--AND RICH AS CROESUS, TOO! SO GRAB YOUR JACKET AND COME OUT ON A DOUBLE DATE WITH US OLD MARRIED FOLKS!
TRUE TO THE MATING GAME, AL IS NATURALLY MORE THAN SOMEWHAT SUSPICIOUS...
PRETTY? BRAINY? AND-- RICH? SOUNDS TOO GOOD TO BE TRUE!
SO-- WHAT'S WRONG WITH HER?
NOT A THING! SHE'S EVERYTHING BETTY SAID SHE WAS--AND THEN SOME!
YOU MEN! YOU MUST THINK YOU'RE THE GREATEST THING NATURE EVER CREATED! I'VE NEVER SEEN ANYBODY SO SUSPICIOUS!
THEN-- WHY IS SHE STILL IN CIRCULATION?
LET'S JUST SAY-- SHE HASN'T MET THE RIGHT MAN YET! SHE MAY BE FUSSY-- JUST LIKE YOU!
AT THE THAYER MANSION, IN THE SWANKY KLAXON WOODS SECTION OF CALVIN CITY...
WAIT'LL YOU OPEN THE FRONT DOOR AND SEE HER, AL--I GUARANTEE SPARKS WILL FLY BETWEEN YOU!
THIS BETTER NOT BE A PUT-ON...
HIS HEART THUMPING EXCITEDLY, AL PRESSES THE DOORBELL...
MAYBE THIS IS THE ONE!
I'VE BEEN SO BUSY AS THE ATOM IN THE PAST-- I'VE SORT OF LET ROMANCE PASS ME BY!
BUT IF MAID MARION IS ONLY HALF AS PRETTY AS--
HI, YOU MUST BE AL PRATT! I'M MARION THAYER--
WHY--WHY ARE YOU STARING AT ME LIKE THAT? IS SOMETHING WRONG?
2

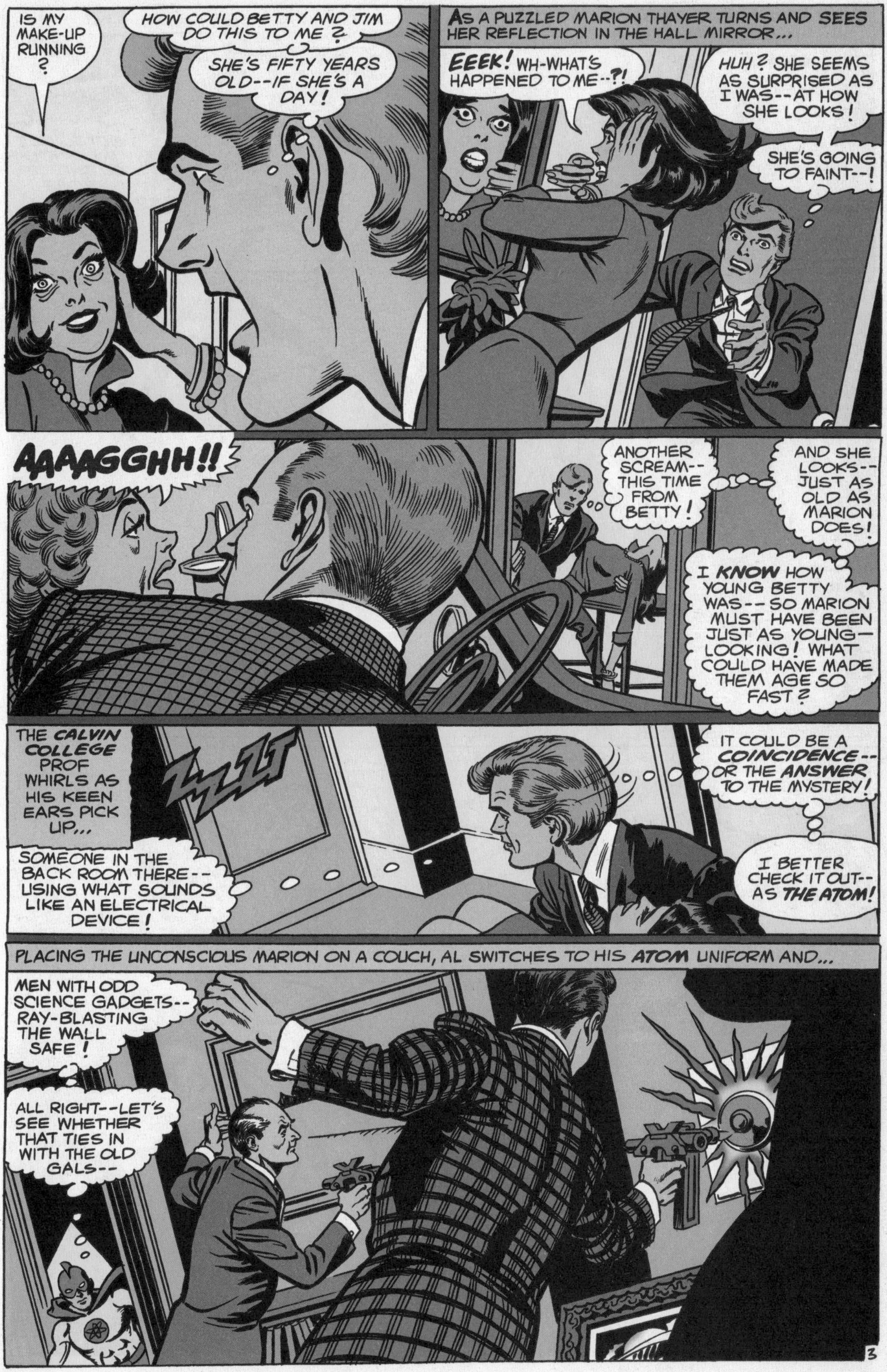
IS MY MAKE-UP RUNNING ?
HOW COULD BETTY AND JIM DO THIS TO ME ?
SHE'S FIFTY YEARS OLD--IF SHE'S A DAY!
AS A PUZZLED MARION THAYER TURNS AND SEES HER REFLECTION IN THE HALL MIRROR...
EEEK! WH-WHAT'S HAPPENED TO ME--?!
HUH ? SHE SEEMS AS SURPRISED AS I WAS--AT HOW SHE LOOKS!
SHE'S GOING TO FAINT--!
AAAAGGHH!!
ANOTHER SCREAM--THIS TIME FROM BETTY!
AND SHE LOOKS--JUST AS OLD AS MARION DOES!
I KNOW HOW YOUNG BETTY WAS--SO MARION MUST HAVE BEEN JUST AS YOUNG-LOOKING! WHAT COULD HAVE MADE THEM AGE SO FAST ?
THE CALVIN COLLEGE PROF WHIRLS AS HIS KEEN EARS PICK UP...
ZZZZT
SOMEONE IN THE BACK ROOM THERE--USING WHAT SOUNDS LIKE AN ELECTRICAL DEVICE!
IT COULD BE A COINCIDENCE--OR THE ANSWER TO THE MYSTERY!
I BETTER CHECK IT OUT--AS THE ATOM!
PLACING THE UNCONSCIOUS MARION ON A COUCH, AL SWITCHES TO HIS ATOM UNIFORM AND...
MEN WITH ODD SCIENCE GADGETS--RAY-BLASTING THE WALL SAFE!
ALL RIGHT--LET'S SEE WHETHER THAT TIES IN WITH THE OLD GALS--
3

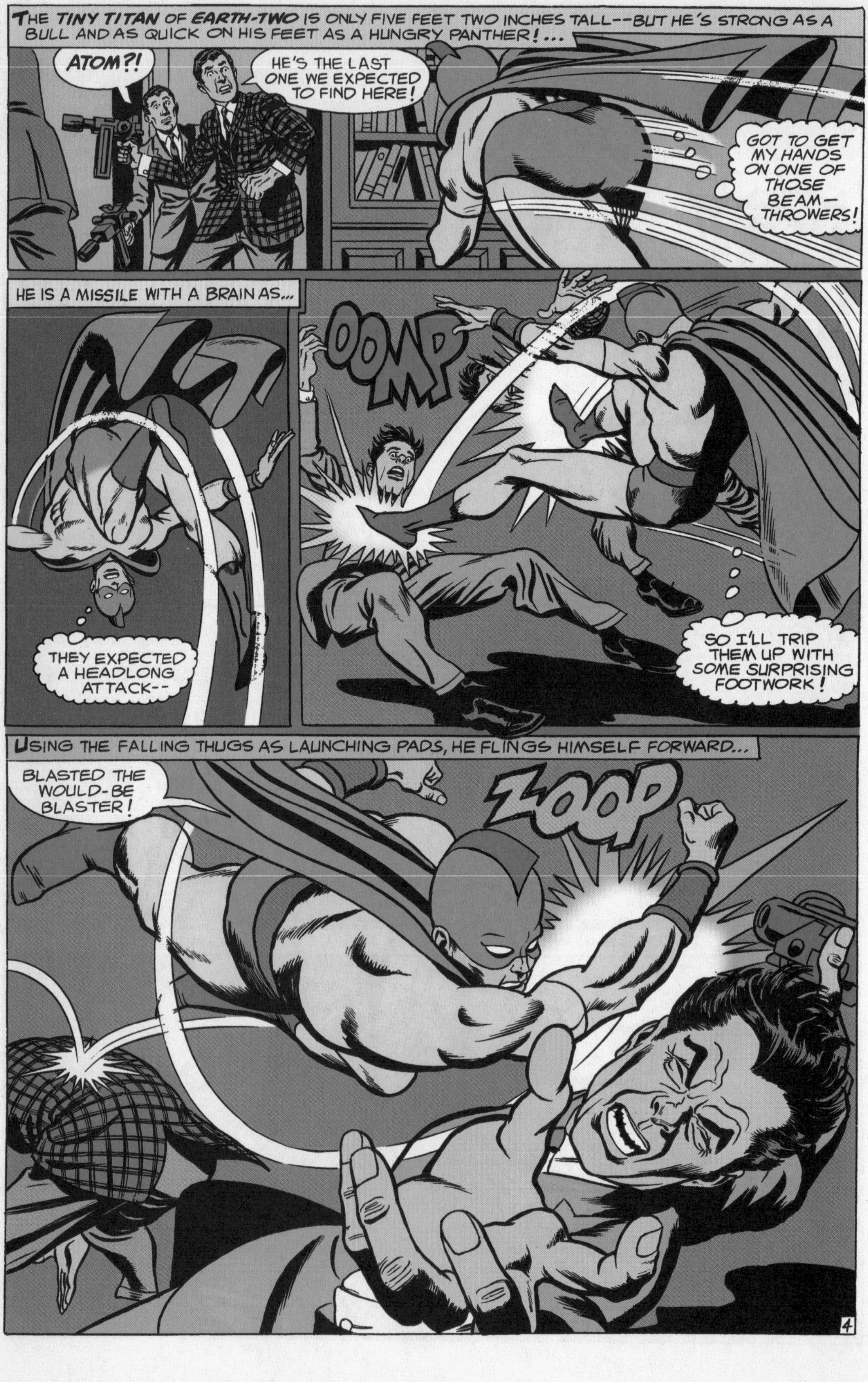
THE TINY TITAN OF EARTH-TWO IS ONLY FIVE FEET TWO INCHES TALL--BUT HE'S STRONG AS A BULL AND AS QUICK ON HIS FEET AS A HUNGRY PANTHER!...
ATOM?!
HE'S THE LAST ONE WE EXPECTED TO FIND HERE!
GOT TO GET MY HANDS ON ONE OF THOSE BEAM-THROWERS!
HE IS A MISSILE WITH A BRAIN AS...
THEY EXPECTED A HEADLONG ATTACK--
OOMP
SO I'LL TRIP THEM UP WITH SOME SURPRISING FOOTWORK!
USING THE FALLING THUGS AS LAUNCHING PADS, HE FLINGS HIMSELF FORWARD...
BLASTED THE WOULD-BE BLASTER!
ZOOP
4

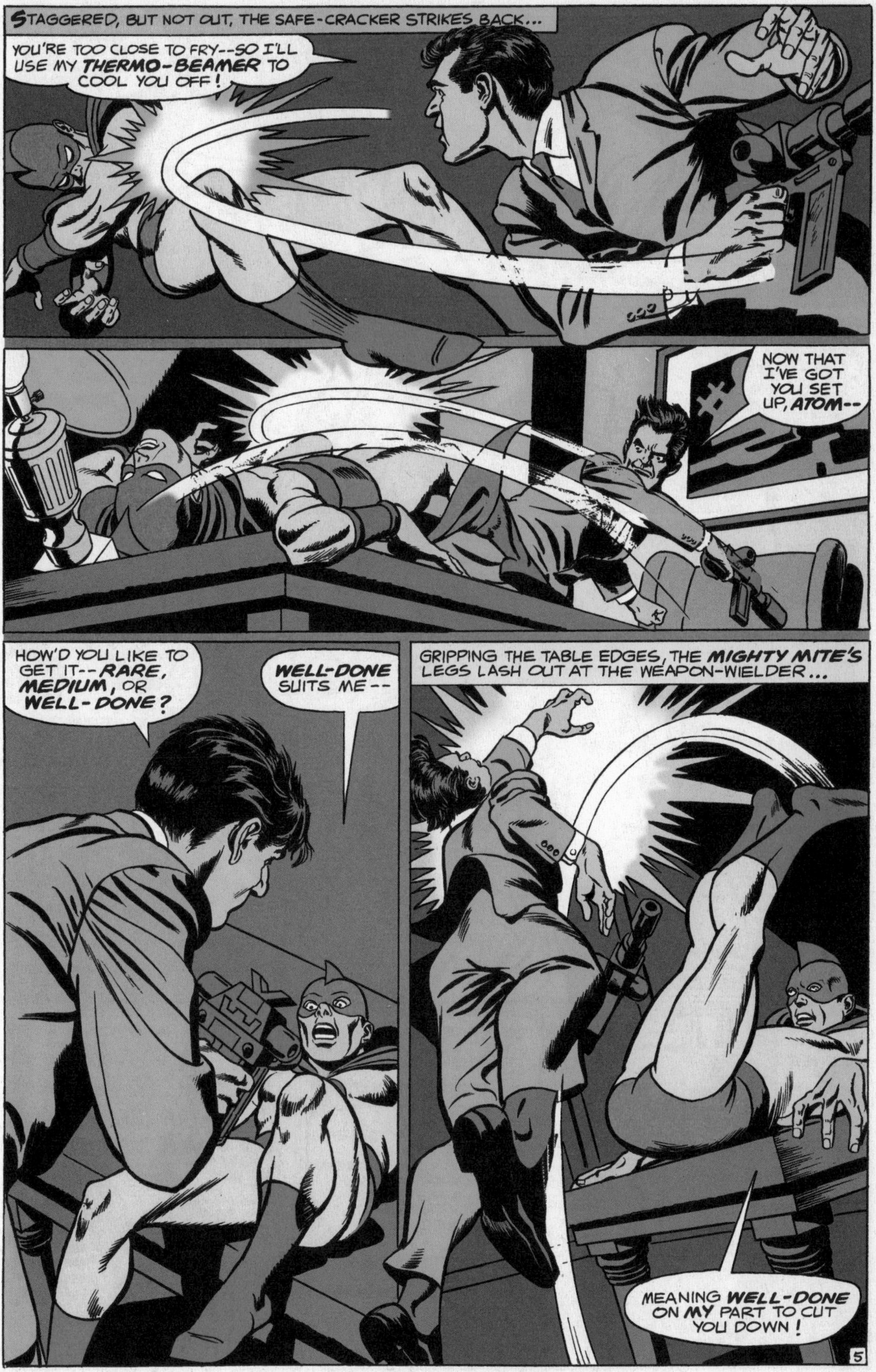
STAGGERED, BUT NOT OUT, THE SAFE-CRACKER STRIKES BACK...
YOU'RE TOO CLOSE TO FRY--SO I'LL USE MY THERMO-BEAMER TO COOL YOU OFF!
NOW THAT I'VE GOT YOU SET UP, ATOM--
HOW'D YOU LIKE TO GET IT--RARE, MEDIUM, OR WELL-DONE?
WELL-DONE SUITS ME--
GRIPPING THE TABLE EDGES, THE MIGHTY MITE'S LEGS LASH OUT AT THE WEAPON-WIELDER...
MEANING WELL-DONE ON MY PART TO CUT YOU DOWN!
5

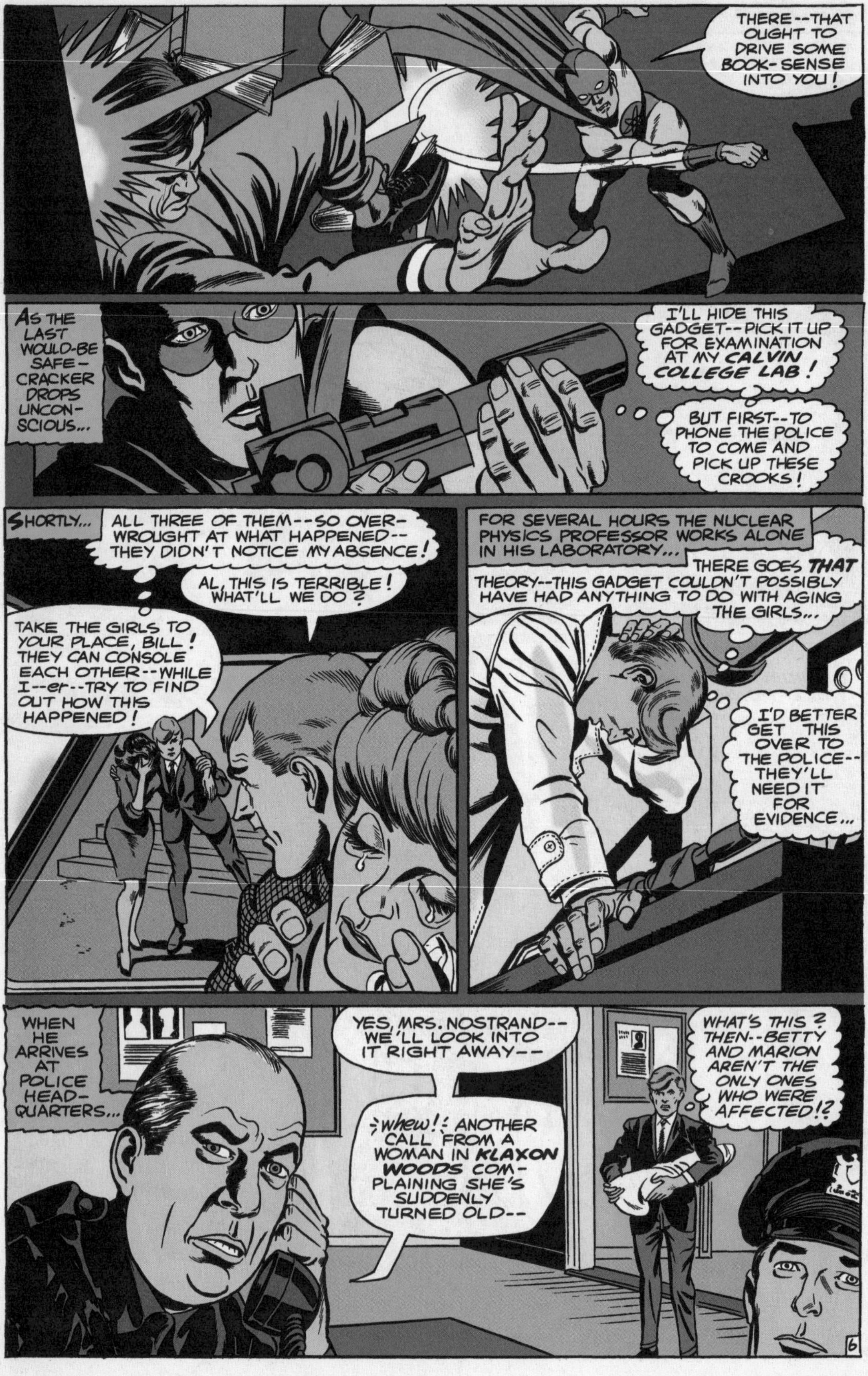
THERE--THAT OUGHT TO DRIVE SOME BOOK-SENSE INTO YOU!
AS THE LAST WOULD-BE SAFE-CRACKER DROPS UNCONSCIOUS...
I'LL HIDE THIS GADGET--PICK IT UP FOR EXAMINATION AT MY CALVIN COLLEGE LAB!
BUT FIRST--TO PHONE THE POLICE TO COME AND PICK UP THESE CROOKS!
SHORTLY...
ALL THREE OF THEM--SO OVERWROUGHT AT WHAT HAPPENED--THEY DIDN'T NOTICE MY ABSENCE!
AL, THIS IS TERRIBLE! WHAT'LL WE DO?
TAKE THE GIRLS TO YOUR PLACE, BILL! THEY CAN CONSOLE EACH OTHER--WHILE I--er--TRY TO FIND OUT HOW THIS HAPPENED!
FOR SEVERAL HOURS THE NUCLEAR PHYSICS PROFESSOR WORKS ALONE IN HIS LABORATORY...
THERE GOES THAT THEORY--THIS GADGET COULDN'T POSSIBLY HAVE HAD ANYTHING TO DO WITH AGING THE GIRLS...
I'D BETTER GET THIS OVER TO THE POLICE--THEY'LL NEED IT FOR EVIDENCE...
WHEN HE ARRIVES AT POLICE HEADQUARTERS...
YES, MRS. NOSTRAND--WE'LL LOOK INTO IT RIGHT AWAY--
whew! ANOTHER CALL FROM A WOMAN IN KLAXON WOODS COMPLAINING SHE'S SUDDENLY TURNED OLD--
WHAT'S THIS? THEN--BETTY AND MARION AREN'T THE ONLY ONES WHO WERE AFFECTED!?
6

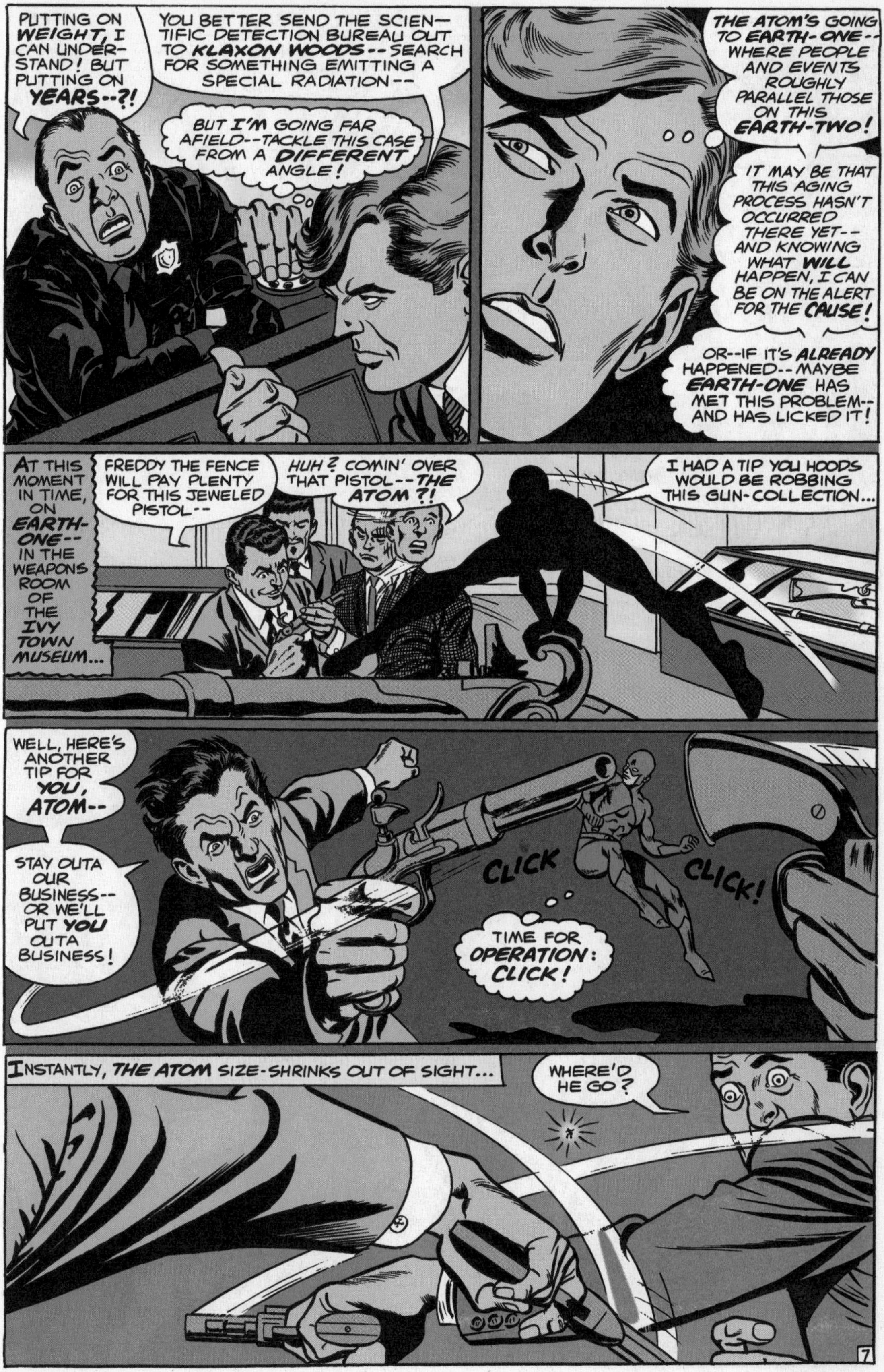
PUTTING ON WEIGHT, I CAN UNDERSTAND! BUT PUTTING ON YEARS--?!
YOU BETTER SEND THE SCIENTIFIC DETECTION BUREAU OUT TO KLAXON WOODS--SEARCH FOR SOMETHING EMITTING A SPECIAL RADIATION--
BUT I'M GOING FAR AFIELD--TACKLE THIS CASE FROM A DIFFERENT ANGLE!
THE ATOM'S GOING TO EARTH-ONE--WHERE PEOPLE AND EVENTS ROUGHLY PARALLEL THOSE ON THIS EARTH-TWO!
IT MAY BE THAT THIS AGING PROCESS HASN'T OCCURRED THERE YET--AND KNOWING WHAT WILL HAPPEN, I CAN BE ON THE ALERT FOR THE CAUSE!
OR--IF IT'S ALREADY HAPPENED--MAYBE EARTH-ONE HAS MET THIS PROBLEM--AND HAS LICKED IT!
AT THIS MOMENT IN TIME, ON EARTH-ONE--IN THE WEAPONS ROOM OF THE IVY TOWN MUSEUM...
FREDDY THE FENCE WILL PAY PLENTY FOR THIS JEWELED PISTOL--
HUH? COMIN' OVER THAT PISTOL--THE ATOM?!
I HAD A TIP YOU HOODS WOULD BE ROBBING THIS GUN-COLLECTION...
WELL, HERE'S ANOTHER TIP FOR YOU, ATOM--
STAY OUTA OUR BUSINESS--OR WE'LL PUT YOU OUTA BUSINESS!
CLICK
CLICK!
TIME FOR OPERATION: CLICK!
INSTANTLY, THE ATOM SIZE-SHRINKS OUT OF SIGHT...
WHERE'D HE GO?
7

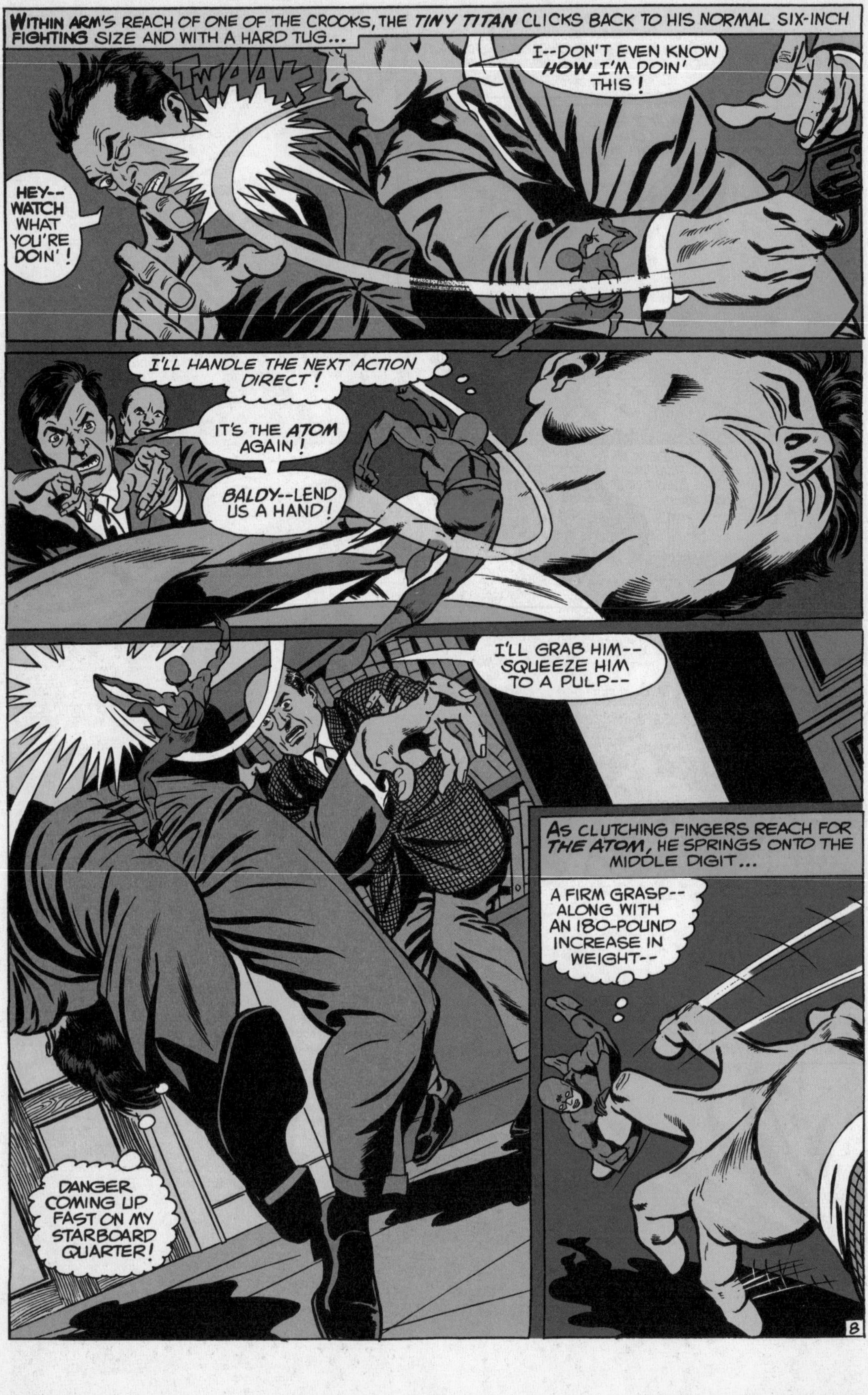
WITHIN ARM'S REACH OF ONE OF THE CROOKS, THE TINY TITAN CLICKS BACK TO HIS NORMAL SIX-INCH FIGHTING SIZE AND WITH A HARD TUG...
TWAAK
I--DON'T EVEN KNOW HOW I'M DOIN' THIS!
HEY--WATCH WHAT YOU'RE DOIN'!
I'LL HANDLE THE NEXT ACTION DIRECT!
IT'S THE ATOM AGAIN!
BALDY--LEND US A HAND!
I'LL GRAB HIM--SQUEEZE HIM TO A PULP--
DANGER COMING UP FAST ON MY STARBOARD QUARTER!
AS CLUTCHING FINGERS REACH FOR THE ATOM, HE SPRINGS ONTO THE MIDDLE DIGIT...
A FIRM GRASP--ALONG WITH AN 180-POUND INCREASE IN WEIGHT--
8

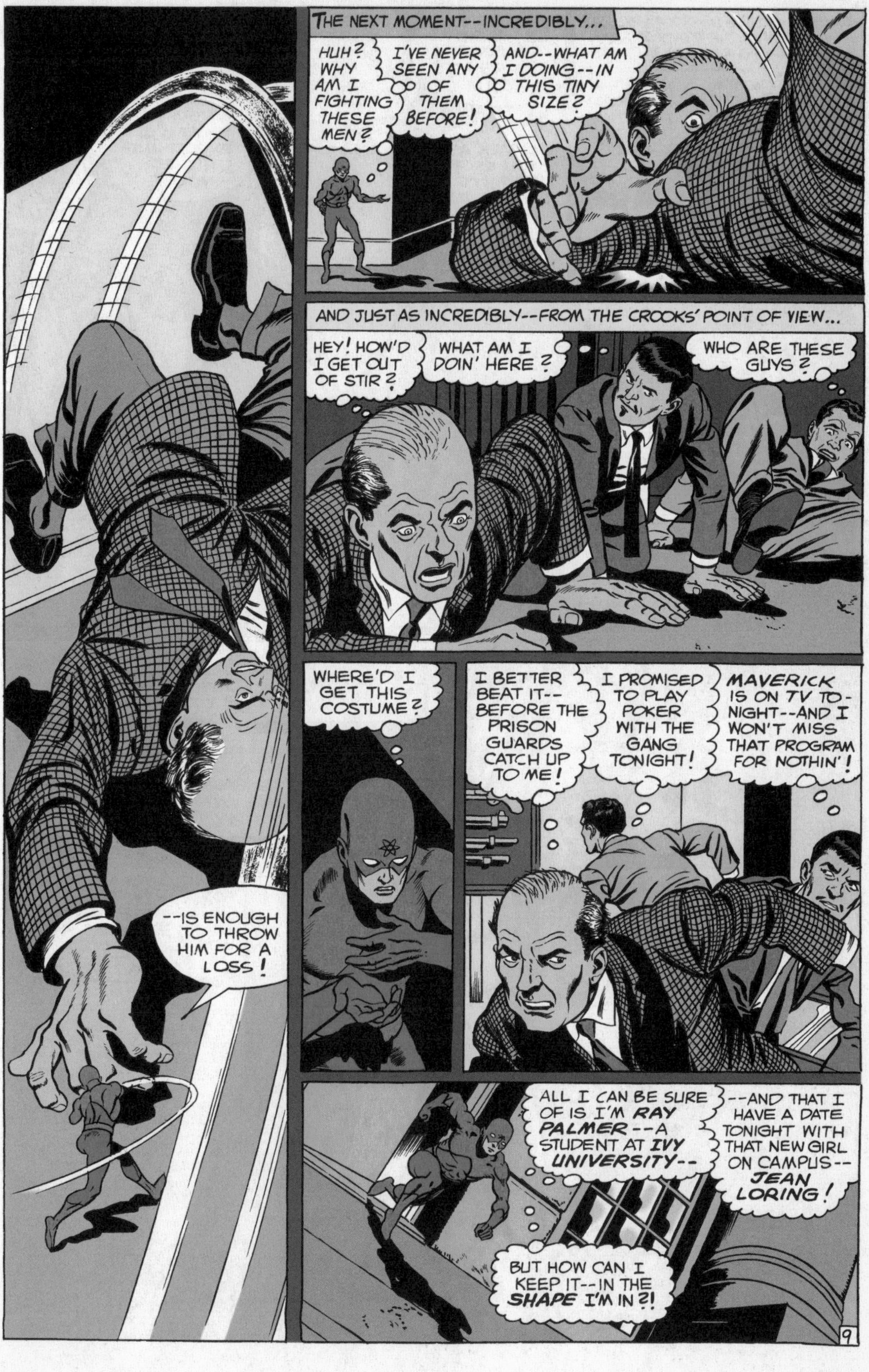

--IS ENOUGH TO THROW HIM FOR A LOSS!
THE NEXT MOMENT--INCREDIBLY...
HUH? WHY AM I FIGHTING THESE MEN?
I'VE NEVER SEEN ANY OF THEM BEFORE!
AND--WHAT AM I DOING--IN THIS TINY SIZE?
AND JUST AS INCREDIBLY--FROM THE CROOKS' POINT OF VIEW...
HEY! HOW'D I GET OUT OF STIR?
WHAT AM I DOIN' HERE?
WHO ARE THESE GUYS?
WHERE'D I GET THIS COSTUME?
I BETTER BEAT IT--BEFORE THE PRISON GUARDS CATCH UP TO ME!
I PROMISED TO PLAY POKER WITH THE GANG TONIGHT!
MAVERICK IS ON TV TO-NIGHT--AND I WON'T MISS THAT PROGRAM FOR NOTHIN'!
ALL I CAN BE SURE OF IS I'M RAY PALMER--A STUDENT AT IVY UNIVERSITY--
--AND THAT I HAVE A DATE TONIGHT WITH THAT NEW GIRL ON CAMPUS--JEAN LORING!
BUT HOW CAN I KEEP IT--IN THE SHAPE I'M IN?!
9

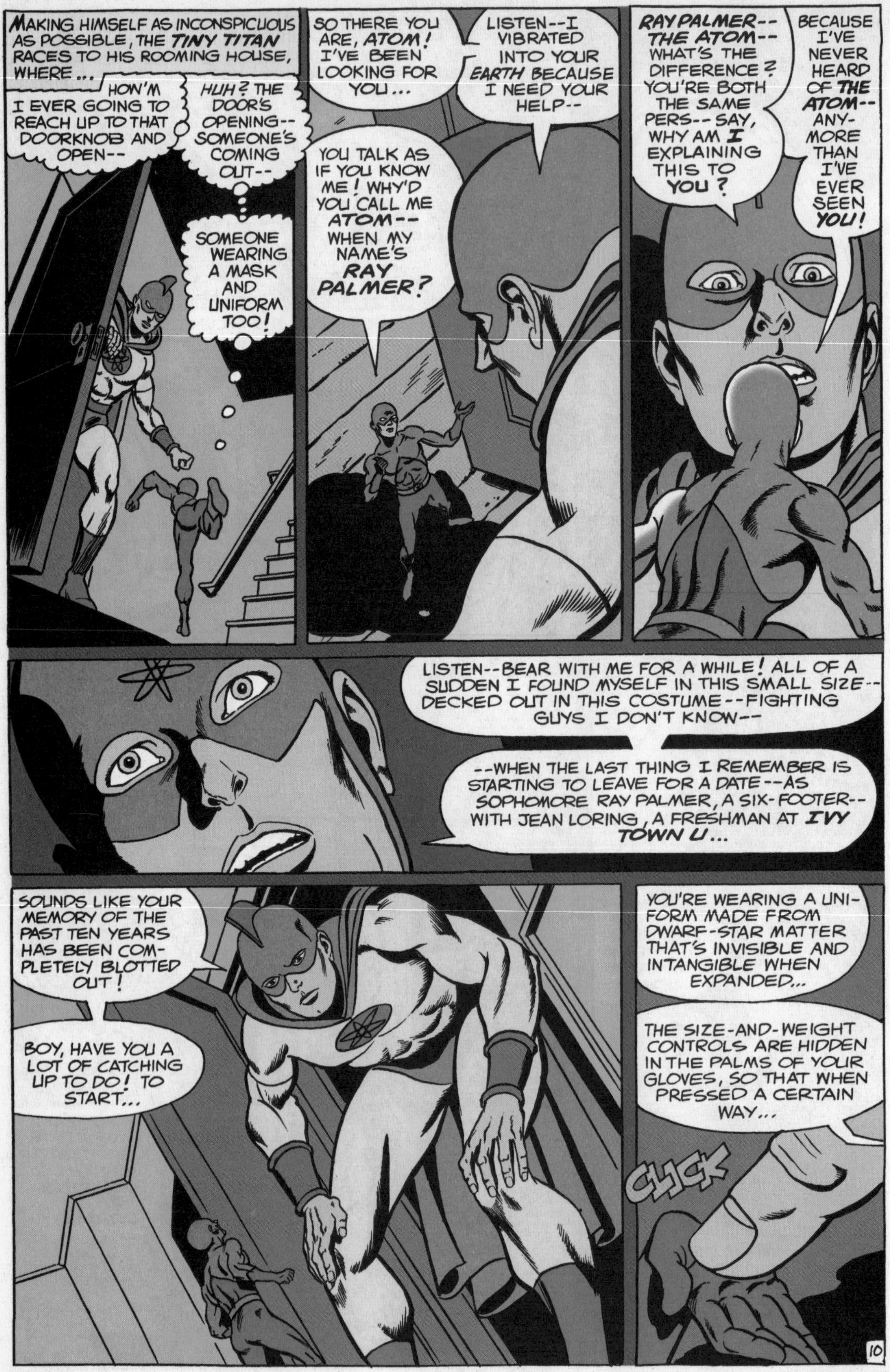
MAKING HIMSELF AS INCONSPICUOUS AS POSSIBLE, THE TINY TITAN RACES TO HIS ROOMING HOUSE, WHERE...
HOW'M I EVER GOING TO REACH UP TO THAT DOORKNOB AND OPEN--
HUH? THE DOOR'S OPENING--SOMEONE'S COMING OUT--
SOMEONE WEARING A MASK AND UNIFORM TOO!
SO THERE YOU ARE, ATOM! I'VE BEEN LOOKING FOR YOU...
LISTEN--I VIBRATED INTO YOUR EARTH BECAUSE I NEED YOUR HELP--
YOU TALK AS IF YOU KNOW ME! WHY'D YOU CALL ME ATOM--WHEN MY NAME'S RAY PALMER?
RAY PALMER--THE ATOM--WHAT'S THE DIFFERENCE? YOU'RE BOTH THE SAME PERS--SAY, WHY AM I EXPLAINING THIS TO YOU?
BECAUSE I'VE NEVER HEARD OF THE ATOM--ANY-MORE THAN I'VE EVER SEEN YOU!
LISTEN--BEAR WITH ME FOR A WHILE! ALL OF A SUDDEN I FOUND MYSELF IN THIS SMALL SIZE--DECKED OUT IN THIS COSTUME--FIGHTING GUYS I DON'T KNOW--
--WHEN THE LAST THING I REMEMBER IS STARTING TO LEAVE FOR A DATE--AS SOPHOMORE RAY PALMER, A SIX-FOOTER--WITH JEAN LORING, A FRESHMAN AT IVY TOWN U...
SOUNDS LIKE YOUR MEMORY OF THE PAST TEN YEARS HAS BEEN COM-PLETELY BLOTTED OUT!
BOY, HAVE YOU A LOT OF CATCHING UP TO DO! TO START...
YOU'RE WEARING A UNI-FORM MADE FROM DWARF-STAR MATTER THAT'S INVISIBLE AND INTANGIBLE WHEN EXPANDED...
THE SIZE-AND-WEIGHT CONTROLS ARE HIDDEN IN THE PALMS OF YOUR GLOVES, SO THAT WHEN PRESSED A CERTAIN WAY...
CLICK
10

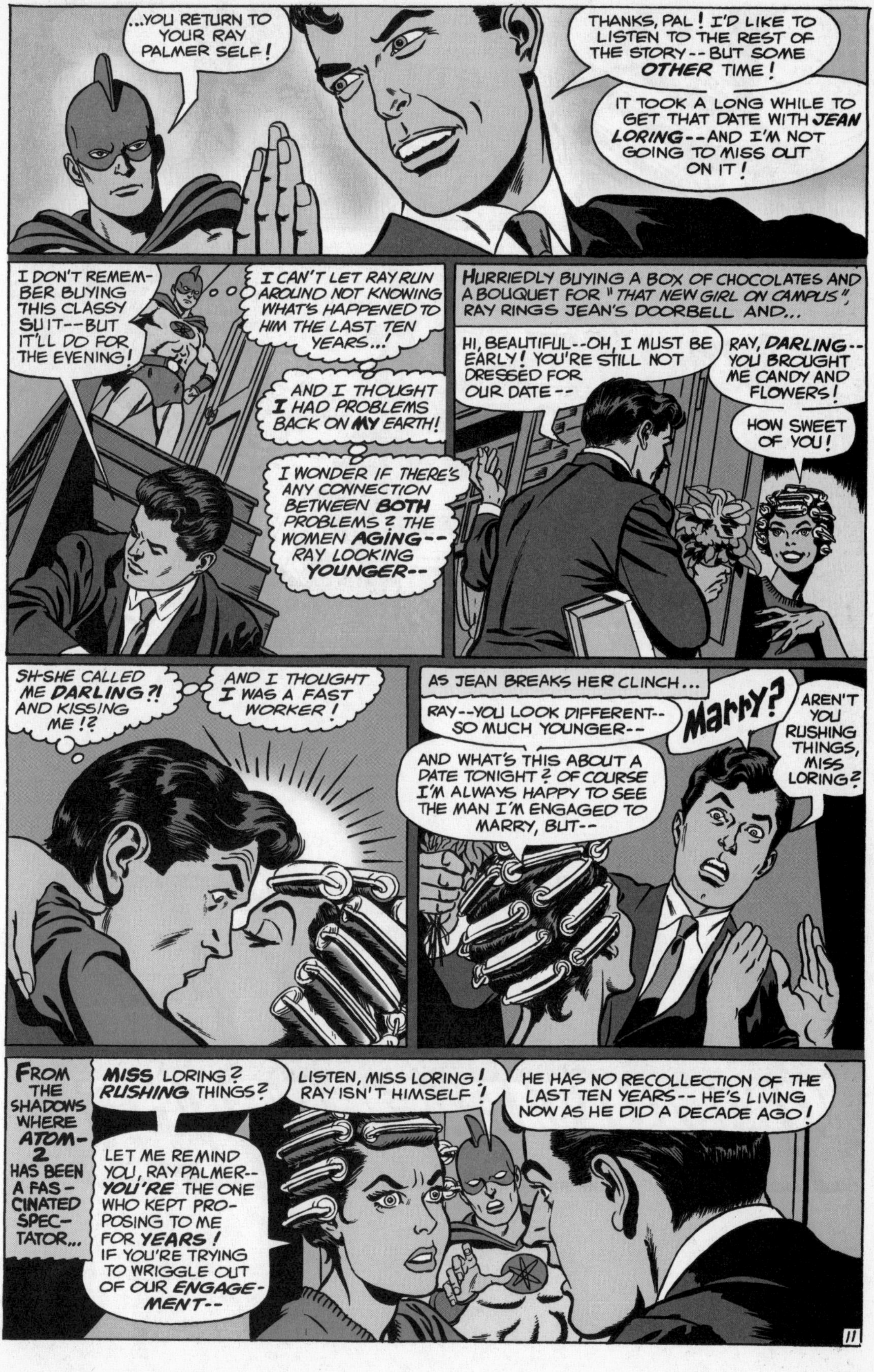
...YOU RETURN TO YOUR RAY PALMER SELF!
THANKS, PAL! I'D LIKE TO LISTEN TO THE REST OF THE STORY--BUT SOME OTHER TIME!
IT TOOK A LONG WHILE TO GET THAT DATE WITH JEAN LORING--AND I'M NOT GOING TO MISS OUT ON IT!
I DON'T REMEMBER BUYING THIS CLASSY SUIT--BUT IT'LL DO FOR THE EVENING!
I CAN'T LET RAY RUN AROUND NOT KNOWING WHAT'S HAPPENED TO HIM THE LAST TEN YEARS...!
AND I THOUGHT I HAD PROBLEMS BACK ON MY EARTH!
I WONDER IF THERE'S ANY CONNECTION BETWEEN BOTH PROBLEMS? THE WOMEN AGING--RAY LOOKING YOUNGER--
HURRIEDLY BUYING A BOX OF CHOCOLATES AND A BOUQUET FOR "THAT NEW GIRL ON CAMPUS", RAY RINGS JEAN'S DOORBELL AND...
HI, BEAUTIFUL--OH, I MUST BE EARLY! YOU'RE STILL NOT DRESSED FOR OUR DATE--
RAY, DARLING--YOU BROUGHT ME CANDY AND FLOWERS!
HOW SWEET OF YOU!
SH-SHE CALLED ME DARLING?! AND KISSING ME!?
AND I THOUGHT I WAS A FAST WORKER!
AS JEAN BREAKS HER CLINCH...
RAY--YOU LOOK DIFFERENT--SO MUCH YOUNGER--
AND WHAT'S THIS ABOUT A DATE TONIGHT? OF COURSE I'M ALWAYS HAPPY TO SEE THE MAN I'M ENGAGED TO MARRY, BUT--
MARRY?
AREN'T YOU RUSHING THINGS, MISS LORING?
FROM THE SHADOWS WHERE ATOM-2 HAS BEEN A FASCINATED SPECTATOR...
MISS LORING? RUSHING THINGS?
LET ME REMIND YOU, RAY PALMER--YOU'RE THE ONE WHO KEPT PROPOSING TO ME FOR YEARS! IF YOU'RE TRYING TO WRIGGLE OUT OF OUR ENGAGEMENT--
LISTEN, MISS LORING! RAY ISN'T HIMSELF!
HE HAS NO RECOLLECTION OF THE LAST TEN YEARS--HE'S LIVING NOW AS HE DID A DECADE AGO!
11

OHHH! SO THAT EXPLAINS WHY HE LOOKS SO MUCH YOUNGER--
LET ME HANDLE THIS, MISS LORING! I'LL HELP HIM--
SO IT'S YOU AGAIN!
GO 'WAY, WILL YOU?
IF ANYTHING'S WRONG HERE, IT'S WITH MISS LORING-- TALKING ABOUT MARRYING ME BEFORE I'VE EVEN HAD MY FIRST DATE WITH HER--
EASY, RAY, EASY! I THINK I KNOW HOW TO BRING YOU UP TO DATE--SO LET'S GO!
MY POOR DARLING--
12
THEN--BEFORE THE LADY LAWYER'S HORRIFIED EYES...
GASP!
THEY SUDDENLY VANISHED OUT OF SIGHT--!

CRISIS ON MULTIPLE EARTHS THE TEAM UPS

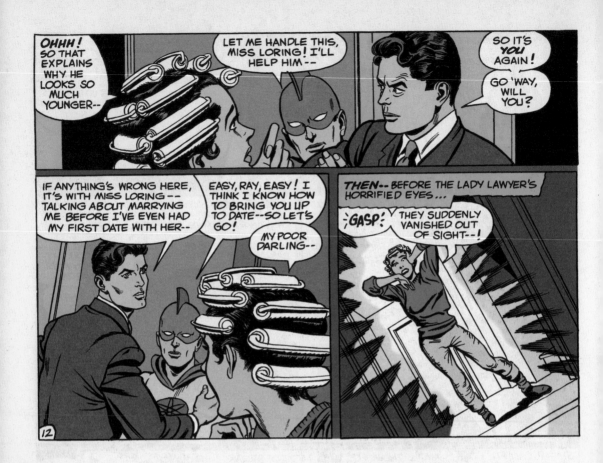

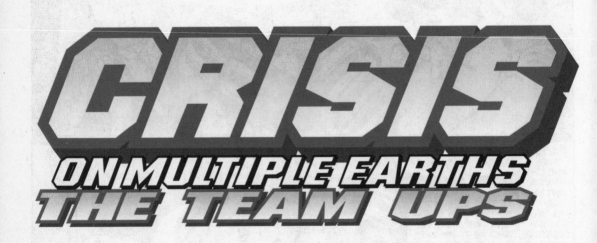

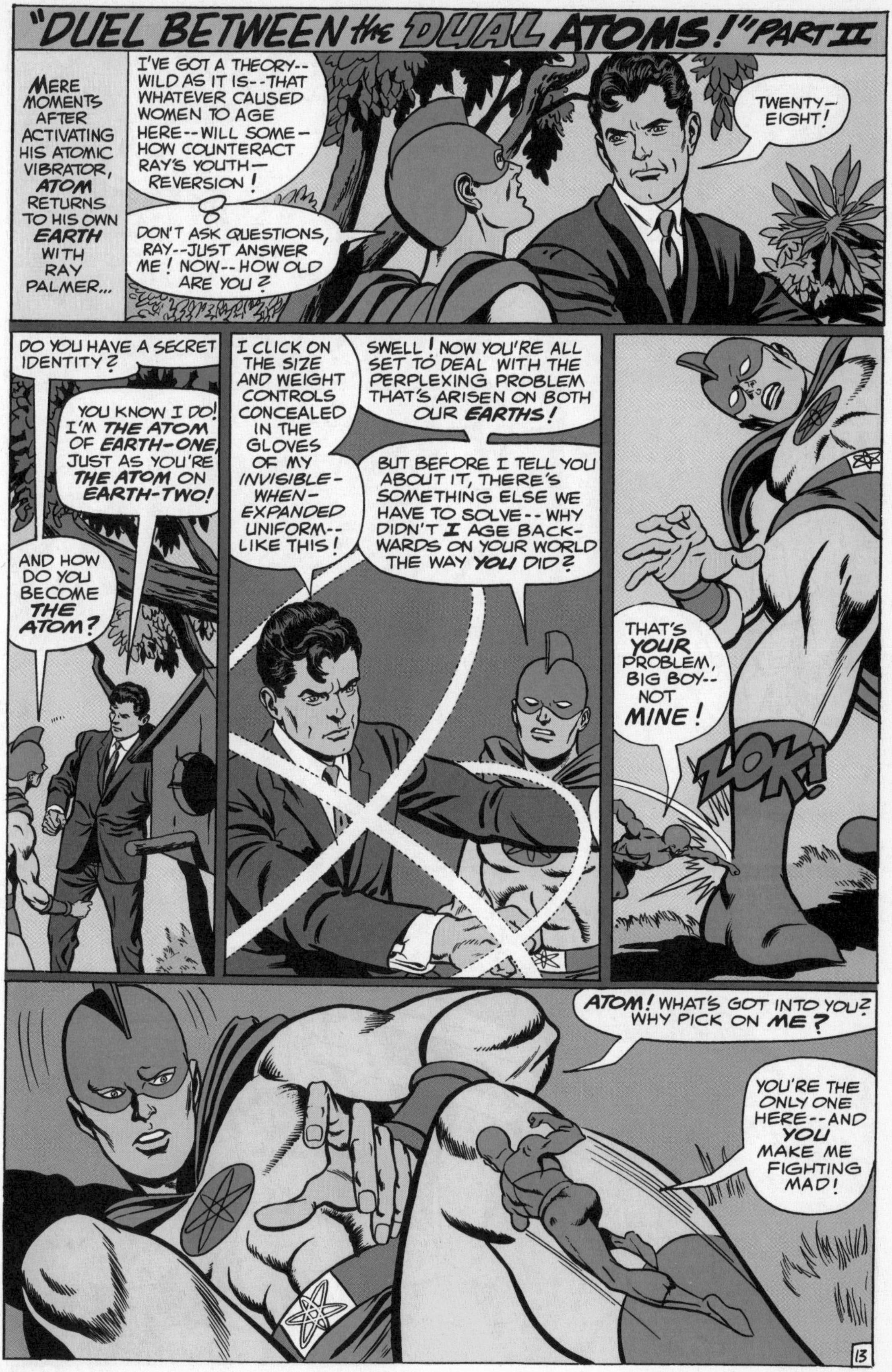
"DUEL BETWEEN the DUAL ATOMS!" PART II
MERE MOMENTS AFTER ACTIVATING HIS ATOMIC VIBRATOR, ATOM RETURNS TO HIS OWN EARTH WITH RAY PALMER...
I'VE GOT A THEORY-- WILD AS IT IS--THAT WHATEVER CAUSED WOMEN TO AGE HERE--WILL SOMEHOW COUNTERACT RAY'S YOUTH-REVERSION!
DON'T ASK QUESTIONS, RAY--JUST ANSWER ME! NOW--HOW OLD ARE YOU?
TWENTY-EIGHT!
DO YOU HAVE A SECRET IDENTITY?
YOU KNOW I DO! I'M THE ATOM OF EARTH-ONE, JUST AS YOU'RE THE ATOM ON EARTH-TWO!
AND HOW DO YOU BECOME THE ATOM?
I CLICK ON THE SIZE AND WEIGHT CONTROLS CONCEALED IN THE GLOVES OF MY INVISIBLE-WHEN-EXPANDED UNIFORM-- LIKE THIS!
SWELL! NOW YOU'RE ALL SET TO DEAL WITH THE PERPLEXING PROBLEM THAT'S ARISEN ON BOTH OUR EARTHS!
BUT BEFORE I TELL YOU ABOUT IT, THERE'S SOMETHING ELSE WE HAVE TO SOLVE--WHY DIDN'T I AGE BACKWARDS ON YOUR WORLD THE WAY YOU DID?
THAT'S YOUR PROBLEM, BIG BOY-- NOT MINE!
ZOK!
ATOM! WHAT'S GOT INTO YOU? WHY PICK ON ME?
YOU'RE THE ONLY ONE HERE--AND YOU MAKE ME FIGHTING MAD!
13

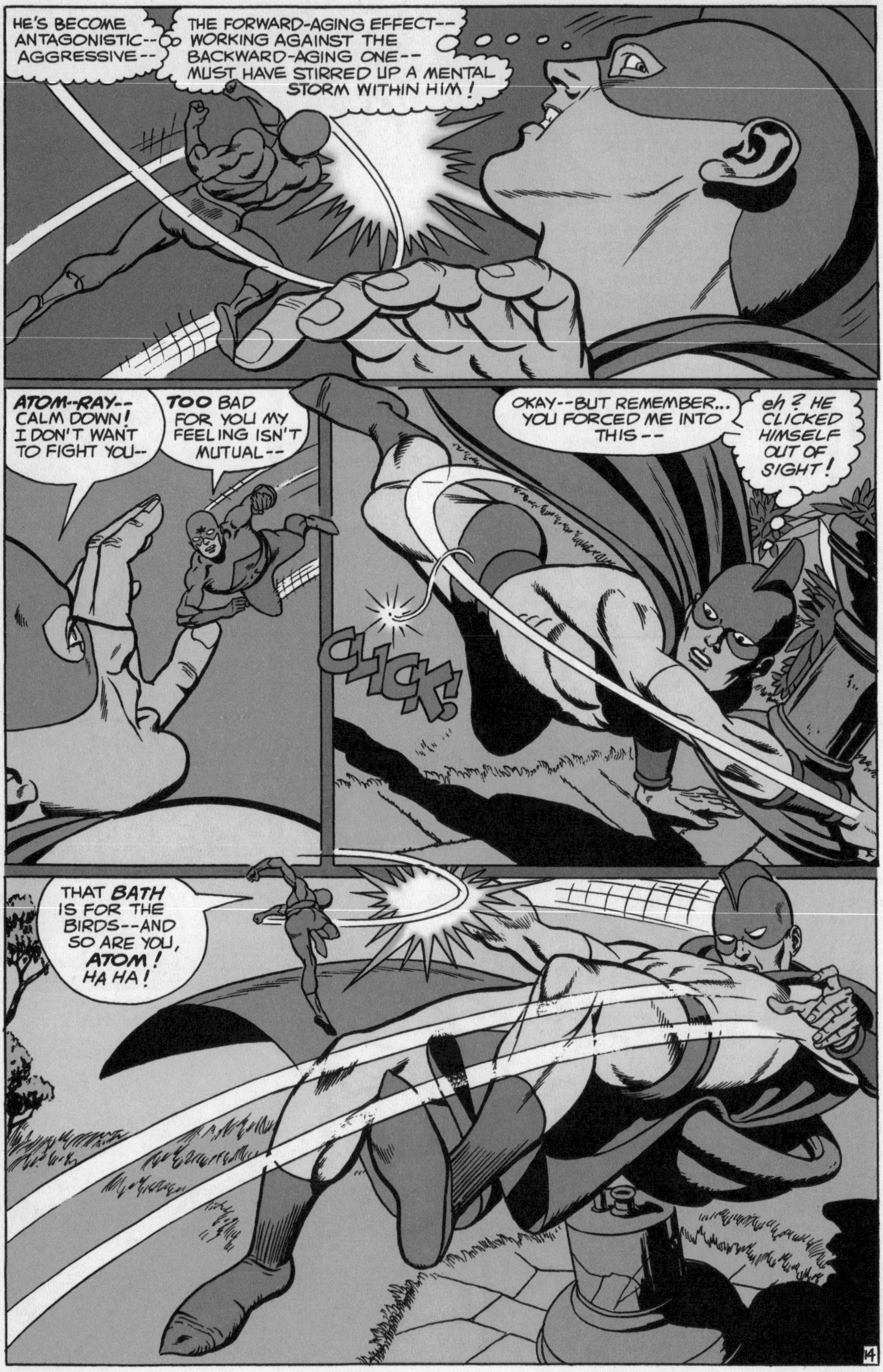
HE'S BECOME ANTAGONISTIC-- AGGRESSIVE--
THE FORWARD-AGING EFFECT-- WORKING AGAINST THE BACKWARD-AGING ONE-- MUST HAVE STIRRED UP A MENTAL STORM WITHIN HIM!
ATOM--RAY-- CALM DOWN! I DON'T WANT TO FIGHT YOU--
TOO BAD FOR YOU MY FEELING ISN'T MUTUAL--
OKAY--BUT REMEMBER... YOU FORCED ME INTO THIS--
eh? HE CLICKED HIMSELF OUT OF SIGHT!
CLICK!
THAT BATH IS FOR THE BIRDS--AND SO ARE YOU, ATOM! HA HA!
14

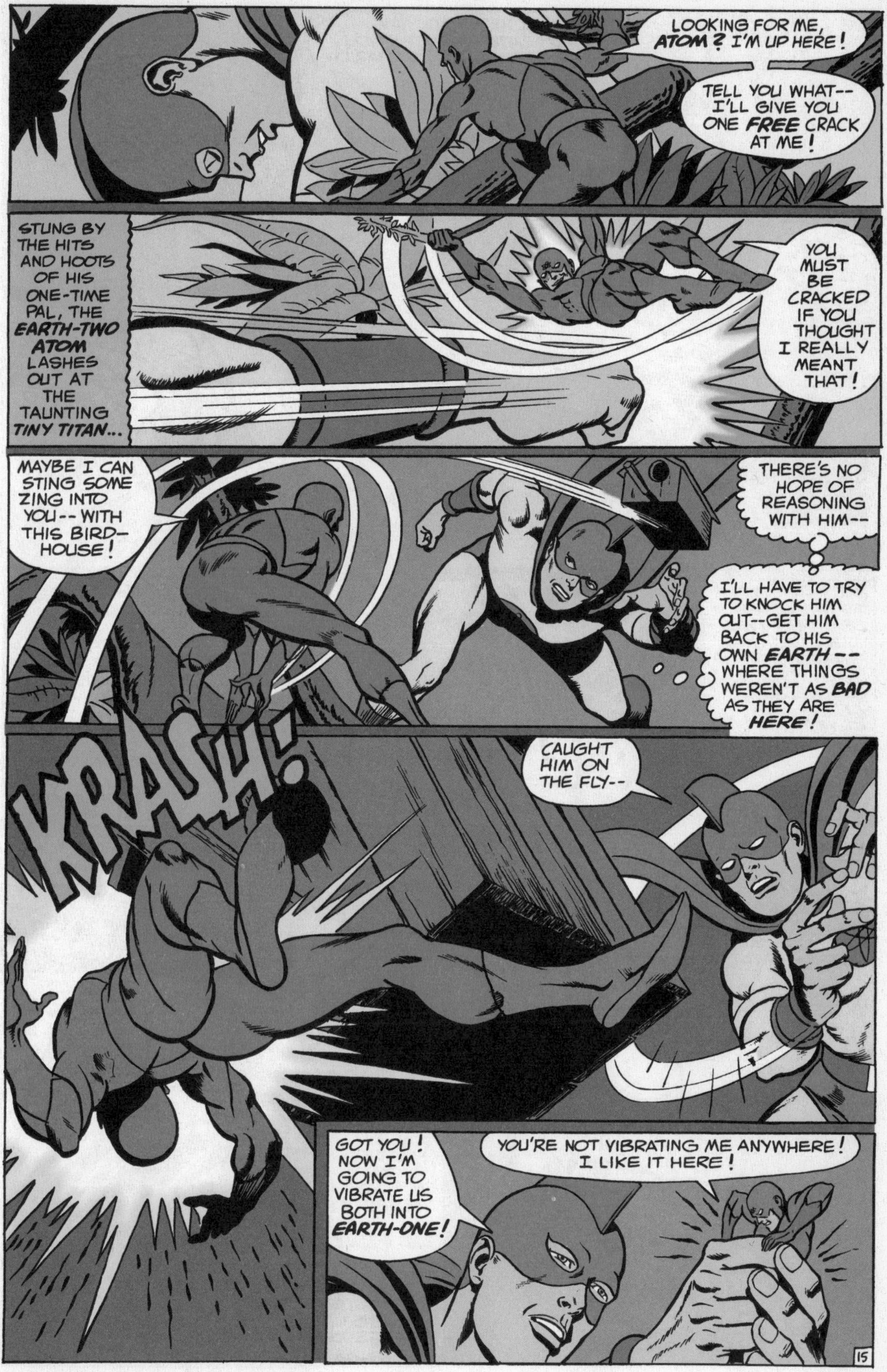
LOOKING FOR ME, ATOM? I'M UP HERE!
TELL YOU WHAT-- I'LL GIVE YOU ONE FREE CRACK AT ME!
STUNG BY THE HITS AND HOOTS OF HIS ONE-TIME PAL, THE EARTH-TWO ATOM LASHES OUT AT THE TAUNTING TINY TITAN...
YOU MUST BE CRACKED IF YOU THOUGHT I REALLY MEANT THAT!
MAYBE I CAN STING SOME ZING INTO YOU-- WITH THIS BIRD-HOUSE!
THERE'S NO HOPE OF REASONING WITH HIM--
I'LL HAVE TO TRY TO KNOCK HIM OUT--GET HIM BACK TO HIS OWN EARTH-- WHERE THINGS WEREN'T AS BAD AS THEY ARE HERE!
KRASH!
CAUGHT HIM ON THE FLY--
GOT YOU! NOW I'M GOING TO VIBRATE US BOTH INTO EARTH-ONE!
YOU'RE NOT VIBRATING ME ANYWHERE! I LIKE IT HERE!
15

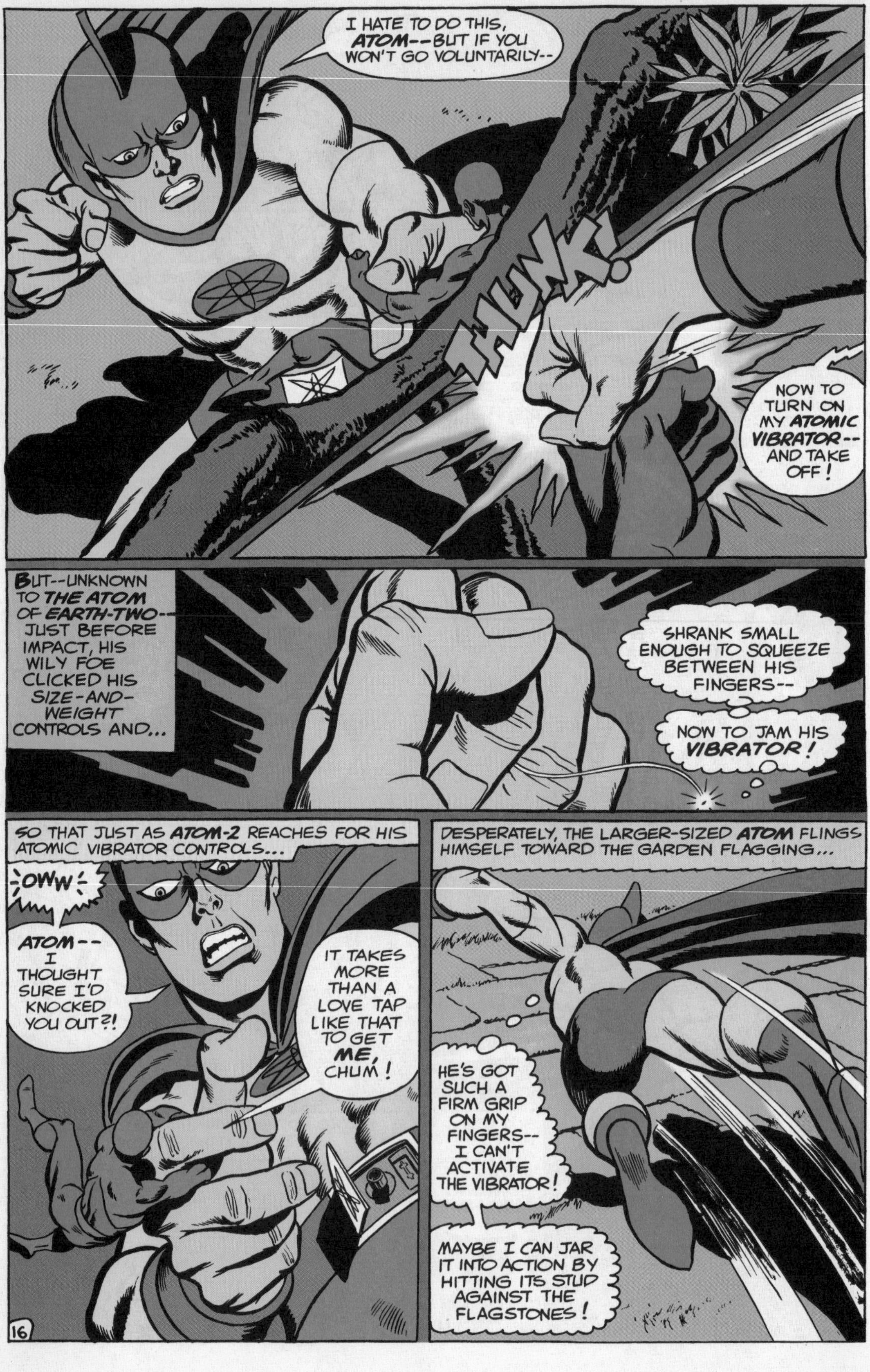

I HATE TO DO THIS, ATOM--BUT IF YOU WON'T GO VOLUNTARILY--
THUNK!
NOW TO TURN ON MY ATOMIC VIBRATOR--AND TAKE OFF!
BUT--UNKNOWN TO THE ATOM OF EARTH-TWO--JUST BEFORE IMPACT, HIS WILY FOE CLICKED HIS SIZE-AND-WEIGHT CONTROLS AND...
SHRANK SMALL ENOUGH TO SQUEEZE BETWEEN HIS FINGERS--
NOW TO JAM HIS VIBRATOR!
SO THAT JUST AS ATOM-2 REACHES FOR HIS ATOMIC VIBRATOR CONTROLS...
OWW
ATOM--I THOUGHT SURE I'D KNOCKED YOU OUT?!
IT TAKES MORE THAN A LOVE TAP LIKE THAT TO GET ME, CHUM!
16
DESPERATELY, THE LARGER-SIZED ATOM FLINGS HIMSELF TOWARD THE GARDEN FLAGGING...
HE'S GOT SUCH A FIRM GRIP ON MY FINGERS--I CAN'T ACTIVATE THE VIBRATOR!
MAYBE I CAN JAR IT INTO ACTION BY HITTING ITS STUD AGAINST THE FLAGSTONES!

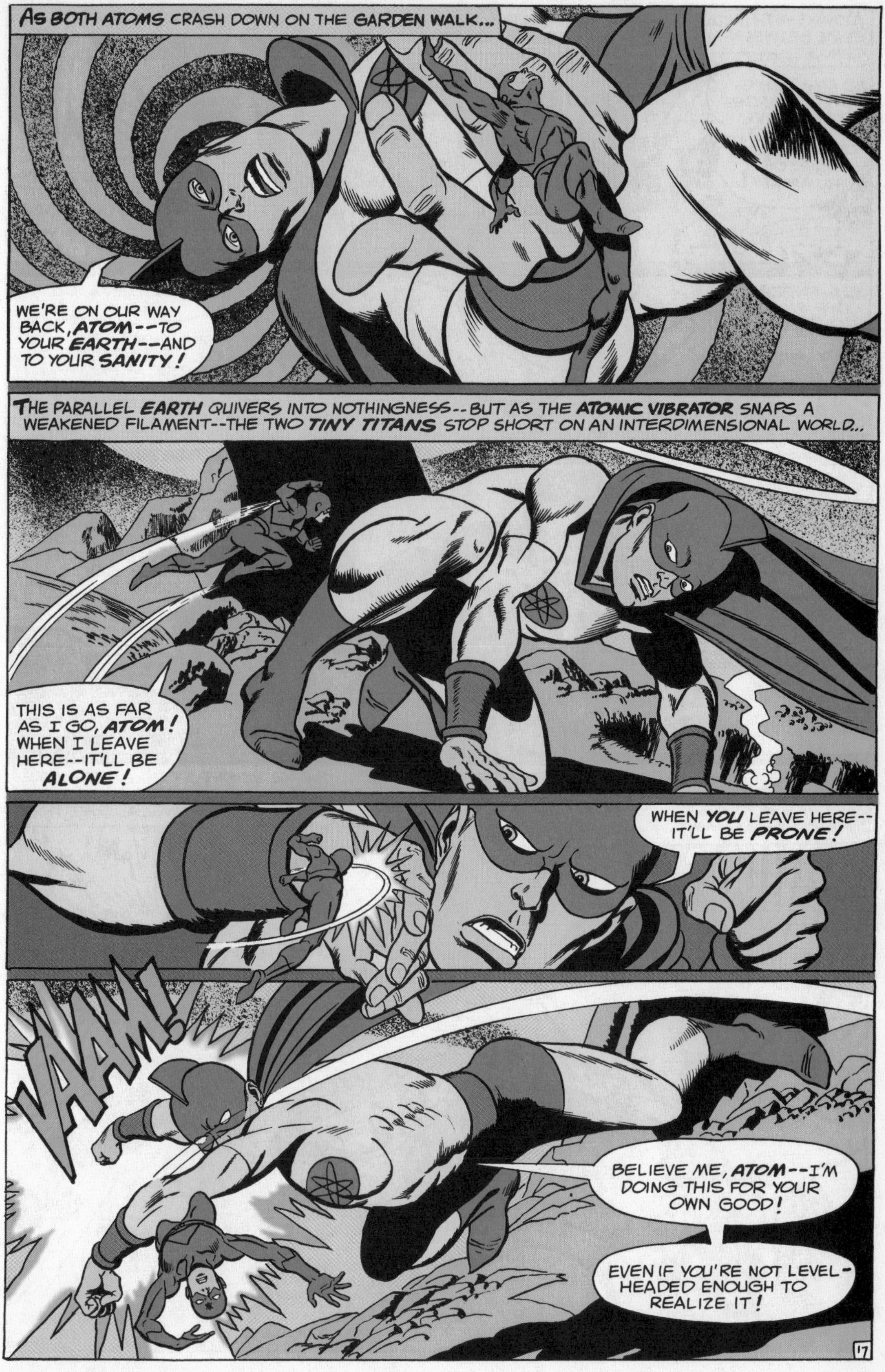
AS BOTH ATOMS CRASH DOWN ON THE GARDEN WALK...
WE'RE ON OUR WAY BACK, ATOM--TO YOUR EARTH--AND TO YOUR SANITY!
THE PARALLEL EARTH QUIVERS INTO NOTHINGNESS--BUT AS THE ATOMIC VIBRATOR SNAPS A WEAKENED FILAMENT--THE TWO TINY TITANS STOP SHORT ON AN INTERDIMENSIONAL WORLD...
THIS IS AS FAR AS I GO, ATOM! WHEN I LEAVE HERE--IT'LL BE ALONE!
WHEN YOU LEAVE HERE--IT'LL BE PRONE!
VAAM!
BELIEVE ME, ATOM--I'M DOING THIS FOR YOUR OWN GOOD!
EVEN IF YOU'RE NOT LEVEL-HEADED ENOUGH TO REALIZE IT!
17

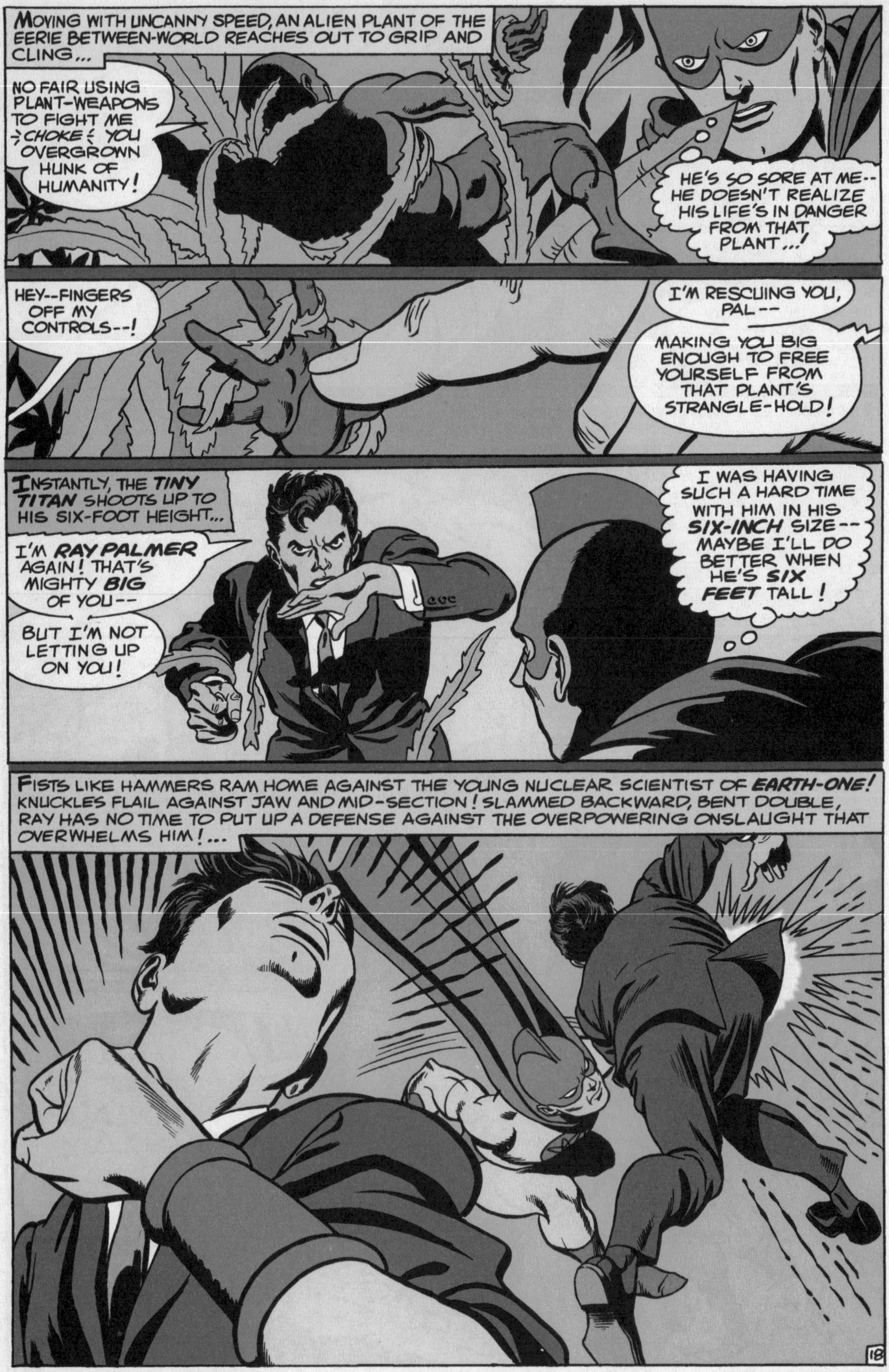
MOVING WITH UNCANNY SPEED, AN ALIEN PLANT OF THE EERIE BETWEEN-WORLD REACHES OUT TO GRIP AND CLING...
NO FAIR USING PLANT-WEAPONS TO FIGHT ME -CHOKE- YOU OVERGROWN HUNK OF HUMANITY!
HE'S SO SORE AT ME--HE DOESN'T REALIZE HIS LIFE'S IN DANGER FROM THAT PLANT...!
HEY--FINGERS OFF MY CONTROLS--!
I'M RESCUING YOU, PAL--
MAKING YOU BIG ENOUGH TO FREE YOURSELF FROM THAT PLANT'S STRANGLE-HOLD!
INSTANTLY, THE TINY TITAN SHOOTS UP TO HIS SIX-FOOT HEIGHT...
I'M RAY PALMER AGAIN! THAT'S MIGHTY BIG OF YOU--
BUT I'M NOT LETTING UP ON YOU!
I WAS HAVING SUCH A HARD TIME WITH HIM IN HIS SIX-INCH SIZE--MAYBE I'LL DO BETTER WHEN HE'S SIX FEET TALL!
FISTS LIKE HAMMERS RAM HOME AGAINST THE YOUNG NUCLEAR SCIENTIST OF EARTH-ONE! KNUCKLES FLAIL AGAINST JAW AND MID-SECTION! SLAMMED BACKWARD, BENT DOUBLE, RAY HAS NO TIME TO PUT UP A DEFENSE AGAINST THE OVERPOWERING ONSLAUGHT THAT OVERWHELMS HIM!...
18

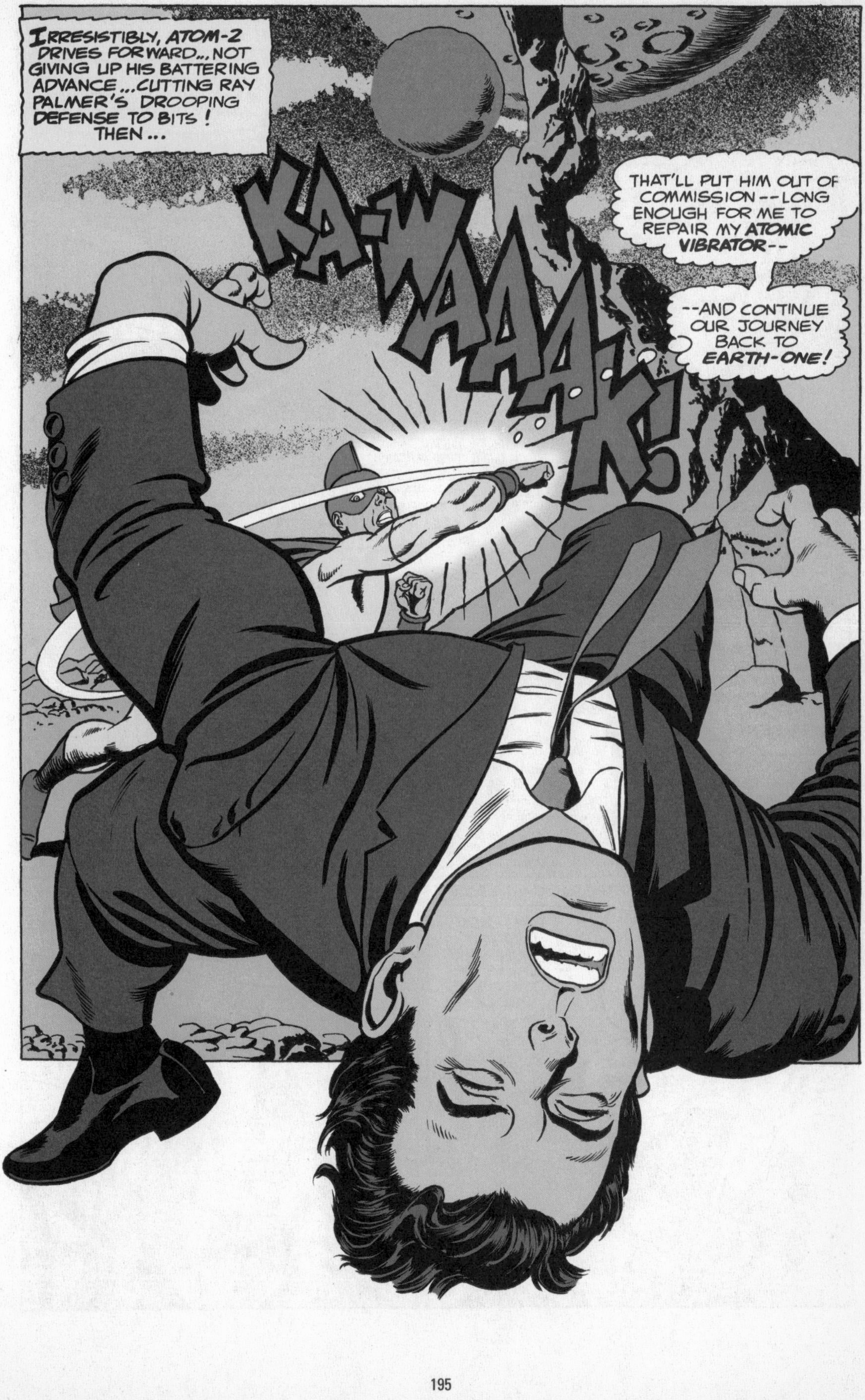
IRRESISTIBLY, ATOM-2 DRIVES FORWARD.., NOT GIVING UP HIS BATTERING ADVANCE ...CUTTING RAY PALMER'S DROOPING DEFENSE TO BITS! THEN ...
KA-WAAAK!
THAT'LL PUT HIM OUT OF COMMISSION --LONG ENOUGH FOR ME TO REPAIR MY ATOMIC VIBRATOR--
--AND CONTINUE OUR JOURNEY BACK TO EARTH-ONE!

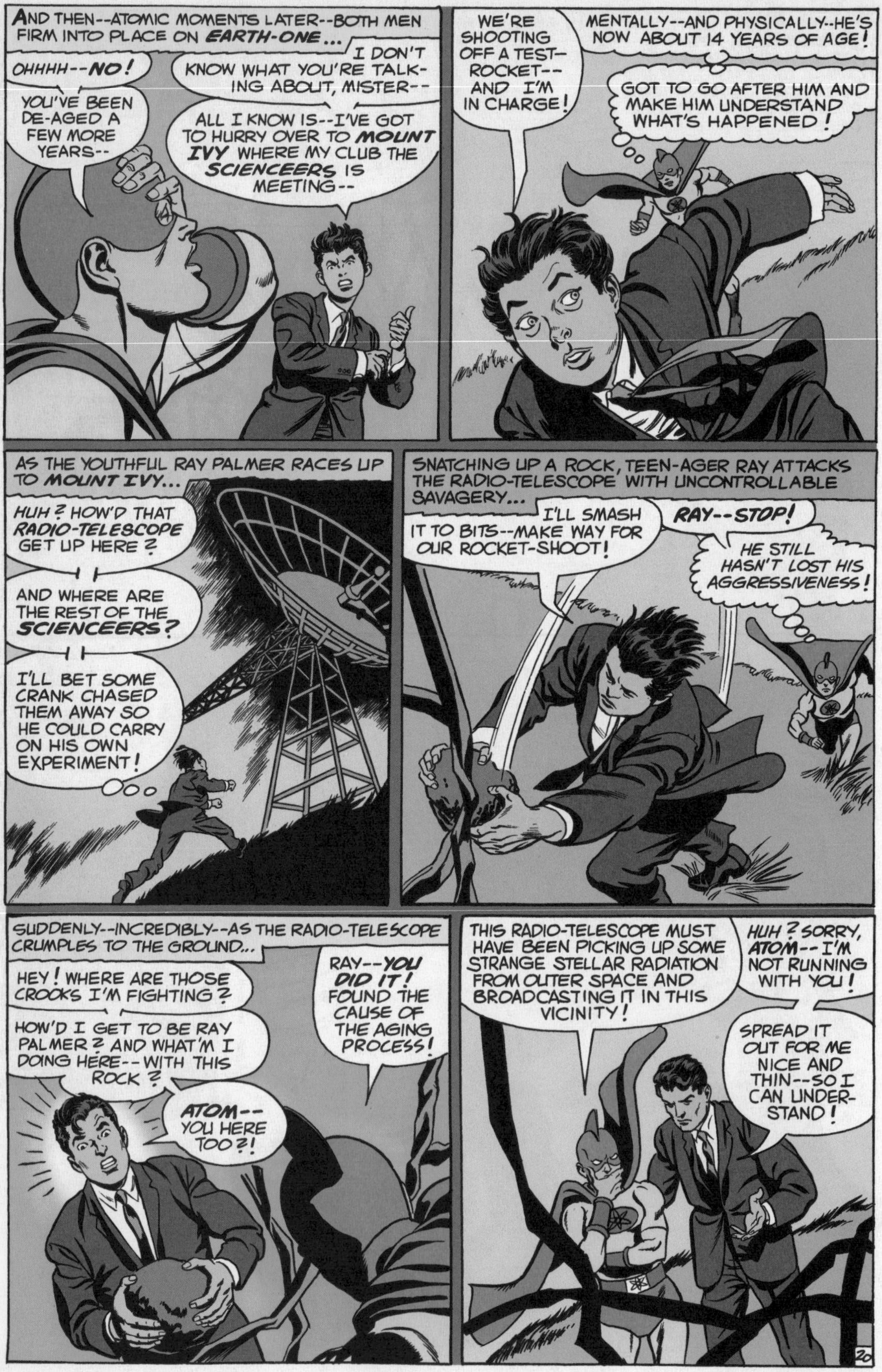

AND THEN--ATOMIC MOMENTS LATER--BOTH MEN FIRM INTO PLACE ON EARTH-ONE...
OHHHH--NO!
YOU'VE BEEN DE-AGED A FEW MORE YEARS--
I DON'T KNOW WHAT YOU'RE TALKING ABOUT, MISTER--
ALL I KNOW IS--I'VE GOT TO HURRY OVER TO MOUNT IVY WHERE MY CLUB THE SCIENCEERS IS MEETING--
WE'RE SHOOTING OFF A TEST-ROCKET--AND I'M IN CHARGE!
MENTALLY--AND PHYSICALLY--HE'S NOW ABOUT 14 YEARS OF AGE!
GOT TO GO AFTER HIM AND MAKE HIM UNDERSTAND WHAT'S HAPPENED!
AS THE YOUTHFUL RAY PALMER RACES UP TO MOUNT IVY...
HUH? HOW'D THAT RADIO-TELESCOPE GET UP HERE?
AND WHERE ARE THE REST OF THE SCIENCEERS?
I'LL BET SOME CRANK CHASED THEM AWAY SO HE COULD CARRY ON HIS OWN EXPERIMENT!
SNATCHING UP A ROCK, TEEN-AGER RAY ATTACKS THE RADIO-TELESCOPE WITH UNCONTROLLABLE SAVAGERY...
I'LL SMASH IT TO BITS--MAKE WAY FOR OUR ROCKET-SHOOT!
RAY--STOP!
HE STILL HASN'T LOST HIS AGGRESSIVENESS!
SUDDENLY--INCREDIBLY--AS THE RADIO-TELESCOPE CRUMPLES TO THE GROUND...
HEY! WHERE ARE THOSE CROOKS I'M FIGHTING?
HOW'D I GET TO BE RAY PALMER? AND WHAT'M I DOING HERE--WITH THIS ROCK?
RAY--YOU DID IT! FOUND THE CAUSE OF THE AGING PROCESS!
ATOM--YOU HERE TOO?!
THIS RADIO-TELESCOPE MUST HAVE BEEN PICKING UP SOME STRANGE STELLAR RADIATION FROM OUTER SPACE AND BROADCASTING IT IN THIS VICINITY!
HUH? SORRY, ATOM--I'M NOT RUNNING WITH YOU!
SPREAD IT OUT FOR ME NICE AND THIN--SO I CAN UNDERSTAND!
20

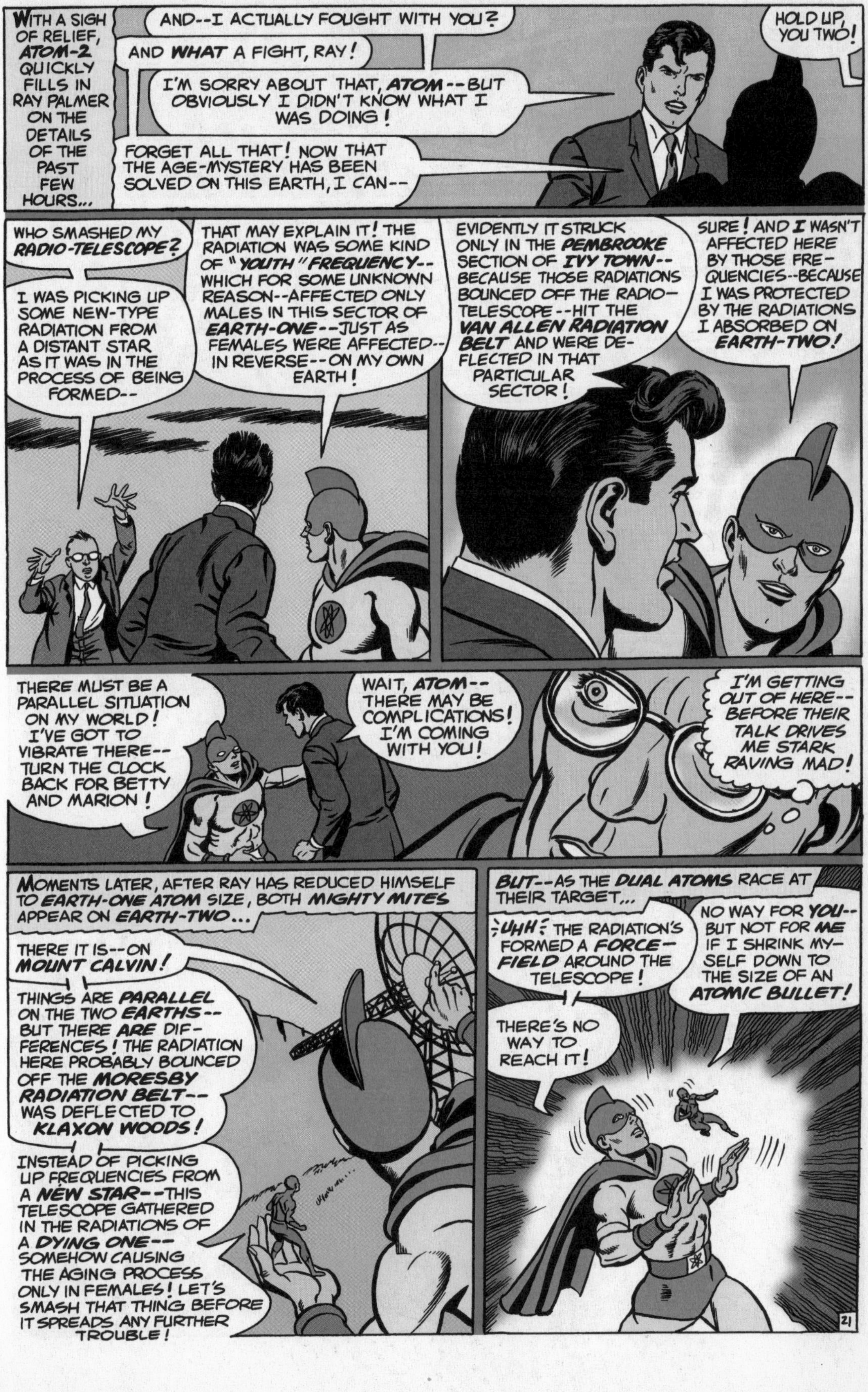
WITH A SIGH OF RELIEF, ATOM-2 QUICKLY FILLS IN RAY PALMER ON THE DETAILS OF THE PAST FEW HOURS...
AND--I ACTUALLY FOUGHT WITH YOU?
AND WHAT A FIGHT, RAY!
I'M SORRY ABOUT THAT, ATOM--BUT OBVIOUSLY I DIDN'T KNOW WHAT I WAS DOING!
FORGET ALL THAT! NOW THAT THE AGE-MYSTERY HAS BEEN SOLVED ON THIS EARTH, I CAN--
HOLD UP, YOU TWO!
WHO SMASHED MY RADIO-TELESCOPE?
I WAS PICKING UP SOME NEW-TYPE RADIATION FROM A DISTANT STAR AS IT WAS IN THE PROCESS OF BEING FORMED--
THAT MAY EXPLAIN IT! THE RADIATION WAS SOME KIND OF "YOUTH" FREQUENCY--WHICH FOR SOME UNKNOWN REASON--AFFECTED ONLY MALES IN THIS SECTOR OF EARTH-ONE--JUST AS FEMALES WERE AFFECTED--IN REVERSE--ON MY OWN EARTH!
EVIDENTLY IT STRUCK ONLY IN THE PEMBROOKE SECTION OF IVY TOWN--BECAUSE THOSE RADIATIONS BOUNCED OFF THE RADIO-TELESCOPE--HIT THE VAN ALLEN RADIATION BELT AND WERE DEFLECTED IN THAT PARTICULAR SECTOR!
SURE! AND I WASN'T AFFECTED HERE BY THOSE FREQUENCIES--BECAUSE I WAS PROTECTED BY THE RADIATIONS I ABSORBED ON EARTH-TWO!
THERE MUST BE A PARALLEL SITUATION ON MY WORLD! I'VE GOT TO VIBRATE THERE--TURN THE CLOCK BACK FOR BETTY AND MARION!
WAIT, ATOM--THERE MAY BE COMPLICATIONS! I'M COMING WITH YOU!
I'M GETTING OUT OF HERE--BEFORE THEIR TALK DRIVES ME STARK RAVING MAD!
MOMENTS LATER, AFTER RAY HAS REDUCED HIMSELF TO EARTH-ONE ATOM SIZE, BOTH MIGHTY MITES APPEAR ON EARTH-TWO...
THERE IT IS--ON MOUNT CALVIN!
THINGS ARE PARALLEL ON THE TWO EARTHS--BUT THERE ARE DIFFERENCES! THE RADIATION HERE PROBABLY BOUNCED OFF THE MORESBY RADIATION BELT--WAS DEFLECTED TO KLAXON WOODS!
INSTEAD OF PICKING UP FREQUENCIES FROM A NEW STAR--THIS TELESCOPE GATHERED IN THE RADIATIONS OF A DYING ONE--SOMEHOW CAUSING THE AGING PROCESS ONLY IN FEMALES! LET'S SMASH THAT THING BEFORE IT SPREADS ANY FURTHER TROUBLE!
BUT--AS THE DUAL ATOMS RACE AT THEIR TARGET...
UHH! THE RADIATION'S FORMED A FORCE-FIELD AROUND THE TELESCOPE!
THERE'S NO WAY TO REACH IT!
NO WAY FOR YOU--BUT NOT FOR ME IF I SHRINK MYSELF DOWN TO THE SIZE OF AN ATOMIC BULLET!
21

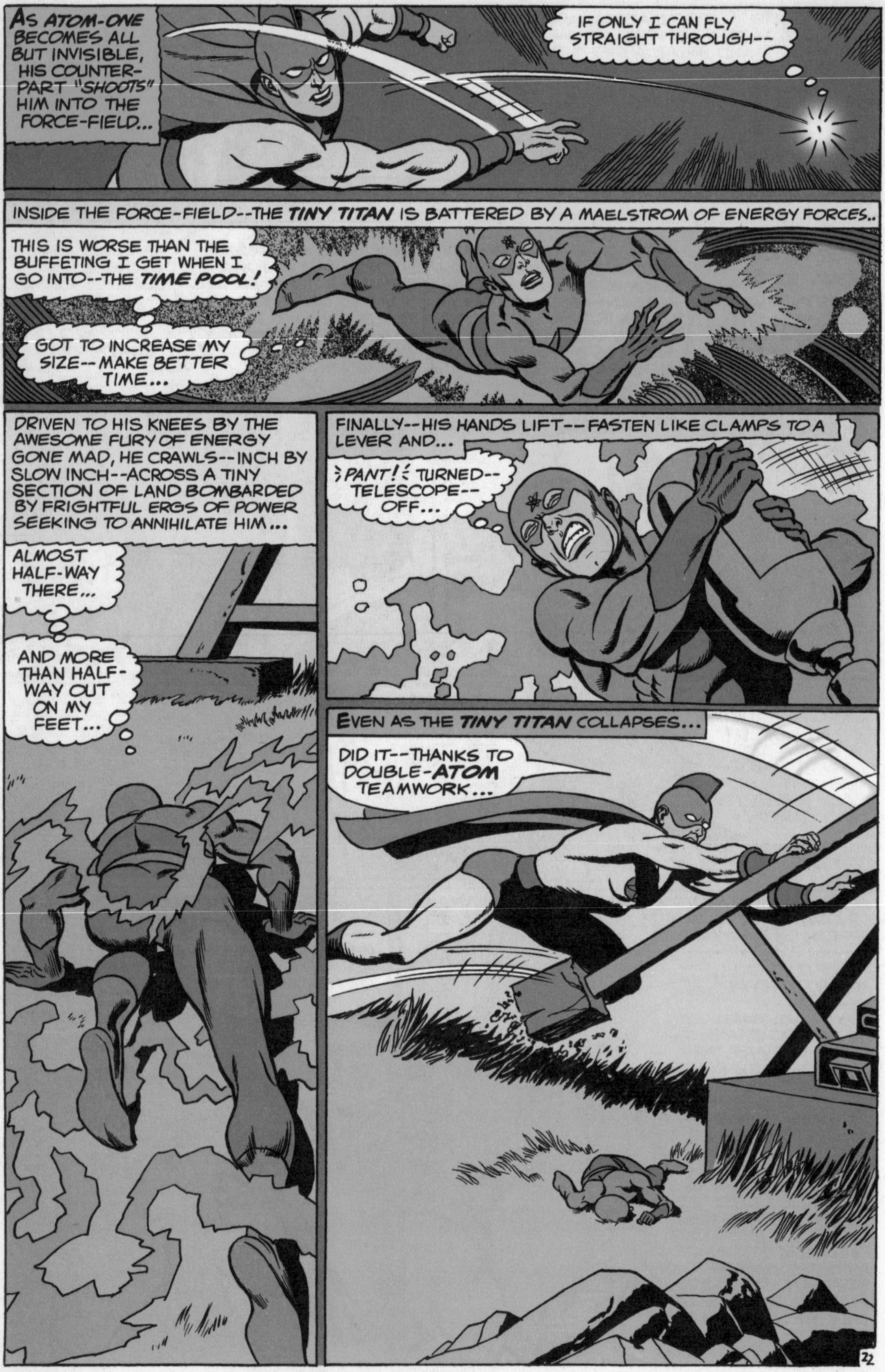
AS ATOM-ONE BECOMES ALL BUT INVISIBLE, HIS COUNTER-PART "SHOOTS" HIM INTO THE FORCE-FIELD...
IF ONLY I CAN FLY STRAIGHT THROUGH--
INSIDE THE FORCE-FIELD--THE TINY TITAN IS BATTERED BY A MAELSTROM OF ENERGY FORCES..
THIS IS WORSE THAN THE BUFFETING I GET WHEN I GO INTO--THE TIME POOL!
GOT TO INCREASE MY SIZE--MAKE BETTER TIME...
DRIVEN TO HIS KNEES BY THE AWESOME FURY OF ENERGY GONE MAD, HE CRAWLS--INCH BY SLOW INCH--ACROSS A TINY SECTION OF LAND BOMBARDED BY FRIGHTFUL ERGS OF POWER SEEKING TO ANNIHILATE HIM...
ALMOST HALF-WAY THERE...
AND MORE THAN HALF-WAY OUT ON MY FEET...
FINALLY--HIS HANDS LIFT--FASTEN LIKE CLAMPS TO A LEVER AND...
PANT! TURNED--TELESCOPE--OFF...
EVEN AS THE TINY TITAN COLLAPSES...
DID IT--THANKS TO DOUBLE-ATOM TEAMWORK...
22

LATER, ON EARTH-TWO, AFTER THE "OLD" WOMEN HAVE REVERTED TO THEIR YOUTHFUL SELVES...
BILL, IT LOOKS LIKE AL AND MARION ARE HITTING IT OFF...
AFTER THAT FANTASTIC FIRST MEETING...THEIR RELATIONSHIP COULD ONLY GO FROM BAD TO BETTER!
AND ON EARTH-ONE...
JUST THINK, RAY--IF IT HADN'T BEEN FOR THE ATOM...
YOU'D BE ENGAGED TO A GIRL-- YOU HADN'T EVEN DATED!
VERY FUNNY, HONEY!
THE END
23

CRISIS ON MULTIPLE EARTHS
THE TEAM UPS

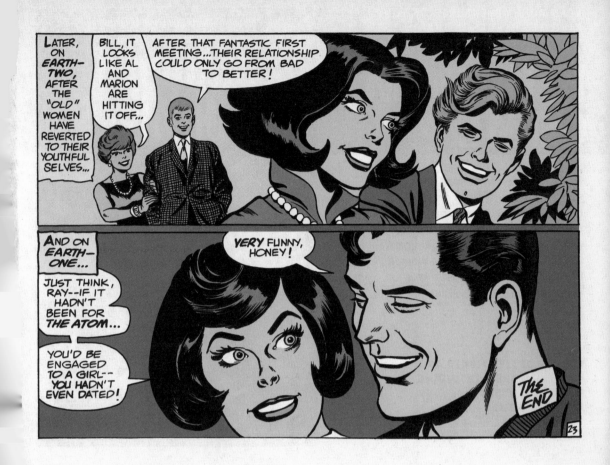

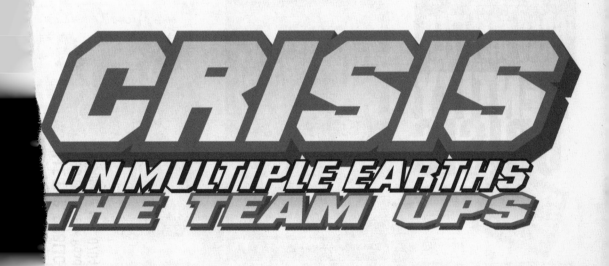

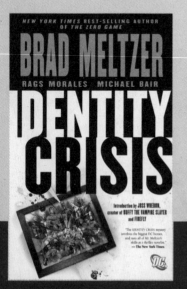